Human Cognitive Abilities
In Theory and Practice

Human
Cognitive Abilities
in Theory and Practice

Edited by
JOHN J. MCARDLE
and
RICHARD W. WOODCOCK
University of Virginia

LEA LAWRENCE ERLBAUM ASSOCIATES, PUBLISHERS
1998 Mahwah, New Jersey   London

Lawrence Erlbaum Associates, Inc., Publishers
10 Industrial Avenue
Mahwah, New Jersey 07430

Cover design by Kathryn Houghtaling Lacey

LIBRARY OF CONGRESS CATALOGING-IN-PUBLICATION DATA

Human cognitive abilities in theory and practice / edited by
    John J. McArdle, Richard W. Woodcock.
        p.   cm.
    Papers presented at a meeting, University of Virginia,
22–24 Sept. 1994.
    Includes bibliographical references and index.
    ISBN 0–8058–2717–X (alk. paper)
    1. Abilities.   2. Cognition.   I. McArdle, John J.   II. Woodcock,
Richard W.
    BF431.H777   1998
    153.9—dc21   97–51455
                                                         CIP

Books published by Lawrence Erlbaum Associates are printed on acid-free paper,
and their bindings are chosen for strength and durability.

Printed in the United States of America
10 9 8 7 6 5 4 3 2 1

This book is dedicated
to the memory of
DICK SNOW
—a talented teacher, a pioneering researcher,
a friend and colleague, and a role model for all of us

HCA Conference Participants.

Contents

Introduction

Research on human intellectual abilities has a long history in psychology and education. This work, unlike many other areas of social science research, has been widely applied to practical work in schools, clinics, and employment settings. These issues are widely discussed by scientists, practitioners, researchers, scholars, writers, clinicians, and other people.

During the past few years, in our discussions with many influential scientists in this area, a common set of concerns were raised—many scientists perceived *an increase in the gap between intellectual abilities theory and practice*. For example, scholars studying intelligence consistently mention the widespread use of single IQ measures in research and clinical practice. Some of these discussions focus on theoretical issues and formal models. Some well-known scholars claim that a general factor of intellectual ability is grounded in the findings of extensive research studies. Other equally respected scholars say the evidence does not support the hypothesis of a single factor of intelligence. Some of this controversy stems from the use of different methods for the analysis of cognitive data. This includes different views about the appropriate design and interpretation of factor analytic research. Personal views on these topics are often a key part of these debates.

Such controversy has important practical outcomes. Some practitioners claim optimal efficiency in the use of a single IQ measure, no matter what behavioral outcome is of interest, and cite only the research consistent with this position. Others conclude that multiple measures of cognitive functioning are required, and again cite evidence consistent with this position. These practical considerations are so important to the public that they often overshadow the original theoretical questions. For example, those who construct intellectual ability tests are compelled by market demand to provide a single composite score, whether or not such a construct is appropriate. Test batteries are questioned for not producing a score called *IQ*, and some new tests are labeled *different* rather than *improved*. In such ways, intellectual ability tests are considerably different than other areas of assessment, such as personality and school achievement.

Questions about the current level of progress in matching of theory and

practice led us to believe that a conference on *human cognitive abilities* (or
HCA) discussing these scientific issues would serve some broadly useful
functions. Our plan was to start this conference with discussions directed at
defining major issues in contemporary research on HCA, and use this to lead
to more practically oriented issues. Our HCA conference was held at the
Dome Room of the Rotunda at the University of Virginia on September 22
through 24, 1994. This book represents the proceedings of this conference.

Just a few months later, it is interesting to look back on the conference
and reflect on the importance of open scientific discussion of these potentially controversial issues. The HCA meeting was opened with a few quotes
ascribed to the founder of the University of Virginia, Mr. Thomas Jefferson:

> And, finally, that truth is great and will prevail if left to herself; that she is
> the proper and sufficient antagonist to error, and she has nothing to fear
> from the conflict unless by human interposition disarmed of her natural
> weapons, free argument of debate; errors ceasing to be dangerous when it is
> permitted freely to contradict them. (from the Virginia Act for Religious Free-
> dom, 1786)

> No experiment can be more interesting than that we are now trying, and
> which we trust will end in establishing the fact, that man may be governed
> by reason and trust. Our first object should therefore be, to leave open to
> him all the avenues of truth. (letter to Judge Tyler, 1804)

> If M. De Becourt's book be false in its facts, disprove them; if false in its rea-
> son, refute it. But, for God's sake, let us freely hear both sides, if we choose.
> (letter to Mr. Dufief, 1814)

> This institution will be based on the illimitable freedom of the human
> mind. For here we are not afraid to follow truth wherever it may lead, nor to
> tolerate error as long as reason is free to combat it. (to prospective teachers,
> University of Virginia, 1822)[1]

In this spirit, each presentation at the meeting was followed by an open
and often lively discussion. Raised here were controversial issues of mental
testing and public policy, crime and social class differences, race differences
in IQ, and the practical uses of behavioral genetic research. Our audience at
the Rotunda was diverse in academic and intellectual background—it even
included one member of a group allegedly investigating the scientific and
personal philosophies of some of the speakers! Only a few short weeks later,
these same issues exploded on the front pages of newspapers and prime time
television as a consequence of the widespread and diverse reactions to the
publication of *The Bell Curve*, written by R. J. Herrnstein and C. Murray

---

[1] For more details, see Merrill D. Peterson, 1984. *Thomas Jefferson: Writings*. New York:
Library of America.

(1994; New York: The Free Press). Clearly, some of the issues discussed by Jefferson in the 19th century remain controversial as we approach the 21st century.

Although readers of these chapters will find some areas of reasonable agreement, this conference and this book also reflect a diversity of methods and reasoning used to examine a diverse set of problems. Because we do not believe the answers to such questions are yet resolved, it is precisely this kind of diversity that we strive to interject into contemporary discussions on human cognitive abilities. All authors submitted drafts of these articles to the editors and, by design, few editorial changes were advised or made. We hope the reader will be encouraged by this Jeffersonian tradition and use these chapters to promote well-reasoned debate on these contemporary topics.

CONTENTS OF THIS BOOK

The contents of this book follow the organization and chronology of the HCA meeting. Three historic figures in the area of human cognitive abilities were invited to give the first HCA conference keynote addresses. These three overviews, as well as a more detailed introduction to each author, are presented in the first section of this book.

The first keynote address was delivered by Dr. John B. Carroll (Professor Emeritus, University of North Carolina). Dr. Carroll's recent 1993 book, *Human Cognitive Abilities: A Survey of Factor-Analytic Studies*, provides a classic reference source on the main topic of the conference. An introduction to this work of Dr. Carroll is given here by Dr. Richard Snow (Stanford University).

The second keynote address was presented by Dr. Raymond B. Cattell (Professor Emeritus, Universities of Hawaii and Illinois). Dr. Cattell's contribution to knowledge and theory in this area is indicated by his 1971 book, *Intelligence: Its Structure, Growth, and Action*. Dr. Cattell is introduced here by Dr. John Horn (University of Southern California).

The third keynote address was given by Dr. Evegny Sokolov (Chairman of Psychology, Moscow State University). Dr. Sokolov is the only foreign member of the National Academy of Sciences, and one of his many books, *Perception and the Condition Reflex* (1958), forms the basis of modern research in psychophysiology. Dr. Sokolov is introduced here by Dr. Steven Porges (University of Maryland).

The second part of this book contains talks based on research of a more focused and contemporary nature. Dr. John Horn (University of Southern California) presents research on the theory of fluid and crystallized intelligence. Horn reviews evidence suggesting that single measures of intellectual abilities are not sufficient—for example, they do not capture the age-related variance in human cognitive functioning. Dr. Richard Snow (Stanford University) discusses current research on abilities regarded as aptitudes and as achievements in school learning situations. Snow discusses the evidence needed for a theory of abilities, and provides evidence on the need for dynamic person-situation interactions in learning. Dr. Sandra Scarr (University of Virginia) discusses theoretical models and empirical research on how families do and do not affect individual differences in intellectual abilities. Scarr compares the goodness of fit of social environmental theories against alternatives provided by those from behavioral genetic theories, and she discusses the social policy implications and misperceptions arising from these kinds of data.

The final two chapters of this section are based on the research of the conference organizers. Richard Woodcock shows how new techniques based on multiple ability measures can be used in a variety of practical settings. Jack McArdle shows how different concepts of test bias may be evaluated and tested using structural equation modeling techniques and logic.

The third section of the book includes some excellent contributions presented at the poster session of this conference. Steven Aggen (University of Virginia) presents research on structural equation models for linking different measurement batteries (the WAIS and the WJ-R), and shows how powerful measurement hypotheses can be tested in the context of large blocks of incomplete data. Steven Boker (University of Viriginia) discusses work on computer-based testing using a remote measurement scheme termed psychotelemetry. Fumiaki Hamagami (University of Viriginia) presents some models for test-retest data where the data are measured at the item level. Patricia Hulick (University of Virginia) examined issues about gender differences using multivariate data from the WJ-R and multivariate models of factorial invariance. Jennie Noll (University of Southern California) discusses an ongoing project on cognitive aging. Thomas Paskus (University of Virginia) discusses methods for creating optimal cutoff scores on psychometric tests using a decision theory framework.

ACKNOWLEDGMENTS

The HCA conference was initially based on an idea from Robert Harrington at the University of Kansas. This and other ideas were eventually turned into a conference by members of the Jefferson Psychometric Laboratory of the Department of Psychology at the University of Virginia. Support for the research of this laboratory has come from grants from the National Institute on Aging (AG-04704 and AG-07137). The HCA conference was also sponsored by a special grant from the Riverside Publishing Company, and we thank Riverside President John Oswald, Vice President Fredrick Shrank, and

National Consultant Barbara Wendling for their support and encouragement of this project.

We also owe a special debt of gratitude to Carolyn Nesselroade and Marilyn Rothstein for their overall assistance in organizing all aspects of the HCA meeting. Finally, we also thank all the University of Virginia students who worked on various aspects of HCA, including Steve Aggen, Steve Boker, Aki Hamagami, Patty Hulick, Paolo Ghisella, Jungmeen Kim, Tom Mulligan, Gina Marshall, Laura Paskus, and Tom Paskus.

It is important to note that many other well-known scholars attended this conference (they are cited in the list of participants at the end). These persons contributed to the lively discussion periods following each presentation, and we are grateful for their attendance and their continued support of this work.

—John J. McArdle
—Richard W. Woodcock
Charlottesville, VA
January 1995

I

KEYNOTE SPEAKERS

Introduction of John B. Carroll

Richard E. Snow
Stanford University

I am pleased and honored to be invited to participate in this conference. The last time I was in Mr. Jefferson's Rotunda was 36 years ago, when I marched through it and down the lawn to receive a B.A. in Psychology from *The University;* it is thus a special treat for me to be here. Above all, however, I am most deeply honored to be asked to introduce John B. Carroll (known to his friends as Jack). I feel that I have been a student of Jack Carroll's ever since my UVa days—not in the sense that I took courses from him or had his supervision in research, but rather as a "distance" learner. I am sure that many others present today feel that way, too.

I have read a good deal of his work and heard him speak many times, and used a lot of his ideas, and yet it is impossible to keep up. He has been such a prolific scholar for so long in the fields I work in—the differential psychology of human abilities and the educational psychology of learning and instruction. But then to recognize that he has also been a pioneering and prolific scholar in several other fields—psychometrics, psycholinguistics, verbal learning and behavior, foreign language learning and teaching, and the teaching of English—it becomes clear that his career has been truly phenomenal. Let me recount it here briefly.

Jack Carroll was born in 1916 in Hartford, Connecticut and attended public schools there. As a young student, he was a language hobbyist and had weekly sessions with Benjamin Lee Whorf, famous for his theory of linguistic relativity. Jack then attended Wesleyan University, graduating in 1937 with a B.A. and highest honors in classics. Through his school years, he became proficient in Latin and classical Greek as well as French and German, and even browsed in the grammars of such languages as Sanskrit and Armenian. I once met him at a conference in Greece and found him teaching himself modern Greek by reading signs, billboard advertisements, and the like.

In 1940, he took his Ph.D. in psychology from the University of Minnesota, but he had also done summer graduate work in linguistics at Michigan
and work on psychometrics and factor analysis with Thurstone at Chicago,
even though he was nominally a student of B. F. Skinner's at Minnesota. His
doctoral dissertation was a factor analysis of verbal abilities. I believe Jack is
thus the only psychologist to have ever studied with both B. F. Skinner and
L. L. Thurstone—a remarkable combination.

In the period 1940 to 1949, he was an instructor at Mt. Holyoke and at
Indiana University, a lecturer at the University of Chicago, and also a U.S.
Navy aviation psychologist and a U.S. Army research psychologist. Then, in
1949, he went to Harvard University, where he rose through the professorial
ranks to become the Roy E. Larsen Professor of Education. After 17 years at
Harvard, moved to spend the years 1967 to 1974 as Senior Research Psychol-
ogist at Educational Testing Service. From 1974 through the present he has
been the William R. Kenan Jr. Professor of Psychology at the University of
North Carolina, Chapel Hill, and has also served as Director of the L.L.
Thurstone Psychometric Laboratory there. He became Professor Emeritus at
North Carolina in 1982; however, no one noticed this step because his pub-
lication rate didn't change.

He has held offices in many professional and scientific organizations, and
won many honors for his work. Just to mention a few: He is a life member of
the Linguistic Society of America, a Fellow of APA and AAAS, and a member of both the Psychometric Society and the Psychonomic Society. He has
been active in AERA, the Modern Language Association, the National
Council of teachers of English and Conference on Research in English, the
American Council of Teachers of Foreign Language, and the Association for
Computational Linguistics. He is a founding member of the National Academy of Education. He has received the E. L. Thorndike Award for Distinguished Contributions to Educational Psychology, the ETS Award for Distinguished Service to Measurement, the Diamond Jubilee Medal from the
London Institute of Linguistics, and an honorary doctorate of science from
the University of Minnesota.

Jack is the author of over 400 journal articles, book chapters, reviews, encyclopedia pieces, and other writings. There is no way to do justice to the
breadth and depth of scholarship represented in that list. In 1985, Lorin An-
derson edited a book that brought together some of Jack's seminal writings
in the field of research on school learning. It included a bibliography of most
of Jack's other work up to that time. However, a range of significant contributions have come out since then, right up to the present.

Beyond all of this, Jack has also written or edited several important books.
I want to mention just two of them. In 1964, he published *Language and
Thought*, a small book in a basics concepts series published by Prentice-
Hall. At the time of its publication I was just out of graduate school and,

having not had any course work in that field, I read the book. I have had occasion to refer back to it since. It I the only book I know that manage to be both a clear, comprehensible introduction for the beginner and an advance in scholarship for the field at the same time—and it accomplishes this in only about 100 pages.

In 1993, Jack published *Human Cognitive Abilities: A Survey of Factor Analytic Studies*. As it happened, the publisher, Cambridge University Press, asked me to be one of the book's reviewers. I wrote them a very positive letter and they ended up quoting from my review on the book cover. I said in that review that:

> Jack Carroll has done a magnificent thing. He has reviewed and reanalyzed the world's literature on individual differences in cognitive abilities, collected over most of a century, to reach an integrated picture. No one else could have done it. No one else would have applied so consistent and impartial a system on the literature, reached so balanced, complete, and useful a conclusion. It is a monumental contribution, destined to be bought and read in every university in the world over that has a psychology or education department, an to be on many an individual scholar's shelf as well. It defines the taxonomy of cognitive differential psychology for many years to come.

We are all tremendously impressed with and tremendously grateful for your work, and we are very happy to be here with you today, Jack. Please join me in welcoming John B. "Jack" Carroll.

REFERENCES

Carroll, J. B. (1964). *Language and thought.* Englewood Cliffs, NJ: Prentice-Hall.
Carroll, J. B. (1993). *Human cognitive abilities: A survey of factor analytic studies.* New York: Cambridge.

1

Human Cognitive Abilities: A Critique

John B. Carroll
University of North Carolina at Chapel Hill

Over the last several years, the most bracing event of my life was the publication of my book *Human Cognitive Abilities: A Survey of Factor-Analytic Studies* (Carroll, 1993a). I would stress the subtitle: The book was intended to be primarily a *survey* of factor-analytic studies. It was never my intention to tell all there is to tell about human cognitive abilities; that would have required more volumes than one, or perhaps an encyclopedia like what Sternberg (1994b) produced. I had to be realistic about what I could cram between the covers of a reasonably sized book.

It was gratifying enough for me just to get the book out into publication, having working on it for something like 10 years. After that, I must confess, I was a little anxious about what reviewers might have to say about it. Would they mark it down as the work of a fanatic of factor analysis, a person totally out of touch with current thinking in psychology, or . . . what? Of course, I might have taken the attitude that many authors adopt, of being pococurante about reactions of reviewers, even to the point of not reading the reviews at all. However, I'm not that kind of author; I'm always curious about what kinds of arguments or dialogues my work might stimulate.

I didn't have to wait too long for reviews. The first that came to my attention was published in England, in the *Times Higher Education Supplement* (Brand, 1993). Overall, it seemed pretty favorable, although the reviewer (a lecturer in psychology at the University of Edinburgh) was prompted to remark that "the methods involved in Carroll's factor-analytic opus are a painfully familiar mixture of the flatfooted and the mildly self-indulgent" (p. 22). I trust that he was referring only to factor analysis, not to me or my book. His major complaint seemed to be that I missed the chance to discuss most of the "more interesting questions about psychometric psychology" (p. 22). Perhaps so, but I had other uses for my limited space. What fascinated me most about this review was that it was entitled "The importance of g"; its author took the occasion to voice opposition to the anti-g, "anti-London school" sentiment that he regarded as pervasive among social scientists in the United Kingdom. He chose to ignore the "three-stratum theory" that I thought was the capstone idea of my book.

Note, by the way, that this review was published in the *Times Higher Education Supplement* of London, which would be faintly analogous to the *New York Times Book Review*. As far as I am aware, no review of my book has yet been published in any edition of the *New York Times*. Apparently, that publication continues to be hostile, as Herrnstein (1982) pointed out, to the idea that intelligence, or g, is of any importance, to say nothing of the idea that g may have some genetic variance.

Then came a review in the journal *Personality and Individual Differences*, by Eysenck (1994), the dean of that very same "London school" that Brand mentioned. Eysenck was extremely generous. "It is difficult," he wrote, "to find anything much to criticize in this book" (p. 199). He mentioned several matters that he felt I should not have neglected, but granted that I "might argue that these issues were somewhat tangential to [my] purpose" (p. 199). I am not sure that I would in fact make this argument; I wish I could have devoted more attention to the issues mentioned by Eysenck, just as I wish I could have added discussion of the "more interesting" questions mentioned by Brand.

Finally, several reviews came out in American publications—a double-header in *Psychological Science* (Brody, 1994; Sternberg, 1994a), and ones in *Contemporary Psychology* (Nagoshi, 1994) and *Educational Researcher* (Burns, 1994). All were what might be characterized as "rave reviews." Burns, for example, called my tome "a remarkable book" (p. 35) and Nagoshi called it "monumental" (p. 617). Sternberg called it "a tour de force" (p. 63) that would be "a classic in the field of human intelligence" (p. 65); Brody wrote that students of individual differences should applaud my efforts on their behalf.

Although all these reviews were in one sense gratifying, in another sense they were disappointing. They didn't tell me what I wanted to know: What was wrong with my book and its ideas, or at least what might be controversial about it, for surely it dealt with a field that has abounded in controversy.

Thus, ever since these reviews came out, I've been brooding about what their authors might have said, but didn't. On some matters, the reviewers may not have been in a position to criticize my work. Even in writing the book, I was aware that I was not always really confident in the statements I made, or that I was perhaps a little too careless about sticking to all the resolutions I had made about how my project should be conducted. Moreover, since publication of the book, I've come across current literature on intelligence and cognitive abilities that suggests questions I might have considered.

My plan here, then, is to attempt a critique of my book and, further, a critique of the field that I proposed to survey, with the hope that my remarks may provoke questions for further thought and research.

A CRITIQUE OF THE BOOK

I mention a number of things in this section concerning problems with the book, giving details as necessary.

Sampling of Datasets

I analyzed some 480 datasets, but these did not include a number of worthy studies that I failed to analyze or report on, even though I knew about some of them. The assembly of datasets was not as systematic as might have been desired—I could have made more use of various bibliographical sources. And since publishing the book, I've discovered the existence of a number of datasets that ought to have been discussed (e.g., one from a doctoral dissertation on memory done at the University of Würzburg; Katzenberger, 1964). But I have no way of knowing whether the failure to include all these datasets would have significantly affected my conclusions, short of remedying this failure.

Methods of Data Analysis

I would have to confess that the methods of data analysis were not as consistent and uniform as might be inferred from the statements I made in the book. Data analyses were conducted over a 5-year period. In the first year or so of that period, my analyses were somewhat experimental, and of a trial-and-error nature while I tried to establish standard procedures. Later, I became aware of some major changes that had been suggested for certain aspects of methodology, such as in Tucker and Finkbeiner's (1981) methods of factor rotation. These changes were implemented for about two thirds of the datasets, but not for all of them. And since the publication of the book, I have discovered that I should have set a stricter criterion for the Tucker-Finkbeiner procedure. Finally, I have become aware that because of what might be called organizational failures, at least one or two of my reanalyses were not properly done according to the rules that my colleagues and I had tried to establish in the early phases of the project.

As I noted in my book, I made little or no use of confirmatory factor analysis (CFA), using LISREL, EQS, or similar structural equation modeling techniques. For one thing, these methods were still under considerable development during my project, and time and resources available to me were not such as to permit their use in such an extensive project as mine. Indeed, it seems that these procedures would have been difficult to apply to the large datasets, with up to 60 or more variables, to which I could easily apply exploratory factor analysis (EFA). However, I pointed out that there were adequate justifications for using only EFA techniques, and in some cases, in my opinion, I was able to show that EFA produced more satisfactory results than did CFA as employed by others (e.g., in my analysis of data from Palmer, MacLeod, Hunt, & Davidson, 1985; see also Carroll, 1995), the inference being that CFA should derive its initial hypotheses with guidance from EFA results, rather than starting from scratch or from *a priori* hypotheses. At the same time, I stressed that CFA analyses should be done to check my EFA analyses, and I hope that students of factor analysis will take this suggestion seriously.

Already in 1989 (Carroll, 1989), I noted my discomfort with using higher-order factor analysis to discover higher-order factors. I felt that higher-order factor analysis relies too much on the assumption that higher-order factors "subsume" lower-order factors. Since then, there have been important developments in CFA theory that relax the assumption of factor subsumption, such as Gustaffson's "nested factors" model (e.g., in a study by Gustafsson & Balke, 1993), and I would suggest that this kind of model be used in trying to confirm or critique EFA findings in my book. Nevertheless, I know of no satisfactory procedure, other than higher-order factor analysis, to identify (at a first approximation) the broad factors that would be hypothesized in CFA reanalyses of datasets—either those that were studied in my book or newly developed ones.

Interpretation, Classification, and Sorting of Factors.

I suspect that few readers of my book have adequately realized what an enormous project it was to classify and sort the several thousand "token" factors that I identified in my reanalyses of datasets. It involved not only the tentative cross-tabulation and interpretation of factors, but also the consideration of the subject samples, the detailed nature of the variables, and other contextual matters involved in the studies from which datasets were derived. The process inevitably entailed a considerable degree of subjectivity. One of the reviewers noted this, remarking that "Carroll admits his operation is essentially one of 'cataloguing' factors . . . but cataloguing by appearance still involves a certain subjectivity and cannot constitute a proof of anything unless the fit of one cataloguing system is somehow compared with the fit of another" (Brand, 1993, p. 22). Somewhere, I recall, Raymond Cattell wrote a pungent statement about the reckless interpretations of factors sometimes made by factor analysts. Whether my sorts and interpretations will stand the test of time, I cannot say. I make no apology for subjectivity in factor analysis, because I know of no way to avoid it: Any faults it produces can be corrected only by testing alternative hypotheses in further research. And even hypotheses, in a sense, are subjective.

Thus, the process of factor interpretation, comparison, and classification remains a basic problem in factor analysis. Certain techniques have been proposed, such as coefficients of factor congruence, but these are applicable only in highly restricted circumstances. I found them almost totally useless in my investigation.

Limitation to Variables Used in Factor-Analytic Studies

One reason my investigation failed to tell as much as it might have about cognitive abilities is that it was necessarily limited to variables that have been employed in factor-analytic studies. I had to limit myself to correlational and factor-analytic studies because these are the only kinds of studies that purvey useful information about associations of variables. That is, I did not find it profitable, in general, to consider studies that focused on only one or a small number of variables, because such studies did not offer much information on the broad structure of cognitive abilities. In this way, I had to ignore large literatures in various domains of ability, such as vocabulary, reading behavior, reasoning abilities, spatial abilities, memory abilities, creativity abilities, and so on. For similar reasons, I largely ignored extensive literatures on group differences in abilities; that is, differences with respect to sex, race/ethnicity, age, occupational and social status, and so on. Such studies are the domain of those who take special interest in them (e.g., Halpern, 1991). I would only hope that my results on the identification of ability factors in the cognitive domain could in the future be more extensively taken account of in the study of group differences. For example, Halpern paid scant attention to studies of gender differences in the structure of cognitive abilities.

It is noticeable, also, that psychological studies of cognitive abilities have made too much use of variables from psychological tests, and too little use of variables derived from direct observation and judgment of intellectual behavior. It is possible that, as a consequence, research has failed to identify entire domains of ability that may actually exist, such as Gardner's (1983) "intrapersonal" and "interpersonal" domains.

SOME MAJOR THEORETICAL PROBLEMS

In this section, I mention and discuss a number of basic problems that must be addressed in the further development of the study of cognitive abilities.

They have, of course, been frequently addressed in the history of the field, but I entertain the idea that the survey I conducted should shed light on these problems and make it possible to find new and more satisfactory answers.

What Are Factors?

Throughout most factor-analytic work, investigators seem to have adopted the premise that factors represent entities, somewhere in the organism, that function in helping to determine performance on psychological tests or in affecting behavior that might be observed in some other way, as in ratings or in a great variety of experimental, clinical, or neurological procedures. I myself have been inclined to accept this premise, with two provisos: first, that these entities are not reified "things" (Gould, 1981) but instead structured patterns of potentialities latent in neurones; and second, that cognitive ability factors must conform to the model of ability implied in item response theory (IRT), where the probability of successful performance on a task (or "item") is a monotonically increasing function of the individual's ability (i.e., score on a particular factor) and three parameters associated with the task itself (a discrimination parameter, a difficulty parameter, and a "chance guessing" parameter).

Cognitive abilities should also conform to this model in the sense of the *person characteristic function* (Carroll, 1990); that is, items or tasks classified under a particular ability should produce reasonable person characteristic functions such that the probability of success on tasks measuring the ability is a monotonically decreasing function of task difficulty, given the individual's ability level. Actually, at the present time we know little about the extent to which the ability factors identified in factor analysis conform to this model, partly because there has been no systematic investigation of the matter and partly because there is, to my knowledge, no adequate theory for testing the conformity of higher-order factors (or even lower-order factors, for that matter) to the IRT model. In my book, I attempted to suggest how this might be done for a presumed general factor and for second-stratum factors, but admittedly my suggestions were not well worked out, and possibly they are impractical.

One advantage of the IRT model is that it is essentially probabilistic; that is, it imples that factors have only a probabilistic effect on behavior. On occasion, I've wondered whether we should think of factors in terms of "fuzzy logic" (Kosko, 1993)—that is, as entities that exist in an indeterminate form —but perhaps IRT as a probabilistic theory already embraces fuzzy logic.

I've recently been involved in a dialogue with Lloyd Humphreys (Carroll, 1994; Humphreys, 1994), who wants to conceive intelligence in terms of a "repertoire" of behaviors. Presumably, Humphreys would apply this concept of repertoire to all factors of cognitive ability, at whatever stratum. I find this concept unappealing, however. For one thing, it might be difficult to define a repertoire operationally. For another, it seems to me that most psychological tests are not intended to define repertoires; they depend, rather, on sampling of repertoires to determine parameters of ability. For example, a pitch discrimination test aims to determine the parameter that specifies the level of difference in pitch that the individual can detect. Similarly, a vocabulary test aims to determine the level of difficulty (in terms of word frequency or familiarity) that an individual can handle; a vocabulary test score says nothing directly about the size of an individual's repertoire of vocabulary.

In factor analysis, the aim is to identify factors that can be associated with parameters (more specifically, factor scores) describing an individual's profile of abilities. We may not be able to specify exactly what in the individual's physiological makeup lies behind these factor scores, but we can infer that *something* is there—perhaps something like Hebb's (1949) "cell-assemblies." Having parameters to predict enables us to assess, for example, the relative amounts of genetic and environmental sources of variance, and it now appears that genetic determinants can be shown to exist for at least some ability factors (Cardon & Fulker, 1993). And almost every month someone reports the discovery of a gene responsible for some behavioral disorder, and some of these behavioral disorders (e.g., Williams' syndrome; Bellugi, Bihrle, Jernigan, Trauner, & Doherty, 1991) might be related to certain established factors.

Is It Possible to Describe the "Cognitive" Aspects of Cognitive Factors?

In my book, it was my intention to relate cognitive factors of ability to current theories and findings of cognitive psychology, but I am not sure that I was very successful in this. One problem is that, in some quarters, cognitive psychology has concentrated on circumstances affecting the *speed* of various kinds of responses (e.g., simple and choice reaction times, mental comparisons, perceptual or mental searches, etc.) rather than the accuracy of those responses. Indeed, some cognitive psychologists prefer to exclude inaccurate responses from their data, so that studies are restricted to data from relatively simple tasks, with little attention to what makes for variations in the difficulty of tasks. Many investigators claim to find significant correlations between speeds of performing these relatively simple tasks and scores on various cognitive ability tests. It is not always clear whether these correlations reflect speeds in performing the cognitive ability tests, as opposed to accuracies in performing them. In any case, the correlations are generally low, just barely beyond statistical significance. In spelling out the structure of cognitive abilities, I found myself inclined, or even forced, to assign many

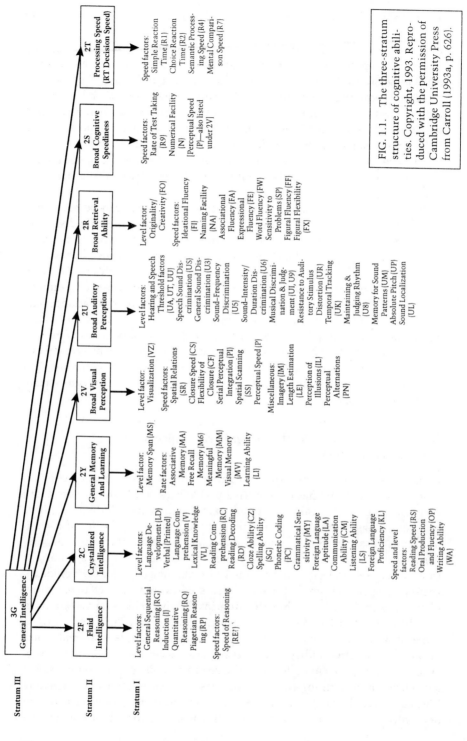

FIG. 1.1. The three-stratum structure of cognitive abilities. Copyright, 1993. Reproduced with the permission of Cambridge University Press from Carroll (1993a, p. 626).

12

of these speed factors to one or the other of two separate second-stratum categories, only remotely related to a general factor (*g*), which I regard as essentially defined as *level* of ability.

This is not the whole story, however. Cognitive psychology should be able to deal with both "level" and "speed" factors. In Fig. 1.1, where I present the structure of cognitive abilities surveyed in my book, it may be noted that most of the stratum II factors embrace both "level" and "speed" factors at stratum I. The second-stratum factors are distinguished from each other not only by content but also by process. In point of fact, cognitive psychology has dealt with both the processes and the contents involved in many tasks subsumed by the cognitive factors identified in my survey. I only regret that because of space and time limitations, I was, for the most part, unable to analyze and show detailed connections between cognitive abilities and relevant findings in cognitive psychology, although I believe I was able at least to suggest some of these connections. In a previous report (Carroll, 1980), I had proposed a set of 8 distinct paradigms and 10 distinct processes that I believed to be potentially useful in analyzing the tasks that underlie cognitive abilities. Possibly these potentialities might be explored in future work.

The Problem of *g* (and Other Higher-Stratum Factors)

In his review, Brand (1993) stressed "the importance of *g*." But Detterman (1982) raised the question of whether *g* exists at all. In my survey, I assumed that the data supported very well the proposition that *g* exists. But Horn (with Noll, chap. 13, this volume) doubted this assumption, insisting that the "general" factors produced in the analysis of different datasets are not necessarily the same, and not necessarily congruent with the general factor assumed by Spearman. Whatever the case may be, the question remains whether a unitary *g* exists, or whether a factorially produced *g* is merely a mathematical artifact. Kranzler and Jensen (1991a, 1991b, 1993) presented evidence purporting to show that *g* is not unitary, but I (Carroll, 1991a, 1991b, 1993b) pointed out that their evidence seems insufficient to permit reaching this conclusion.

The developmental psychologist Ceci (1990) raised interesting questions about the singularity of *g*. He suggested that it may be an artifact resulting from "partially overlapped sampling of [microlevel] cognitive components" (p. 227). In an endnote, he presented a hypothetical scenario:

> Suppose that a battery of three tests (arithmetic, vocabulary, and spatial reasoning) is administered to children and that their scores are factor analyzed and *g* is extracted. Suppose also, for the sake of illustration, that the arith-

metic performance depends on just three microlevel cognitive components
a, *b*, and *c*. (For example, *a* could be verbal encoding of the word problems,
b could be a spatial mapping skill that is relevant for some of the geomet-
ric problems, and *c* could be some highly specific quantitative skill that is
useful for a broad array of arithmetic problems, but not relevant for non-
arithmetical problems.) Now, suppose that the two other tests (vocabulary
and spatial reasoning) also sample some, but not all, of these same microlevel cognitive components, in addition to some components that are highly
specific to themselves. (For example, maybe vocabulary requires *a* [verbal
encoding] as well as *d*, which is the ability to "compare representations"
and *e*, which is a highly specific vocabulary skill.) Finally, suppose that spatial reasoning requires *b*, in order to engage in spatial mapping, *d*, in order to
compare representations, and *f*, which is a highly specific spatial skill. The
vocabulary and arithmetic performances might be correlated because they
share verbal encoding resources (*a*), arithmetic and spatial reasoning might
be correlated because they share a mapping resource (*b*), and vocabulary and
spatial reasoning might be correlated because they share the need to compare representations (*d*). . . . According to this task analysis, *g* could end up
being substantial in magnitude without actually representing a single
source of processing variance that is common to each of the three tasks!
(Ceci, 1990, pp. 226–227)

It seemed to me that it would be useful to investigate Ceci's proposal by
constructing a plasmode in accordance with his hypothetical scenario. Such
a plasmode is shown in Table 1.1 as a hypothetical orthogonal factor matrix,
resulting in a reproduced correlation matrix as shown further on in the table.

TABLE 1.1
Analysis of a Plasmode Constructed to Represent
Ceci's (1990) Scenario for Generating a *g*

	Plasmode						
	Verbal Encoding	*Spatial Mapping*	*Quantitative*	*Comparing Representations*	*Lexical Knowledge*	*Spatial Skill*	h^2
Arith 1	.5	.5	.5	—	—	—	.75
Arith 2	.5	.5	.5	—	—	—	.75
Arith 3	.5	.5	.5	—	—	—	.75
Vocab 1	.5	—	—	.5	.5	—	.75
Vocab 2	.5	—	—	.5	.5	—	.75
Vocab 3	.5	—	—	.5	.5	—	.75
Spatial 1	—	.5	—	.5	—	.5	.75
Spatial 2	—	.5	—	.5	—	.5	.75
Spatial 3	—	.5	—	.5	—	.5	.75

(Continued)

TABLE 1.1
(Continued)

Reproduced Correlation Matrix
(diagonals replaced by 1.00)

	1	2	3	4	5	6	7	8	9
Arith 1	1.00	.75	.75	.25	.25	.25	.25	.25	.25
Arith 2	.75	1.00	.75	.25	.25	.25	.25	.25	.25
Arith 3	.75	.75	1.00	.25	.25	.25	.25	.25	.25
Vocab 1	.25	.25	.25	1.00	.75	.75	.25	.25	.25
Vocab 2	.25	.25	.25	.75	1.00	.75	.25	.25	.25
Vocab 3	.25	.25	.25	.75	.75	1.00	.25	.25	.25
Spatial 1	.25	.25	.25	.25	.25	.25	1.00	.75	.75
Spatial 2	.25	.25	.25	.25	.25	.25	.75	1.00	.75
Spatial 3	.25	.25	.25	.25	.25	.25	.75	.75	1.00

Principal Component Factor Matrix

	1	2	3	4	5	6	7	8	9
Arith 1	.667	−.101	.615	−.361	−.191	.000	.000	.000	.000
Arith 2	.667	−.101	.615	.303	−.136	−.031	.049	−.158	−.167
Arith 3	.667	−.101	.615	.058	.327	.031	−.049	.158	.167
Vocab 1	.667	−.483	−.395	.000	.000	.334	.105	.136	−.160
Vocab 2	.667	−.483	−.395	.000	.000	−.333	−.125	.157	−.124
Vocab 3	.667	−.483	−.395	.000	.000	−.001	.020	−.293	.284
Spatial 1	.667	.583	−.221	.100	−.189	.109	−.284	.107	.131
Spatial 2	.667	.583	−.221	−.119	.225	.008	−.079	−.218	−.219
Spatial 3	.667	.583	−.221	.019	−.036	−.117	.362	.111	.088
Roots	4.000	1.750	1.750	.250	.250	.250	.250	.250	.250

Principal Factor Matrix
(iterated for communalities)

	1	2	3	h^2
Arith 1	.646	−.462	.347	.750
Arith 2	.646	−.462	.347	.750
Arith 3	.646	−.462	.347	.750
Vocab 1	.646	−.070	−.573	.750
Vocab 2	.646	−.070	−.573	.750
Vocab 3	.646	−.070	−.573	.750
Spatial 1	.646	.531	.226	.750
Spatial 2	.646	.531	.226	.750
Spatial 3	.646	.531	.226	.750
Roots	3.750	1.500	1.500	

(Continued)

TABLE 1.1
(Continued)

Varimax Factor Matrix

	1	2	3	h^2
Arith 1	.137	.844	.137	.750
Arith 2	.137	.844	.137	.750
Arith 3	.137	.844	.137	.750
Vocab 1	.143	.137	.843	.750
Vocab 2	.143	.137	.843	.750
Vocab 3	.143	.137	.843	.750
Spatial 1	.845	.138	.131	.750
Spatial 2	.845	.138	.131	.750
Spatial 3	.845	.138	.131	.750
Sums of squares	2.260	2.250	2.240	

Simple Structure Rotated Factor Matrix

	1	2	3
Arith 1	.000	.791	.000
Arith 2	.000	.791	.000
Arith 3	.000	.791	.000
Vocab 1	.000	.000	.791
Vocab 2	.000	.000	.791
Vocab 3	.000	.000	.791
Spatial 1	.791	.000	.000
Spatial 2	.791	.000	.000
Spatial 3	.791	.000	.000

First-Order Factor Correlations

	1	2	3
1	1.000	.333	.333
2	.333	1.000	.333
3	.333	.333	1.000

Hierarchical Orthogonalized Factor Matrix

	g	1	2	3	h^2
Arith 1	.500	.000	.707	.000	.750
Arith 2	.500	.000	.707	.000	.750
Arith 3	.500	.000	.707	.000	.750
Vocab 1	.500	.000	.000	.707	.750
Vocab 2	.500	.000	.000	.707	.750
Vocab 3	.500	.000	.000	.707	.750
Spatial 1	.500	.707	.000	.000	.750
Spatial 2	.500	.707	.000	.000	.750
Spatial 3	.500	.707	.000	.000	.750
Sums of squares	2.250	1.501	1.501	1.501	

The only modification I have made in Ceci's scenario is to posit three examples of each kind of test (i.e., three arithmetic tests with the same factorial composition, three vocabulary tests, and three spatial reasoning tests) in order to ensure that there would be common variance among the three tests of each kind. Now, one problem is immediately apparent: The correlation matrix is only of rank three, and obviously the three factors that could be derived and rotated to simple structure would be correlated, producing a general factor, even though the plasmode is postulated to contain six independent orthogonal factors.

Actually, the plasmode with which we started was only of rank three, and thus couldn't have produced more than three orthogonal factors. I tried to fix this problem by varying some of the weights in the plasmode. The resulting rank six plasmode is shown in Table 1.2, with the generated correlation ma-

TABLE 1.2
Analysis of a Revised Plasmode Constructed to Represent
Ceci's (1990) Scenario for Generating a *g*

| | Plasmode | | | | | | |
	Verbal Encoding	Spatial Mapping	Quantitative	Comparing Representations	Lexical Knowledge	Spatial Skill	h^2
Arith 1	.5	.3	.5	—	—	—	.59
Arith 2	.4	.5	.5	—	—	—	.66
Arith 3	.3	.4	.5	—	—	—	.50
Vocab 1	.5	—	—	.3	.5	—	.59
Vocab 2	.4	—	—	.5	.5	—	.66
Vocab 3	.3	—	—	.4	.5	—	.50
Spatial 1	—	.5	—	.3	—	.5	.59
Spatial 2	—	.4	—	.5	—	.5	.66
Spatial 3	—	.3	—	.4	—	.5	.50

Reproduced Correlation Matrix
(diagonals replaced by 1.00)

	1	2	3	4	5	6	7	8	9
Arith 1	1.00	.60	.52	.25	.20	.15	.15	.12	.09
Arith 2	.60	1.00	.57	.20	.16	.12	.25	.20	.15
Arith 3	.52	.57	1.00	.15	.12	.09	.20	.16	.12
Vocab 1	.25	.20	.15	1.00	.60	.52	.09	.15	.12
Vocab 2	.20	.16	.12	.60	1.00	.57	.15	.25	.20
Vocab 3	.15	.12	.09	.52	.57	1.00	.12	.20	.16
Spatial 1	.15	.25	.20	.09	.15	.12	1.00	.60	.52
Spatial 2	.12	.20	.16	.15	.25	.20	.60	1.00	.57
Spatial 3	.09	.15	.12	.12	.20	.16	.52	.57	1.00

(Continued)

TABLE 1.2
(Continued)

Principal Component Factor Matrix

	1	2	3	4	5	6	7	8	9
Arith 1	.585	−.553	−.256	−.285	−.017	.290	−.113	.330	.001
Arith 2	.621	−.589	−.107	−.047	−.089	.120	.083	−.474	−.002
Arith 3	.551	−.608	−.105	.366	.201	−.353	−.015	.132	.000
Vocab 1	.585	.351	−.498	−.259	−.101	−.291	.260	.039	−.236
Vocab 2	.621	.456	−.388	−.063	−.007	−.127	−.324	−.086	.350
Vocab 3	.551	.473	−.395	.393	.079	.366	.125	.031	−.075
Spatial 1	.585	.055	.607	.090	−.391	−.020	.228	.132	.236
Spatial 2	.621	.202	.564	.044	−.113	−.016	−.341	−.032	−.351
Spatial 3	.551	.213	.579	−.202	.496	.036	.148	−.028	.075
Roots	3.093	1.666	1.664	.494	.477	.459	.399	.380	.368

Principal Factor Matrix
(iterated for communalities)

	1	2	3	4	5	6	h^2
Arith 1	.545	−.489	−.205	−.099	.045	.002	.590
Arith 2	.594	−.438	−.333	.045	−.037	−.029	.660
Arith 3	.496	−.394	−.305	.065	.022	.032	.500
Vocab 1	.545	−.113	.518	−.075	−.079	.002	.590
Vocab 2	.594	.021	.550	.027	.051	−.029	.660
Vocab 3	.496	.023	.498	.068	.004	.032	.500
Spatial 1	.545	.422	−.322	.011	−.109	.002	.590
Spatial 2	.594	.508	−.213	.010	.057	−.029	.660
Spatial 3	.496	.461	−.189	−.051	.045	.032	.500
Roots	2.684	1.250	1.250	.030	.030	.006	

Varimax Factor Matrix

	1	2	3	4	5	6	h^2
Arith 1	.039	.739	.166	.105	−.057	.007	.590
Arith 2	.148	.791	.091	−.020	.056	−.030	.660
Arith 3	.112	.693	.055	−.056	.002	.030	.500
Vocab 1	.044	.159	.741	.103	.050	.005	.590
Vocab 2	.155	.085	.790	−.026	−.058	−.029	.660
Vocab 3	.118	.050	.692	−.060	−.001	.030	.500
Spatial 1	.740	.165	.035	−.002	.116	−.000	.590
Spatial 2	.791	.090	.145	−.036	−.050	−.029	.660
Spatial 3	.693	.053	.109	.025	−.051	.034	.500
SSQR	1.731	1.725	1.725	.032	.031	.006	

(Continued)

TABLE 1.2
(Continued)

Simple Structure Oblique Rotated Factor Matrix

	1	2	3	4	5	6
Arith 1	−.006	.533	.006	.013	−.000	.014
Arith 2	.007	.533	.001	−.013	.027	−.080
Arith 3	−.001	.525	−.007	−.076	−.027	−.014
Vocab 1	−.007	.005	.552	.009	.134	.004
Vocab 2	.008	.001	.561	−.009	−.018	−.017
Vocab 3	−.001	−.005	.547	−.076	.018	.013
Spatial 1	.553	.002	−.007	−.004	.134	−.009
Spatial 2	.562	.001	.008	.016	−.018	.009
Spatial 3	.547	−.003	−.001	−.012	.018	.080

First-Order Factor Correlations

	1	2	3	4	5	6
1	1.000					
2	.215	1.000				
3	.283	.301	1.000			
4	−.121	.356	.568	1.000		
5	−.349	.298	−.351	−.035	1.000	
6	−.573	−.193	.109	.602	.018	1.000

Oblique Procrustes Rotation to Plasmode

	1	2	3	4	5	6
Arith 1	.500	.300	.500	.000	.000	.000
Arith 2	.400	.500	.500	.000	.000	.000
Arith 3	.300	.400	.500	.000	.000	.000
Vocab 1	.500	.000	.000	.300	.500	.000
Vocab 2	.400	.000	.000	.500	.500	.000
Vocab 3	.300	.000	.000	.400	.500	.000
Spatial 1	.000	.500	.000	.300	.000	.500
Spatial 2	.000	.400	.000	.500	.000	.500
Spatial 3	.000	.300	.000	.400	.000	.500

Transformation Matrix From PF Matrix to the Above

	1	2	3	4	5	6
1	.491	.491	.304	.491	.304	.304
2	−.464	.023	−.529	.441	−.028	.556
3	.241	−.522	−.337	.281	.627	−.289
4	−.616	.412	.169	.203	.344	−.513
5	−.121	−.473	.495	.593	−.394	−.101
6	−.304	−.304	.491	−.304	.491	.491

trix, the principal component matrix (note roots), and the principal factor matrix (note roots). Now, we know that this principal factor matrix is an orthogonal transformation of the plasmode (the transformation matrix is shown in the table). However, applying standard rotation and Schmid-Leiman orthogonalization procedures to the principal factor matrix, we do not "recover" anything like the plasmode with which we started; we recover only what looks like a three-factor solution, similar to what was obtained from the rank three plasmode.

The conclusion I draw from this is that *if* psychological tests reflect a series of "partially overlapping microlevel processes" (Ceci, 1990, p. 227), standard procedures of factor analysis will not ordinarily reveal this, and the *g* factor we ordinarily derive is an artifact resulting from the operation of these partially overlapping processes. This is a disappointing result, if it is valid. I am not sure how to proceed to provide a remedy for the artifactual results. Possibly a remedy would come out of designing tests or tasks that would have convergent and divergent validity for exclusively measuring each of the presumptive microlevel processes; that is, they would be loaded only on factors for each of the microlevel processes. Note that the scenario Ceci presented assumed that all the presumed microlevel processes were orthogonal to each other. One could still conceive a valid *g* factor derived from the correlations of microlevel processes, if they are not actually orthogonal to each other. Obviously, what we need at the present time is a full-scale investigation of possible microlevel cognitive processes and the ways in which they affect performance on more traditional types of tests in various cognitive domains. It appears that Kyllonen and Christal (1989) initiated a program of such studies.

Note that the problem I have described as applying to the computation and interpretation of *g* may also apply to the computation and interpretation of *any* higher-order factor, such as those in stratum II of my model.

The Problem of Development

In my book, I called for greater attention to "cross-sectional, or even better, longitudinal studies to investigate the 'normal' development of factors over age, that is, development that takes place in the course of normal maturation without any special intervention that is designed to improve abilities" (Carroll, 1993a, p. 694). I could have pointed out, of course, that numerous longitudinal studies exist; I could mention, for example, the longitudinal studies of talented individuals covered in a recent volume edited by Subotnik and Arnold (1994). But many of these studies concern the development, essentially, of *g* or IQ; with some exceptions, they take little account of specific abilities identified by factorial studies. I would hope that, in the future, the analysis of ability structure presented in my book could serve as a guide for those planning cross-sectional and longitudinal studies.

Problems of Nature and Nurture:
Behavioral Genetics and Ability Modification Studies

Similarly, I would insist that studies of heritability, ability modification, and related issues are more likely to lead to detailed understanding if they are guided by an orientation to the structure of abilities as presented in my book.

Problems of Validity.   What is the eventual meaning and relevance of individual differences in abilities? This is a question that I deliberately avoided trying to answer in my book, partly because I believed that I would be staggered by any attempt to survey the vast field of validity studies, if by that phrase one means studies attempting to show the predictive power of ability measurements in various fields of practical endeavor—education, military training, occupational success, and the like. Currently accepted wisdom maintains that the validity of ability measurements depends mostly on the predictive powers of general intelligence, g (Hunter, 1986). I am inclined to believe, however, that this point of view is unsatisfactory, for several reasons. First, even if test validity primarily depends on g, it is intellectually unsatisfying to leave it at that, because it fails to provide an explanation of why g produces validity, particularly in view of the debate about whether g exists, or about of what it consists.

Second, it is my impression that there is much evidence, in various places, that special abilities (i.e., abilities measured by second- or first-stratum factors) contribute significantly to predictions. This has been my experience, for example, in predicting success in foreign- or second-language learning (Carroll, 1974). Using structural modeling techniques, Gustafsson and Balke (1993) showed that differentiation among at least a limited number of broad abilities may be worthwhile in predicting school success in different domains. In publishing a handbook relating many different human abilities to job task requirements, Fleishman and Reilly (1992) appeared to assume that measurements of these abilities are significantly valid in selecting and placing individuals in various occupational categories, and one can presume that they had adequate empirical evidence for their statements. At this point I can only say that there is need for assembling presently available data on the validity of factor-analytically defined abilities in various contexts, and for using new knowledge on the definition and structure of abilities to pursue further studies on the validity of those ability measurements.

CONCLUSION

Whether or not my book on human cognitive abilities can be regarded as an important milestone in its field, I hope that it can at least serve as a guide and reference for future researchers. However, I also think that my book leaves much to be desired, in that it fails to answer a plethora of fundamental questions about cognitive abilities—their structure, sources and meanings.

REFERENCES

Bellugi, U., Bihrle, A., Jernigan, T., Trauner, D., & Doherty, S. (1991). Neuropsychological, neurological, and neuroanatomical profile of Williams Syndrome. *American Journal of Medical Genetics Supplement, 6*, 115–125.

Brand, C. (1993, October 22). The importance of the *g* factor [Review of Carroll, 1993a]. *Times Higher Education Supplement,* October 22, p. 22.

Brody, N. (1994). Cognitive abilities [Review of Carroll, 1993a]. *Psychological Science, 5* (63), 65–68.

Burns, R. B. (1994). Surveying the cognitive terrain [Review of Carroll, 1993a]. *Educational Researcher, 23*(2), 35–37.

Cardon, L. R., & Fulker, D. W. (1993). Genetics of specific cognitive abilities. In R. Plomin & G. E. McClearn (Eds.), *Nature, nurture, and psychology* (pp. 99–120). Washington, DC: American Psychological Association.

Carroll, J. B. (1974). The aptitude-achievement distinction: The case of foreign language aptitude and proficiency. In D. R. Green (Ed.), *The aptitude-achievement distinction: Proceedings of the Second CTB/McGraw-Hill Conference on Issues in Educational Measurement* (pp. 286–311). Monterey, CA: CTB/McGraw-Hill.

Carroll, J. B. (1980). *Individual difference relations in psychometric and experimental cognitive tasks* (Report No. 163). Chapel Hill, NC: The L. L. Thurstone Psychometric Laboratory, University of North Carolina (NTIS Doc. AD-A086 057; ERIC Doc. ED 191 891).

Carroll, J. B. (1989). Factor analysis since Spearman: Where do we stand? What do we know? In R. Kanfer, P. L. Ackerman, & R. Cudeck (Eds.), *Abilities, motivation, and methodology: The Minnesota Symposium on Learning and Individual Differences* (pp. 43–67). Hillsdale, NJ: Lawrence Erlbaum Assocates.

Carroll, J. B. (1990). Estimating item and ability parameters in homogeneous tests with the person characteristic function. *Applied Psychological Measurement, 14*, 109–125.

Carroll, J. B. (1991a). No demonstration that *g* is not unitary, but there's more to the story: Comment on Kranzler and Jensen. *Intelligence, 15*, 423–436.

Carroll, J. B. (1991b). Still no demonstration that *g* is not unitary: Further comment on Kranzler and Jensen. *Intelligence, 15*, 449–453.

Carroll, J. B. (1993a). *Human cognitive abilities: A survey of factor-analytic studies.* New York: Cambridge University Press.

Carroll, J. B. (1993b). The unitary *g* problem once more: On Kranzler and Jensen. *Intelligence, 17*, 15–16.

Carroll, J. B. (1994). An alternative, Thurstonian view of intelligence. *Psychological Inquiry, 5*, 195–197.

Carroll, J. B. (1995). On methodology in the study of cognitive abilities. *Multivariate Behavioral Research, 30,* 429–452.

Ceci, S. J. (1990). *On intelligence . . . more or less: A bioecological treatise on intellectual development.* Englewood Cliffs, NJ: Prentice-Hall.

Detterman, D. K. (1982). Does "g" exist? *Intelligence, 6,* 99–108.

Eysenck, H. J. (1994). [Special review of Carroll, 1993a]. *Personality and Individual Differences, 16,* 199.

Fleishman, E. A., & Reilly, M. E. (1992). *Handbook of human abilities: Definitions, measurement, and job task requirements.* Palo Alto, CA: Consulting Psychologists Press.

Gardner, H. (1983). *Frames of mind: The theory of multiple intelligences.* New York: Basic Books.

Gould, S. J. (1981). *The mismeasure of man.* New York: Norton.

Gustafsson, J.-E., & Balke, G. (1993). General and specific abilities as predictors of school achievement. *Multivariate Behavioral Research, 28,* 407–434.

Halpern, D. F. (1991). *Sex differences in cognitive abilities* (2nd ed.). Hillsdale, NJ: Lawrence Erlbaum Associates.

Hebb, D. O. (1949). *The organization of behavior: A neuropsychological theory.* New York: Wiley.

Herrnstein, R. J. (1982, August). IQ testing and the media. *Atlantic Monthly,* pp. 68–74.

Humphreys, L. G. (1994). Intelligence from the standpoint of a (pragmatic) behaviorist. *Psychological Inquiry, 5,* 179–192.

Hunter, J. E. (1986). Cognitive ability, cognitive aptitudes, job knowledge, and job performance. *Journal of Vocational Behavior, 29,* 340–362.

Katzenberger, L. (1964). *Dimensionen des Gedächtnisses* [Dimensions of memory]. Unpublished doctoral dissertation, Universität Würzburg.

Kosko, B. (1993). *Fuzzy thinking: The new science of fuzzy logic.* New York: Hyperion.

Kranzler, J. H., & Jensen, A. R. (1991a). The nature of psychometric *g:* Unitary process or a number of independent processes? *Intelligence, 15,* 397–421.

Kranzler, J. H., & Jensen, A. R. (1991b). Unitary *g:* Unquestioned postulate or empirical fact? *Intelligence, 15,* 437–448.

Kranzler, J. H., & Jensen, A. R. (1993). Psychometric *g* is still not unitary after eliminating supposed "impurities": Further comment on Carroll. *Intelligence, 17,* 11–14.

Kyllonen, P. C., & Christal, R. E. (1989). Cognitive modeling of learning abilities: A status report of LAMP. In R. F. Dillon & J. W. Pellegrino (Eds.), *Testing: Theoretical and applied perspectives* (pp. 146–173). New York: Praeger.

Nagoshi, C. T. (1994). The factor-analytic guide to cognitive abilities [Review of Carroll, 1993a]. *Contemporary Psychology, 39,* 617–618.

Palmer, J., MacLeod, C. M., Hunt, E., & Davidson, J. E. (1985). Information processing correlates of reading. *Journal of Memory and Language, 24,* 59–88.

Sternberg, R. J. (1994a). 468 factor-analyzed data sets: What they tell us and don't tell us about human intelligence [Review of Carroll, 1993a]. *Psychological Science, 5,* 63–65.

Sternberg, R. J. (1994b). *Encyclopedia of human intelligence.* New York: Macmillan.

Subotnik, R. F., & Arnold, K. D. (Eds.) (1994). *Beyond Terman: Contemporary longitudinal studies of giftedness and talent.* Norwood, NJ: Ablex.

Tucker, L. R., & Finkbeiner, C. T. (1981, December). *Transformation of factors by artificial personal probability functions* (ETS Report RR-81-58). Princeton, NJ: Educational Testing Service.

Introduction of
Raymond B. Cattell

John L. Horn
University of Southern California

Raymond Cattell was born in 1905 in Staffordshire, England. In 1924, he earned a Bachelor of Science Degree in Chemistry from Kings College of the University of London. But then, as he wrote: "On a cold and foggy London morning in 1924 I turned my back on the shining flasks and tubes of my well-equipped chemistry bench and walked over to Charles Spearman's laboratory to explore the promise of psychology, . . . my broader reading having led me to see that psychology was the really new, challenging frontier of science, and the source of rational hopes for human progress" (Cattell, 1984, p. 121).

His principal advisor in graduate work was Spearman, but he also studied with Cyril Burt. Cattell finished a Ph.D. in psychology in 1929. His dissertation topic was "The Subjective Character of Cognition" (Cattell, 1930). In 1939, the University of London awarded him the Doctor of Science (D.Sc.) degree.

His first professorial position was at the University of Exeter. Then, from 1934 through 1937, he directed the child guidance clinic for the city of Leicester. He also served as psychologist and teacher at the Dartington Hall School. In 1937, he came to the United States to be a research associate with E. L. Thorndike at Columbia University. He gained citizenship in the first year of his residence in this country. From 1938 to 1941, Cattell was G. Stanley Hall Professor of Genetic Psychology at Clark University. From 1941 to 1944, he was a Lecturer and Fellow in Psychology at Harvard University. From 1944 to 1945, Cattell served as a civilian consultant to the Adjutant General's Office, Personnel Research Division, developing tests and research on personality. As World War II came to an end in 1945, he took a much-coveted Research Professorship in Personality at the University of Illinois in

Urbana, where he founded and directed the Laboratory of Personality Assessment. He remained in that position for 27 years.

Cattell's retirement from University of Illinois in 1973 enabled him to leave a climate he never liked and move to Hawaii, where year-round he could enjoy sailing, a favorite pastime. There, at the University of Hawaii, he turned his immense energies to further refining and specifying personality theory, particularly parts dealing with motivation and the relationship between personality and learning.

Cattell's writings on theory and method, as well as his findings from empirical research, have contributed immensely to the breadth and depth of modern scientific psychology. He has been, as Lewis Goldberg characterized him, psychology's master strategist. In more than 50 books and 500 articles, he has put forth a theory of human behavior rivaled in comprehensiveness only by the theory of Freud, and rivaled by no other theory in adherence to evidence derived from empirical research. He must rank among the 20th century's most influential behavioral scientists.

Cattell's premier theoretical contribution was his book *Personality, A Systematic, Theoretical, and Factual Study*, published in 1950, when the author was 45 years old. The book was a comprehensive description and developmental explanation of human individual differences. For the development of a science of personality, this book is among the most influential publications of this century. In it Cattell developed a methodologically sophisticated and theoretically comprehensive program of research for systematically studying the phenomena of human behavior through measures derived from self-reports, ratings of others, and objective test performances. This plan of attack had massive influence on the entire field of psychology. The theory of the book came to be characterized as *trait theory*—in particular, *multivariate trait theory*—but it was much more than an account of enduring characteristics whereby one person is distinguished from another; it also took into account phenomena of evanescent states and of systematic changes in behavior brought about through motivation and learning, and it dealt with short-term and over-a-lifetime changes associated with physiological functions and agents that affect physiological functions.

This 1950 book, two other books published in 1946 and 1949, and 41 studies published between 1940 and 1950 were widely recognized as providing basic evidence of organization among variables indicating personality, which includes intelligence and psychopathology. The regularities identified in Cattell's research of this period, although now appearing in other guises, remain among the principal contributions to theoretical analysis of personality. These regularities and the theory Cattell put together to help describe and explain them are embodied in contemporary conceptions of cognitive capabilities, learning, memory, perception, emotion, and motivation.

A strongly attractive feature of Cattell's approach is his combination of cultural, sociological, neurophysiological, and psychological constructs to promote a complete understanding of human behavior. This approach may be too ambitious to be fully realized in practice, but as indication of the phenomena to be described in a science of personality, it provides an immensely valuable template for the design of research.

Cattell has been among the more controversial psychologists of this century. The nature of much of this controversy is illustrated by two books he wrote in 1937. In one book, *The Fight for Our National Intelligence*, he put forth, first, a theory that major cognitive capabilities stem from genetic factors and, second, an argument (based on findings from large sample studies he had done in previous years) that because people of low ability were reproducing at a more rapid rate than were people of high ability, dysgenic influences were producing a societal decline in the genetic potential for developing high levels of intelligence. Appearing in the years when Adolf Hitler was putting forth programs of sterilization of the "unfit" and proclaiming that an "Aryan super race" should run the world, Cattell's arguments for eugenics aroused much discussion and led many to give him the same brand as was given Hitler.

The other 1937 book that represents ideas that have made Cattell so controversial is *Human Affairs From the Standpoint of the Social Sciences* (edited with Travers and Cohen). In this book, Cattell brought together writings of Haldane, Katz, Malnowski, Mannheim, Ellis, and McDougall to develop a thesis that the findings and methods of science should be applied to solve political and social problems. This thesis and his arguments for eugenics were carried forward in other writings. They were brought to focus in what was called *A New Morality From Science: Beyondism* (Cattell, 1972). In this writing, Cattell argued that the findings of science indicate that the development of large political organizations—large nations—is inimical to the maintenance and advancement of the human species. Instead, he maintained, humans should be organized in small, independent communities that peacefully compete in advancing particular views about the correct way to live. A principle of survival of the fittest communities, analogous to the Darwinian principle of survival of the fittest individuals, would then operate to enable human societies to adapt and improve. The more successful of such communities would, Cattell reasoned, adopt eugenic policies.

These writings were both praised and reviled. The book has "the power to provoke thought . . . the first trait of a classic" wrote Thoern Haag (1973) in a review. In contrast, Cardiss Collins (1993), a congresswoman in the U.S. House of Representatives, opined that: "I personally find Dr. Cattell's views on eugenics and his ideas of a future world abhorrent." Such reactions illustrate the provocative and controversial quality of Cattell's writings.

Always thinking, hardworking, hugely imaginative, and creative, but at the same time low key and humorous, Cattell has had great ability to inspire students and younger colleagues. There is not time here to do justice to this feature of his contributions, but the evidence of this influence can be seen in the long list of former students and colleagues who have become respected scientists. Impressive evidence can also be found in the affection, admiration, and high respect these people show for Cattell.

In his chapter, Cattell writes from the perspective of his studies of human abilities. These studies are among his earliest works, but his statement of a theory of fluid and crystallized intelligence, first sketched in 1941, has been most influential. In that 1941 paper, he summarized evidence suggesting that abilities regarded as indicating intelligence are not unitary, but instead appear to indicate separate intelligences. Abilities of reasoning that are required to attain understanding of novel relationships and acquire concepts indicate one form of intelligence, which he called *fluid* (g_f). Abilities of maintaining and accessing concepts, and reasoning with these concepts, indicate a second form of intelligence, which Cattell labeled *crystallized* (g_c). He suggested that the abilities of fluid intelligence are highly sensitive to neurological damage and factors associated with aging in adulthood, but the abilities of crystallized intelligence are much less affected by the influences of aging and neurological damage. (A line of research founded on these observations, launched some 20 years later, would keep one of his students— namely, this one—more or less gainfully occupied for most of his professional career.) In his chapter, Cattell gives his current thoughts on what has become of g_f-g_c theory and where we have come in developing a scientific understanding of human cognitive abilities.

REFERENCES

Cattell, R. B. (1930). The subjective character of cognition. *British Journal of Psychology Series*, No. 5. Cambridge, England: Cambridge University Press.

Cattell, R. B. (1937). *The fight for our national intelligence*. London: King.

Cattell, R. B., Travers, R. M., & Cohen, J. (Eds.). (1937). *Human affairs from the standpoint of the social sciences*. New York: Macmillan.

Cattell, R. B. (1941). Some theoretical issues in adult intelligence testing. *Psychological Bulletin, 38,* 592.

Cattell, R. B. (1946). *The description and measurement of personality*. New York: Harcourt, Brace, & World.

Cattell, R. B. (1949). *An introduction to personality study*. London: Hutchinson.

Cattell, R. B. (1950). *Personality, a systematic, theoretical, and factual study*. New York: McGraw-Hill.

Cattell, R. B. (1972). *A new morality from science: Beyondism*. New York: Pergamon.

Cattell, R. B. (1984). The voyage of a laboratory, 1928–1984. *Multivariate Behavioral Research, 19,* 121–174.

Collins, C. (1993, December 13). *Letter to Mr. Joseph N. Crowley, President, National Collegiate Athletic Association*. Washington, DC: United States House of Representatives, Subcommittee on Commerce, Consumer Protection, and Competitiveness (pp. 1–7).

Haag, T. (1973). Review: A new morality from science: Beyondism, by Raymond B. Cattell. *Faith and Freedom, 26,* 9–23.

2

Where Is Intelligence?
Some Answers
From the Triadic Theory

Raymond B. Cattell
University of Hawaii, Emeritus

Modern intelligence theory begins in the year 1904, in which, simultaneously, Binet put forward the first practical intelligence test (Binet & Simon, 1905) and Spearman published his theoretical breakthrough in the article, "Intelligence Objectively Determined and Measured" (Spearman, 1904).

The difference between the practical and the theoretical streams has curiously persisted down to the present day. For most of a century, many psychologists have followed the Binet tradition of adding test to test according to a commonsense idea of what intelligence is. Meanwhile, on a different level, Spearman's introduction of factor analysis has bloomed into a vast field of multivariate experimental attacks on theory. The bankruptcy of the alleged practical approach is shown in the response of the WAIS, WISC, and other Binet derivatives to the question, "What is intelligence?" Their innocent reply is, "Intelligence is what intelligence tests measure."

Spearman, on the other hand, asked the basic questions, "Is intelligence a single power?" and "If so, what operations will measure it, with concept validity?" He answered the first positively by intercorrelating a large number of cognitive performances and showing that the universal positive correlations implied the existence of a single power. The technical proof of this lay in the fact that correlation tables could be arranged in a hierarchy falling from left to right and from above down. He noted that the highest correlations were for complex performance in mathematics, classical grammar and the like.

However, Thurstone and Burt noticed that such perfect matrices were found only by rejecting many performances that would not fit the hierarchy. They developed the use of the new multifactorial analysis. In the 1930s, Thurstone found a set of primary abilities—verbal, mathematical, spatial, perceptual, and so on. This caused great excitement in the educational world. Many rebels against individual differences held the discovery as the end of the individual IQ. For a few years, they cried that the IQ was dead. In 1940, however, Spearman and Thurstone reconciled their difference by the further discovery that the primaries correlated positively and yielded Spearman's g as a second-order factor among them.

At the APA Annual Meeting in 1942, however, I examined these intercorrelations and came up with the startling finding that a single general factor was not enough; there were two general factors. These are related as shown in Fig. 2.1.

When this two general factors model was confirmed a few years later by

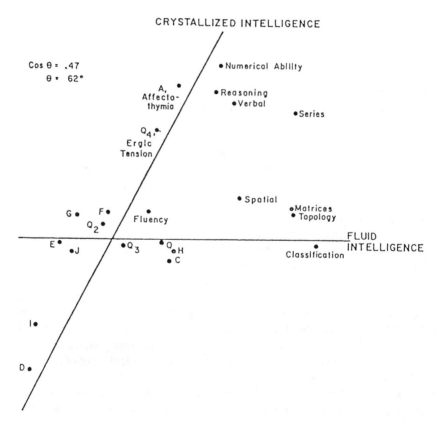

FIG 2.1.   Plot of g_f and g_c intelligence factors showing simple structure and correlation of abilities. Capital letters refer to primary personality factors (from Horn & Cattell, 1967).

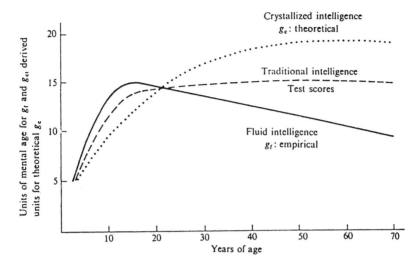

FIG 2.2. Age plots of the investment theory of fluid into crystallized intelligence. Age: 5, 15, 25, 35, 45, 55, 65, 75; g_f values: 9, 15, 14, 13, 12, 11, 10, 9; g_c values: 6.7, 13.0, 16.2, 17.9, 18.8, 19.3, 19.5, 19.6; g_{ct} traditional intelligence test curve.

the work of Horn, we called them "fluid and crystallized" intelligences. Fluid intelligence, termed g_f, showed its highest correlations in performing complex analyses where there was no advantage from previous knowledge. Crystallized intelligence, termed g_c, was found on cultural performances and the use of what one has learned and stored up. Fluid intelligence occurred in what were called *culture fair intelligence tests*, which gave the same mean score in Britain, France, Germany, China, and India, but this culture fairness was only a secondary advantage.

The scientifically interesting feature of the fluid and crystallized distinction is that although the division was first revealed by factor analysis, it soon showed all sorts of other differences. Four of the most obvious are:

1. The age plot curve is quite different. Both reach a maximum between 16 and 21, but thereafter fluid intelligence steadily declines throughout adulthood. Crystallized intelligence, as Horn (Horn, 1972; Horn & Cattell, 1967) showed, slowly improves throughout active life (see Fig. 2.2). I return to this important difference later in this chapter.

2. Second, there is a striking difference in the standard deviation of IQs. We are accustomed to a sigma of 16 points of IQ in old-fashioned crystallized intelligence tests, whereas the new g_f showed a startling variance of 24 points—a 50% increase.

3. Studies by both the twin methods and the new MAVA method show

that fluid intelligence is far more heritable. The heritability stands at 80% plus, whereas for crystallized intelligence it reaches about 40%. Incidentally, this accounts for the long arguments about inheritance of intelligence because past tests have been an uneven mixture of g_f and g_c.

4. There is suspicion of a neural, physiological difference, which was first noticed by Hebb (1942) and Lashley (1963) and more recently by Horn (Horn, 1972; Horn & Cattell, 1967). Lashley found with rats that ablation of a part of the brain removed *specific* capacities but also reduced *general* learning ability directly in proportion to the mass removed. Clinical work with humans suggests that g_f is affected no matter which part of the cortex is injured, whereas the loss in g_c is specific to a given area and a given performance.

I discuss later the evidence on these four differences and their implication. The last of the four suggests that g_f intelligence is the action of the whole cortex. It is, however, the least confirmed of the four, but evidence that brain size is proportional to intelligence supports it. This comes from many sources: First, the relation of brain to body weight seems to predict the differing intelligences of animal species. Second, archaeologists find in the evolution of humans a continuous increase in brain size from homo-erectus onward. Finally, among humans there is a correlation of about + 0.3 between measured head size and intelligence. It may be low because head size does not perfectly predict brain size, or because hormone conditions in the brain also affect neural efficiency.

Returning to the high heritability of fluid intelligence, we get further evidence of the neural basis. It points to the need to measure g_f rather than g_c in most predicting situations.

As to the difference of g_f and g_c in standard deviations of IQ (measured in the classical way), we must surely suppose that in the genesis of g_c from investing in life and classroom experience, there is pressure toward the mean. The busy teacher puts upward pressure on the dull and leaves the really bright more to their own devices. This tendency in g_c to regress toward the mean has been clearly shown in MAVA method studies of heredity. The old twin method of studying heredity has the defect that it yields no term for the covariance of genetic and environmental influences. This latter I have called the *genothreptic* correlation. The first determination of its value, by MAVA, shows that it is negative, not only in intelligence, but in all 16 personality traits in the 16 PF (Cattell, Eber, & Tatsuoka, 1970). We might have expected such pressure in, say, the dominance trait, to suppress the more dominant and lift the esteem of the downtrodden, but it is surprising in intelligence. However, it is not only the classroom, but in the whole culture (e.g., as seen on TV) that pressure is all toward equality.

Finally, we come to the first finding—the downward trend in fluid intelligence after the age of 21. This truth is so distasteful that it has been most criticized, but it stands very firm in statistical surveys, showing a fall of about 3 points of IQ every 10 years. In the first place, it should surely not surprise us when we know of the life curve of all measures of physiological vitality. Exactly the same course is shown by hearing acuity, greatest strength of handgrip, oxygen consumption per pound of body weight, and so on. When we partial out general speed of reaction, however, the trend is still there.

One speculation is that the trend is not innate but is the effect of culture, particularly of a society that smokes and drinks to excess. A more general environmental theory is that blows on the head (e.g., in football, attacks of fever, poor nutrition, minor strokes, etc.) become cumulatively more effective the longer we live. These propositions have not been tested, and we can probably attribute most of the downward trend as part of the inevitable course from birth to death. It does raise the question, however, of why we put our fate in the hands of elderly politicians rather than in younger men and women.

I turn to the general structure of abilities, which I have expressed in the Triadic Theory (Cattell, 1987). When we factor a wide collection of primary abilities we find some six or seven secondary abilities of a global kind. They are g_f, g_c, immediate or short-term memory and retrieval (SAR), distant memory and retrieval (LER), visual capacity, and perceptual speed. In the Triadic Theory we go beyond the immediate factor revelation of order, yielding what we call the *general factors*, to separate a specific subgroup, which we call the smaller *provincial factors*. These have been known for some time as *visual ability* and *kinaesthetic ability*, and have been added to recently by the discovery by Horn and Stankov (1989) of *auditory ability*. These provincial abilities may be regarded as sensory centers that accumulate immediate interpretive abilities around the sensory center. For example, when hearing declines it is not just in sensory alertness, but also in the interpretation of words and common sounds. These *ps* (or provincials), which need to be supplemented by the study of smells and tastes, are much narrower than the *gs* (or general abilities), but are wider and different in form from the primary abilities, which may be called agencies (*as*).

Thus, instead of a two-rank hierarchical theory we find, in the Triadic Theory, a peculiar three-rank structure, in which provincials operate between the *gs* and the *as* as shown in Fig. 2.3. That is to say, the *ps* are essential to the birth and growth of *as*, but are themselves integrated by action of the six broad general factors.

We have still to explain the fact that in spite of g_c elements being sporadically learned they nevertheless appear as a unitary factor. There are two reasons for this unitariness. First there is what we may call the Investment Theory, which says that the unitariness of g_c is due to the fact that it expresses the unitary factor g_f invested in a host of random unorganized expe-

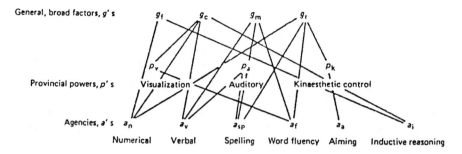

FIG 2.3.   Model of the triadic theory of ability structure. The diagram would become a tangle if all directions of influence were drawn as path coefficients. A sufficient sample is drawn to indicate, as in the text, the agencies draw on both ps and gs, and that some degree of recursive action accurs between g and ps. This last prevents a ready separation of g and ps by simple factor analysis.

riences. This produces a correlation of about 0.5 between g_f and g_c (as illustrated in Fig. 2.1). But then we notice that, at least as far as school experience is concerned, there is already a uniform learning exposure to all elements of a curriculum. Uneven exposure to school life would thus produce a unitary factor, representing the curriculum. But why does this pattern blend with that due to g_f investment? The fact is that since time immemorial—since the trivium and quadrivium curricula of the Middle Ages—schools have always imposed more demands on g_f than does random life experience. Thus, there is a true unitariness to g_c, due to the simultaneous action of social factors, curricula choice, and investment of g_f in progress in anything requiring intellect.

However, this view imposes a problem in measuring g_c beyond the school age. As Horn (1972) pointed out, g_c represents the storage of all clever things we have learned. It continues with a moderate increase through life not only because of new g_f investments, but also because work is continually done on stored skills to organize their memories better for immediate retrieval. I have put forward a formula that describes the growth of g_c in terms of (a) new additions from g_f action, and (b) forgetting of acquisitions. I have written this (see Cattell, 1987) as

$$g_{c.x} = \sum_{k=0}^{x} [g_f^{-x} g_{f.x}^{(1-k)}],$$

where $g_{c.x}$ is the level of g_c in the years x, $g_{f.x}$ is the strength of the (declining) g_f in the same year x, and g_f^{-x} is the result of continual loss of g_f, which is the forgetting rate of what one once has acquired. The expression thus gives us the level of g_c at year x from opposed tendencies. The plot from this equation agrees reasonably well with the empirical plot of g_c.

There is one big practical problem to accurately measuring g_c: After the school years are over, the areas in which people get experience differ considerably. The same g_c test would not do for comparing a doctor and a lawyer. Psychometric ingenuity and extensive comparisons of fields may eventually overcome this, but at present we have to rely on harking back to the end of high school data, when life investments were very similar for all. The main argument, however, for measurement of intelligence after high school is in g_f tests. Besides, g_f looks forward, whereas g_c looks backward in making the predictions of criteria. Surveys of the loading patterns of g_f and g_c are shown in Table 2.1.

A survey such as this presentation, of the structure and origin of abilities, would not be complete without a quick glance at social implications. In an

TABLE 2.1
Some Empirical Relationships for Fluid and Crystallized Intelligence

Seventh- and Eighth-Grade Boys and Girls (N = 277 14- to 15-Year-Olds)		
Primaries	Fluid Intelligence g_f	Crystallized Intelligence g_c
Thurstone primaries:		
Verbal ability	.15	.46
Spatial ability	.32	.14
Reasoning ability	.08	.50
Numerical ability	.05	.59
Fluency	.07	.19
IPAT Culture Fair:		
Series	.35	.43
Classification	.63	−.02
Matrices	.50	.10
Topology	.51	.09
Personality, HSPQ:		
A Cyclothymia	−.04	.52
C Ego strength	.21	−.07
D Excitability	−.04	−.44
E Dominance	−.15	−.01
F Surgery	−.05	.09
I Premsia	−.09	−.29
Q Ergic tension	−.04	.37

Fourth- and Fifth-Grade Boys and Girls (N = 306 10- to 11-year-olds)		
Primaries	Fluid Intelligence g_f	Crystallized Intelligence g_c
Culture Fair Intelligence		
IPAT	.78	.09
Verbal ability	.22	.63
Numerical ability	.47	.35
Spatial ability	.73	.03

age alert to sexist implications, for example, we want to know whether males and females differ in intelligence. The answer is a definite "No," although there has been a curious indication within persons of African origins that the women tend to be slightly more intelligent than the men. But everywhere else the tests show males and females have indistinguishable results.

There are real differences, however, in the lower-order factors, women being higher on verbal ability and men on spatial ability. There are also suggestions of racial differences from the work of Lynn and of Jensen in that Mongolians are higher on spatial ability and Europeans on verbal ability.

A matter of more immediate concern is the distribution of ability by classes, and any indications of change over time. For example, it has been known since Heron measured it in 1900 that the birth rate decreases with higher social status. (As the old song goes, "The rich get richer and the poor get children.") However, no effect of this on intelligence could be inferred from status. Thus, in 1935, I made a survey of intelligence and size of family in Britain and came out with the alarming finding that whereas in the 80–95 IQ range the mean family size was 3.5, in the 105–120 range it was only 1.5. As Leonard Darwin, Darwin's son, pointed out, this must mean a dysgenic, backward evolution if it continued. I calculated that it would produce a fall of average IQ at the rate of 1 point every 10 years. Just the same value has been recently found for the American population by the population statistician named Vining (1982).

The heredity of g_f being what we know it to be—80% between families—points to alarming conclusions, which I predicted in 1936, in the form of decline of school standards, an increase of violent crime, and a permanent unemployment at the unskilled level. This work led to a finding that has sometimes been called "Cattell's paradox": Re-testing at intervals over the last 50 years shows no decline and even a fair improvement. Unfortunately, most testing was done by g_c tests, like the WAIS and the Binet, before Culture Fair tests arrived. But it is clear that the dysgenic rate is being corrected, perhaps largely by selective marriage and by a death rate that must be higher for the less intelligent. Sociologists who are serious, and who give up the prejudices that everything is environmental, should be concentrating research on this problem, to remove our anxiety.

Among the social problems of intelligence testing is, first, the clinging to old g_c tests like the WAIS. There is also a rather widespread opposition to using tests to examine individual inequality. During the 19th century there was a widespread application to human life of the advances in the physical sciences. We now face a different problem in the acceptance of the results of psychological science, in its impact on privacy and on prepsychological political ideas.

A final social problem of intelligence arises in the field of science. In recent years, reasoning has been unable to keep up with experimental findings. Schrodinger and Derek spoke of an *indeterminacy* principle, in which nature seems insusceptible to human logic. They said, "God plays dice," but Einstein had faith to say, "God does not play dice. He is subtle but not vindictive." Alas, Einstein died before reaching his uniform theory.

As a final personal note, let me add that it seems to me that the prejudice against anything being subject to heredity is quite widespread among uneducated people. When they lectured on heredity and intelligence, both Jensen and my friend Eysenek in England were physically attacked by apparently left-wing student groups. The same happened to Herrnstein at Harvard and to me personally last year when I spoke at the University of Munich. The recent medical findings on the action of particular genes has, however, done much to make calm discussion of the problems easier.

The necessary reaction is obvious. We must watch the mutations among our most eminent intelligences and foster an increase of brain size and of intelligence. Then we may understand what eludes our present lower intelligence. A movement in this eugenic direction I have called "Beyondism." This philosophy of mine admits that much of mankind is obsolete and that continuing the past course of evolution, from Austrolopethesus to Cromagnon man, we need to go beyond ourselves.

To conclude this chapter, I list some references to the work described. I am also aware, as the reader should be, that my personal views stated here are not shared by either the conference organizers or the other conference presenters.

REFERENCES

Binet, A., & Simon, T. (1905). Methodes Nouvelles pour le diagnostic des virience intellectuel des amormaux. *L'Annee Psychologiche, 11*, 191–244.

Boyle, G. J., & Start, K. B. (1989). Sex differences on the prediction of academic achievement. *British Journal of Educational Psychology, 59*, 245–252.

Burt, C. L. (1940). *Factors of the mind.* London: London University Press.

Carroll, J. B. (1993). *Human cognitive abilities.* Cambridge, England: Cambridge University Press.

Cattell, R. B. (1937). *The fight for our national intelligence.* London: King.

Cattell, R. B. (1982). *The inheritance of personality and ability.* New York: Academic Press.

Cattell, R. B. (1987). *Intelligence: Its structure, growth and action.* Amsterdam: Elsevier.

Cattell, R. B., Eber, H. J., & Tatsuoka, M. (1990). *Handbook for the sixteen personality factor questionnaire.* Champaign, IL: the Institute for Personality and Ability Testing.

Cattell, R. B., & Horn, J. L. (1978). A check on the theory of fluid and crystallized intelligence with descriptions of new sub-test designs. *Journal of Educational Measurement, 15*, 139–164.

Hakstian, R., & Cattell, R. B. (1978). Higher stratum ability factors on a basis of twenty primaries. *Journal of Educational Psychology, 74*, 657–669.

Hebb, R. Q. (1942). The effects of early and late brain injury upon test scores. *American Philosophical Society, 89*, 275–292.

Horn, J. L. (1972). State, trait and change dimensions of intelligence. *British Journal of Educational Psychology, 42,* 159–186.

Horn, J. L., & Cattell, R. B. (1966). Age differences in primary mental ability factors. *Journal of Gerontology, 21*(2), 210–220.

Horn, J. L., & Stankov, L. (1982). Auditory and visual factors of intelligence. *Intelligence, 6,* 165–185.

Jensen, A. R. (1969). How much can we boost I.Q. and scholastic achievement. *Harvard Educational Review* (Winter Issue), 1–125.

Lashley, K. S. (1963). *Brain mechanisms and intelligence.* New York: Dover.

McNemar, Q. (1964) Lost: Our intelligence. Why? *American Psychologist, 19,* 871–882.

Spearman, C. (1927). *The abilities of man.* London: McMillan.

Terman, L. M. (1925). *Mental and physical traits of a thousand gifted children.* London: Harrap.

Thurstone, L. L. (1938). *Primary mental abilities.* Chicago: University of Chicago Press.

Vernon, P. E. (1961). *The structure of human abilities.* London: Methuen.

Vining, D. P. (1982). On the possibility of the emergence of a dysgenic trend with respect to intelligence in American fertility differentials. *Intelligence, 6,* 261–264.

Introduction of E. N. Sokolov

S. W. Porges
University of Maryland

Professor Sokolov's work is known to most American psychologists, and represents an important legacy of the influence of Russian psychology on American science. Evgeny Nikolaevich Sokolov, like other great Russian behavioral scientists such as Pavlov and Luria, has had a great impact on our science. This is remarkable given the political barriers and the lack of scientific communication between our countries.

One of his books, *Perception and the Conditioned Reflex* (published in English in 1963) helped develop several areas of psychology. The book introduced to American psychologists the concepts of orienting and defensive responses. This book provided the theoretical stimulus for much of American psychophysiology during the 1960s and 1970s. Moreover, interest in Sokolov's template model, explaining habituation as a matching of stimulus features on both neuronal and subjective levels, stimulated the rapid growth of cognitive sciences. In the specialized area of cognitive development, the Sokolovian principles of habituation evolved into the "habituation" paradigm to evaluate visual memory in preverbal infants. Applications of "Sokolovian" orienting and habituation even influenced polygraphy, and the concepts created a theoretical basis to refine polygraph examinations from subjective judgments to the quasi-experimental procedures associated with the guilty knowledge and control question tests.

Contemporary psychophysiology gained much of its current theoretical perspective from the intriguing ideas introduced by Sokolov (1963) regarding the interaction among autonomic, sensory, and mental processes. The Sokolovian model presented an integrative theory relating autonomic function to psychological state. The model included: (a) acknowledgement of both sensory and motor components of both autonomic and somatic systems, (b) an autonomic feedback loop (i.e., autonomic tuning) to regulate

39

sensory thresholds, (c) an interface between autonomic processes and psychological phenomena (i.e., orienting and defensive reflexes), and (d) brain regulation of the autonomic reactivity via habituation.

In the 1960s, many of us were intrigued with the Sokolovian view of autonomic processes facilitating or "tuning" receptor systems to engage or disengage with the external environment. In many ways, we were looking for a type of physiological *g* factor, which would be sensitive to the regulatory capacity of the nervous system in the intake and processing of novelty. This "neural"-based *g* factor would not only be culture free, but also would not require language.

To many of us, *Perception and the Conditioned Reflex* was not a textbook but instead a book of epic proportions. Research was always compared to the Sokolovian model and expectations. At meetings there would be electrifying debates about whether ideas, interpretations, and even data were consistent with "Sokolov." The name *Sokolov* became a construct, an unobtainable metric of comparison for the American psychophysiologist. Although most of us believed that we would never have the opportunity to meet Professor Sokolov, he became our mentor and our model scientist.

I feel very fortunate to know Evgeny, to share ideas, and to discuss science and politics with him. Evgeny is a complex and compassionate person with a great love for science. He is dedicated to extending his energies to ensure that Russian science survives in these difficult economic times in Russia.

We met about a year ago when he was invited by the Federation of Behavioral, Psychological and Cognitive Sciences to address the Forum on Research Management (FORM) on the impact of the economic crisis in Russia on behavioral sciences. We attempted at that meeting to stimulate interest on the part of funding units to help support research with our colleagues in the former Soviet Union. Evgeny addressed our committee, discussed the possibility of a joint postgraduate training program, and encouraged collaborations.

This past June I visited Evgeny in Moscow. It did not take me long to understand the difference between Russian and American psychology. Russians are interested in theory, and their research evolves from theory. They search for methods and constructs to explain integrative concepts. Application is not fundamental to their research; rather, it provides a "living" laboratory to test specific assumptions regarding their models. In contrast, much of American research is driven by available funds, and most of the funded research is atheoretical. As Congress continues to influence funding priorities, the mission of research is explicitly shifting to specific problems determined by Congressional staffers—funds are seldom allocated for theory-based research or method development. Thus, to maintain active research programs, many American psychologists have become applicators, using techniques that do not quite match the populations being tested or the questions being addressed. In a way, Russian psychology maintains the optimistic view that American psychology had during the first half of this century.

Professor Sokolov's chapter is an example of this integrative approach. Professor Sokolov's research agenda deals with, perhaps, the most fundamental question of psychology, a question similar to other researchers of human cognitive ability: He is, and has always been, interested in describing subjective experiences. His interests in psychophysiological techniques and, more recently, neurophysiological techniques have been approaches to evaluate subjective experiences without requiring verbal descriptions or motor behaviors.

During one of our many discussions, Evgeny shared with me why he titled his book *Perception and the Conditioned Reflex*. Initially, he thought of entitling the book *The Theory of Orienting and Defensive Reactions*. However, he believed that he was studying broader processes, processes that related to perception and subjective experiences. From Evgeny's theoretical viewpoint, psychophysiology is the natural outgrowth of psychophysics. For Professor Sokolov, psychophysiology is the science of understanding mechanisms of subjective phenomena, functional states, and individual differences. These categories have echoed in all the previous presentations; however, Professor Sokolov effectively argues that to have an understanding of mechanisms of subjective experiences there is a need to integrate behavioral, neuronal, and molecular levels of observations.

In 1988, with the relaxation of travel restrictions between our countries, Professor Sokolov was honored by the Society for Psychophysiology and presented the Distinguished Contributions to Psychophysiology Award. It was at this meeting that I met him briefly, and had the opportunity to hear about his new research on a multimethod approach to describe the subjective experience of color vision.

The transcript of the citation to Professor Sokolov, written by Frances Graham, appeared in volume 26 of the journal *Psychophysiology* (Graham, 1989). I have extracted the following from this article:

> The western world first encountered [Professor Sokolov] in 1954 when an 11-person team of Soviet psychologists, "traveling outside their own country for the first time" attended the 14th International Congress of Psychology in Montreal. The meeting attracted newspaper attention because Soviet and Western scientists had virtually no communication since the 1920s. The *New York Times* featured the symposium which included Sokolov and two other Soviet speakers, as well as John Lacey and Hans Eysenck.
>
> Sokolov's presentation at the Congress was titled "Higher nervous activity and the problem of perception" and the abstract indicates that he had already formed many of his ideas about the role of orienting. The importance of the work was immediately recognized. Citations by esteemed western psychologists — Sharpless, Berlyne, and Morrell — appeared in 1956 and 1957

in major western journals. . . . Professor Luria, in the 1957 London University Lectures, described Sokolov as an outstanding member of the young, postwar generation of Soviet psychologists.

Sokolov's publications were important to psychophysiology and cognitive science. They provided a coherent theory of the orienting reflex as a system, responsive to change or novelty, which served as an information regulator or filter. As a cognitive theory, the work linked psychophysiology to an emerging major theme in experimental psychology. . . . It, thus, broadened the base of American psychophysiology, whose previous ties had been closer to clinical psychology and to physiology.

By 1966, Sokolov had extended his research on orienting into more detailed [modeling] of memory mechanisms and into neurophysiology.

In 1974 Sokolov again [traveled] to the USA to be a visiting professor at MIT.

In 1975 Professor Sokolov's impact was recognized by our National Academy of Sciences and he was elected as a foreign member; there are only seven living psychologists so honored. In 1976, he became a Foreign Member of the American Academy of Arts and Sciences; in 1984, a Foreign Member of the Finnish Academy of Sciences and Letters; and, in 1985, a member of the Soviet Academy of Pedagogical Science and the recipient of Pavlov's Gold Medal Award from the Soviet Academy of Science.

In his research, applying multidimensional scaling techniques, Sokolov has identified striking commonalities among the vector representation of behavioral, physiological, and neuronal levels. He has conducted comparative research on color vision with fish, monkeys, and humans. Professor Sokolov has asked me to summarize his chapter to help in the communication of these important concepts.

First, his objective is to use the multimethod study of color vision as an example of modeling a subjective experience. The methods include subjective report, reaction time discrimination of target stimulus and background, and actual neuronal activity in animal models.

Second, the subjective experience of color vision is understood via the use of psychophysics. Color vision maps onto a spherical space generated by the orthogonal vectors corresponding to the subjective aspects of colors: hue, lightness, and saturation.

Third, in animal models the behavior of neurons elicited via a color discrimination task generate a similar spherical space.

Fourth, the spherical shape of the subjective space changes when individuals with specific genetic color vision deficits are tested for color discrimination via verbal report and reaction time.

Fifth, the spherical shape derived by the vectors is the same for subjective report, reaction time for color discrimination, and neuronal activity. The Cartesian coordinates of the color space extracted from the matrix of subjective differences closely match excitation values of real neurons in primates.

This means that vectors derived by multidimensional scaling correspond to excitation vectors elicited by color stimuli in color-coding neurons, thus demonstrating the continuity of organization between the subjective experience of color vision and neuronal activity.

It now gives me great pleasure to introduce to you, one of the most distinguished and influential psychologists of our century, Professor Evgeny Nikolaevich Sokolov.

REFERENCES

Graham, F. K. (1989). For distinguished contributions to psychophysiology: Evgeny Nikolaevich Sokolov. *Psychophysiology, 26,* 385–391.

Sokolov, E. N. (1963). *Perception and the conditioned reflex.* Oxford, England: Pergamon. (Originally published in Russian in 1958)

3

Higher Mental Activity and Basic Physiology: Subjective Difference and Reaction Time

E. N. Sokolov
Moscow State University

Psychophysiology is a science concerned with physiological mechanisms of subjective phenomena. A new direction in the development of psychophysiology is an integration of cognitive psychology with neurophysiology, which deals with processing information in neuronal nets. In the framework of this trend, *vector psychophysiology* is suggested.

Vector psychophysiology is a branch of psychophysiology based on a principle of vector coding in neuronal nets. A stimulus acting on an ensemble of neurons results in a particular magnitude of excitation in each member of the ensemble. A combination of these excitations within the ensemble constitutes an excitation vector that is a code of the input stimulus. The excitation vector is normalized in neuronal networks. The normalization procedure is a reason that different stimuli influencing the neuronal ensemble generate excitation vectors that are represented geometrically as equal in their lengths. It means that the input stimuli are coded geometrically by orientations of corresponding excitation vectors, and that the total set of stimuli affecting the ensemble is projected on a surface of a sphere in metric space. Dimensionality of this space is determined by a number of independent neurons of the ensemble (Sokolov & Vaitkyavichus, 1989).

In this chapter, a vector code is proposed as an operational mode in neuronal nets. It is conceived as a basis for reconstruction of perceptual space from a matrix of subjective differences. The latter are regarded as absolute values of differences between excitation vectors of a test and a background. Such differences are considered to determine reaction time: The greater the subjective difference is, the shorter the reaction time is. Measurement of reaction time is conceived to evaluate excitation vectors generated in neuronal nets. Dependence of reaction time on subjective difference in a color detection task can be explained using vector coding network. At first, within visual field areas occupied by figure and background in color-coding ensembles, four-dimensional excitation vectors are generated. These excitation vectors are locally normalized. The local normalization procedure is described as a city block metric generated by the summation of absolute values of vector components in a summating unit, which in turn influences color-coding neurons. Normalized excitation vectors are responsible for identification of colors of figure and of background, respectively. These normalized vectors are responsible for detection of subjective difference.

In parallel, absolute values of figure and background vector components are subtracted to generate absolute values of their respective differences. Outputs of subtracting units are connected via plastic synapses with a command neuron triggering a motor response under detection of a target. A command neuron summating these absolute values is excited in accordance with a module of vector differences given in a city block metric: The greater the excitation of the command neuron is, the shorter the reaction time is. Excitation of the command neuron, in turn, is determined by the absolute value of the difference between excitation vectors generated by figure and background. At the same time, a module of vector differences is equal to subjective differences between colors of figure and background. In this way two different operations—that is, evaluation of subjective difference and target detection—become connected. Some experiments are described to demonstrate how this connection is based on vector codes of color stimuli within neuronal nets.

VECTOR CODE AND SUBJECTIVE DIFFERENCE

A scheme of realization of vector coding can be tested either directly by microelectrode recording from single neurons constituting an ensemble, or by using a psychophysical approach. The psychophysical principle of testing vector coding is based on an assumption that the subjective difference between stimuli perceived by a subject is directly proportional to a Euclidian distance between the ends of geometrically represented respective excitation vectors generated in the neuronal ensemble. Such a suggestion implies a possibility to infer information on excitation vectors from a matrix of subjective differences between respective stimuli. The problem of extraction of information on implicit excitation vectors can be solved using multidimensional scaling. Typically, the minimum of orthogonal axes is preferred, but in this case one has to find out a real number of axes corresponding to independent neurons in the ensemble. An orientation of axes cannot be chosen at will, but instead has to correspond to neuron outputs. Additionally, an assumption concerning the normalization of excitation vectors in real neuronal nets predicts that vectors calculated from a matrix of subjective differences have to be of equal lengths.

Consequences following an acceptance of the vector code principle were tested using color stimuli of different wavelengths in a series of experiments carried out at the Department of Psychophysiology at the Faculty of Psychology at Moscow State University (for details, see Izmailov & Sokolov, 1991). In one experiment colors were presented pairwise, with short intervals between stimuli in each pair. After presentation of each pair, a subject was requested to report the subjective difference between the colors using a numerical rating from 0 (completely identical) to 9 (maximally different). Subjective differences constituted a matrix that was processed using a multidimensional scaling procedure.

The resulting spatial configuration showed that each color stimulus was characterized by a four-dimensional vector. These vectors were almost equal in their lengths, implying that different color stimuli are located in a thin spherical layer. Orthogonal axes of the color space were rotated in such a way that they coincided with projection of stimuli of constant hues (green—500 *nm*, blue—470 *nm*, and yellow—475 *nm*). This procedure revealed coordinates that corresponded to excitations of four neuronal channels in the lateral geniculate body of monkeys. The coordinates along red-green and blue-yellow axes corresponded to responses of red-green and blue-yellow opponent neurons at respective wavelengths. The coordinates of two achromatic axes of the color space corresponded to reactions of achromatic neurons also known as *brightness* and *darkness cells*.

Thus, Cartesian coordinates of the color space extracted from the matrix of subjective differences closely matched excitation values of real neurons in primates. This means that vectors revealed by multidimensional scaling indeed correspond to excitation vectors evoked by color stimuli in color-coding neuronal ensembles. To test how close subjective differences between colors coincide with distances between ends of the vectors extracted from the matrix of subjective differences, Euclidian distances between color points were calculated from the four-dimensional vectors. A correlation between initial subjective differences and calculated Euclidean distances was very high, supporting the hypothesis that differences between stimuli are coded by absolute values of differences between excitation vectors evoked by respective stimuli.

It has to be emphasized that achromatic (white, grey, and black) stimuli do not excite opponent color neurons. Thus, they are coded exclusively by brightness and darkness neurons. To test this at a psychophysical level, a matrix of subjective differences for different lightness of achromatic stimuli was obtained under intensity contrast in a disk and ring stimulus configuration. It was shown that achromatic colors are located on a semicircle being characterized by two coordinates that closely correspond to excitation of brightness and darkness neurons. This result reinforces a notion that subjective differences are coded by absolute values of differences between excitation vectors. Thus, Cartesian coordinates of color space correspond to excitations of neurons of color-coding ensembles.

A question arises concerning the interpretation of spherical coordinates. To answer this question, let us project color points on three planes. A projection of color points on a plane comprising red-green and blue-yellow orthogonal axes has demonstrated that monochromatic stimuli are situated in a circular manner, according to wavelength sequence. White color is located in the center of the plane. Angular coordinates correspond to hue. A comparison of angles of color stimuli with hue coordinates taken from the Munsell color body demonstrated their high correlation. The projection of color points on the plane defined by two orthogonal achromatic axes showed that white color is shifted from the center of the plane. Monochromatic colors are located in such a way that the closer they are to the center, the higher their saturation is. An angle in this plane characterizes lightness of a color. A comparison of the angle with the Munsell measure of lightness (value) demonstrates high correlation.

The plane constructed from axes obtained by combinations of the two chromatic and the two achromatic axes was used to demonstrate a relation of the third angle of hypersphere to saturation. One combined axis composed from red-green and blue-yellow axes is a common chromatic axis. The other combined axis composed from the two achromatic axes is a common achromatic one. On the plane built up by these combined axes, all projected colors are located on a circumference of the first quadrant in accordance with their saturation. The comparison of the angle with saturation (according to Munsell chroma) has also shown this coincidence.

This model of color coding is based on the notion that excitation vectors are representing stimuli in neuronal nets. The model integrates neuronal mechanisms of color coding with subjective aspect of perceived colors. Cartesian coordinates correspond to excitations of color-coding neurons, and spherical coordinates (three angles) correspond to subjective aspects of colors: hue, lightness, and saturation.

The most important characteristic of the color space is its spherical organization. From a neurophysiological standpoint, the mechanism of such a spherical projection is determined by normalization of excitation vectors. Psychophysical evidence for this statement was obtained from investigations of color vision deficiency related to genetic modification of visual pigments.

A study of color differences in "protan" and "deutan" persons by application of multidimensional scaling has, in all cases, shown a spherical structure of color space. Location of color points on a sphere was valid for various forms of color deficiency despite different modifications of pigments at the receptor level. A retention of sphericity of color-deficient space implies the presence of a normalization process in the color-coding network. Normalization of the excitation vector results in the reduction of any excitation vector component accompanied by amplification of other components. Thus, protan color vision is characterized by a reduction of red-green axis contribution due to substitution of red pigment by a green one. At the same time, contributions of blue-yellow and achromatic axes are amplified. In deutan vision, due to the substitution of green pigment by a red one, an impact of red-green and blue-yellow axes is reduced and compensated by an increase of achromatic axis (Paramei, Izmailov, & Sokolov, 1991).

The process of normalization is connected with a multistage transition from three types of cones to four types of neurons generating excitation vectors of constant length. In this way, three independent variables at the receptor level are transformed into three independent angle–spherical coordinates of a four-dimensional hypersphere.

VECTOR CODE AND REACTION TIME

The notion of vector code opens a new perspective in analysis of reaction time. Reaction time in a detection task is greater as the subjective difference between a figure (target stimulus) and a background is smaller. Assuming that subjective difference between stimuli is a function of an absolute value of vector difference between respective excitation vectors, one can use reaction time to obtain information about excitation vectors. To do this, one has to find a relationship between reaction time and the subjective differences between targets and backgrounds.

In two independent experiments, subjective differences and reaction time for each target-background combination were obtained. Excitation vectors for figure and background were derived from the matrix of their subjective differences. Since reaction time is dependent on subjective differences, an absolute magnitude of excitation vectors can be derived from the reaction times.

A hypothesis concerning the dependence of reaction time in the detection task on absolute magnitude of difference between excitation vectors was tested using color stimuli in a figure-background configuration. The contribution of brightness contrast to reaction time was minimized by equalization of the figure and the background with respect to color intensity. Specification of a test stimulus as equiluminant with a background was achieved by sequentially changing the test-stimulus intensity against a constant background (see Figs. 3.1, 3.2, 3.3).

GREEN stimulus, BLUE background

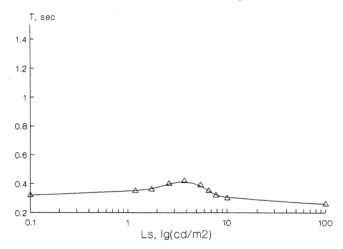

FIG. 3.1.   Dependence of reaction time on intensity of green (535 *nm*,
2 × 2 *mm*) test stimulus (arbitrary units) presented on blue (480 *nm*)
background with intensity 3 *cd/m* 520. Horizontal axis is intensity of
test stimulus (arbitrary units). Vertical axis is reaction time (sec). Reaction time reaches its maximum at particular intensity when test
and background become equiluminant. The most important feature of
the graph is its symmetry: Reaction time drops with both increase and
decrease of test-stimulus intensity. Reaction time is influenced not
by absolute intensity of test stimulus but by its contrast against background.

The test stimulus that produced maximal reaction time is regarded as
"equiluminant" with the background. In an experiment, subjects estimated
subjective color differences of such equiluminant combinations of test and
background stimuli. Subjective differences between equiluminant colors
were represented as a matrix that was processed by a multidimensional scaling program. It appeared that all tested color stimuli were characterized by
four-dimensional vectors with lengths almost equal to each other. The following formula permits the calculation of subjective differences equal to absolute values of excitation vector differences using reaction time:

$$T = A + B/S$$

where T is the reaction time, S is the subjective difference equal to an absolute value of excitation vector difference, $A + B = 0.96$ reaction time for $S = 1$,
and $A = 0.3$ — nonreducible reaction time under infinite increase of S (see
Figs. 3.4 and 3.5).

The matrix of subjective differences obtained indirectly from reaction
times was processed in order to construct a color space using multidimen-

sional scaling. The comparison of color space constructed on the basis of direct estimation of subjective differences with the color space based on reaction times has demonstrated their coincidence.

Projections of color points obtained via direct estimation and of those inferred indirectly from reaction times are very similar to each other on a plane comprising red-green and blue-yellow axes. Angular coordinates for both types of color points correspond to hue. Thus, reaction time in the detection task for color stimuli depends on subjective differences between figure and background, and this in turn is determined by absolute magnitude of excitation vector difference. One must emphasize that reaction time does not depend on specific characteristics of a figure, but rather only on its difference with respect to a background.

The previous results imply that motor response in a detection task is controlled at a level where operation of subtraction of excitation vectors from test and background areas is already completed. Excitation reaching the trig-

BLUE stimulus, BLUE background

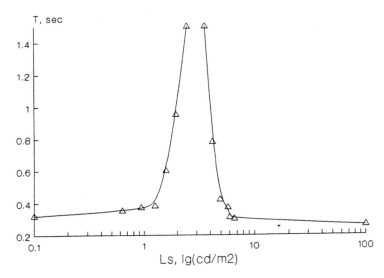

FIG. 3.2. Dependence of reaction time on intensity of blue (480 nm, 2 × 2 mm) test stimulus (arbitrary units) presented against blue background of the same wavelength with intensity 3 cd/m. Horizontal axis is intensity of test stimulus (arbitrary units). Vertical axis is reaction time (sec). Test stimulus is not detected (reaction time is greater than 1500 ms) at the point of test and background equality. Reaction time drops symmetrically both with increase and decrease of intensity of test stimulus with respect to the point of its equality with background. Reaction time is suggested to be a function of brightness contrast but not of absolute intensity of test stimulus.

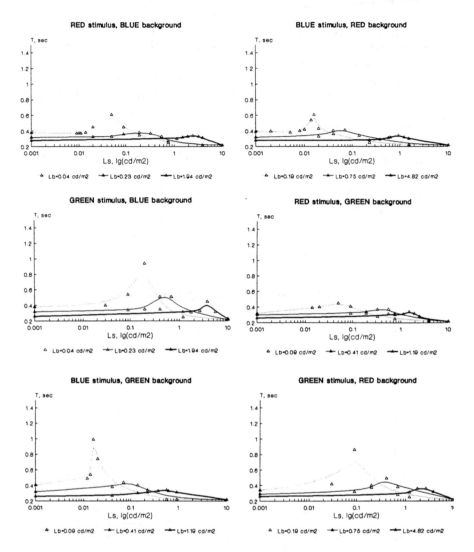

FIG. 3.3. Dependence of reaction time on intensity of test stimulus (2 × 2 *mm*) under different levels of background intensity for all combinations of blue (480 *nm*), green (535 *nm*), and red (615 *nm*) colors. Horizontal axis is intensity (arbitrary units). Vertical axis is reaction time (sec). For all test-background combinations there exists reaction time maximum at the point where test stimulus is equiluminant with background. Increase of background intensity results in reduction of reaction time maximum at the point where test stimulus has the same intensity as background. The reduction of reaction time under an increase of background intensity suggests an increase of subjective color differences. At the same time, increases of background intensity lead to decreases in the range between the nonreducable reaction time and the reaction time maximum.

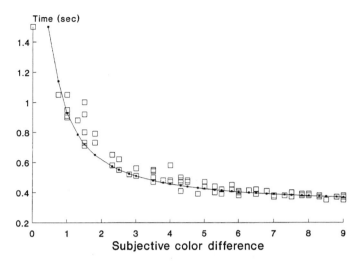

FIG. 3.4.   Relationship between subjective differences obtained by direct estimations for 78 combinations of 13 equiluminant test and 13 background stimuli. Horizontal axis stands for subjective differences (rantings). Vertical axis is reaction time (sec). Increase of subjective difference corresponds to progressive reduction of reaction time to a non-reducable minimum, irrespective of particular lights for test and background. The graph can be approximated by a hyperbolic function (dots) according to the formula, $T = A + B/S$, where T is reaction time, S is the subjective difference, A is the asymptotic value of reaction time (nonreducable minimum) when S reaches its maximum, and $A + B$ is initial magnitude of reaction time for $S = 1$. For the given experiment: $T = 0.3 + 0.63/S$. Subjective differences calculated from reaction times according to this formula closely correspond to directly estimated subjective differences $(r = 0.96)$.

gering mechanism of a motor response is "depersonalized" with respect to specific color characteristics of the figure. Neurophysiological studies of motor responses show that they are controlled by command neurons supplied by sensory inputs via plastic synapses. In animals, sensory neurons are connected to a command neuron, and their inputs are modified due to conditioning. In humans, such an operation can be performed under the influence of verbal instruction. In detection tasks, synapses of command neurons that lead from "subtracting units" are activated. These latter determine absolute magnitudes of differences in separate color-coding channels affected by figure and by background, respectively. The command neuron receiving absolute magnitudes from "subtracting units" sums them up. A sum of absolute magnitudes is a module of excitation vector difference expressed in a city block metric.

When excitation vectors of figure and background are equal, the module of their difference is equal to zero; therefore, excitation does not protract to

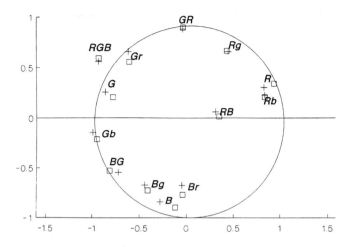

FIG. 3.5. Projection of color points on plane composed from red-green (horizontal) and blue-yellow (vertical) axes for directly estimated subjective differences (squares) and for subjective differences calculated from respective reaction times (crosses). Color stimuli are located closely to a circle corresponding to their hue. Equivalent wavelengths are the following: $R = 615$ nm, $G = 535$ nm, and $B = 480$ nm. White color (RGB) composed from lights with 480, 535, and 615 nm was subjectively perceived as greenish and is located close to green point (G) both for directly estimated color differences and for those inferred from reaction times. Purple color (RB), perceived as having low saturation, is shifted closer to the center of the plane. Comparability of the results obtained by direct estimation of color differences and by reaction time measurement within a common color space strongly supports the notion that reaction time in detection task is a function of absolute values of differences of excitation vectors.

the command neuron and no motor response is triggered. With increase of difference between excitation vectors, excitation reaching the command neuron increases, and reaction time shortens due to reduction of spike initiation latency in the command neuron. Thus, reaction time is a measure of excitation reaching the command neuron that, in turn, is determined by the sum of absolute differences of excitations in color-coding neurons affected by figure and background. Dependence of reaction time on excitation vector difference opens very efficient pathways for operative testing of visual functions.

Accuracy of measurements can be improved by elimination of brightness contrast in color. Elimination of brightness contrast results in the reaction time being determined mainly by perceived color difference. Reduction of brightness contrast reveals in deuteranomalous, glaucomic, and albino persons a profound reduction of color discrimination expressed in an increase of reaction time, not only for equiluminant stimuli but also in wide range of neighboring intensities of compared stimuli. Of a special interest is an asymmetrical graph of a glaucoma patient (see Fig. 3.6).

Reaction time reaches its maximum at the point where test stimulus is equiluminant with the background and is substantially longer than in normal subjects. Under increase of intensity of test-stimulus, reaction time drops to a level close to the normal one. Decreased test-stimulus intensity

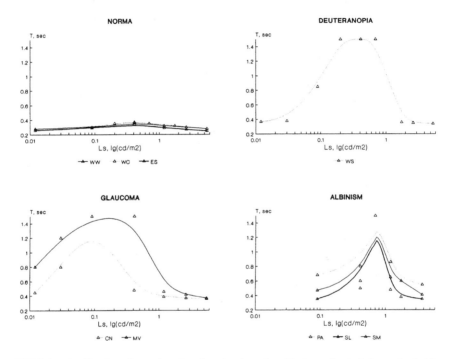

FIG.3.6.   Application of reaction time for visual testing. Horizontal axis is intensity (arbitrary units) of test stimulus (535 *nm*) presented against purple background (480 *nm* + 615 *nm*). Vertical axis is reaction time (sec).

• Subjects with normal color vision demonstrate a small increase of reaction time at the point of equal luminance of test stimulus and background that corresponds to subjectively large color differences.

• The deuteranomalous subject demonstrates substantial increases in reaction time not only under equal luminance of test stimulus and background but also for a wide range of neighboring intensities. This corresponds to reduction of perceived color difference.

• The glaucoma patient demonstrates substantial increase in reaction time in a wide range of intensities that corresponds to subjectively small color differences. Asymmetrical increase in reaction times by decrease of intensity of test stimulus corresponds to weakness of the darkness system in comparison with the brightness system.

• Albino persons demonstrate increases in reaction times in a wide range of intensities around the point of the equal luminance for target and background that correspond to decreases in subjective color differences.

in all nonglaucoma subjects results in a decrease in reaction time symmetrical to that provided by increases of intensity. In glaucoma patients, this is not the case; under decreases of test-stimulus intensity, reaction time remains similar to the maximum during the equiluminant condition. This increase of reaction time results in a reduction of subjective differences for stimuli with intensity lower than intensity of the background. In terms of excitation vectors, this means that the excitation vector of the test stimulus does not change with decreases in stimulus intensity. Perception of darkness of a local self-illuminating surface on a monitor is due to signals coming from brightness neurons of the induction field. Asymmetrical reduction of subjective differences under decrease of intensity of test field implies that lateral interaction between different areas of the visual field is weakened. This results in poor perception of targets darker than background, including printed texts and drawings.

This short presentation can offer only a brief description of a variety of experiments on these topics. Interested readers can obtain more technical details on this and other related research by contacting the author.

AUTHOR'S NOTE

The project "Comparative neurobiological investigation of color vision in humans and animals" is supported by "Russian Fund of Fundamental Investigations" Grant N 93–04–20511. I thank Doctors A. M. Shamshinova and S. N. Yeudirkhovskiy for their contribution to the project.

REFERENCES

Izmailov, C. A., & Sokolov, E. N. (1991). Spherical model of color and brightness discrimination. *Psychological Science, 2,* 249–259.

Paramei, G. V., Izmailov, C. A., & Sokolov, E. N. (1991). Multidimensional scaling of large chromatic differences by normal and color-deficient subjects. *Psychological Science, 2,* 244–248.

Sokolov, E. N., & Vaitkyavichus, G. G. (1989). *Neyrointellect: ot neirona k neirokompjuteru* [Neurointellegence: from a neuron towards neurocomputer]. Moscow: Nauka (in Russian).

II

INVITED TALKS

4

A Basis for Research
on Age Differences
in Cognitive Capabilities

John Horn
University of Southern California

This chapter is a review of scientific theory of human intelligence. It summarizes current knowledge as a basis for indicating where further empirical research is needed. A study illustrating such further research is described by Noll and Horn in chapter 13 of this volume.

BACKGROUND

It has become clear that the phenomena referred to as *human intelligence* is a mosaic of many cognitive capabilities. This mosaic can be partitioned into a finite set of dimensions that fairly completely account for individual differences among a large number of such capabilities. The abilities that psychologists have become able to measure probably do not represent the entire range of capabilities that constitute human intelligence, but they are a good sample. Thousands of different tests have been designed to measure hundreds of features of intelligence. Analyses of these different tests indicate that what these thousands of tests measure in common are actually fewer than 100 dimensions called *primary mental abilities.* Further analyses and descriptions of links to developmental and physiological variables indicate that fewer than a dozen broad dimensions describe all major kinds of cognitive capability.

Thus, scientific understanding has moved away from the idea that intelligence can be well represented by a single factor (often referred to as *g*) and be measured with commercial IQ tests such as the Stanford Binet and the Wechsler Adult Intelligence Scales. To a very large extent, this movement away from the simple idea of IQ (i.e., g) has been led by the two people honored with this symposium—Raymond Cattell and John Carroll.

Cattell did his Ph.D. studies with Spearman, and thus came to understand early the elegance of Spearman's substantive theory of intelligence and his mathematical/statistical model for testing the major hypothesis of this theory. Cattell (1933) put forth evidence relating to this theory in his earliest research. However, as the evidence of studies in the 1930s and 1940s came forward again and again to indicate that a single common-factor theory was not adequate to explain the diversity of human intellectual capabilities, Cattell (1941, 1943, 1957, 1971) proposed and put forward evidence that supported a theory of two intelligences—fluid (g_f) and crystallized (g_c). That theory, and the evidence produced in the research it sparked over the next 50 years, has led to the current theory of several intelligences.[1]

Carroll's (1993) work has structured the definitive foundation for current theory. His tour-de-force summary and integration of over 400 studies (i.e., 477 data sets) makes it clear that the reliable variation humans display in thousands of diverse tests[2] cannot be described in terms of g, but can be organized in terms of a three-stratum system of 75 abilities (analogous to Mendelyev's first presentation of a periodic table of elements in chemistry).

Abilities identified at the first stratum of this system are often referred to as *primary mental abilities*, after Thurstone (1938), who identified the first set of such abilities. Table 4.1 provides a summary description of major primary abilities found in replicated factor analytic studies.

Second-stratum abilities are described in summary form in Table 4.2. As mentioned previously, Cattell identified two intelligences (g_f and g_c) at the second stratum. As evidence accumulated, Cattell's early findings and explanations evolved into a theory of several cognitive capabilities. Each is de-

---

[1]Thurstone's (from 1938) presentations of evidence indicating primary mental abilities, Thorndike's (from 1921) developments of four-dimensional theory of intellect, Thomson's (from 1919, 1948) analysis of g and theory of bonds, Burt's (from 1909) questioning of the theory of g, and Guilford's (from 1956) findings of common factors of intellect also contributed notably to modern structural theory of multiple human intelligences.

[2]Measures that have been designed to indicate human intelligence include tests of eduction of relations and correlates (basic elements of Spearman's theory), problem solving, reasoning, induction, deduction, abstracting, concept formation, concept attainment, learning, knowledge, comprehension, decoding, encoding, communication, creativity, insight, sensitivity to problems, originality, associational fluency, expressional fluency, word naming, figural fluency, flexibility, associative memory, free recall, nonsense memory, visual memory, auditory memory, visualization, perceiving spatial relations, visual closure, visual integration, spatial scanning, sound localization, loudness discrimination, pitch discrimination, resistance to auditory distraction, judging rhythm, temporal integration, perceptual (visual, auditory, tactile) speed, reaction time speed, choice reaction time speed, semantic processing speed, and information processing speed.

scribed in Table 4.2. The second-stratum factors are basic elements of the theory of several intelligences.

The factors at the second stratum are positively correlated. This has led Carroll and others to compute a factor (or occasionally two factors) at a third stratum. However, a single factor defined at this level varies greatly across different studies, as seen in the Carroll (1993) review. No single principle—

TABLE 4.1
Factors at the First Stratum or First-Order Primary Mental Abilities

	Symbols Used To Represent Ability	
Abilities of acculturational knowledge:		
General information: Science, humanities, social sciences, business	Vi	
Verbal comprehension: Demonstrate understanding of words, sentences and paragraphs	V	CMU
Sensitivity to problems: Suggest ways to deal with problems (e.g., improvements for a toaster)	Se	EMI
Syllogistic reasoning: Draw logically permissible conclusions when given stated premises, even when these are nonsensical	Rs	EMR
Behavioral relations: Make judgments about how people interact and behave; estimate others' feelings		CBI
Semantic relations (esoteric concepts): Demonstrate awareness of analogic relationships among abstruse bits of information		CMRe
Number facility: Do basic operations of arithmetic quickly and accurately	N	NSI
Estimation: Use incomplete information to estimate what is required for problem solution		CMI
Mechanical knowledge: Information about industrial arts (mechanics, electricity, etc.)	Mk	
Verbal closure: Show comprehension of words and sentences when parts are omitted		CSU
Abilities of reasoning under novel conditions:		
Induction: Indicate a principle of relationships among elements	I	NSR
General reasoning: Find solutions for problems having an algebraic quality	R	CMS
Figural relations: Demonstrate awareness of relationships among figures		CFR
Semantic relations (common concepts): Demonstrate awareness of analogic relationships among common bits of information		CMRc
Symbolic classifications: Show which symbol does not belong in a class of several symbols		CSC
Concept formation: Given several examples of a concept, identify new instances		CFC
Short-term apprehension and retrieval abilities:		
Associative memory: When immediately presented with one element of previously associated but otherwise unrelated elements, recall the associated element after up to approximately 1 minute	Ma	MSR

(Continued)

TABLE 4.1
(Continued)

	Symbols Used To Represent Ability	
Span memory: Immediately recall a series of randomly related elements (letters, numbers) after a few seconds—up to approximately 1 minute	Ms	MSU
Meaningful memory: Immediately recall a set of items that are meaningfully related	Mm	MSR
Chunking memory: Immediately recall elements by categories into which the elements can be classified		MC
Memory for order: Immediately recall the position of one element within a set of elements		MASS
Long-term storage and retrieval abilities:		
Delayed retrieval: Recall material learned several minutes or hours before	Dr	
Associational fluency: Produce words similar in meaning to a given word	Fa	DIR
Expressional fluency: Produce different ways of saying much the same thing	Fe	DDS
Ideational fluency: Produce ideas about a stated condition or object (e.g., a lady holding a baby)	F	DMZ
Word fluency. Produce words meeting particular structural requirements (e.g., ending with a particular suffix)	F	DIR
Originality: Produce "clever" expressions or interpretations (e.g., titles for a story plot)	O	DDT
Spontaneous flexibility: Produce diverse functions and classifications (e.g. uses for a pencil)	Xs	DMC
Visualization and spatial orientation abilities:		
Visualization: Mentally manipulate forms to "see" how they would look under altered conditions	Vz	CFT
Spatial orientation: Visually imagine parts out of place and put them in place (e.g., solve jigsaw puzzles)	S	CFS
Speed of closure. Identify gestalt when parts of whole are missing	Cs	CFU
Flexibility of closure: Find a particular figure embedded within. distracting figures	Cs	NFT
Spatial planning: Survey a spatial field and find a path through the field (e.g., pencil mazes)	Ss	CFI
Figural adaptive flexibility: Try out possible arrangements of elements of visual pattern to find one arrangement that satisfies several conditions	Xa	DFT
Length estimation: Estimate lengths or distances between points	Le	
Figural fluency: Produce different figures using the lines of a stimulus figure		DFI
Seeing illusions: Report illusions of such tests as Muller-Lyer, Sanders, and Poggendorff		DFS

(Continued)

TABLE 4.1
(Continued)

	Symbols Used To Represent Ability	

Abilities of listening and hearing:

Listening verbal comprehension: Show understanding of oral communications — Va

Temporal tracking: Demonstrate understanding of sequence of auditory information (e.g., reorder a set of tones) — Tc

Auditory cognitive relations: Show understanding of relations among tones (e.g., identify separate notes of a chord) — Acor

Discriminate sound patterns: Show awareness of differences in different arrangements of tones — DASP

Auditory span memory: Immediately recall a set of notes played 10 to 30 seconds previously — Msa

Perception of distorted speech: Demonstrate comprehension of speech against a background of noise or when it is distorted in several ways — SPUD

Maintain and judge rhythms: Continue an established beat; judge whether two beats are the same or different — MaJR

Speed of thinking abilities:

Perceptual Speed: Under highly speeded conditions, distinguish similar visual patterns and find instances of a particular pattern — P   ESU

Numerical facility: Do simple arithmetic operations (adding, subtracting) as quickly as possible — N   NSI

Writing and printing speed: As quickly as possible, write cursive letters or print manuscript letters — Ws

Choice reaction time: As quickly as possible, press a lever or button to indicate one among several possible patterns presented tachistoscopically — CRT

Decision speed: Demonstrate speed in finding correct answers to problems of low difficulty level — CDS

Simple reaction time: As quickly as possible, press a lever or button to indicate a stimulus presented tachistoscopically — SRT

Abilities of quantitative thinking:

Applied problems: Given information about a quantitative problem, indicate the analyses that need to be done to solve the problem — APP

Sensitivity to problems: Given information about desired outcomes, indicate the nature of the quantitative problems that must be solved to yield the desired outcomes — SEP

Quantitative concepts: Demonstrate understanding of quantitative concepts — CA

Number facility: Do basic operations of arithmetic quickly and accurately — N   NSI

General reasoning: Find solutions for problems having an algebraic quality — R   CMS

Taken from Ekstrom, French, and Harman (1979), French, Ekstrom, and Price (1963), and Guilford (1956).

TABLE 4.2
Second-Stratum Cognitive Capabilities (Intelligences)

Acculturation knowledge (Gc), measured in tasks indicating breadth and depth of the knowledge of the dominant culture.

Fluid reasoning (Gf), measured in tasks requiring inductive, deductive, conjunctive, and disjunctive reasoning to arrive at understanding relations among stimuli, comprehend implications, and draw inferences.

Short-term apprehension-retention (SAR) [also called *short-term memory (Gsm)*], measured in a variety of tasks that mainly require one to maintain awareness of, and be able to recall, elements of immediate stimulation (i.e., events of the last minute or so).

Fluency of retrieval from long-term storage (TSR) [also called *long-term memory (Glr)*], measured in tasks that indicate consolidation for storage and mainly require retrieval, through association, of information stored minutes, hours, weeks, and years before.

Visual processing (Gv), measured in tasks involving fluency and visual closure and constancy in "imaging" the way objects appear in space as they are rotated and flip-flopped in various ways.

Auditory processing (Ga), measured in tasks that involve perception of sound patterns under distraction or distortion; maintaining awareness of order and rhythm among sounds; and comprehending elements of groups of sounds, such as chords and the relations among such groups.

Processing speed (Gs), although involved in almost all intellectual tasks (Hertzog, 1989), this is measured most purely in rapid scanning and reaction in responding to intellectually simple tasks (in which almost all people would get the right answer if the task were not highly speeded).

Decision speed (CDS), measured in quickness in providing answers, both correct and incorrect, in problems of moderate difficulty.

Quantitative knowledge (Gq), measured in tasks requiring understanding and application of the concepts and skills of mathematics.

Although IQ tests and neuropsychological batteries are not necessarily described as involving these abilities, nevertheless the abilities that are reliably measured in such tests are mainly predicted and accounted for by these nine factors of Gf-Gc theory.

---

no single factor—has been found to define the factors of the lower strata. Current evidence suggests that each of the second stratum factors is formed by and represents several distinct processes that are linked to different genetic and environmental determinants.

Gf-Gc THEORY OF SEVERAL INTELLIGENCES

The term *intelligence* is used to describe the second-stratum factors because psychologists, researchers, and others refer to the abilities of these factors as indicating the essence of intelligence. This use of language can be a problem because the word *intelligence* is singular and thus implies that there is a single intelligence. However, the evidence suggests that there is more than one such capability. This means that we must change our use of the word *intelligence* to have a plural form.

EVIDENCE IN SUPPORT OF THE THEORY

There are five kinds of evidence that indicate different construct validities for separate indicators of intelligence: (a) evidence of individual differences covariation, called *structural evidence;* (b) evidence of developmental change from infancy to old age, called *developmental evidence;* (c) evidence of relationships to indicators of physiological and neurological functioning, called *neurocognitive evidence;* (d) evidence of relationships among persons related biologically in different degrees, called *heritability* or *behavioral-genetic evidence;* and (e) evidence of predictions of school performance, educational levels, and occupational performance, called *achievement evidence.*

Structural Evidence

This is the kind of evidence Carroll (1993) summarized.

The Nature of the Evidence. The major results of structural studies are summarized in Tables 4.1 and 4.2, indicating primary and second-stratum abilities. The tables summarize results from many studies indicating that the different capabilities of the first and second stratum have different distributions.

Practically, the structural evidence indicates that persons said to be intelligent when the measure is one of the cognitive capabilities of the second stratum are different from persons said to be intelligent when the measure is one of the other factors at this level. The correlations between the capabilities are positive, but substantially below the reliabilities of measurement

The abilities of IQ tests and neuropsychological batteries of tests are accounted for by these second-stratum abilities; that is to say that IQ and neuropsychological tests are a combination of some of these abilities, with different combinations in different tests. The abilities are construct independent. The best-weighted linear combination of any set of eight of the factors at the second stratum does not fully predict the reliable variance of the ninth factor. This evidence shows that each factor measures capabilities not measured in the other factors.

Critical Perspective on Structural Evidence. It is important to recognize that although the structural theory just outlined provides an empirically based system for describing the phenomena of human cognitive capabilities, it is not the only system that can describe and summarize the lawful regularity thus far found. In the long run, knowing that science is a neverending search for better explanations and that no model of reality is reality, we can be sure that the current system will be replaced by a better system. Limitations in the theory should be kept in mind. The following are among the major limitations.

In accordance with structural analyses, cognitive capabilities are described in terms of Cartesian coordinates or factors. The factors may be rotated into an infinity of different positions, each equally adequate for merely summarizing the data. A metatheory of simple structure has guided the rotation that has been accepted as the basis structure of Gf-Gc theory. This metatheory requires that, at the primary and second-stratum levels, no ability relates to all the factors and no factor affects all abilities. This is a reasonable requirement for studies designed to indicate it—and many studies have been so designed—but it is not an indication of how abilities must be organized to account for the relationships or how they must function in the practice of thinking.

The order of factors (as primary factors and second-stratum factors) is not intrinsic to the phenomena; it is a matter of the design of studies (Humphreys, 1976). For example, a primary factor, F, defined by tests of the form x, y, and z, can be identified as a second-stratum factor if the study is designed at the primary level to have three tests of the x type (x_1, x_2, x_3), three tests of the y type (y_1, y_2, y_3), and three of the z type (z_1, z_2, z_3). Three primary factors (x, y, and z) will then be identified at the primary level, and these will define the factor F at the second stratum.

Structural theory is not of a form that well describes natural phenomena. The phenomena of nature are usually rounded and irregular, not well described by the linear equations of a Cartesian coordinate system. A system of factors is not a set of structural formulas, such as those for the hydrocarbons, the chief constituents of living things. Nor is it a system for representing rounded structures, such as we see in the configurations of plants and animals. The human-constructed rectangular blocks of city streets are well described in terms of Cartesian coordinates, but nature's construction of the brain is not well described by such coordinates. The equations that describe the outer structure and convolutions of the brain must include parabolas, cycloids, cissoids, spirals, foliums, exponentials, and hyperboles. It is likely that human capabilities, which are grounded in brain structure, are best described with similar equations, not in terms of linear equations of the kind that describe city blocks.

The factors of structural theory do not represent biological functional relationships. A functional theory would indicate how abilities interact and work together to produce the behavior of adaptation and adjustment. Structural theory does little to help indicate such workings together.

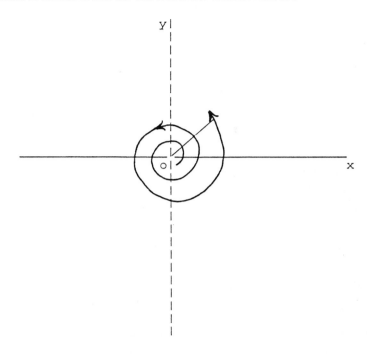

FIG. 4.1.   Spiral of Archimedes (the kind of equation that might represent development of human abilities).

The kind of system that ultimately will best describe human abilities and their development will be functional and more nearly of the form of carbon compounds. It will map on to brain functions. To represent development, it will be more nearly of the form of a spiral of Archimedes or equiangular spiral (Fig. 4.1).

Snow, Kyllonen, and Marshalek (1984) demonstrated that the regularities summarized with a Cartesian system of factors can also be understood in terms of the circular system of a radex. The full array of evidence summarized with Gf-Gc theory has not been summarized with a radex theory, but, if it were, such a theory could well turn out to be a better system for understanding cognitive capabilities.

The limitations of structural theory should be attended to, but this should not lead one to reject the evidence indicated by factor analytic studies. This evidence provides the basis for the understanding we currently have of the organization for the phenomena of human cognitive capabilities. The likelihood that another system will ultimately be found to be better does not discount the fact that the structural system represents what has been indicated by empirical research better than any other system thus far proposed. It indicates what must be accounted for in a better system.[3]

Developmental and Neurocognitive Evidence

Results from a variety of different kinds of studies indicate that separate cognitive capabilities have different relationships to age and brain damage. This evidence has come from case studies of brain damage, studies of average age differences at autopsy in brain structures, average age changes and age differences in cognitive performances, and process studies of neural and cognitive functions.

Case Studies.   The results of single-subject case studies of cognitive performance before and after various kinds of brain damage (e.g., stroke, surgery, blows to the head, brain tumors) indicate that brain damage is associated with declines in attaining and maintaining awareness in reasoning with novel concepts (the abilities of Gf, SAR, and Gs). The results also indicate that although there are declines in the abilities of Gc and TSR immediately following brain damage, these declines are largely reversed and abilities return to pre-injury levels in a period of recovery following the injury, whereas this is not the case for the abilities of Gf, SAR, and Gs.

Brain damage occurring in humans is never precisely the same in all cases. It is necessary to pool over diverse cases. Many changes accompany the damage and could be responsible for some of the observed changes in cognitive performance. It is thus impossible to be pointedly precise about which neurological variable is related to which aspect of cognitive performance.

Studies of Averages.   Evidence from the study of aging is based on averages computed over samples of subjects of different ages. The two kinds of variables for which evidence of relationship is desired—neurological and cognitive behavioral—have not been obtained on the same persons. Analyses thus cannot provide direct evidence that brain damage in a particular person is associated with decline of cognitive function in that person. Results indicate that brain damage increases with age and some abilities decline with age, but the results do not show that the brain damage and the decline in

---

[3]Although it is known that the regularities of navigation on the earth are more precisely described and best understood with the terms of spherical geometry, the Cartesian system of dimensions of Euclidean geometry has for centuries provided a useful basis for navigation, and even today is often adequate for much description and explanation. So, too, the phenomena of abilities described with the Cartesian system of primary and second-stratum cognitive capabilities can be sufficient even as a more adequate system ultimately will be developed.

ability covary over the same persons. The results from averages suggest that this is likely.

Cross-sectional analyses in measures (at autopsy) of neural tissue and of anatomical, histological, neurochemical, and metabolic indicators of brain function suggest that with increase in age in adulthood there is loss of brain tissue and increase in brain malfunction. Similar cross-sectional averages of cognitive performances indicate that, for several kinds of measures of Gf, SAR, and Gs, older adults perform at a lower level than do younger adults. In the same samples of subjects, results in the averages for measures of Gc and TSR indicate either no decline (in some studies) or increase (in other studies) over a period that extends to 60 to 65 years of age, and little decline thereafter (substantially less than for measures of Gf, SAR, and Gs).

Results from longitudinal studies of cognitive performances are, for the most part, consistent with the results from cross-sectional analyses, although the indicated declines observed in longitudinal data appear at somewhat older ages. This may reflect a practice effect (Horn & Donaldson, 1980).

Results from case studies and studies of age differences in averages—both longitudinal and cross-sectional—thus are consistent in suggesting that wasting and deterioration of the brain accumulates with age in a substantial proportion of people (thus registers in averages), and produces irreversible declines in the abilities of Gf, SAR, and Gs. But along with deterioration there is also learning and consolidation. Thus, over most of the years of adulthood there is built up improvement in the abilities of Gc and TSR. Some abilities improve, whereas others decline. The results point to distinct kinds of abilities of human intelligence.

Process studies. Several accumulations of evidence suggest that neural circuits and pathways in the brain are linked to separate sets of abilities. There is evidence indicating that the left and right hemispheres of the brain are associated with different features of perceptual capabilities that, in turn, are associated with particular cognitive abilities (Hellige, 1990). Right hemisphere function is linked to visual and auditory perceptual sensitivities of the kind that underlie Gv and Ga and, possibly, also Gf and SAR. Left hemisphere function, on the other hand, is associated with the perception of verbal stimuli and other skills that appear to be linked to Gc and/or TSR.

There is evidence, too, that the top-to-bottom and front-to-back divisions of the brain also represent separate functions related to separate cognitive performances (Blackwood & Corsellis, 1976; Bourne, Ekstrand & Dominowski, 1971; Prohovnik, 1980). Separate behavioral organizations are associated with anatomically and functionally different neural organizations of the frontal lobe, the parietal lobe, the occipital pole, the cerebellum, and the hippocampus (Thompson, 1992). Research results also indicate distinct neural foundations for short-term apprehension and retention. One line of research points to the cerebellum as the site of the essential memory trace for aversive classical conditioning of discrete responses (Lavond, Kim, & Thompson, 1993). Other evidence indicates that short-term retention is linked to receptor binding in the hippocampus (Berger & Thompson, 1978; Thompson, 1990, 1991). Still other pieces of evidence point to the amygdala as an essential substrate for emotional learning (Amaral, 1987; Rosen, Hitchcok, Sananes, Miserendino, & Davis, 1991).

The brain houses different neurotransmitter systems linked to different circuits of neuron interconnections and associated with distinct behaviors that relate to cognition in different ways (Thompson, 1991). A norepinephrine system—centered around the locus coeruleus, branching largely into the hypothalamus and adjacent areas—is associated with behavioral indicators of arousal and apprehension memory (as Ms and SAR). A serotonin circuit along the brain stem from the medulla to the midbrain with projections into the hypothalamus and cerebral cortex is associated with the behaviors of alertness (as in Gs). A dopamine system (one of three) centered along a path from the substantia nigra to basal ganglia is associated with regulation of hand movements of the kind that are required in reaction time measures of cognitive speed.

The brain is a complex system of many circuits and pathways that are distributed and configured in somewhat different ways in different individuals, rather in the way external features of physiognomy are distributed and configured. These different circuits and pathways are the substrates—the physical housing—for manifest abilities. Individual differences in such "housing" stem from structure given at conception and modified through experience throughout life. Just as people look different in virtue of having different configurations of cheekbones, noses, eyes, and so on, so too they have different highs and lows of abilities that are associated with different configurations of neural circuits and pathways.

Evidence from Studies of Genetic Influences

Evidence that genetic factors determine, in part, different abilities and configurations of abilities derives mainly from comparison studies of samples of people of different degrees of biological relationship—identical (monozygotic, or MZ) twins compared with fraternal twins and/or ordinary siblings, or children compared with parents. The variance in measurements of individual differences (T) is partitioned into estimates of two proportions: a proportion, G, interpreted as heritability, associated with the differences in biological relatedness (MZ twins compared with siblings) and a nonerror proportion, E, interpreted as representing environmental influences. Thus $T =$

$G + E$ (plus an error component), and heritability, HB, is defined as the proportion of T associated with G: $HB = G/T$.[4]

Any cognitive ability might be studied to estimate genetic and environmental influences, and some of the primary abilities have been so studied (DeFries, Kuse, & Vandenberg, 1979; Nichols, 1978; Plomin, DeFries, & McClearn, 1980; Vandenberg, 1962, 1971), but most of the research and discussion of heritability has centered on measures of IQ and most theoretical distinctions have concerned Gf and Gc.

Heritability of IQ and Limitations of the BG (behavioral genetic) Evidence. Analysis in accordance with the BG model, together with the assumptions of the model, constitute a paradigm in the sense that Kuhn (1970) used this concept to describe implicit world views. A paradigm permits particular kinds of understandings—statements of lawful relationships—but does not permit some other kinds of understandings. The BG model in particular provides evidence of relationship between observed (i.e., phenotypic) variability in measurements and variability in biological relatedness. It does not provide information for understanding of how genetic factors determine the observed measurements.

Estimates of heritability (based on the BG model) are very much dependent on the extent of variability of influences operating in a particular sample, and the reliable variability of the measurements. The reliable G and E components of variance sum to a constant. If one is small, the other must be large. If a sample is homogeneous, particularly in respect to environmental opportunities (e.g., composed of White middle-class children of a particular country, say, Sweden), the G component will be large relative to the E component. In a sample of wide diversity (racially, ethnically, economically, in styles of life, etc.), the E component will be large relative to the G component. In a racially and ethnically homogeneous egalitarian society well organized to ensure that everyone develops a trait, the heritability of the trait will be large; in a society in which there are large racial, ethnic, and economic differences in opportunities to develop a trait, heritability will be small. If samples are representatively drawn, they will show these conditions of societies. If not, then heritability estimates need not reflect features of societies. Heritability estimates thus are descriptions of samples, not measures of individuals.

Heritability estimates are confounded with environmental influences. That is, heritability does not reflect simply genetic variability; it also re-

---

[4]Given this simple equation, there are different ways to obtain the variances terms that enter into the calculations. Some computations used in published research provide illogical estimates (see Schonemann, 1994, for a review).

flects environmental variability. Estimates of environmental influences are associated with heritable influences, and estimates of genetic influences are associated with environmental influences. This is true because genetic and environmental influences cannot be separated by the sampling of people of different degrees of relatedness: environmental and genetic determinants cannot be randomly assigned to different groupings of people (Plomin et al., 1980). The confounding is illustrated with results from studies of the intraclass correlation between IQ scores of people that are genetically related in different degrees.

For samples of identical twins (who have the same genetic structure) reared in the same home, the correlation between the IQ score of one twin compared with the IQ score of the other twin has been found to be about 0.8 to 0.9. A correlation of about 0.6 to 0.7 has been found for samples of fraternal twins (for whom an average of 50% of their genes are the same, which is true also for ordinary siblings and a child compared with a parent). The correlation between IQs of MZ twins reared apart is smaller than the correlation for MZ twins reared together, but larger than the correlation for fraternal twins reared together (Bouchard & Propping, 1993). For samples of ordinary siblings and parent-child pairs, the correlations have hovered around 0.5. For half siblings, the correlations have been roughly 0.3 to 0.4. The correlations for pairings of first cousins, uncle-nephew, aunt-niece, and child-grandparent have been in the neighborhood of 0.20 to 0.35. For unrelated people raised in the same home or orphanage, the correlations have ranged between 0.0 and 0.3.

Similarity in IQ thus relates to biological similarity, which suggests that IQ stems partly from genetic factors. But the inseparability and thus confounding of genetic and environmental influences should lead one to qualify this interpretation. The greater the degree of biological relationship, the more similar environments are likely to be. The environments are likely to be most similar for identical twins, next-most similar for fraternal twins, next-to-this-most similar for ordinary siblings, and so on for other degrees of biological similarity. The similarities expected for environments decrease monotonically with decrease in similarities in genetic structure. Genetic and environmental influences thus are mixed; however, to what extent is not known or reliably estimable. It is known that the influences are not unmixed by partitioning the variance into a part that is correlated with the biological similarity of related people, because this part also includes environmental similarity.

If environments could be assigned randomly, the confounding of genetic and environmental influences would be more nearly eliminated (e.g., if MZ twins could be separated at birth—or ideally before this—and randomly assigned to environments). This is not possible, of course, and thus is not done in BG research. MZ twins separated at birth are placed in similar kinds of homes, usually with relatives, usually with people of the same race and religion, and usually with people in similar economic circumstances. For example, one twin is placed with Aunt Mary, the other with Aunt Jane—the assignment is not random.

Even random assignment at birth would not entirely control for environmental influences in estimating genetic determination, because intrauterine environmental influences could still operate and there could be the environmental reactions (of people, of society) to the similar characteristics of twins (or other biologically similar people). For example, the environment is similar for African American twins (African American people) regardless of how they might be placed in adoption. Even when African American children are adopted by White parents and raised in what is ostensibly the environment of White children, they experience an environment that is in some respects similar to that experienced by other African American children not raised in what is ostensibly an environment of White children. Heritability estimates in these ways reflect (to some unknown degree) the similarities of environments.

IQ measures contain different mixtures of Gf, Gc, and other cognitive capabilities, and the proportions of these different capabilities vary with different IQ measures. Heritability estimates of IQ thus are ambiguous with respect to which component capabilities are most and least heritable.

With the qualifications outlined previously, the results of BG studies of IQ indicate that genetic factors influence the development of cognitive capabilities throughout the life span. The results also suggest that what is measured with indices of social economic class (usually a mixture of mother's educational level and family income) does not account for much of the variance of IQ that is not associated with estimation of G: The principal environmental determinants of IQ are not well indicated by conglomerate measures of income and education.

Findings for Gf and Gc.   Cattell (1941, 1957) put forth the theory that has been most influential in BG studies of different intelligences. According to this theory, Gf potential is inherited at birth and this inherited capacity is invested, along with influences of the environment, in the development of Gc. Individual differences in environmental opportunities arise throughout development, and Gf capabilities build on these opportunities to produce Gc, which then fosters further development of Gc. Gc thus becomes somewhat independent of Gf as individual differences in environmental influences accumulate. If reliabilities of measurement are equal (or correcting for attenuation of correlation due to unreliability), the heritability of Gf thus should be larger than the heritability of Gc. The following three hypotheses derive from this theory:

1. Gf primarily reflects genetic influences, and Gc reflects (to a larger extent than Gf) environmental influences: The heritability of Gf is larger than the heritability of Gc.[5]

2. Gf precedes development of Gc and thus can predict this, but Gc follows development of Gf and thus will not predict it.

3. For measurements obtained in the earliest period of life, there should be virtually no distinction between Gf and Gc, because there would be few individual differences in environmental influences, and little time for such influences to operate. Insofar as Gc can be distinguished at all, it will correlate very highly with Gf. As development proceeds beyond the earliest years, individual differences in environmental influences should accumulate and the distinction between Gf and Gc should become clearer and the correlation between these abilities should become smaller.

Does the evidence support these hypotheses? The answer is no—not definitively and not entirely, but generally no.

The heritability of Gf has not been found to be larger than the heritability of Gc (DeFries et al., 1979; McArdle, Goldsmith, & Horn, 1981; Nichols, 1978; Plomin et al., 1980). This is seen in results from Nichols collation of findings from several studies of twins (Table 4.3). The difference between the intraclass correlations for MZ twins and fraternal twins provides Falconer's (1960) estimate of heritability. Nichols' (1978) results indicate that this heritability estimate is virtually the same for Gc abilities as for Gf abilities. This was the finding also of the McArdle et al. (1981) study of MZ and fraternal twins. The summaries of DeFries et al. (1979) and Plomen et al. (1980) led to the same conclusion. The average of the heritabilities for abilities that define Gf was no larger than the corresponding average for the abilities of Gc.

Results from a pioneering study (Schmidt & Crano, 1974) appeared to support the investment hypothesis of Cattell's theory. It turned out, however, that when differences in the reliabilities of measures were taken into account, Gf was no more predictive of Gc than Gc was predictive of Gf.

In a second study that tests this hypothesis, the sampling was across a major portion of the life span (McArdle & Hamagami, 1995). Results indicated that Gf was no more a precursor of Gc than Gc was a precursor of Gf in either childhood or adulthood. However, the span of age in childhood was a jump from early childhood to adolescence. It would seem that the major investments of Gf in the development of Gc would occur in the earliest period of childhood—a period from birth to early childhood. The McArdle study

---

[5]Frank Schmidt (personal communication) pointed out that if the investment of Gf in the development of Gc is directed by interests, values, and other qualities of personality, and if these qualities are substantially heritable (as indicated by some recent evidence), then it is not clear that Gc measures should show lower heritabilities than do Gf measures.

TABLE 4.3

Primary Ability Average Intraclass Correlations Within Samples
of Fraternal and Identical Twins (After Nichols, 1978)

Crystallized Markers	MZ	DZ	Dif.*	2 Dif.
Knowledge: Social studies	.83	.57	.26	.52
Natural Sciences	.80	.64	.16	.32
V: Verbal comprehension	.82	.61	.21	.42
Vocabulary	.84	.60	.24	.48
N: Number facility	.80	.60	.20	.40
Fw: Word fluency	.65	.51	.14	.28
Fe: Expressional fluency	.60	.49	.11	.22
Averages	.76	.58	.18	.37
Fluid Markers				
I: Inductive Reasoning	.70	.55	.15	.30
S: Spatial Reasoning	.64	.40	.24	.48
P: Perceptual Speed	.70	.53	.17	.34
N: Number Facility	.80	.60	.20	.40
Ma: Associative Memory	.53	.39	.14	.28
Averages	.67	.49	.18	.36

*Dif. represents difference. 2 Dif. is Falconer's estimate of
broad-sense heritability.

did not test this hypothesis. A more thorough analysis of the early childhood
period of development might yield support for the investment hypothesis.

The results of the McArdle study indicated that, in adulthood, Gc was a
precursor to Gf. This was not predicted by the early statement of the investment hypothesis, but is consistent with a form of that hypothesis that stipulates that knowledge developed in Gc includes knowledge about how to
maintain health and avoid conditions that destroy neurons and decrease Gf
abilities (conditions of inebriation, inhalation of carbon monoxide, anes-
thetics, drugs, etc.). Thus, development of Gc may be an investment in
maintenance of Gf.

Also not supported by the evidence is the hypothesis that the distinction
between Gf and Gc will not be seen (will be difficult to find) in samples of
young children, and the hypothesis that the correlation between Gf and Gc
will increase as the average age within samples increases. In samples of 4-
year-olds and 7-year-olds, Ellison, Horn, and Browning (1983) found a clear
distinction between dimensions very much like the factors of Gf, Gc, SAR,
and TSR that have been found in samples of adults, and the correlations
among the dimensions were no smaller in the sample of younger children
than in the sample of older children or in samples of adults.

Generally, then, results from heritability studies suggest different heritabilities for different abilities: Different abilities are determined to about
the same extent by separate sets of genes. Studies specifically focused on the

major hypotheses of investment theory do not lend strong support for the theory. On the other hand, findings from various sources indicate that measures obtained early in childhood that are indicative of Gf are predictive of measures obtained later in childhood and adulthood that are indicative of Gc (e.g., Cattell, 1971; Simonton, 1988).

Achievement Evidence

In reviewing evidence of prediction of educational and occupational achievements, it is important to recognize that the abilities measured with tests, referred to as *aptitudes* and regarded as predictors of important outcomes, are themselves achievements and at the upper extremes indicate expertise. Aptitude tests are achievement tests (Humphreys, 1974).

A substantial body of evidence indicates that outstanding ability achievements in a variety of different areas are realized through deliberate practice that starts at a young age, extend over a long period of development, and are well guided and encouraged by good instruction and coaching (Ericsson & Charness, 1994). The differences between those who reach the highest levels of expert performance and those at lower levels are in knowledge, skills, and physiological adaptations that are affected by intensive and extended training. And what is seen most clearly at the extremes of developing expertise is seen also at lower levels in the distributions of achievements: the more sustained, deliberate, and well-guided the practice, the higher the level of achievement attained, both in narrow and broad abilities (Ackerman, 1987; Charness, Krampe, & Mayr, 1996; Ericsson, 1996; Ericsson, Krampe, & Tesch-Romer, 1993; Ericsson & Lehmann, 1996; Hoffman, 1992; Radford, 1990; Simonton, 1988).

In evaluating the evidence on the prediction of achievement outcomes, it is also important to attend to whether or not distinct features of outcomes are measured. What are regarded as achievement criteria are often ratings that are mixtures of different factors—conglomerates of overall performance. Raters are not helped to, or even allowed to, distinguish among and separately assess different qualities of outcome. Similarly, when measured with tests, outcomes are often comprised of several component abilities and other qualities all mixed together in an overall assessment.

If an outcome is measured as a mixture of different capabilities, then a conglomerate predictor that mirrors the mixture will best predict it (Anastasi, 1989; Austin & Hanisch, 1990; Hartigan & Wigdor, 1990; Larson & Wolfe, 1995; Schmidt, Hunter, & Larson, 1988; Schmidt, Ones, & Hunter, 1992; Welsh, Watson, & Ree, 1990). For example, if performance in electrical engineering is an expression of abilities of visualization (Vz), numerical skill (N), and verbal comprehension (V), and the criterion measure is simply a global rating of job performance, then the best predictor is likely to be a conglomerate that contains or predicts all three components—Vz, N, and V—not any one of these components as such. In this kind of prediction situation it has been found again and again (e.g., Campbell, 1990; Schmidt et al., 1988) that broad conglomerate measures are better predictors than a primary or second-stratum factor, and usually is as good as a best-weighted linear combination of several such factors. Also, after the prediction obtained with the conglomerate measure is taken into account, primary or second-stratum abilities provide little or no additional predictability. Such results are necessary consequences of not distinguishing separate components of outcome in criterion measurements.

It is difficult to identify the separate abilities involved in educational and occupational achievements, and it is difficult, in practice, to measure them. It is not done in most studies of predicting important outcomes. In the majority of prediction studies, therefore, a conglomerate measure, often unfortunately referred to as representing g, has been found to be the best predictor of important outcomes. But when, and to the extent that, different dimensions of outcome are distinguished, these distinct features usually are best predicted by separate predictor dimensions—dimensions that are most similar to the separate features of outcome (Ackerman, 1992; Anastasi, 1989; Carretta, 1989; Colberg & Nestor, 1987; Larson & Wolfe, 1995; Prediger, 1989; Schmidt et al., 1992). Different kinds of achievements are themselves different cognitive abilities and combinations of abilities (Berman, 1992; Lave, 1989; Nunes, Carraher, & Schliemann, 1993). To most accurately predict such outcomes it is necessary to reliably measure different abilities in both the outcome and the predictors. For example, in studies of developing proficiency in complex air traffic control simulation, Ackerman (1992) found that estimates of a general factor provide stable overall prediction, but different abilities are required to predict different components of performance over the learning sequence.

In general, the best predictor of educational and occupational achievements are very similar achievements (regarded as predictors) (Glaser & Bassock, 1989; Perkins & Solomon, 1989; Reif & Allen, 1992). Vocabulary and information learned in high school social studies are the best predictors of performance in college social studies courses. Mathematics achievement at one level is the best predictor of mathematics achievement at the next level. The best predictors of component abilities of achievements are similar abilities measured in predictors. For example, in a study of performance in physics, Levidow, Hunt, and Hinman (1996) distinguished in the outcome between knowledge and reasoning, and they found that Gc best predicted knowledge and Gf best predicted reasoning.

Over short periods of time—a few years between predictor measurement and assessment of criterion achievement—the best second-stratum ability predictors of academic criteria are usually conglomerate estimates containing much Gc, TSR, and Gq; measures that indicate Gf, SAR, and Gs are among the weaker predictors. There is some evidence, although it is not fully convincing, that this order of predictor validities becomes reversed as length of time increases between measurement of predictors and measurement of outcome—that measures indicating Gf and SAR become better predictors relative to measures that primarily indicate Gc and TSR (Ackerman, 1987, 1989; Austin, Humphreys, & Hulin, 1989; Cattell, 1957, 1971; Simonton, 1988).

Overall, the results from prediction studies indicate that usually only broad conglomerate measures of outcome are obtained, and that the best predictors of such outcomes are broad conglomerate measures of predictor abilities. However, when different abilities are distinguished in criterion measures, predictors that are most similar to these achievements are the best predictors.

Summary: Evidence From Five Sources

Results from a variety of studies thus add up to indicate that humans express distinctly different patterns of the achievements that are said to indicate intelligence. Different intelligences stem from different combinations of genetic and environmental determinants. They are affected in different ways by influences associated with injuries, childrearing, education, and the practices that make up different lifestyles. They are brought about by different patterns of practice that are more or less provided and encouraged through formal and informal educational systems. The practice varies over individuals in intensity, length, and quality. The different intelligences that emerge thus reflect a variety of neurological, experiential, developmental, genetic, and life achievement influences.

THE FATE OF GENERAL INTELLIGENCE

Despite the evidence just reviewed indicating multiple cognitive functions of the kind that are said to indicate human intelligence, the idea has persisted that general intelligence is a good concept, well supported by scientific evidence. There is widespread belief that one of the major achievements of psychological science is the discovery and measurement of general intelligence, often referred to as *Spearman's g* (e.g. Carroll, 1992; Estes, 1992; Jensen, 1992). It seems that the brain should be organized as a whole, and that this should be manifested in a behavioral organization that can be measured in a single factor. The primary factors and the second-stratum factors of structural analysis are positively correlated, and it seems that this should indicate a general factor at the third stratum that represents a functional system—intelligence.

Positive manifold (positive intercorrelations among abilities) provides a prima facie case for a hypothesis that a unifying principle unites all cognitive abilities; positive intercorrelations among second-stratum abilities are consistent with a hypothesis that a single factor at the third stratum represents a principle of general intelligence. But although consistent with this hypothesis, the evidence of positive test intercorrelations is not sufficient to support the hypothesis. Three kinds of additional evidence are needed. First, there should be evidence that the same general factor can be identified in different samples of people and tests—evidence that a general factor computed at the third order is the same under different conditions in which it may be computed. Call this the *same factor requirement*. Second, the general factor should represent how the different abilities of the second and first strata are united; how these variables are organized at the third stratum. Call this the *requirement for a unifying principle*. Third, the general factor should relate to other variables in a consistent way. It should have consistent construct validity. Call this the *construct validity requirement*. No general factor of intelligence has been identified that meets these three requirements.

Positive Manifold Related to Evidence of Spearman's *g*

The findings of many studies have shown that almost all measures of cognitive abilities are positively intercorrelated. The exceptions (Guilford, 1964) are rare. The major exceptions appear to be for highly speeded measures of abilities that require little resolution of complexity compared to unspeeded measures that do require resolution of difficult complexities in the immediate testing situation (in contrast to in the past). When these kinds of measures have been studied in homogeneous samples of people (all about the same age, same educational level, etc.), particularly samples of infants or very young children, near-zero and even negative correlations among cognitive abilities have been found (Guilford, 1964; McCall, 1979). Generally, however, cognitive ability measures are positively correlated.

Under conditions of positive manifold among the intercorrelations for measures of different abilities, a general factor that correlates positively with all the measures can always be calculated. Indeed, it can be determined in a way that yields a general factor that, linearly, has maximum variance. This maximum-variance factor is the principal component (PC). The PC or a simple sum of several ability measures is often calculated to obtain what is called a large and general factor of intellectual ability. It is claimed that the factor so calculated represents Spearman's *g* or something like it (Carroll, 1992; Herrnstein & Murray, 1994; Jensen, 1992).

But positive manifold, and the general factor that can always be calculated on it, does not, in itself, support Spearman's hypothesis of *g* or even a hypothesis of "something like it." Positive manifold and calculation of a PC or simple sum does not meet the same factor requirement, the unifying principle requirement, or the construct validity requirement for support of a hypothesis of general intelligence.

Spearman's (1927) theory of g has two major parts: one a substantive theory describing the cognitive components of g, and one a mathematical-statistical model specifying the conditions that must be obtained in measurements of abilities if the theory is valid. The substantive part of Spearman's theory is a behavioral complement to Lashley's (1935) theory of mass action, which stipulated that injury anywhere in the brain will result in decline of cognitive capabilities and the amount of decline will be proportional to the amount of brain tissue lost, not a function of particularly where the injury occurs. As indicated in previous sections of this chapter, the results from studies of the aftermath of brain injury have not supported Lashley's theory.

Spearman's equivalent of mass action is a form of mental energy that pervades all cognitive functions. It is manifested behaviorally through three primary processes: apprehension of experience, eduction of relations, and the eduction of correlates. Spearman regarded apprehension of experience as subjective and thus not distinguishable in objective measurement, but he thought that eduction of relations and correlates can be, and indeed are, varied in cognitive tasks and thus provide a basis for measure of g. According to Spearman's theory, eduction of relations and correlates are the necessary and sufficient within-person factors for causing behavior indicative of what is generally identified as intelligence (what he called g). Thus, all measures of human cognitive capability will reflect the operation of these processes, and individual differences in performance on cognitive tasks will reflect individual differences in g.

Spearman's model for testing this substantive theory stipulated that if cognitive tasks are chosen in a manner that ensures that they measure g and no other factor in common, then it will be found that the intercorrelations among these tasks will be accounted for with one common factor. Specifically, the model specifies that in any sample of $i = 1, \ldots, N$ people, a task measuring cognitive capabilities will involve a common factor, g_i and another specific factor, s_{ij}, that may, with proper design of research, be unique to each particular task j. The extent to which the common factor is measured by different tasks, j and k, can be symbolized G_j and G_k. The model specifies, and the design for research should aim to ensure, that to within chance the intercorrelations among the specific factors will be zero. Under these conditions, the correlation between any two tests will be

[1] $$r_{jk} = G_j G_k.$$

The model thus stipulates that the manifest variable correlations are produced by one and only one common factor, and the magnitude of this correlation is the product of the G_j and G_k proportions indicating the extent to which the manifest variables measure this factor. The model does not require that the correlations among tests be large (contrary to what is sometimes said). If the specific factors overlap and thus correlate, group factors—other common factors—will be indicated and statistical test will indicate rejection of a hypothesis of one common factor. But if the g hypothesis is correct and data are carefully gathered to ensure that there is no overlap in measure of specific factors, then the intercorrelations among different measures of cognitive capabilities will be fully reproduced with one common factor. Thus, the model for g is demanding but quite testable.

Many studies have been carried out with aim of demonstrating support for Spearman's model. Some of the studies were not well designed to avoid overlap of specific factors, but some were. Without exception, the well-designed studies failed to support the theory (Horn, 1976, 1988, for full reviews). It is not simply that the evidence of these studies requires rejection of a hypothesis specifying no group factors (an early interpretation of Spearman's theory); the evidence more fundamentally indicates that a g-factor model does not fit intercorrelations for sets of abilities that are well chosen to avoid the kind of overlap that determines group factors (provided only that the sets are representative samples of the abilities that are acknowledged to be indicative of intelligence). When care was taken to ensure that specific factors did not overlap and the sample tasks were representative of the range of capabilities regarded as indicating human intelligence, it was found that one common factor would not reproduce the intercorrelations. More than one common factor was indicated.

Thus, Spearman's model requires more than positive manifold among the correlations among measures of cognitive abilities, and the evidence of this manifold is not sufficient support for the hypothesis of g. As Thomson (1919) and Thurstone (1938, 1947) pointed out earlier in this century, there are many ways in which variables can be positively correlated and yet not measure a single common factor. The following symbolic representation of a common factor solution indicates one way this can occur:

Variables	Common Factor Coefficients				Intercorrelations Among Variables			
					V1	*V2*	*V3*	*V4*
V1	a	b	c	0	( )	$ad + ce$	$bg + ch$	bj
V2	d	0	e	f	$da + ec$	( )	eh	fk
V3	0	g	h	0	$gb + hc$	he	( )	gj
V4	0	j	0	k	jb	kf	jg	( )

Here it is seen that if a, b, c, d, e, f, g, h, j, and k are positive, the intercorrelations among the variables are all positive, but four common factors are indicated (required to reproduce the correlations).

The fact that positive manifold is not sufficient evidence of g is indicated by the fact that many tests that do not measure cognitive abilities nevertheless correlate positively with ability tests. For example, measures of ego strength (absence of neuroticism), sanity (absence of psychosis), and law abidance (absence of criminality) correlate positively with abilities, as do measures of athletic, artistic, and musical skills. Such measures thus are part of a positive manifold that includes cognitive abilities, but a score computed over a collection of such measures does not represent a single factor of intelligence.

Other Structural Evidence

In theory, the intercorrelations among the second-stratum factors could fit the Spearman model and thus indicate a g-factor at the third stratum. But the results of research do not support this theory. Carroll (1993) identified a general factor at the third stratum in 33 separate analyses, but the factor of 1 analysis was not the same as the factor of other analyses. Some of these general factors were conceptually similar to Spearman's substantive theory of g; some were not. Even those that were conceptually similar differed notably. Some involved Gc and TSR to a major extent; some involved mainly Gf and Gv. The factors did not meet the standards of even the weakest form of factor invariance (namely, configural invariance; Horn & McArdle, 1992). Although referred to as the (singular) general factor, the third-stratum factors were not replications of one factor; they were different factors.

This has been the case for other calculations to obtain a measure of general intelligence. In Jensen's (1980) book on test bias, for example, the general factor identified in one chapter was similar to Gc, the general factor referred in another chapter was similar to Gf, and the general factor of still another chapter was similar to Gv (Horn & Goldsmith, 1981). As noted in previous sections, Gc, Gf, and Gv have different construct validities. Also different are the single factors found at the third stratum in the studies of McArdle and Horn (1983; Horn, 1985, 1988), Gustafsson (1984, 1985), and Undheim and Gustafsson (1987, 1992). In all of these studies, as in the analyses of Carroll, ability measures intercorrelated positively and a general factor could be calculated, but that general factor was not the same from one study to another.

The Undheim and Gustafsson (1987) results suggest that, in at least some hierarchical solutions, the common factor at the highest order cannot be distinguished from one of the factors (Gf in their solution) at the next order down. That is, the Gf second-stratum factor and the third-stratum factors were not significantly different in their study. This means that the third-stratum factor did not account for the common variance among the second-stratum factors; it accounted for the variance of only one of these factors.

Thus, the third-stratum factor was not a general factor. It is not, therefore, supportive of an hypothesis of general intelligence. As Gf, it is indicative of *one form* of intelligence.

Indifference of Indicators

Jensen (e.g., 1984, 1993) argued that a "principle of indifference of the indicator" supports a claim that combining the scores on any goodly sample of ability tests will yield a measure of g that is invariant across different samples of tests and subjects. The argument is circular and not supported by evidence. The claim that there is principle of indifference of indicator is no more than an assertion that all ability tests measure g as specified in Spearman's model. As we have seen, that claim is not supported by evidence. The claim that combinations of scores on different batteries of tests will measure the same g factor is based on an assumption that in each combination other factors measured in a battery of tests will cancel out, leaving only g. This could occur if all other factors were specific and thus randomly related to each other and to the g factor. This is not generally true, however. Common factors other than g are measured in different batteries of tests, these other factors are not the same from one battery to another, and different common factors make up different proportions of the total in different batteries. If more than one common factor is present in a battery, these factors, too, will accumulate in a composite computed over the several tests of the battery. They will not cancel out to leave only g. The composites will not measure just one factor; however, they will measure conglomerates of several factors. Thus, even if g were measured in each of several batteries, each battery would yield measure of g plus whatever the other factors in that battery were. For example, if Battery A measured g plus primary factors Vi, Rs, and Ma, while Battery B measure g plus Fa, Cs, Ws and P (described in Table 4.1), the measures obtained with A and B would be notably different. This would be particularly the case if, for example, the Ma measures were a particularly large proportion of Battery A, and Cs measures were a large proportion of Battery B.

Jensen and others have argued that findings of substantial correlations between the composite measures of different batteries is evidence that the same g is measured in different batteries. But such correlations may be large not because they measure g alone, but because they measure similar sets of other common factors. Some batteries do sample many of the same primary and second-stratum factors.

It has been argued, too, that one factor g is indicated by evidence showing that composite scores based on different batteries of tests provide comparable predictions of different criteria, and by evidence that when a general factor estimate is entered first in a prediction equation, other ability predictors add little—often a statistically insignificant amount—to the prediction. But again, for several reasons, this evidence does not really indicate g. The different criterion measures that are predicted by different predictors are often heterogeneous mixtures of different abilities, and the predictor measures, too, are conglomerates of different abilities. One such heterogeneous predictor will predict some of the different abilities in heterogeneous criteria as well as another such predictor, even when somewhat different abilities are involved in both the predictors and criteria. Two predictors can predict equally well, for example, even though they are not predicting the same sets of abilities. For example, if the criterion is comprised of u, v, w, x, y, z, and one predictor is comprised of u, v, and w, whereas another is comprised of x, y, and z, the two predictor composites can have about the same predictability even as they predict different things. In any case, the evidence of prediction from conglomerate predictors to heterogeneous criteria does not indicate g.

If an ability relevant to prediction is already contained within a general composite, a separate measure of that ability will not (cannot be expected to) add to the prediction achieved with the general composite. Findings that a separate measure does not add to the prediction achieved with a composite measure thus do not indicate that only a general factor is at work in the prediction.

Gf Related to Spearman's Theory of g

Among the second stratum factors, Gf appears to best represent Spearman's substantive theory of intelligence and model for g. It is comprised of components that to a considerable extent represent the processes Spearman specified as essential (necessary and sufficient) for g. Measures of these processes intercorrelate in a manner that indicates support for Spearman's model. Measures of apprehension, retention, and encoding in short-term memory, and comprehension of conjunctions (eduction of relations) and of drawing inferences (eduction of correlates) appear to function together to indicate a unity. By selecting operational definitions of process variables designed to indicate Gf and satisfy the conditions of a g model, with careful attention to avoid overlap of specific factors, it is found that the intercorrelations among the process components very nearly fit the Spearman model. This kind of evidence suggests that Gf represents Spearman's concept of g.

For example, in a sample of 146 subjects, the intercorrelations among the following seven measures approximate fit to the Spearman model:

1. Immediate awareness, measured with an adaptation of the Sperling (1960) paradigm.
2. Primacy memory, measured as immediate recall of the first two elements (numbers and letters) of serial recall tests.

3. Working memory, measured as recall in reverse order after 5 seconds of elements presented in serial order.
4. Inductive reasoning, measured under power conditions with a letter series test.
5. Cognitive speed, measured with a crossout test.
6. Concentration, measured with slow tracing test.
7. Carefulness, measured as few incorrect answers in various speeded tests in which the items are of nontrivial difficulty.

We have found similar approximations to Spearman's model in different samples of subjects with different combinations of tasks designed to indicate features of fluid intelligence.

As pointed out in discussing the results of Undheim and Gustafsson (1992), this Gf factor is not general to all measures accepted as indicating human intelligence. The tasks that indicate Gf are different from tasks that indicate Gc, for example, and as soon as Gc tests are introduced into the battery of Gf indicators, the fit to a Spearman model is lost. If several Gc tests are included in the battery, the model of fit must have at least two common factors. If indicators of Gv and Ga are introduced, at least four common factors are required to fit the data.

The Gf concept of cognitive capabilities thus might be said to indicate g, but this g does not include all the features of intelligence that are represented in other second-stratum factors. It does not account for the full range of positively intercorrelated cognitive abilities. These abilities, too, are indicative of intelligence. No single integrating principle among abilities indicative of human intelligence has been found in structural research.

Cognitive Speed Theory of General Intelligence

Spearman (1927) hypothesized that neural speed is a principal feature of the eduction processes underlying manifestations of human intelligence. Eysenck (1985, 1987) and Jensen (1982, 1987, 1993) since proposed that speed of information processing, reflecting a process of speed of transmission throughout the neural system, is the essence of a g-factor of human intelligence: The level of ability manifested in any and all measures of human intelligence is determined by neural speed. Research based on this theory has focused on identifying correlations between chronometric measures (reaction time, response time, time to complete) and measures regarded as indicative of general intelligence.

The evidence-derived study of chronometric measures and other measures of cognitive capabilities is clear in indicating that cognitive speed is not a general factor, and no broad factor among chronometric measures accounts for the relationships among cognitive measures in general. Results from several studies suggest at least three cognitive speed factors (Nettel-beck, 1994), and a few studies (e.g., Cunningham-Tomer, 1990) suggest as many as five common-factor speed dimensions. These factors are not general in the sense that they account for the variation in all measures of cognitive capability: They have different patterns of correlations with Gf, SAR, and Gc.

The factors also are not general in the ways in which they relate to age variance in measured cognitive factors (Horn et al., 1981). For example, a Gs factor correlates negatively with age and positively with cognitive measures (Gf, SAR) that decline with age, whereas a TSR factor correlates positively with age and with cognitive measures (Gc) that do not decline with age. A factor of decision speed (DS) correlates negatively with age, but correlates near zero both with cognitive measures that decline and cognitive measures that do not decline with age.

Cognitive speed factors also are not general in the way they relate to other variables. Hertzog (1989), for example, found that for different operational definitions of cognitive speed there were different patterns of relationships to primary abilities and different components of cognitive processing. There appears to be no one uniform process of cognitive speed. It depends on where in cognition speed is required, or permits individuals to express their characteristic rate of responding.

Walsh (1982, 1986) found evidence of independence of speeded functions in highly reliable measures of peripheral and central cognitive processing, each measured under conditions in which the subject's motivation and alertness could have very little influence. The measures, based on Turvey's (1973) paradigm, were of time to escape the effects of a backward mask in visual processing. In peripheral processing, the mask must be presented to the same eye as the target, the energy of the mask must exceed the energy of the target, and the mask may be simply white noise. The masking appears to produce interference in the retina, lateral geniculate nucleus, and terminal connections of the striate cortex that disrupt neural nets attuned to figural characteristics. In central processing, the masking can be produced when the mask is presented to a different eye than is the stimulus target. The pattern of the mask must be similar to the pattern of the target. Escape from the mask is determined by the time separating onset of the target and the mask, but the energy of the mask need not exceed the energy of the target. The masking appears to produce interference in the cortex of the brain.

The reliabilities of both peripheral and central processing were in excess of .80, and there was notable cross-sectional age decline in speed of both kinds of processing, but the correlation between the two kinds of measures was less than .20. Thus, each measure had much reliable variance that was not shared with the other measure. Such evidence again suggests that cognitive speed is not a general factor. There is general age-related decrease in the averages for measures of the speed people do a wide variety of different tasks, but this is not the same as, or indicative of, a general common factor of individual differences in speed of doing different tasks.

SUMMARY

The results of many studies thus indicate that human intelligence is comprised of many separate abilities. Structural evidence suggests that abilities are organized at different levels of generality. At a low level of generality, independent factors representing as many as 66 separate abilities have been identified in separate replicated studies. At the second level the findings of many studies indicate nine broad sets of abilities (second-stratum factors), each of which individually represents a form of human intelligence.

The second-stratum factors are positively intercorrelated, as are first-stratum factors and most elementary cognitive ability measures. This evidence is necessary but not sufficient to indicate organization among all human abilities in a factor of general intelligence. A basis for such organization has not been adduced, however, and most of the evidence of construct validation suggests that there are functionally distinct forms of intelligence. It is not yet clear how many such forms of intelligence there are.

Thurstone (1947) pointed out that more than structural evidence is needed to build understanding of the concepts indicated by structural evidence—an early statement of what has become known as the *need for construct validation*. Important in considering the hypothesis of general intelligence is evidence of developmental change, of relationships to indicators of physiological and neurological functioning, of heritability, and of studies of achievements.

The evidence of developmental research suggests that three second-stratum factors—Gf, Gs, and SAR—are components of one form of (vulnerable) intelligence: Each declines with age in adulthood, and each is affected adversely and irreversibly by known injuries to the central nervous system (CNS). TSR and Gc, on the other hand, appear to be components of another form of intelligence that is relatively invulnerable to influences associated with aging.

SAR, Gf, and Gs appear to be interconnected processes of reasoning. In order to comprehend relationships and make decisions about them (i.e., reason effectively, as in Gf), it is necessary to apprehend information and hold it in the span of immediate awareness (as in SAR) and cycle through various possible relationships quickly (as in Gs). A process of concentration is also necessary. When requirements for reasoning of a cognitive ability test are small, answers are provided quickly and automatically. In difficult reasoning tasks, on the other hand, it is necessary to sustain concentration. Individual differences in capacity for concentration become important.

The organizational relationship between Gc and TSR appears to be one of storage and access, respectively. The first, Gc, is a storage network of many nodes of knowledge, and TSR represents a process of moving through the network to access and recover the knowledge of particular nodes. It's as if Gc is a library of books and TSR is the system for obtaining the books.

There appears to be no general factor of cognitive speed. Rather, there are several such factors. These factors, considered singly or collectively, do not fully predict, or account for, either the age differences or the individual differences, generally, of cognitive abilities that do and do not decline with age.

Although not discussed in any detail in this review, the separate processes of visual cognition and auditory cognition, as seen in the second-stratum factors of Gv and Ga, also appear to represent different forms of intelligence. More research is needed to build the network of evidence that will support such a conclusion.

A broad collection of evidence from different sources thus adds up to indicate several organizations of cognitive processes. No single factor of intelligence is indicated. Some of the abilities that have a good claim on the connotations of the concept of intelligence relate to age in a manner opposite to the relationships for other abilities that also well represent these connotations. If Gf and Gc are combined in one conglomerate measure, the distinction between the aging decline of some intellectual abilities and the aging improvement of other such abilities is lost. Studies of the neurological basis for cognitive capabilities also provide little support for a one-factor hypothesis. There appear to be at least two distinct organizations for short-term memories. There are distinct organizations of anatomical structures and neuroprocessor systems underlying other behavioral organizations. This is indicated also by evidence from behavioral genetics and studies of achievements.

There may be a single unifying principle pervading all human cognitive capabilities. It is reasonable that there should be, and it would be valuable to have a measure of it, but the evidence adduced thus far does not indicate that principle. Positive manifold is not sufficient to indicate it. Spearman's g-model does not represent it. Spearman's substantive theory is best represented by Gf. But Gf is not equivalent to general factors (plural) calculated at the third stratum. A functional unity might be identified at the third stratum, but it has not been identified thus far. If there is such unity, we have yet to be clear about what it is. The quest for a principle of general intelligence must continue.

AUTHOR'S NOTE

I thank Jennie Noll, Jack McArdle, Anders Ericsson, Gerald Larson, Phillip Ackerman, and Frank Schmidt for suggestions concerning the content and writing of this chapter. Preparation of the chapter was supported by grants from the National Institute on Aging (AG00156–06, AG09936–05).

REFERENCES

Ackerman, P. L. (1987). Individual differences in skill learning: An integration of psychometric and information processing perspectives. *Psychological Bulletin, 102,* 3–27.

Ackerman, P. L. (1989). Within-task intercorrelations of skill performance: Implications for predicting individual differences? *Journal of Applied Psychology, 74,* 360–364.

Ackerman, P. L. (1992). Predicting individual differences in complex skill acquisition: Dynamics of ability determinants. *Journal of Applied Psychology, 77,* 598–614.

Amaral, D. G. (1987). Memory: Anatomical organization of candidate brain regions. In F. Plum (Ed.)., *Handbook of physiology, vol. 5, higher functions of the brain* (pp. 211–294). Baltimore: Williams & Williams.

Anastasi, A. (1989). Ability testing in the 1980's and beyond: Some major trends. *Public Personnel Management Journal, 18,* 471–484.

Austin, J. T., & Hanisch, K. A. (1990). Occupational attainment as a function of abilities and interests: A longitudinal analysis using project TALENT data. *Journal of Applied Psychology, 75,* 77–86.

Austin, J. T., Humphreys, L. G., & Hulin, C. L. (1989). Another view of dynamic criteria: A critical reanalysis of Barrett, Caldwell, Alexander. *Personnel Psychology, 42,* 593–596.

Berger, T. W., & Thompson, R. F. (1978). Neuronal plasticity in the limbic system during classical conditioning of the rabbit nicitating membrane response: The hippocampus. *Brain Research, 145,* 323–346.

Berman, J. (Ed.). (1989). *Nebraska symposium on motivation: Cross-cultural perspective.* Lincoln: University of Nebraska Press.

Blackwood, W., & Corsellis, J. A. (Eds.). (1976). *Greenfield's neuropathology.* London: Arnold.

Bouchard, T. J., & Propping, P. (1993). *Twins as a tool of behavioral genetics.* West Sussex, England: Wiley.

Bourne, L. R., Ekstrand, B. R., & Dominowski, R. L. (1971). *The psychology of thinking.* Englewood Cliffs, NJ: Prentice-Hall.

Burt, C. (1909). Experimental tests of general intelligence. *British Journal of Psychology, 3,* 94–177.

Campbell, J. P. (1990). An overview of the army selection and classification project (Project A). *Personnel Psychology, 43,* 231–239.

Carretta, T. R. (1989). USAF pilot selection and classification systems. *Aviation Space Environment, 60,* 46–49.

Carroll, J. B. (1992). Cognitive abilities: The state of the art. *Cognitive Science, 5,* 278.

Carroll, J. B. (1993). *Human cognitive abilities: A survey of factor analytic studies.* New York: Cambridge University Press.

Cattell, R. B. (1933). *The Cattell Intelligence Test. Scales 1, 2, and 3.* London: Harrap.

Cattell, R. B. (1941). Some theoretical issues in adult intelligence testing. *Psychological Bulletin, 38,* 592.

Cattell, R. B. (1943). The measurement of adult intelligence. *Psychological Bulletin, 40,* 153–193.

Cattell, R. B. (1957). Personality and motivation structure and measurement. New York: World Book.

Cattell, R. B. (1963). Theory of fluid and crystallized intelligence: A critical experiment. *Journal of Educational Psychology, 54,* 1–22.

Cattell, R. B. (1971). *Abilities: Their structure, growth and action.* Boston: Houghton Mifflin.

Charness, N., Krampe, R., & Mayr, U. (1996). The role of practice and coaching in entrepreneurial skill domains. In K. A. Ericsson (Ed.), *The road to excellence* (pp. 51–80). Mahwah, NJ: Lawrence Erlbaum Associates.

Colberg, M., & Nestor, M. A. (1987, September). The use of illogical biases in psychometrics. Paper presented at the Eighth International Congress on Logic, Methodology, and Philosophy of Science, Moscow.

Cunningham, W. R., & Tomer, A. (1990). Intellectual abilities and age: Concepts, theories and analyses. In A. E. Lovelace (Ed.), *Aging and cognition: Mental processes, self-awareness and interventions* (pp. 279–406). Amsterdam: Elsevier.

DeFries, J. C., Kuse, A R., & Vandenberg, S. G. (1979). Genetic correlations, environmental correlations and behavior. In J. R. Royce & L. P. Mos (Eds.), *Theoretical advances in behavior genetic* (pp. 389–421). Alpen aan den Rijn, Netherlands: Sijthoff Noordhoff.

Eckstrom, R. B., French, J. W., & Harman, M. H. (1979). Cognitive factors: Their identification and replication. *Multivariate Behavioral Research Monographs, 79*(2), 84.

Ellison, P. H., Horn, J. L., & Browning, C. (1983). A large-sample, many variable study of motor dysfunction of infancy. *Journal of Pediatric Psychology, 8*, 345–357.

Ericsson, K. A. (1996). The acquisition of expert performance: An introduction to some issues. In K. A. Ericsson (Ed.), *The road to excellence* (pp. 1–49). Mahwah, NJ: Lawrence Erlbaum Associates.

Ericsson, K. A., & Charness, N. (1994). Expert performance: Its structure and acquisition. *American Psychologist, 49*, 725–747.

Ericsson, K. A., Krampe, R. T., & Tesch-Romer, C. (1993). The role of deliberate practice in the acquisition of expert performance. *Psychological Review, 100*, 363–406.

Ericsson, K. A., & Lehmann, A. C. (1996). Expert and exceptional: Evidence of maximal adaptation to task constraints. *Annual Review of Psychology, 47*, 273–305.

Estes, W. K. E. (1992). Ability testing. Postscript on ability tests, testing, and public policy. *Cognitive Science, 5*, 278.

Eysenck, H. J. (1986). The theory of intelligence and the psychophysiology of cognition. In R. J. Sternberg (Ed.), *Advances in the psychology of human intelligence* (Vol. 3, pp. 1–34). Hillsdale, NJ: Lawrence Erlbaum Associates.

Eysenck, H. J. (1987). Speed of information processing, reaction time, and the theory of intelligence. In P. A. Vernon (Ed.), *Speed of information processing and intelligence* (pp. 21–68). Norwood, NJ: Ablex.

Falconer, D. S. (1960). *Introduction to quantitative genetics.* New York: Ronald Press.

French, J. W., Eckstrom, R. B., & Price, L. A. (1963). *Manual and kit of reference tests for cognitive factors.* Princeton, NJ: Educational Testing Service.

Glaser, R., & Bassock, M. (1989). Learning theory and the study of instruction. *Annual Review of Psychology, 40*, 631–666.

Guilford, J. P. (1956). The structure of the intellect. *Psychological Bulletin, 53*, 276–293.

Guilford, J. P. (1964). Zero intercorrelations among tests of intellectual abilities. *Psychological Bulletin, 61*, 401–404.

Gustafsson, J. E. (1984). A unifying model for the structure of intellectual abilities. *Intelligence, 8*, 179–203

Gustafsson, J. E. (1985). Measuring and interpreting g. *The Behavioral and Brain Sciences, 8*, 231–232.

Hartigan, J. A., & Wigdor, A. K. (Eds.). (1990). *Fairness in employment testing: Validity generalization, minority issues, and the general aptitude test battery.* Washington, DC: National Academic Press.

Hellige, J. B. (1990). Hemispheric asymmetry. *Annual Review of Psychology, 41*, 55–80.

Herrnstein, R. J., & Murray, C. (1994). *The bell curve: Intelligence and class structure in American life.* New York: Free Press.

Hertzog, C. (1989). Influences of cognitive slowing on age differences in intelligence. *Developmental Psychology, 25,* 636–651.

Hoffman, R. R. (1992). *The psychology of expertise: Cognitive research and empirical results.* New York: Springer-Verlag.

Horn, J. L. (1976). Human abilities: A review of research and theory in the early 1970s. *Annual Review of Psychology, 27,* 437–485.

Horn, J. L. (1985). Remodeling old models of intelligence: Gf-Gc theory. In B. B. Wolman (Ed.), *Handbook of intelligence* (pp. 267–300). New York: Wiley.

Horn, J. L. (1988). Thinking about human abilities. In J. R. Nesselroade (Ed.), *Handbook of multivariate psychology* (pp. 645–685). New York: Academic.

Horn, J. L., & Donaldson, G. (1980). Cognitive development in adulthood. In O. G. Brim & J. Kagan (Eds.), *Constancy and change in human development* (pp. 445–529). Cambridge, MA: Harvard University Press.

Horn, J. L., & Goldsmith, H. (1981). Reader be cautious: *Bias in mental testing* by Arthur Jensen. *American Journal of Education, 89,* 305–329.

Horn, J. L., & McArdle, J. J. (1992). A practical and theoretical guide to measurement invariance in aging research. *Experimental Aging Research, 18,* 117–144.

Humphreys, L. G. (1974). The misleading distinction between aptitude and achievement tests. In D. R. Green (Ed.), *The aptitude achievement distinction* (pp. 262–274). Monterey, CA: CTB/McGraw-Hill.

Humphreys, L. G. (1976). A factor model for research on intelligence and problem solving. In L. B. Resnick (Ed.), *The nature of intelligence* (pp. 329–340). New York: Wiley.

Jensen, A. R. (1980). *Bias in mental testing.* New York: Free Press.

Jensen, A. R. (1982). Reaction time and psychometric g. In J. J. Eysenck (Ed.), *A model for intelligence* (pp. 93–132). New York: Springer-Verlag.

Jensen, A. R. (1984). Test validity: g versus the specificity doctrine. *Journal of Social and Biological Structures, 7,* 93–118.

Jensen, A. R. (1992). Commentary: Vehicles of g. *Psychological Science, 5,* 275–278.

Jensen, A. R. (1993). Why is reaction time correlated with psychometric g? *Current Directions in Psychological Science, 2*(2), 53–56.

Kuhn, T. S. (1970). *The structure of scientific revolutions* (2nd ed.). Chicago: University of Chicago Press.

Larson, G. E., & Wolfe, J. H. (1995). Validity results for g from an expanded test base. *Intelligence, 20,* 15–25.

Lashley, K. S. (1935). The mechanism of vision. XII. Nervous structures concerned in the acquisition and retention of habits based on reactions to light. *Comparative Psychological Monographs, 11,* 43–79.

Lave, J. (1989). Cognition in practice: Mind, mathematics and culture in everyday life. New York: Wiley.

Lavond, D. G., Kim, J. J., & Thompson, R. F. (1993). Mammalian brain substrates of aversive classical conditioning. *Annual Review of Psychology, 44,* 317–342.

Levidow, B. B., Hunt, E., & Hinman, H. (1996). *The relation between fluid and crystallized intelligence and learning in introductory high school physics.* Seattle, WA: University of Washington, Department of Psychology.

McArdle, J. J., & Hamagami, F. (1995, July 3). *A dynamic-structural analysis of the theory of fluid and crystallized intelligence.* Paper presented at the IV European Congress of Psychology, Athens, Greece.

McArdle, J. J., Goldsmith, H. H., & Horn, J. L. (1981). Genetic structural equation models of fluid and crystallized intelligence. *Behavior Genetics, 60,* 607.

McArdle, J. J., & Horn, J. L. (1983). Validation by systems modeling of WAIS-R abilities. *Na-*

tional Institute of Aging Grant #AG-04704. Department of Psychology, University of Denver.

McCall, R. B. (1979). The development of intellectual functioning in infancy and the prediction of later IQ. In J. B. Osofsky (Ed.), *Handbook of Infant Development* (pp. 170–215). New York: Wiley.

Nettelbeck, T. (1994). Speediness. In R. J. Sternberg (Ed.), *Encyclopedia of Intelligence* (pp. 1014–1019). New York: Macmillan.

Nichols, R. (1978). Twin studies of ability, personality, and interests. *Homo, 29,* 158–173.

Nunes, T., Carraher, D. W., & Schliemann, A. D. (1993). *Street mathematics and school mathematics*. New York: Cambridge University Press.

Perkins, D. N., & Solomon, G. (1989). Are cognitive skills context- bound? *Educational Research, 18,* 16–25.

Plomin, R., DeFries, J. C., & McClearn, G. E. (1980). *Behavioral genetics*. San Francisco: Freeman.

Prediger, D. J. (1989). Ability differences across occupations: More than g. *Journal of Vocational Behavior, 34,* 1–27.

Prohovnik, I. (1980). *Mapping brainwork*. Malmo, Sweden: CWK Gleerup.

Radford, J. (1990). *Child prodigies and exceptional early achievers*. New York: Free Press.

Reif, F., & Allen, S. (1992). Cognition for interpreting scientific concepts: A study of acceleration. *Cognitive Instruction, 9,* 1–44.

Rosen, J. B., Hitchcock, J. M., Sananes, C. B., Miserendino, M. J. D., & Davis, M. (1991). A direct projection from the central nucleus of the amygdala to the acoustic startle pathway: Anterograde and retrograde tracing studies. *Behavioral Neuroscience, 105,* 817–825.

Schmidt, F. L., & Crano, W. D. (1974). A test of the theory of fluid and crystallized intelligence in middle- and low-socioeconomic-status children: A cross-lagged panel analysis. *Journal of Educational Psychology, 66,* 255–261.

Schmidt, F. L., Hunter, J. E., & Larson, M. (1988). *General cognitive ability versus general and specific aptitudes in the prediction of training performance: Some preliminary findings*. Report for Navy Personnel Research Development Center. San Diego, CA: Office of Naval Research.

Schmidt, F. L., Ones, D. S., & Hunter, J. E. (1992). Personnel selection. *Annual Review of Psychology, 43,* 627–670.

Schonemann, P. H. (1994) Heritability. In R. Sternberg (Ed.), *Encyclopedia of human intelligence*. New York: MacMillan.

Simonton, D. K. (1988). *Scientific genius: A psychology of science*. New York: Cambridge University Press.

Snow, R. E., Kyllonen, P. C., & Marshalek, B. (1984). The topology of ability and learning correlations. In R. J. Sternberg (Ed.), *Advances in the psychology of human intelligence* (vol. 2, pp. 47–103). Hillsdale, NJ: Lawrence Erlbaum Associates.

Spearman, C. (1927). *The abilities of man: Their nature and measurement*. London: Macmillan.

Sperling, G. (1960). The information available in brief visual presentations. *Psychological Monographs, 74,* 498.

Thomson, G. A. (1919). On the cause of hierarchical order among correlation coefficients. *Proceedings of the Royal Society, A, 95,* 400–408.

Thomson, G. A. (1948). *The factorial analysis of human abilities* (3rd ed.). Boston: Houghton Mifflin.

Thompson, R. F. (1990). The neurobiology of learning and memory. *Science, 233,* 941–947.

Thompson, R. F. (1991). *The brain: An introduction to neuroscience*. New York: Freeman.

Thompson, R. F. (1992). Memory. *Current Opinion in Neurobiology, 2,* 203–208.

Thorndike, E. L. (1921). Intelligence and its measurement: A symposium. *Journal of Educational Psychology, 12,* 123–147.

Thurstone, L. L. (1938). Primary mental abilities. *Psychometric Monographs, 1,* 97.

Thurstone, L. L. (1947). *Multiple factor analysis.* Chicago: University of Chicago Press.

Turvey, M. T. (1973). On peripheral and central processes in vision: Inferences from and information processing analysis of masking with patterned stimuli. *Psychological Review, 80,* 1–52.

Undheim, J. O., & Gustafsson, J. E. (1987). The hierarchical organization of cognitive abilities: Restoring general intelligence through the use of linear structural relations (LISREL). *Multivariate Behavioral Research, 22,* 149–171.

Vandenberg, S. G. (1962). The hereditary abilities study: Hereditary components in a psychological test battery. *American Journal of Human Genetics, 14,* 20–237.

Vandenberg, S. G. (1971). What do we know today about the inheritance of intelligence and how do we know it? In R. Cancro (Ed.), *Intelligence: Genetic and environmental influences* (pp. 99–125). New York: Grune and Stratton.

Walsh, D. A. (1982). The development of visual information processes in adulthood and old age. In F. I. M. Craik & S. Trehub (Eds.), *Aging and cognitive processes* (pp. 99–125). New York: Plenum.

Walsh, D. A. (1986). Aging and human visual information processing. *Geriatric Ophthalmology, 2,* 29–35.

Welsh, J. R., Watson, T. W., & Ree, M. J. (1990). *Armed Services Vocational Battery (ASVAB). Predicting military criteria from general and specific abilities.* Brooks Air Force Base, TX: Air Force Human Resources Laboratory.

5

Abilities as Aptitudes and Achievements in Learning Situations

Richard E. Snow
Stanford University

This chapter considers cognitive ability constructs as both aptitudes and achievements in learning situations of the sorts found in schools. It first addresses some definitional matters that have posed confusions in the past. It then reviews a proposed framework for identifying and organizing evidence needed for a theory of abilities as aptitudes and achievements; and provides some examples of current evidence on two of the most important issues for such a theory. Finally, it sketches some process mechanisms that might explain the operation of individual differences in abilities in this context, and might help to guide further research in this direction.

TERMS AND CONCEPTS

Ability, Aptitude, and Achievement

Despite clear definition in the literature, people still confuse these terms, so I begin with some distinctions that also outline my own research interests. To be concrete, these distinctions are here couched in terms relating to research on learning and instruction. There are, of course, somewhat different usages in other walks of psychology.

Aptitude, as a construct, refers to relatively stable psychological characteristics of individuals that predispose and thus predict differences in later learning under specified instructional conditions. Abilities are cognitive characteristics that fit this definition; they represent an important class of aptitudes for learning. But there are also other aptitudes; examples include specific knowledge and skills that represent prior achievements that predict future achievements, and also personality and motivational differences, such as anxiety, achievement motivation, independence versus conformity, and a host of other dispositional and style constructs. The inclusion of personality, motivation, and prior achievements in the definition of aptitude is still controversial in some circles, so it is worth noting that Carroll (1974) recommended much the same position over 20 years ago. He also made the important point that constructs and their measures must be distinguished:

> We must carefully distinguish between aptitude as a construct and indicants of aptitude. An "aptitude test" is only one indicant of aptitude. Other indicants of aptitude could include scores on achievement tests, data on prior performance in activities similar to those for which we wish to predict success, and information derived from procedures for assessing personality, interest, attitude, physical prowess, physiological state, etc.
>
> With a definition of aptitude that identifies it with the *present* state of the individual as symptomatic of *future* performance, it is difficult to see why there should be any great difficulty in distinguishing between aptitude and achievement *as concepts* . . . information on past or present achievement might indeed be an indicant of present state (aptitude), and as such, a predictor of future achievement. (p. 287, emphasis in original)

Thus, aptitude is present readiness to benefit, to profit, to perform well, and to succeed in specified future performance situations. The objective of my research program is to understand, considering all relevant personal characteristics, what makes a person ready to profit from a given kind of instruction, why persons differ in this readiness, and how instruction can be designed to fit each person's readiness in order to promote optimal achievement, under specified conditions. Abilities are thus just one important category of aptitude; they need to be studied jointly with other sources of individual differences as aptitudes as well.

Abilities are also an important category of achievement. In my view, educators and psychologists can no longer treat achievement as an undifferentiated mass to be assessed as a total score after instruction and interpreted, for example, simply as "the amount of science or mathematics or history knowledge possessed." Modern cognitive psychology forces on us a much richer conception of achievement than the educational and psychological measurement field has heretofore embraced. Achievement should be defined as multidimensional, composed of psychological constructs representing thinking, reasoning, understanding, and performance in particular domains (as well as attitudes, interests, and motivations about that domain). During learning, knowledge and skills are acquired, organized, changed into functional systems, and tuned for use in thought and further learning. These systems transfer to performance in similar situations to help produce new achievements. The organization, generalization, facile adaptation, and reasoned application of these functional systems in new contexts constitutes cognitive ability development, or to use Cattell's terms, the growth of crystallized intelligence (G_c).

Cattell's G_c is a complex, multivariate, hierarchical structure. There are thus multiple cognitive abilities to be identified and distinguished, not only as aptitudes but also as outcomes of educational development; these are important ability constituents of achievement. Again, however, cognitive outcomes are not the only important constituents of achievement; positive attitudes, motivation for further learning, interest, persistence, and self-regulation in further learning, for example, are also achievements in this broad sense. We are thus led to a broad conception of multivariate aptitude input to a learning situation and multivariate achievement outcome from it, wherein the combined product of aptitude, learning, and achievement across this one period of educational development constitutes aptitude input to the next period. Aptitude and achievement as constructs differ only in time relation to instructional treatment.

In short, cognitive abilities are important constituents of aptitude as inputs to learning. They are also important constituents of achievement as outcomes of learning. In each case they may blend in interesting and important ways with conative and affective dispositions of learners.

But the concept of aptitude still contains one further implication. In its origins, it means readiness for a particular situation and thus mutual person-situation suitability in this condition. The original European definition stressed *apt, appropriate,* and *suitable.* The term *aptitude* came to us from Latin via French. In French, it is associated with *apropos*—the appropriate matching of person and situation. Even in old English there is clearly implied a relational quality between person and situation, or person and person. John Milton (in his treatises on divorce) referred to "that sociable and helpful aptitude between man and woman." Unfortunately, the relational quality was lost in English over the last 200 years. Aptitude became equated with intelligence and interpreted as a quantity inside persons' heads, rather than as a quality of the interrelation or interface between persons and situations (Snow, 1991b).

Interpreting aptitude as an interface between person and situation is a radical idea, not yet much accepted. In the same vein, achievement can be considered the product of the person-situation union. But these ideas fit with other new theorizing about situated cognition, distributed cognition, and the like (for discussion beyond that possible here, see, e.g., Greeno, 1994; Lave & Wenger, 1991; Salomon, 1993; Snow, 1992, 1994a, 1994b). This movement represents an important new frontier for ability theory (at least when ability is studied as aptitude and achievement in learning).

Learning Situations and Instructional Treatments

This view of aptitude and achievement also forces a reanalysis of the characteristics of situations in which learning occurs. Of particular interest are situations expressly designed to promote learning; that is, instructional treatment situations. The term *treatment* is used here because it is a general term typical in descriptions of experimental design conditions in psychology and statistics, but also in descriptions of medical and psychotherapeutic interventions, as well as educational programs. It refers to any set of systematically designed conditions in which persons are expected to learn and perform. Systematically manipulated instructional variations are treatment variables. In educational research and also in research on psychotherapy, there are also usually correlational aspects of the treatment contexts that are confounded with the experimental manipulation and contrast, and of course these are inexorably part of the treatment variable as well.

There have been various attempts to produce taxonomies of learning situations and their distinctive characteristics. These attempts focus at different levels: stimulus conditions influencing response over seconds or minutes; individual task characteristics experienced in a single sitting; situations as configurations of tasks, conditions, and contexts that span a space of hours or days; and instructional programs involving sequences of situations over weeks or months. As yet, no taxonomy fully serves its purpose, although several have interesting and useful features for the purpose of analyzing particular treatments or treatment variables (see Snow, 1994b).

The instructional treatment characteristics usually discussed in public debates about educational reforms and focused on by most research are what we might call "main effect" characteristics—defining features of treatments that are thought to have major beneficial effects on learning for all students. Unfortunately, the list of main effect treatment characteristics on which most researchers, educators, and the public can agree is quite short. Rather, the newspapers and even the journals are typically filled with argument and evidence on the merits of one instructional treatment over all others, written as though the one best way was clear. Examples of treatment contrasts about which people have argued recently are discovery learning versus direct instruction, whole language instruction versus phonics, emphasis on basic skills versus higher-order thinking skills, teacher-centered versus student-centered instruction, homogeneous versus heterogeneous grouping or tracking, and whole group instruction versus cooperative small group learning versus individualization.

Empirical evaluations of such contrasting treatments may or may not show main effects favoring one or the other, but such evaluations almost always show vast individual differences in learning among students within any one treatment. They usually show that a particular treatment is effective only for a subgroup of students, if any. They sometimes even show that each treatment is effective for different subgroups of students. In turn, aptitude differences assessed prior to instruction always predict individual differences in learning in general, usually predict individual differences within any treatment, and sometimes also predict which treatment is best for which individual. However, different combinations of aptitudes often do the predicting in each case.

Beyond the understanding of main effects, then, an important goal for research is to understand the treatment characteristics that operate jointly with learner characteristics in the person-situation interface to produce differential learning effects. Individual differences in learning, and thus in achievement, are presumed to arise because different situations fit different learners more or less well. In other words, there are aptitude by treatment interactions.

Aptitude by Treatment Interactions

Research on aptitude by treatment interactions (or ATI for short) has turned up many, many examples; ATI appear to be ubiquitous in education (Cronbach & Snow, 1977; Snow, 1977). They are also increasingly an interest and concern in research comparing psychotherapeutic treatments (Shoham-Salomon & Hanna, 1991; Snow, 1991a). Unfortunately, ATI are complex phenomena that are difficult to study and understand. Contemporary methodology, and the conventional thinking of investigators and journal editors, has been limiting in various ways (Snow, 1989). But more important, there has not been much theoretical advance to help us think about ATI in ways productive of new research.

Within the confines of this chapter, I cannot review the problems and potentials of ATI methods in treatment evaluations or the value of ATI concepts in finding person-treatment matches in instruction. But it is important to note at least briefly two general principles that derive from ATI research that I think have major implications for ability theory. One concerns identifying the boundary conditions (i.e., the set of situations) within which a particular ability construct serves as an aptitude for learning. Unless an ability construct is truly general, there must be situations in which its relation to learning is low, perhaps even zero. ATI appear when a situation variable spans such a boundary and thus demarcates the limits of that ability construct as aptitude. In other words, the boundary defines a class of treatments within which the ability serves as aptitude for learning. The second principle points to the experimental manipulation of ability-learning, ability-achievement, or ability-ability relations as a demonstration of construct validity for the ability construct. To demonstrate that the relation of an ability measure to other measures can be manipulated experimentally is to show that the ability construct is understood, at least to that extent (see

Snow, 1992; Underwood, 1975). ATI are thus additional criteria for construct validation beyond convergent, discriminant, predictive, and content considerations.

THEORETICAL FRAMEWORK AND EVIDENCE

Given that cognitive ability constructs are useful for understanding aptitude, learning, and achievement interrelationships in particular instructional situations, the next step is to amass the evidence that will advance ability theory and research in this direction, and improve our understanding of the nature of abilities in the process. Elsewhere I have discussed the kinds of evidence and propositions based on them that I think form the constituents of an aptitude theory for cognitive abilities, at least in outline form. The lists shown in Table 5.1 provide this outline. In the left column are the numbered constituents of any aptitude theory (from Snow, 1992). For the present purpose, we can think of them as constituents of an ability theory, wherein ability constructs serve in either the aptitude or the achievement role in educational settings. In the right column are propositions designed to reflect general evidence about cognitive abilities in this regard (from Snow,

TABLE 5.1
Constituents of a Theory of Cognitive Abilities as Aptitudes
and Achievements in Learning Situations, With Related Propositions
from Present Evidence (Adapted From Snow, 1992, 1994a)

Constituents of an Ability Theory	Propositions from Present Evidence
	Cognitive abilities . . .
1. Convergent and discriminant relations	. . . are multifaceted and hierarchically organized, not modular.
2. Prediction	. . . predict learning from instructional treatment and are predictable from treatment variables.
3. Differential prediction	. . . predict differentially for different treatments, not for different groups.
4. Process explanation	. . . are multileveled, personal, relational, selective, constructive, and adaptive.
5. Boundary conditions	. . . are both pervasive and situated.
6. Short-term malleability	. . . have learnable components.
7. Long-term development	. . . differentiate and specialize with experience.
8. Measurement model	
9. Methodological model	
10. Selection decision rules	. . . can be measured, used, and evaluated as aptitudes and achievements according to the conditions of particular educational treatment situations.
11. Classification decision rules	
12. Education decision rules	

1994a). Here I review this outline briefly. I will then return to theory and research examples related to those aspects of most concern in my own research project at present: building a process description of individual differences in abilities, particularly as these function in the person-situation interface; and identifying and validating ability distinctions in complex achievement tests.

Convergent and Discriminant Relations

Point 1 of Table 5.1 concerns the need for convergent and discriminant validation, and more generally, a structural organizational representation of ability interrelationships. There is massive evidence that intelligence is multifaceted and that intellectual abilities and their interrelations are best represented as organized in a hierarchical structure. Cattell's (1971) hierarchical model is well known. Carroll's (1993) review and reanalysis of most of this century's evidence yielded a hierarchy similar to Cattell's and also to Horn's (1989) model. Furthermore, Gustafsson (1984, 1988) demonstrated that fluid intelligence (G_f) can be equated with the general factor (G) and also with Thurstone's (1938) primary induction factor, in a hierarchy approximating Vernon's (1950) model. One can discriminate among special abilities at lower levels in these hierarchical models, but each construct remains subordinate to g. Abilities seem not to be modular in the biological sense proposed by Gardner (1983), although they may be conceived as acquired contextual modules in the sense intended by Bereiter (1990). When measures specifically designed to represent achievement outcomes are included in factor analyses with traditional ability measures, they typically help define G, particularly G_c, and also some more intermediate combination factors such as mathematical or reading ability. Tests of more specific kinds of knowledge have only rarely been included in ability factor studies, but should be investigated more thoroughly in this way.

Prediction

Point 2 of Table 5.1 requires that ability measures be valid predictors of school learning, and again massive evidence shows that they are indeed strongly related to learning measures. There is controversy as to whether or not special abilities offer unique prediction beyond that afforded by G measures in many situations. Certainly it is often the case that many ability-learning correlations can be accounted for by an underlying general ability factor. Yet there are clearly situations, such as spatial-mechanical, auditory, or language learning conditions in which special abilities play a role aside from G. Measures of prior achievement also certainly predict further achievement in a field of study, but again it is often unclear whether domain specific or general knowledge is the primary predictor. In turn, cognitive abilities as achievements should be predictable from instructional treatment variables and other background indicators relevant to learning, as well as from general and special aptitudes.

Differential Prediction

Point 3 of Table 5.1 brings in the differential prediction issue with respect to both different groups and different treatment situations. Differential prediction for treatments is the basic ATI point. By demonstrating that certain treatment variables interact with certain ability differences, one can claim understanding of both the ability and the treatment constructs. Furthermore, considering an ability construct as aptitude means that describing the treatments or learning situations in which it predicts is part of defining the ability as aptitude. As noted before, the ATI evidence demarcates a boundary separating those situations in which the ability relates to learning from those in which it does not. Differential prediction for groups would similarly demarcate portions of the population in which an ability is more versus less relevant to learning. To date, there is much evidence for *ability* by treatment interaction, but not much for ability by group membership interaction. Achievement tests similarly show much evidence for differential validity by treatment, but not by group. However, some ability measures representing either aptitudes or achievements do show average differences for gender and ethnic groups. Differential relationships within and across groups have been less well studied for specialized aptitude and achievement constructs.

Process Explanation

Point 4 of Table 5.1 requires process description of the ability differences at hand. The aim is to reach a theory that explains in process terms why differences in initial ability translate into differences in learning and subsequent achievement, and do so differently in different instructional treatments. The evidence in hand does not go that far. It does, however, offer a much richer description of ability differences than is provided by correlational analyses of test scores standing alone. It is clear that ability differences involve multiple levels; there are component processing skills but there are also metacognitive level strategies concerned with when, where, and how to use component skills. Abilities can also be seen as personal combinations, deriving in part from each individual's unique learning history; they are thus idiosyncratic even while also reflecting the trends of socialization in a particular culture. Following the ATI point, abilities are also relational—they need to be interpreted in person-situation interactional terms. Person-in-situation—the person-situation union—is the appropriate unit for process analysis. Because persons sample situations as they perceive them, they are also selective with respect to the characteristics of situations they choose to use, constructive of the personal meaning of these situations, and adaptive to the demands and opportunities provided by them.

Boundary Conditions

Point 5 of Table 5.1 points to boundary conditions beyond those involved directly in the differential relationships explicit in Point 3. Any ability construct may be situated within conditions of culture, context, era, and locale, and thus be meaningful primarily within these bounds. All of these limits need to be spelled out eventually.

One finds that G is often interpreted as pervasive, even universal, and thus involved in all learning. Yet it is also situated and specialized in the sense that some learning situations demand much more agile adaptation, inferential structuring, and self-evaluation than do others. Some instructional situations require construction of meaning under incomplete and relatively unstructured learning conditions. Resnick and Glaser (1976) even defined G as the ability to learn from incomplete instruction. Thus, when treatments differ in incompleteness in these ways, G enters ATI. Furthermore, over time the functional properties of abilities become adapted to the specialized mixture of demands and opportunities provided by different types of learning situations; abilities become tuned to each such situation and thus specialized and situated for each. Also, in Cattell's (1971) theory, G_f is invested in school learning situations to produce G_c and various kinds of specialized achievements within the G_c network.

Malleability and Development

Points 6 and 7 of Table 5.1 address the malleability and development issues. An ability theory needs to include an account of both long-term development and responsiveness to short-term training. General ability develops with good health, nutrition, and early learning experience. But abilities also differentiate through learning experiences in development, and specialized learning experience leads to specialized patterns of abilities. The result is an expanding array of abilities both specialized and generalized—increasingly tuned to the pattern structures of many particular, familiar situations, yet ready for attunement to the structures of new situations. Situations that share aspects of structure in common afford use of the same abilities. Situations that show no common structure afford use of different abilities. But situations that share only the need to overcome novelty still afford use of those abilities that are attuned to that purpose. One might say that G_f ability reflects this attunement or accommodation to novelty, whereas the network of G_c abilities reflects the assimilation of many now-familiar learning demands and opportunities (Snow, 1981). Intervention studies also show that some components of abilities can be directly trained, and these transfer to other task performances. In Ferguson's (1954, 1956) theory, abilities emerge through the coalescence of skill acquisition among specific tasks due to differential transfer functions among the tasks. The breadth of transfer of skills among tasks determines the breadth of the emergent ability. Verbal, reasoning, and metacognitive skills transfer broadly, whereas certain perceptual, memory, and spatial skills transfer among a narrow range of tasks. These transfer functions account for the hierarchy of ability correlations usually obtained in factor analytic research. Further, more general abilities appear to transfer to earlier stages of new skill learning, whereas more specialized abilities transfer to later stages of new skill learning, as Ackerman's (1989) theory suggests.

Measurement and Methodological Decisions

Points 8 through 12 of Table 5.1 justify choices of measurement and methodological models in an ability theory and decision rules for using the theory in practical selection, classification, and education systems. These practical issues need not be belabored here.

RESEARCH EXAMPLES

Abilities as Aptitudes

As noted previously, there is massive evidence supporting the convergent, discriminant, and predictive relations for abilities as aptitudes—Points 1 and 2 in Table 5.1. There is less evidence and more controversy concerning Points 3 through 7. The first example addresses Points 3 and 5—the issue is ATI.

Among the ATI results that have been reported, one of the strongest findings concerns general ability (G or G_c) in relation to instructional treatments that differ in structure, directness, and completeness. For simplicity, I label this treatment contrast *high-structure* (HS) versus *low-structure* (LS) instruction. Treatments described as direct instruction, mastery-oriented, or teacher-controlled would typically be considered HS, whereas those described as indirect, inductive, discovery-oriented, or learner-controlled would be considered LS. Glaser and Bassok (1989) used essentially the same contrast to summarize a large amount of current research on two major kinds of computerized instructional designs, called "mastery" (HS) and "guided discovery" (LS) for short.

The frequent finding is that HS helps low G learners; they benefit from the external control of learning activities, pacing, and feedback; the small step sequence; and the explicit content and procedure. LS provides insufficient guidance for low G learners. However, HS is irrelevant, even interfering and boring, for high G learners who benefit more from the independent, self-regulated, and self-constructed learning conditions afforded by LS. The resulting ATI pattern has been seen at various grade school and college levels, in a variety of subject matters, and with different measures of G and achievement outcome, so it is apparently robust and relatively unbounded in these respects.

But the pattern does not always occur and often it is moderated by other factors (see Snow, 1989, 1994a). Some studies have included measures of personality constructs to show that G by personality by treatment interactions occur. For example, test anxiety has been shown to interact with G and HS versus LS. Personality measures contrasting achievement via conformance versus achievement via independence, and also a measure of mindfulness or effort investment in mental processing, have shown the same ATI patterns as G with the HS versus LS contrast. One might conclude that LS is good for high G, nonanxious, more mindful, and more independent learners, whereas HS is good for low G, anxious, less mindful, and more conforming learners. But no studies have systematically studied all these aptitude variables jointly (e.g., as profiles), nor has any research satisfactorily distinguished G_f and G_c in this contrast. Some specific prior achievements have seemed to operate somewhat differently than G, and socioeconomic status differences may also sometimes moderate. Clearly, one needs to pursue hypotheses about aptitude complexes (Snow, 1987) in further research along these lines. Abilities do not operate in isolation in these ATI patterns, and so far there has not been great progress in process analysis of the complex.

Abilities as Achievements

Points 6 and 7 of Table 5.1 also deserve much more attention. There is scattered but increasing evidence from attempts to train ability components directly. There is also evidence on long-term developmental curves from both longitudinal and cross-sectional studies, although this work only rarely reflects the influence of instructional treatment variables.

But another tack is to look for ability distinctions embedded in achievement assessments that can in turn be related to treatment variables as well as to other preceding or background variables. Unfortunately, most achievement measures are built without considering distinguishable ability components within them. Also, most instructional research relies on narrow achievement measures specifically related to immediate instruction, and uses samples too small for correlational analysis. However, some educational surveys have used broad achievement measures in large, longitudinal samples. These might be used to investigate the development of abilities as achievements as well as their differential prediction.

A case in point is the *National Educational Longitudinal Study* of 1988 (NELS:88), which followed a national sample of eighth graders through tenth and twelfth grades with achievement tests in four subject matters and student, teacher, parent, and school questionnaires. My colleagues and I have studied the math and science achievement tests. We applied a new method of item factor analysis (Bock, Gibbons, & Muraki, 1988) to each grade test separately to obtain distinguishable ability components, and then built regression models to shows different patterns of background predictors for each component. (For details, see Hamilton, Kupermintz, & Snow, submitted; Hamilton, Nussbaum, Kupermintz, Kerkhoven, & Snow, 1995; Kupermintz, Ennis, Hamilton, Talbert, & Snow, 1995; Kupermintz & Snow, submitted; Nussbaum, Hamilton, & Snow, submitted).

In brief, the results were as follows. At each grade level, math reasoning (MR) ability could be distinguished from math knowledge (MK). When separate factor scores for these dimensions were predicted from background variables, with prior achievement controlled statistically, markedly different patterns were obtained. In contrast to results typically reported when overall achievement scores are studied, average differences favoring males occurred only on MR; females actually showed a small advantage on MK. The average advantage for Asian American students occurred only on MK, whereas the average disadvantage for African American students appeared much more on MR than on MK. Furthermore, earlier positive attitude toward math related to MK, not MR. Course taking (e.g., advanced algebra, geometry) and most instructional variables related more to MK than to MR. However, teacher emphasis on high-order thinking and understanding and possession of a computer for educational work at home related substantially to MR. It was also clear that many effects would be misrepresented by analysis of total math achievement scores without the component subscores.

In science, four ability factors were identified in eighth grade. These seemed to collapse into two at tenth grade, where a new third factor emerged from items added at that level. These same three factors were obtained also at twelfth grade. The eighth-grade factors were called everyday or elementary science (ES), chemistry knowledge (CK), scientific reasoning (SR), and reasoning with knowledge (RK). At tenth and twelfth grades, the CK and SR factors collapsed into a new factor termed quantitative science (QS), involving items that either required quantitative operations or related to areas of science (specifically, chemistry) that are heavily quantitative in nature. The second factor was termed basic knowledge and reasoning (BKR), involving items assessing knowledge of scientific concepts and the ability to apply these concepts to simple reasoning situations; it appeared to combine ES and RK from the eighth-grade analysis. The third, new factor was called spatial-mechanical reasoning (SM), defined by items that required interpreting diagrams or reasoning about pictured physical devices. Thus, the abilities involved in science achievement may become consolidated as students move from middle school through high school, as science courses and course-taking patterns change.

Regression analyses showed that MK in eighth grade predicted only QS later, whereas eighth-grade MR predicted all later science abilities. Regression analyses were also conducted to relate student and instructional variables to the science factors, and again it was clear that using the total score alone would have hidden many important differential relationships. Different patterns of prior achievement factors predicted later science achievement factors. Average differences favoring males over females appeared heavily on spatial-mechanical reasoning (SM), slightly on quantitative science, but not at all on basic knowledge and reasoning (BKR). On average, Asian American students were disadvantaged on SM by twelfth grade, but showed no other important contrasts with other ethnic groups. African Americans showed average disadvantage mostly on SM and BKR. Course-taking patterns showed strong and distinct effects; in tenth grade, chemistry related to QS, biology to BKR, and earth science to SM. Also here, teacher emphasis on problem solving and understanding related to BKR and trips to science museums related to SM. At twelfth grade, some of these relations changed, some remained, and some new relations appeared; for example, having a computer at home related to QS, as did positive confidence about one's ability in math.

In brief, the analysis clearly showed that the NELS:88 math and science tests are multidimensional; that a simple, stable, and reliable factor structure emerges in tenth and twelfth grades; and that these ability factors are differentially related to other important student, course-taking, and instructional variables. Given the stability of the factor structure, future achievement tests could be explicitly designed to distinguish these dimensions and thus to study ability development through instruction more directly. Achievement tests have always been built using content by process specification tables. Unfortunately, the usual process distinctions have been taken for granted and never validated. The results for the NELS:88 tests suggest that they can be defined and validated as ability distinctions.

TOWARD A PROCESS THEORY

Research on abilities in ATI and in achievement assessment is continuing as exemplified previously, but the biggest stumbling block remains Point 4 in Table 5.1—the problem of process explanation. What kind of theory of ability-learning-achievement processes can be fashioned that will incorporate all that has been discussed here? Can it be made to describe intra-individual as well as interindividual differences in the dynamics of person-situation interactions, particularly in instructional learning performances?

My attempt is, in part, a generalization of Thomson's (1919, 1939) response sampling model (as updated and advocated also by Humphreys, 1979, 1981). Then I add the concepts of affordances (Gibson, 1979), artifacts (Simon, 1969), and performance assemblies (Simon, 1976). For other related origins and constituents, see Snow (1991b, 1992, 1994a, 1994b).

In my construction, the basic event at the interface of person and situation is a sampling, of person by situation and situation by person. This sampling is governed by associative networks of stimulus and response components residing in the inner environment of the person and the outer environment of the situation. In effect, these associative networks provide a bank of components from which different sorts of mental structures, procedures, and representations can be assembled as needed in a particular person-situation interaction. Each individual's inner environment contains a vast assortment of potential response components, probabilistically interconnected in multiple networks. Individuals differ in what components are present or absent, and also in the strengths of the connections between them. One can think of components as productions interconnected in a production system or as nodes in a connectionist network; either model works at this stage of theoretical development. Also, although these components are described here as bits and pieces of ability, the term applies as well to aspects of conative and affective aptitudes.

Many sorts of assemblies of these components can be constructed in different ways by different persons in different situations. These assemblies are also decomposable, so parts can be transferred to other assemblies as needed. The products of past learning are component assemblies stored as units to be triggered anew by situations similar to those previously faced. The products of continuing learning are additional components, new assemblies of both new and old components, and strengthened connections between them. Continuing learning also exercises and strengthens the assembly and control functions themselves. The system is loosely coupled and flexible in assembling and reassembling components into performance programs (i.e., actions) to meet varying situational needs. The details of each person's learning history also makes each such system highly idiosyncratic.

Each performance situation samples from each person in the sense that the demands and opportunities it presents will draw forth whatever response component assemblies each person can muster. But the person also samples from the situation, in the sense that stimulus components are perceived, selected, and used. Particular stimulus components may suggest a demand for particular response components or assemblies, and may also provide opportunities to use particular response components or assemblies.

The situation may also provide components for assembly into the perform-ance as prosthetic devices, so that the person need not produce them. The two-way sampling process will be conditioned by the demands and opportu-nities afforded by the situation, and by the possibilities and constraints af-forded by the assembly and control history of the performing person. These situational components are there to be perceived and used by persons whose history tunes them to do so.

Considering the person's learning history suggests some further distinc-tions between several kinds of situational demands and opportunities. Some situations require or allow the retrieval and reuse of old component assem-blies, a process reflected in crystallized (G_c) ability differences. On the other hand, some situations require or allow the construction and use of novel component assemblies, a process more central to fluid (G_f) ability differ-ences. Complex tasks typically involve some of both kinds of process, and will further require the flexible reassembly of components as learning pro-ceeds. To simplify the language and bring out some other implications, it helps to see these person-situation connections as "affordances," as in Gib-son's (1966, 1979) theory of perception, and also "artifacts," as in Simon's (1969) design science.

The theory of affordances concerns the mutuality of person and situation in the control of perception-action sequences. To paraphrase Gibson (1979), the affordances of a situation are what it offers the person, what it provides or furnishes, for good or ill. There is a complementarity of person and situ-ation, as in an ecological niche. A niche is a place or setting that is appropri-ate for a person, that offers a combination of situational components into which the person "fits." However, a situation is an assembly of affordances only with respect to some persons. Affordances reflect the invitation, de-mand, or opportunity structures of a situation for those persons who are tuned or prepared to perceive them. Gibson's concept of affordances is thus close to the old meanings and roots of the concept of aptitude (see Snow, 1991b, 1992), which brings in the individual differences aspect directly. A situation provides a suitable niche only for those persons who are prepared to meet and use its affordances effectively. Those not properly tuned or pre-pared will in some way fail to perform effectively in the situation as given. Only rarely will a situation be completely suitable for all persons. Instruc-tional treatment situations, in particular, cannot usually be designed to fit optimally all of the diversity of persons entering them.

Thus, research on individual differences in abilities as aptitudes requires a detailed analysis of the affordance-effectivity matches of different learners and different instructional treatments. This analysis emphasizes the oppor-tunities offered by a particular treatment to be detected and capitalized on by a particular person to reach some achievement. The analysis also remains at a level that identifies the unique person-situation synergy in local ecological terms, rather than reducing to physical or biological description or abstracting to generalized principles. Because ecological information is personal, it is unique to particular person-situation units. There is therefore no detached or abstracted list of qualities of instructional treatments that will be equally important for all persons, or of persons that will be equally important for all treatments. Aptitude is thus the unique coalition of affordances and effectivities in particular person-treatment systems.

If abilities are also considered as achievements (i.e., the result of this unique coalition), then research in this direction requires a reconstruction of achievement assessment. The reconstruction would focus on producing ability distinctions of import in the domain of achievement under consideration. It would especially link analysis of the affordance-effectivity matches in the person-situation interaction to instructional treatment design. Affordances need to be built into instruction to promote ability developments as outcomes. Again, there may be unique designs for each person.

This analysis of abilities as affordances emphasizes the important ways in which person and situation are tuned to one another—to be in harmony for successful performance. But an equally important question for ability theory is the analysis of the disharmonies in the person-situation interface that result in failure. Some aspects of these disharmonies can be described as failures of tuning the person to perceive affordances. But other aspects seem better described in Simon's (1969) language of artifacts and interface design. Artifacts are interfaces between inner and outer environments. If these two environments are appropriate to one another—if they are adapted or designed to fit one another optimally—then the artifact serves its purpose unnoticed. However, interface design is often only approximate. Then the limiting properties of the inner environment appear in the failure to match the demands of the taxing outer environment.

For a particular person in a particular instructional treatment, the empirical evidence of aptitude arises from the inabilities of the behavioral system to adapt perfectly to its treatment. Aptitude differences between persons in particular treatments "show through" at the interface as inabilities. For a person who is perfectly suited to a treatment or a treatment that is perfectly suited to a person, the achievement goal is reached successfully; the presence of aptitude is inferred from this fact, but it is attributable to *both* person and environment. For a person who is not perfectly adapted to a treatment or a treatment that is not perfectly adapted to a person, the goal is not successfully reached; this fact shows that inaptitude of some kind is present. But again, inaptitude is attributable to the interface; either the inner or the outer environment, or both, need redesign to bring them into adaptive harmony. Research aimed at system redesign thus needs to find the key inabilities in the interface that constitute the mismatch. The redesign then proceeds by reshaping the treatment, adding opportunities or eliminating demands and thereby circumventing limitations, or by removing limitations directly by retraining the person.

Following Simon's ideas, future research on abilities in learning requires a detailed analysis of the treatment design features that seem mismatched to the person. The analysis is geared to detect inabilities so as to remove or circumvent them in treatment redesign. Following Gibson's ideas, future research on abilities requires a detailed analysis of the affordance-effectivity matches in different person-treatment unions. The analysis is geared to detect abilities so as to capitalize on them in treatment redesign. The two views are complementary, because the most successful instructional treatments will be those that capitalize both on strengths and compensate for weaknesses for each individual treated.

Thus, ability is situated. It is reflected in the tuning of particular persons to the particular demands and opportunities of a situation. It thus resides in the union of person in the situation, not "in the mind" alone. It is a two-way sampling of performance components and their assembly between person and situation and is also distributed between person and situation; the situation contains some pieces of what the person needs or can use to accomplish a given task. But individuals need to be tuned to perceive and use those pieces, and also need to supply some pieces from their own learning history. Some individuals are prepared to perceive these affordances—to use the pieces provided by the situation—but some are not. Among those who are so tuned, each may supply slightly different pieces, although each piece thus supplied may be equally effective. The result is that some persons succeed in learning in a given situation; they are in harmony with it. Others do not, because they are not tuned to use what the situation affords or to produce what it demands.

ATI result when the affordance profiles of person-situation interfaces differ. An LS treatment samples just the kinds of assemblies that persons described as able, independent, mindful, flexible, and the like are tuned to produce. HS instruction does not provide that opportunity for such persons. It does, however, provide some of the assemblies and controls that less able, less independent, less mindful learners cannot provide for themselves, and it does not sample what such learners cannot produce.

Considering abilities as achievement outcomes, however, not just as aptitude inputs, adds further analysis to these instructional treatments. LS is good for able learners partly because it affords exercise and extension of relevant abilities; it helps build these abilities as achievement outcomes, and thus as aptitudes for the future, even as it simultaneously uses these abilities as aptitudes for the present. The same cannot often be said about HS treatments. Designs that only circumvent inabilities to focus on short-term achievement do not build abilities as aptitudes for future learning. Thus, HS treatments need to be designed to develop abilities as long-range goals even as they compensate for inabilities in the short run. That is perhaps the most difficult instructional design problem faced today.

CONCLUSION

Abilities can be understood as stable dimensions—as factors arranged in a hierarchical model. But they also need to be understood as aptitudes for learning from particular instructional treatment situations and as components of achievement outcome from instruction as well as development. Continuing research toward these goals is producing new kinds of ability theory in which organized systems of cognitive processing components are analyzed as they operate in the dynamic person-situation interaction, and as they combine therein with other person characteristics related to learning.

REFERENCES

Ackerman, P. (1989). Individual differences and skill acquisition. In P. L. Ackerman, R. J. Sternberg, & R. Glaser (Eds.), *Learning and individual differences* (pp. 164–217). New York: Freeman.

Bereiter, C. (1990). Aspects of an educational learning theory. *Review of Educational Research, 60,* 603–624.

Bock, E., Gibbons, R., & Muraki, E. (1988). Full information item factor analysis. *Applied Psychological Measurement, 12,* 261–280.

Carroll, J. B. (1974). Fitting a model of school learning to aptitude and achievement data over grade levels. In D. R. Green (Ed.), *The aptitude-achievement distinction* (pp. 53–78). Monterey, CA: CTB/McGraw-Hill.

Carroll, J. B. (1993). *Human cognitive abilities.* New York: Cambridge University Press.

Cattell, R. B. (1971). *Abilities: Their structure, growth, and action.* Boston: Houghton Mifflin.

Cronbach, L. J., & Snow, R. E. (1977). *Aptitudes and instructional methods: A handbook for research on interactions.* New York: Irvington.

Ferguson, G. A. (1954). On learning and human ability. *Canadian Journal of Psychology, 8,* 95–112.

Ferguson, G. A. (1956). On transfer and the abilities of man. *Canadian Journal of Psychology, 10,* 121–131.

Gardner, H. (1983). *Frames of mind: The theory of multiple intelligences.* New York: Basic Books.

Gibson, J. J. (1966). *The senses considered as perceptual systems.* Boston: Houghton Mifflin.

Gibson, J. J. (1979). *The ecological approach to visual perception.* Boston: Houghton Mifflin.

Glaser R., & Bassock, M. (1989). *Learning theory and the study of instruction.* (Tech. Rep. No. 11). Pittsburgh, PA: Learning Research and Development Center.

Greeno, J. G. (1994). *The situativity of learning: Prospects for syntheses in theory, practice, and research.* Unpublished report, School of Education, Stanford University.

Gustafsson, J. E. (1984). A unifying model for the structure of intellectual abilities. *Intelligence, 8,* 179–203.

Gustafsson, J. E. (1988). Hierarchical models of the structure of cognitive abilities. In R. J.

Sternberg (Ed.), *Advances in the psychology of human intelligence* (vol. 4, pp. 35–71). Hillsdale, NJ: Lawrence Erlbaum Associates.

Hamilton, L. S., Kupermintz, H., & Snow, R. E. (submitted). Enhancing the validity and usefulness of large-scale educational assessments: V, NELS:88 mathematics and science achievement and affective interrelationships.

Hamilton, L. S., Nussbaum, E. M., Kupermintz, H., Kerkhoven, J. I. M., & Snow, R. E. (1995). Enhancing the validity and usefulness of large-scale educational assessments: II. NELS:88 science achievement. *American Educational Research Journal, 32,* 555–581.

Horn, J. L. (1989). Cognitive diversity: A framework of learning. In P. L. Ackerman, R. J. Sternberg, & R. Glaser (Eds.), *Learning and individual differences* (pp. 61–116). New York: Freeman.

Humphreys, L. G. (1979). The construct of general intelligence. *Intelligence, 3,* 105–120.

Humphreys, L. G. (1981). The primary mental ability. In M. P. Friedman, J. P. Das, & N. O'Connor (Eds.), *Intelligence and learning* (pp. 87–102). New York: Plenum.

Kupermintz, H., Ennis, M. M., Hamilton, L. S., Talbert, J. E., & Snow, R. E. (1995). Enhancing the validity and usefulness of large-scale educational assessments: I. NELS:88 mathematics achievement. *American Educational Research Journal, 32,* 525–554.

Kupermintz, H., & Snow, R. E. (submitted). Enhancing the validity and usefulness of large-scale educational assessments: III. NELS:88 mathematics achievements to twelfth grade. Paper submitted for publication.

Lave, J., & Wenger, E. (1991). *Situated learning.* New York: Cambridge University Press.

Nussbaum, E. M., Hamilton, L. S., & Snow, R. E. (submitted). Enhancing the validity and usefulness of large-scale educational assessments. IV. NELS88 science achievement to twelfth grade. Paper submitted for publication.

Resnick, L. B., & Glaser, R. (1976). Problem solving and intelligence. In L. B. Resnick (Ed.), *The nature of intelligence* (pp. 205–230). Hillsdale, NJ: Lawrence Erlbaum Associates.

Salomon, G. (Ed.). (1993). *Distributed cognition.* Hillsdale, NJ: Lawrence Erlbaum Associates.

Shoham-Salomon, V., & Hannah, M. T. (1991). Client-treatment interactions in the study of differential change process. *Journal of Consulting and Clinical Psychology, 59,* 217–225.

Simon, H. A. (1969). *The sciences of the artificial.* Cambridge, MA: MIT Press.

Simon, H. A. (1976). Identifying basic abilities underlying intelligent performance of complex tasks. In L. B. Resnick (Ed.), *The nature of human intelligence* (pp. 65–98). Hillsdale, NJ: Lawrence Erlbaum Associates.

Snow, R. E. (1977). Research on aptitudes: A progress report. In L. S. Shulman (Ed.), *Review of research in education* (vol. 4, pp. 50–105). Itasca, IL: Peacock.

Snow, R. E. (1981). Toward a theory of aptitude for learning: Fluid and crystallized abilities and their correlates. In M. P. Friedman, J. P. Das, & N. O'Connor (Eds.), *Intelligence and learning* (pp. 345–362). New York: Plenum.

Snow, R. E. (1987). Aptitude complexes. In R. E. Snow & M. J. Farr (Eds.), *Aptitude, learning, and instruction, Vol. 3: Conative and affective process analyses* (pp. 13–59). Hillsdale, NJ: Lawrence Erlbaum Associates.

Snow, R. E. (1989). Aptitude-treatment interaction as a framework of research in individual differences in learning. In P. L. Ackerman, R. J. Sternberg, & R. Glaser (Eds.), *Learning and individual differences* (pp. 11–34). New York: Freeman.

Snow, R. E. (1991a). Aptitude-treatment interaction as a framework for research on individual differences in psychotherapy. *Journal of Consulting and Clinical Psychology, 59,* 205–216.

Snow, R. E. (1991b). The concept of aptitude. In R. E. Snow & D. F. Wiley (Eds.), *Improving inquiry in social science* (pp. 249–284). Hillsdale, NJ: Lawrence Erlbaum Associates.

Snow, R. E. (1992). Aptitude theory: Yesterday, today, and tomorrow. *Educational Psychologist, 27,* 5–32.

Snow, R. E. (1994a). A person-situation interaction theory of intelligence in outline. In A. Demetriou & A. Efklides (Eds.), *Intelligence, mind and reasoning: Structure and development.* Amsterdam: Elsevier.

Snow, R. E. (1994b). Abilities in academic tasks. In R. J. Sternberg & R. K. Wagner (Eds.), *Mind in context: Interactionist perspectives on human intelligence.* New York: Cambridge University Press.

Thomson, G. H. (1919). On the cause of hierarchical order among correlation coefficients. *Proceedings of the Royal Society.* A, 95.

Thomson, G. H. (1939). *The factorial analysis of human ability.* London: University of London Press.

Thurstone, L. L. (1938). Primary mental abilities. *Psychometric Monographs, 1.*

Underwood, B. J. (1975). Individual differences as a crucible in theory construction. *American Psychologist, 30,* 128–140.

Vernon, P. E. (1950). *The structure of human abilities.* London: Methuen.

6

How Do Families Affect Intelligence? Social Environmental and Behavior Genetic Predictions

Sandra Scarr
University of Virginia

A theory is a good theory if it satisfies two requirements:
It must accurately describe a large class of observations
on the basis of a model that contains only a few arbitrary
elements, and it must make definite predictions
about the results of future observations.
—Hawking, 1988, p. 10

Competing theories about family determinants of intellectual differences offer a challenging opportunity to test theoretically required predictions with available observations. Predictions about crucial research results are generated by social environmental theories and by behavior genetic theory, and those predictions are quite different. The critical observations to test the adequacy of predictions from these competing theories have been made. Data collections (particularly with behavior genetic designs) have accelerated in recent years, so that more than a critical mass of observations is available. Yet, there has been little direct theoretical confrontation. That the theories have not been tested with existing data in a systematic fashion is either a sign of mutual ignorance or an aversion to being challenged. Now is an opportune time to bring together the observations that bear on competing theories, and to test them.

Forcing Competition

> Each time new experiments are observed to agree with the predictions the theory survives, and our confidence is increased; but if ever a new observation is found to disagree, we have to abandon or modify the theory. At least that is what is supposed to happen, but you can always question the competence of the person who carried out the observation. (Hawking, 1988, p. 11)

Battles between theories are seldom won on the mere merits of the evidence. Something like an intellectual revolution is required of the adherents of inadequate theories. Rather than admit defeat, advocates of losing theories more often "question the competence" of the study or the investigator who challenges the prevailing orthodoxy. When pressed, adherents of an empirically contradicted theory may modify the theory to accommodate new results, if it is possible to do so, or they may bury their heads, ignore the conflict, and communicate exclusively among themselves. In psychotherapeutic practice, there are isolated pockets of neo-Freudians, Jungians, Rational-Emotivists, Rankians, adherents to primal screams, and so forth. They speak their own languages and talk with other true believers. In global science, an island mentality is not an acceptable way to avoid theoretical revisions. The requirements of theoretical revision are that the theory must remain internally consistent, and "it must accurately describe a large class of observations on the basis of a *model that contains only a few arbitrary elements*" (Hawking, 1988, p. 11, emphasis added), and it should predict new classes of observations.

This review presents social environmental and behavior genetic theories of intellectual development and academic achievement, and evaluates the adequacy of the theories' predictions to account for existing observations.

Observations are scientifically credible (reliable, valid) measurements of phenomena that are the subject matter of a theory. Under the term *observation* I include all kinds of measurements, such as tests, ratings, self-reports, and behavioral observations. Both socialization and behavior genetic theory focus on processes that transmit behaviors from one generation to the next, so that observations of family influences are crucial to both theories. What is observed are co-occurrences or correlations between one event and another.[1] Observations are shaped into "facts" by theories, by making "sense" of the observation in terms of the theory (Scarr, 1985). Many observations can be made into different facts by different theories.

---

[1]Experimental studies of the core processes posited by both theories are not possible in human populations. Laboratory simulations can be experimentally arranged, but the phenomena studied are trivial reflections of the powerful processes posited by the theories to occur in everyday life. Parents have pervasive, longitudinal effects on child development that cannot easily be manipulated in short-term, artificial experiments on social learning, nor can artificial selection experiments be used to test genetic hypotheses.

SOCIAL ENVIRONMENTAL THEORIES
COME IN TWO BROAD CLASSES:
OPPORTUNITY AND SOCIALIZATION

Opportunities. Opportunities are available and accessible aspects of the environment that afford chances for experiences to be coded and for learning to occur. I (Scarr, 1992, 1993; Scarr & McCartney, 1983) have argued that social environments should be seen as sets of opportunities from which people make their own experiences, by which I mean that individuals create experiences from available environments in their own developmentally and individually different ways. What environments provide, therefore, are opportunities for experience. In opportunity theory, it is proposed that different locations in the social structure afford different kinds of opportunities for experience and learning that are related to people's intellectual and academic achievements. Social class—defined by parents' educational, occupational, and income characteristics—is often thought to afford different amounts of opportunity to children born into families at different locations in the social structure, but social classes are sometimes thought to have cultural components, as in the "culture of poverty" or in class-differentiated childrearing attitudes and practices (e.g., Kohn, 1969). Thus, social classes may be conceived of as more than opportunity differences and may involve socialization components as well (these are dealt with in the discussion of socialization theory). At root, any version of opportunity theory focuses on between-family differences, because social class and parental characteristics are shared by siblings in the same home but differ among families. Thus, opportunity theory appeals primarily to social environmental causes that differ among groups at different locations in the social structure.

Socialization. For the past 50 years, thousands of articles and books have been written in the field of psychology about the effects of parents as socializing agents on their children (see, e.g., Bandura, 1977; Baumrind, 1993). Parents are, of course, not the only socializing influence on children, because other adults in the family, siblings, peers, and schools all transmit cultural knowledge to developing persons. Socialization can be thought of as a lifelong learning experience, because people continue to be socialized into new niches throughout life. But parents of young children have special status as socializing agents (Maccoby, 1992), because of their status and competence superiorities to their children, and because early experiences are believed to be especially powerful in determining later behaviors. In the context of socialization theory, socialization researchers stress the many ways that parental behaviors directly affect their children's development, through modeling, social reinforcement, and interactions that either promote or discourage learning. Socialization theory is at root a description of parental behaviors and their association with child outcomes. In this review, the term *parental influences* includes the many characteristics of schools, neighborhoods, and communities to which parents expose children, as part of the correlated family environment.

Socialization theory appeals primarily to differences *between families* — differences in the environments that parents provide, including the parents themselves. Differences between families are hypothesized to make siblings alike in intelligence and academic achievement (because they are reared by the same parents in the same household) and different from children reared in other families. The concept of social class is sometimes invoked to characterize average differences in childrearing attitudes and practices by parents with different educational, occupational, and income characteristics. Social disadvantage, a frequently evoked concept, is clearly a difference between low-income and/or minority families and more affluent and/or majority-group families.

Parental rearing styles would seem to be primarily between-family differences, because siblings share the same parents. Socialization research has rarely included siblings, so that characterizations of parental rearing styles have been based on parent reports and behaviors with one child per family and, thus, are de facto between-family differences. It is not clear whether parents' basic style is expected to vary much from one child to another. The theory is moot on this issue. Increasingly, socialization researchers have written about within-family environmental differences (e.g., Hoffman, 1991), but their studies have not included siblings or twins until very recent collaborations with behavior geneticists (e.g., Plomin, Reiss, Hetherington, & Howe, 1994).

Behavior genetic theory, derived from evolutionary theory, is focused on causes of individual variation in intelligence and other characteristics in populations (see Plomin, DeFries, & McClearn, 1990). Behavior genetics is not the study of species invariants or of gene action pathways that affect behaviors; rather, behavior genetics studies sources of variation in populations. It makes predictions about parental influences on children from both genetic and environmental (both biological and social) transmission (see Rowe, 1994). Environmental transmission includes both social environmental differences between families in opportunities and parental styles, and other, often unknown, environmental differences between siblings in the same family. Behavior genetic studies aim to sort out what influences have what effects in what populations.

In truth, generalizations from both socialization and behavior genetic research are limited to the populations, measures, and methods sampled in studies. This limitation applies to all behavioral research, although it is often ignored in socialization studies. By incorporating both genetic and environmental sources of variation, between and within families, behavior genetic theory can in principle subsume both opportunity and socialization theories in a more comprehensive framework. To do so, it must generate predictions that fit and explain observations generated not only within its own research tradition, but observations generated by investigations inspired by social environmental theories.

Most observations about determinants of intellectual differences can be fit to both social environmental and behavior genetic theories and, thus, do not provide a critical test between them. Studies in the tradition of social environmental theories typically sample one child per family and include only biologically related families, thus confounding genetics with social transmission of behavioral traits from parents to children (Scarr, 1992, 1993). Studies of biological families *only*, even if they include siblings, are not theoretically informative, because the observations of modest similarities among family members and correlations of family "environments" with children's intellectual differences can be fit as well, or better, to other theories. Other observations, mostly from behavior genetic studies, do provide tests of different predictions that must be made by the two theories.

Competing Models

To make entirely explicit the tests of socialization and behavior genetic theories that are to be made, Fig. 6.1 shows models derived from the two theories. Models are shown for biologically related families, adoptive families, and identical (MZ) twins reared by different families. Three kinds of relationships are shown in the models: a solid line with one arrow for a causal path; a solid line with two arrows for a correlation that exists "in nature," apart from other elements in the model; and a dashed line with two arrows to indicate correlations created by the causal relations of other elements in the model.

First, in the socialization and behavior genetic models for biological families, the paths have different causal status. In the opportunity and socialization models, parental social class or rearing style and parental intelligence are correlated (in nature). Hundreds of studies document positive correlations between children's social class background and IQ scores, and social class background and academic achievements, which many social environmentalists have interpreted as opportunity effects. There is no question that parents' IQ scores are correlated with their own social class status, largely through the correlations of IQ with educational levels. Although socialization researchers seldom mention that authoritative parents are more intelligent than are authoritarian ones, there are two reasons this must be so. First, authoritarianism is substantially, negatively correlated with IQ (−.5 in most studies). Second, to explain the observed correlation between parent and

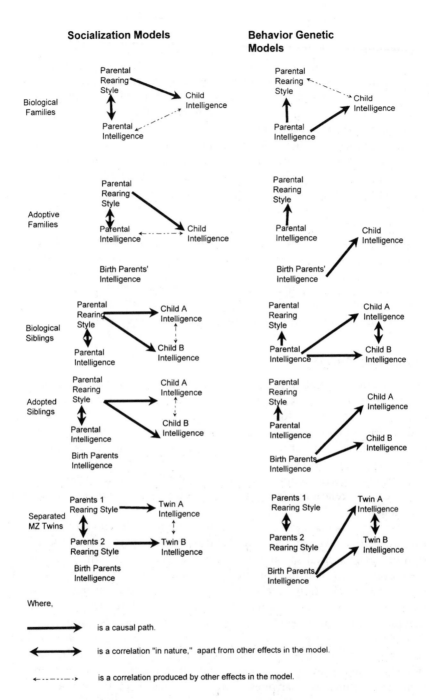

FIG. 6.1. Socialization and behavior genetic models of effects of parental intelligence and rearing style differences on children's intelligence.

child intelligence in hundreds of studies, the only potential path is through parental rearing styles. Thus, socialization researchers must predict that the parent-child IQ correlation is produced by the correlation between parental intelligence and rearing styles. In the socialization model, parental rearing styles have the causal effect on child intelligence.

Although behavior genetic theory posits both environmental and genetic transmission of intelligence from parents to children, the following models stress genetic transmission to maximize their contrast with those derived from social environmental theory. Quantitative estimates of both environmental and genetic sources of intellectual and achievement differences are used. In Fig. 6.1, the behavior genetic model for biological families shows causal paths from parental to child intelligence and from parental intelligence to parental rearing styles. In this model, parental rearing styles are correlated with child intelligence as a product of the two causal paths, and are thus indicated by a dashed line with two arrows. In behavior genetic theory, parents of different levels of intelligence are predicted to use different rearing styles and predicted to have children of different intelligence levels, on average, such that rearing styles are *associated with*, but do not cause, differences in children's intelligence.

Note that observations of the relationships among parental rearing styles, parental intelligence, and children's intelligence *in biological families* cannot distinguish between social environmental and behavior genetic models. Although the models are causally different, they specify the same observed correlations. Data that fit one model will fit all three. As asserted earlier, biological families are not informative for these competing theories.

Thus, let us turn to competing models for adoptive families. Here we can choose between the social environmental and behavior genetic models, based on what is observed. Social environmental researchers must predict the same observed correlations in adoptive as in biological families, because theirs is an environmental transmission theory, whose effects are not dependent on genetic relatedness. Opportunity theorists must predict that children reared in different locations in the social structure have different amounts or kinds of learning opportunities. Socialization theory is at root a social learning theory, whereby parents' rearing styles are posited to affect their children's learning directly through processes described by Baumrind (1993). Birth parents' intelligence should have no effect on adopted children's intelligence when there is no social contact.

By contrast, the predicted observations about genetic transmission of parent-child effects from behavior genetic theory are entirely different for adoptive and biological families. Neither adoptive parental intelligence nor rearing styles are predicted to affect adopted children's intelligence, but birth parents' intelligence must be predicted to affect the rank order of adopted children's IQ scores. Environmental variance in the behavior genetic model is not predicted to arise from systematic differences in parental rearing styles.

Similarly, biological sibling studies alone are not informative for theory testing, because the two theories predict the same observed correlations, albeit for different theoretical reasons. Adopted sibling studies are informative, because the theories predict different observations. Again, the social environmental theory model for biological and adopted siblings must be the same, and adopted children's birth parents' intelligence must be irrelevant in predicting the adopted child's intelligence. Behavior genetic theory must predict a genetic effect for birth parents' intelligence on their offspring, even though the child was adopted away. The model does not predict substantial effects for rearing parents' intelligence because the adoptive parents are not genetically related to the child, nor for adoptive parents' rearing style, which is only a manifestation of other parental characteristics.

An additional test of the competing models is shown for identical (MZ) twins reared in different adoptive homes. Here, for simplicity, adoptive parental intelligence has been left out of the model, because neither theory would predict any causal effect on child intelligence. Social environmental theories predict that the social class or rearing style of each set of parents has an effect on the child they rear, and there is no effect for birth parents' intelligence. To the extent that the rearing families are similar in social class or rearing style, the twins will resemble each other in intelligence; if their rearing styles are not correlated, the twins will not have similar intelligence. Predictions from behavior genetic theory are quite different: Birth parents' intelligence is predicted to have an effect on the twins' intelligence, and the twins genetic correlation is predicted to make their IQs similar, despite being reared in different homes. Parental rearing styles are predicted to have no causal effect on the twins' intelligence.

In science, theories must subsume observations and remain internally consistent; that is, assumptions and predictions cannot contradict each other. A theory cannot predict all possible outcomes or it is not testable, nor can it adopt inconsistent, post hoc hypotheses to accommodate unexpected observations that contradict its predictions. Socialization theory has been particularly guilty of post hoc revisionism, as shown in Hoffman's (1991) apologia for the observed lack of similarity in personality among children reared in the same homes, and in Baumrind's (1993) and Jackson's (1993) attempts to explain away incompatible family results (Scarr, 1993). Predictions from the long history of socialization research are clear: Parents have important effects on their children through proximal interactions with them, regardless of genetic relatedness. Opportunity theories have largely ignored the possibility of genetic transmission in families and social classes, and thus, are unchallenged by behavior genetic results. This review may help to alter that isolation.

OBSERVATIONS FROM
SOCIALIZATION STUDIES

Parental rearing styles, observed and reported by family members, have often been found to correlate with child outcomes, including intelligence and school achievement. A recent study (DeBaryshe, Patterson, & Capaldi, 1993) serves as an exemplar of the genre. I examine this well-designed study in detail, because its problems with causal inference, in the face of competently conducted causal analyses, is acute, but no more so than problems in any other study inspired by socialization theory.

This study (DeBaryshe et al., 1993) predicted academic achievement among 206 youths at risk for conduct disorder with parental rearing styles, parental WAIS-R IQ and education, and earlier measurements of the youths' own behavior problems and academic achievement. The authors proposed seven latent variable models to be tested for best fit. The report made clear that their preferred a priori model, which focused on parental discipline and conduct disorder, was not the best model fit to predict academic achievement differences among these boys. In these respects, and in its careful measurements, the study was exemplary. Fig. 6.2 shows estimated correlations among the latent variables in their models.

Correlations. In Fig. 6.2, correlations among the latent variables in their models are given. *These are the observations to be modeled;* thus, inspect-

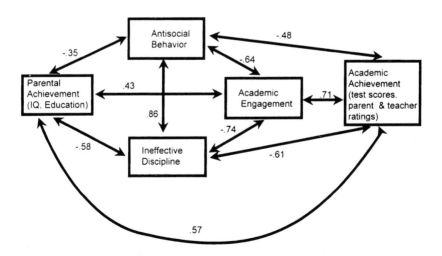

FIG. 6.2. Correlations among latent variables (DeBaryshe et al., 1993).

ing and understanding them is important. Note first the large correlations among some of the variables. Antisocial behavior was correlated .86 with ineffective parental discipline, which implies that they are measuring the same construct, because their correlation must be at the limit of the reliabilities of the two latent variables ($r = .86$ implies reliabilities of .927). Seven of the 10 correlations in this study exceed .50, and 9 of the 10 > .40, implying excellent measurement of the manifest variables that are summarized in these latent variables. How should they be modeled to make theoretical sense of these observations?

Authors' Models. At the top of Fig. 6.3 is the authors' hypothesized model, for which coefficients were not provided, but which was not a good fit to the observed correlations (Fig. 6.2). In the middle of Fig. 6.3 is the best of the seven models the authors tried, whose fits they tested competitively with chi-square. Seven does not exhaust the number of possible models for these observations, of course. *DeBaryshe et al.'s best-fit model was the only one that included a direct path from parents' IQ and education to youths' academic achievements.* The other predictive path in the best-fit model was from youths' academic engagement (effort at school) to their own achievement. Even this model was "cluttered up" with antisocial behavior (which did not contribute directly or indirectly to the prediction of academic achievement) and with ineffective discipline (whose indirect effect was through academic engagement). In no model did the authors drop both antisocial behavior and ineffective discipline to test for a best fit. Despite the authors' best modeling efforts, the evidence for causal effects from socialization practices was not compelling.

Models Not Tested. More important, no direct path was tested from parental IQ and education to youths' academic engagement in DeBaryshe et al.'s best-fit model or in any other model. The not-tested model is shown at the bottom of Fig. 6.3. Based on the correlations shown in Fig. 6.2, I suspect that a still-better fit would be obtained with the very simple causal model of the transmission of parental achievements (IQ, education) to adolescents' academic engagement and academic achievement. One direct effect and one indirect effect (via academic engagement) of parental intelligence and education on their offspring's academic achievement are shown. One could, of course, go further and predict academic achievement and academic engagement simply from parental achievement, with a correlation between the two adolescent variables; this would imply that smart, achieving parents have smart, achieving offspring. What else is new?

By eliminating parental discipline and conduct disorder from my more parsimonious model, I have removed the core socialization theory variables that were supposed to explain the correlations between parental and child characteristics (in these biological families).

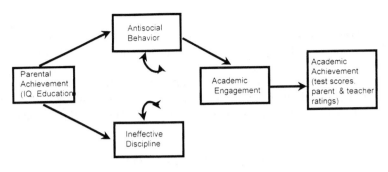

Authors' Hypothesis

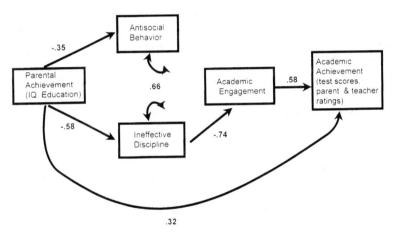

Authors' Best Model

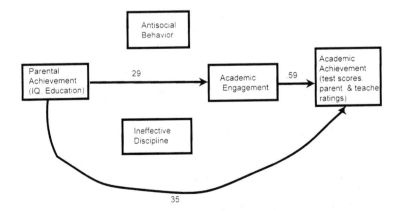

Model Not Tested

FIG. 6.3. Structural equation models of parental achievements, parental discipline, adolescents' antisocial behaviors, and school involvement on adolescents' school achievements (DeBaryshe et al., 1993).

A dispassionate reading of the DeBaryshe group's report reveals that they tried very hard, with seven different models, to avoid the inference that higher-IQ parents have higher-achieving offspring, even among youths at risk for conduct disorder. The observation they ultimately could not avoid, and they included in just one of the seven models, was that the highest correlate of youths' academic test scores was parental WAIS-R IQ (r = .424).

OBSERVATIONS FROM
BEHAVIOR GENETIC STUDIES

Behavior genetic studies are characterized by designs that allow inferences about both environmental and genetic sources of variation. If the ecology of rearing environments (including home environments, neighborhoods, communities, and social classes, all of which are shared by family members) are important determinants of variation, then people reared together will resemble each other intellectually and in academic achievement, to some extent, regardless of genetic relatedness. If, in addition, genetic resemblance plays a role in determining phenotypic resemblance, then genetic relatives will resemble each other, regardless of whether they were reared in the same ecology or not. If family members are individually variable apart from their environmental and genetic variability, then unique or nonshared environments (including biological as well as social environments) and measurement error are implicated. As described earlier, there have been studies of adoptive and biologically related families (MZ and DZ twins) reared in the same and different homes, and more recently stepfamilies with full-, half-, and unrelated siblings.

Table 6.1 provides a summary of family correlations on IQ tests and the first principal component from batteries of tests of cognitive abilities; the results are equivalent, so I do not dwell on possible distinctions. These data have been summarized and discussed so often in textbooks, review articles, and other books, that it is not necessary to repeat here what can easily be found elsewhere (e.g., Bouchard, 1997; Plomin, 1990; Scarr, 1992, 1993).

Correlations of Relatives: IQ and Achievement

Relatives resemble each other intellectually to the extent they are genetically related, and genetic relatives reared in different homes are somewhat less similar intellectually than are those reared in the same homes. Adopted adolescent and adult siblings, reared together since early infancy, are no more similar in intelligence than are randomly chosen people in the same populations. In North American and Western European populations, the heritability of IQ past childhood is quite high (about 70%), with small ef-

TABLE 6.1
Intelligence Test Correlations of Siblings, From Behavior Genetic Studies
of Biological and Adoptive Families and Twins (Adolescents and Adults)

Genetic r	Relationship	Same Home?	IQ Correlation	Number of Pairs
1.00	Same person, tested twice	Yes	.90	—
1.00	Identical twins	Yes	.86	4,672
1.00	Identical twins	No	.76	158
0.50	Fraternal twins	Yes	.55	8,600
0.50	Fraternal twins	No	.35	112
0.50	Biological siblings	Yes	.47	26,473
0.50	Biological siblings	No	.24	203
0.00	Adopted siblings	Yes	.02	385

Sources: Bouchard (1997); Loehlin (1997); Loehlin, Horn, and Willerman (1989); Pedersen et al. (1992); Plomin, DeFries, and McClearn (1990); Scarr and Weinberg (1978, 1994); Teasdale and Owen (1985).

fects of differences between families, which would include opportunity differences by social class and most parental socialization differences. Genetic variation in school achievement is less than in IQ test scores (Scarr & Yee, 1980; Thompson, Detterman, & Plomin, 1993).

The unexpected finding is that most of the environmental variation is found in unique, individual experiences that siblings do not share (i.e., environments that make siblings dissimilar). Analyses of these family data in simple heritability and in multivariate models can be found in many sources (e.g., Bouchard, 1997; Plomin, 1990; Scarr, 1992), and are not repeated here.

Socialization theory, focused on parental rearing practices, which presumably vary mostly *between* families, accounts for less than 10% of the variation in intelligence in these populations. As Jensen (1997) argued, even these "environmental" effects may not be the psychosocial variables of which psychologists primarily think when they consider sources of nongenetic variance. Rather, various biological insults, both pre- and postnatal, may account for a large part of the nonshared environmental effects on intelligence in populations studied. By examining IQ differences between MZ co-twins, Jensen showed that larger intrapair differences are strongly associated with the lower-scoring twin falling below IQ expectations, not by the higher-scoring twin exceeding expectations. Other studies of birth weight differences between MZ co-twins have shown that the lighter twin more often scores lower on later IQ tests than does the heavier twin, thereby implicating prenatal developmental environments to account for intrapair IQ variability (Guttman, 1994; Scarr, 1993). Being genetically identical, the only sources of MZ within-pair variability are environmental, and at least some of the environmental differences are prenatal.

Bouchard and colleagues (Bouchard et al., in press) provided a stunning

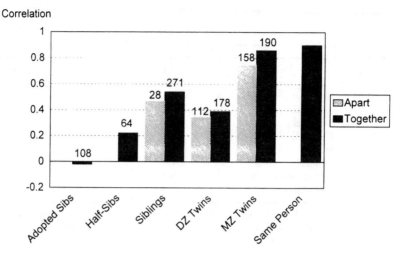

FIG. 6.4.   Kinship IQ correlations in the Minnesota study of twins reared apart and together (Bouchard, 1997).

summary of the pattern of family correlations *for adults* in their samples of five critical kinships, under two rearing conditions—same and different families—as shown in Fig. 6.4.

These observations yield broad heritabilities (including nonadditive genetic effects) of .70 to .94 for IQ differences in White North American and European populations from which the samples were drawn. Estimates of IQ heritability in these populations can be as low as .50 (Plomin, 1994), if one includes data on large numbers of young adopted siblings, whose IQ correlation average .24, versus five studies of late adolescent and young adult siblings (adopted in infancy), whose IQ correlation is 0. If one includes only data from late adolescents and adults for all family relationships, the heritability of IQ in North American and Western European populations is 70% to 90% (Bouchard & McGue, 1990; Scarr, 1997).

IQ results from the Minnesota study of twins reared apart were replicated exactly by the Swedish study of aging twins (SATSA; Pedersen, Plomin, Nesselroade, & McClearn, 1992). In the SATSA sample, MZ twins reared in different homes correlated .78 on the first principal component from a battery of cognitive tests. The SATSA MZ twins reared apart were much more similar than were their DZs reared apart (*r* = .32) and as similar in IQ as the MZs reared together (*r* = .80), thus providing no evidence for any shared environmental effect on general intelligence in late adulthood. Taking all of their data on twins' intelligence into account in a biometrical model, Pedersen et al. (1992) found that genetic differences accounted for 80% of the variability; nonshared environment, 19%; and shared environments, 0%, in this Swedish sample of older adults.

In fact, data on IQ resemblance between MZ co-twins reared in different homes are so remarkably consistent across nations and decades that they bear reprinting. Table 6.2 gives a summary of the five studies of MZs reared apart from the 1937 U.S. study of Newman and colleagues, to the Danish study of Juel-Nielson (1965) and the British study by Shields (1962) in the 1960s, to the ongoing Minnesota and Swedish studies.

Note that each of the five studies included more than one set of cognitive tests or IQ tests, which further reinforce the overall consistency of the results. The general intelligence correlations of MZ twins reared in different homes range from .74 to .78, with a median value of .76. Rarely can one find such consistency in social science data across time, history, and cultures. The implications of these results are that the heritability of general intelligence in these European and North American populations over this half-century accounts for about three quarters of the variance, and nonshared environments (and measurement error) accounts for about one quarter.

Critics of the studies of separated twins often focus on alleged similarities in the co-twins' rearing experiences, on the fact that most pairs have met in adulthood, and on other contact and environmental correlations in their backgrounds. The Minnesota and SATSA investigators dealt systematically with such criticisms (Bouchard, Lykken, McGue, Segal, & Tellegen,

TABLE 6.2
IQ Correlations of Monozygotic Twins Reared Apart. Samples Sizes, Intraclass Correlations, and Weighted Averages in Six Studies

Study and Test Used	N for Each Test	Primary Test	Secondary Test	Tertiary Test	Mean of Tests
Primary/Secondary/ Tertiary					
Newman et al. (1937) (Stanford-Binet/Otis)	19/19	0.68	0.74		0.71
Juel-Nielson (1965) (Wechsler-Bellvue/ Raven Matrices)	12/12	0.64	0.73		0.69
Shields (1962) (Mill-Hill/Dominoes)	38/37	0.74	0.76		0.75
Bouchard et al. (1990) (WAIS/Raven + Mill-Hill/1st Principal Component)	50/45/44	0.69	0.78	0.78	0.75
Pedersen et al. (1992) (First Principal Component)	45.00	0.78			0.78
Weighted Average	164/113/44	0.73	0/76	0.78	0.75

1990; Pedersen et al., 1992) and showed them to have little or no effect on the IQ and personality test results. In addition to gathering data about the objective circumstances of the twins' rearing environments (parental educational and occupational levels, material possessions in the homes), these investigators also gathered *perceptions* of the twins about their rearing environments, using instruments such as the family environment scales (Moos & Moos, 1981).

Younger and Older Adoptees

Earlier studies of adopted children, which examined their similarities to their rearing families compared to biological offspring to their families, included only young children with an average age of 8 years (see Scarr & Weinberg, 1983). Studies of young adoptees found the genetically unrelated children's IQ scores correlated .24 on average with their adoptive parents and .34 with unrelated siblings. Although biological relatives had correlations in the .40 to .55 range, heritability estimates based on adopted children were lower (.40 to .60) than those based on twins reared together and apart. Furthermore, the correlations of unrelated siblings *are* a direct estimate of the magnitude of shared environmental effects, which were found to be negligible in twin studies but accounted for about 25% of the variation in adoption studies. The mystery of inconsistent results was solved when Scarr and Weinberg's (1978, 1983) study of older adolescent and young adult adoptees found IQ correlations of −.03 for older, unrelated sibling pairs, and adoptive parent-child correlations of < .10. Shared environmental effects for young adults match the null to small estimated from twin studies, With biological siblings' IQ correlations at .35, and biological parent-child correlations at .40, heritability estimates for WAIS IQ in the older samples approached those of the twin studies (.76 and .70).

Results of the Minnesota adolescent adoption study have been replicated by three other adoption studies of older adolescents and adults adopted in infancy. Two adoption studies have reported longitudinal data from childhood to adulthood. The Texas adoption project (Loehlin, 1997; Loehlin, Horn, & Willerman, 1989) found that genetically unrelated siblings' IQ correlations declined from .17 at the age of 8 years to −.02 at the average age of 18 years. The Minnesota Transracial Adoption Study (Scarr, Weinberg, & Waldman, 1993; Weinberg, Scarr, & Waldman, 1992), which included adoptive families with at least one child of African American origin, found that adopted siblings' IQ correlations declined from .34 to .13, which was significantly different from zero, but was smaller at age 18 years than was the IQ correlation of the transracial adoptees at the average age of 7 years (Scarr & Weinberg, 1976).

The original finding (Scarr & Weinberg, 1978) of null resemblance between adopted siblings in late adolescence and early adulthood inspired the theory of genotype → environment effects (Scarr & McCartney, 1983: Scarr & Weinberg, 1983). The theory predicts increasing heritability and declining effects of shared environments as people increasingly choose and make their own environments, rather than being strongly influenced by the home environment provided by parents. To test the theory, McCartney (McCartney, Harris, & Bernieri, 1990) conducted a meta-analysis of twin studies on IQ and personality to evaluate the effects of subjects' age on heritability estimates. She found a correlation of .30 between increasing age and increasing heritabilities, and evidence for declining effects of shared environments, in keeping with our theory (Scarr, 1992; Scarr & McCartney, 1983).

Differences in socialization history have negligible effects on development of intelligence past childhood in European and North American populations that are not specially deprived of opportunities to acquire developmentally appropriate experiences (Bouchard, 1997; Scarr, 1992, 1993). The implication of these results is that any redistribution of existing environments considered favorable to those in environments considered unfavorable can have limited effects on culturally approved intellectual development, because environments experienced by these samples are largely functionally equivalent. Although heritability estimates for IQ variation in these populations range from .7 to .9, there is environmental variance (e^2) that ranges from .06 to .30. All or nearly all of this environmental effect, however, is due to unique individual experiences, which cannot be programmed.

Thus, opportunity theory, which relies on correlations in biologically related families to make inferences about social class difference in opportunities, fails to account for the data from behavior genetic studies of twins and adoptive families. Observed differences in intelligence by social class in European and Euro-American populations are not primarily due to differences in opportunities to acquire the skills and knowledge valued by the dominant culture. Similarly, socialization theory, which focuses on shared rearing environments, fails to account for the lack of such effects on intelligence past childhood.

GENETICS CREEPS
INTO SOCIALIZATION STUDIES

More and more socialization researchers recognize the ubiquitous influence of genetic individual differences in intelligence and personality on the "socialization" variables they study, and the need to take genetic variability into account. The need to incorporate environmental measures in behavior genetic studies has been recognized (e.g., Plomin, 1994; Scarr, 1993), but the need to include genetically informative designs in socialization studies is less often mentioned. The omission of genetically informative families in socialization studies has produced only uninterpretable results. With only these data, there is no way to test competing theories about sources of individual differences, as was shown in Fig. 6.1.

Socialization theory has been moot on possible effects of genetic variability on intellectual development, and it ignores the confounding of genetic and environmental variability reported for the most common measures of family "environment" (Chipuer, Plomin, Pedersen, McClearn, & Nesselroade, 1993; Plomin & Bergeman, 1991; Plomin & Daniels, 1987; Plomin, Loehlin, & DeFries, 1985; Plomin, McClearn, Pederson, Nesselroade, & Bergeman, 1988, 1989; Rowe, 1994). Because family members report *perceptions* of the family environment, and because individual differences in social perception are partly genetic, measures of family "environments," such as the Family Environment Scales (Moos & Moos, 1981) and the HOME scale (Caldwell & Bradley, 1984), are partly heritable.

In fact, there is considerable evidence that popular measures of family "environments," such as the HOME scale, and the Family Environment Scales (FES), are confounded by genetic differences among parents (Bouchard & McGue, 1990; Jang, 1993; Plomin, 1994; Plomin et al., 1985, 1988, 1989; Plomin & Bergeman, 1991; Plomin & Neiderhiser, 1992; Rowe, 1981, 1983, 1994). By comparing the similarities in perceptions of the family environment among families with genetically identical twins, first-degree relatives, and adopted relatives, behavior genetic analyses show that genetic similarities affect the similarity of perceptions of relationships in the family on major dimensions of parenting (warmth and control) and on intellectual stimulation in the home.

Most striking is the finding that, as adults, identical twins reared apart (MZAs) perceived their rearing families to have been as similar as those of fraternal twins reared together, even though the MZAs were reporting on *different* families! The MZAs were not as similar as the MZs reared together, but were considerably more similar than DZs reared apart. Thus, the heritability estimates for various FES scales for the adult twins' rearing environments ranged from .15 to .35 (Plomin et al., 1988). When reporting on rearing practices with their own children, the adult MZAs were as similar as adult MZTs (those pairs reared together), and both MZ groups reported more similar childrearing practices than did DZ twins (Plomin et al., 1989). Heritabilities of the FES for adult twins rating their offspring families ranged from .12 to .40 (median = .26). Both parents' and offspring perceptions, measured when the offspring were adolescents to older adults, show that 25% to 50% of the variability in measures of perceived family environments are due to genetic variability.

Perhaps, one could dismiss these results as *perceptions* of the family environment that show merely that genetic differences affect people's perceptions of relationships and emotional climates in their homes. (Actually getting socialization researchers to admit that much would be a triumph for empirical theory testing.) Fortunately, there are four observational studies of parent–child interactions that provide similar evidence of genetic effects on family environment. In the largest study ever done of genetic contributions to family "environments," Reiss, Hetherington, and Plomin (reported in Plomin, 1994) found large effects for genetic differences (52% to 64% of the variance) and nonshared environments (25% to 37%) in adolescents' positivity and negativity in interactions with family members, scored from videotaped observations. Strangely enough, the shared environment (all of the sibling and twin pairs in this study were reared in the same homes) accounted for only 0% to 23% of the variance in adolescents' interactions. Parental positivity and negativity in interactions with their adolescent children showed more shared environmental effect (34% to 63%) and lesser effects of genetic differences among the children (0% to 38%) and nonshared environments (19% to 34%).

Additional data about genetic effects on other aspects of children's rearing environments are also revealing. Peer relationships and the choice of peers have been shown to be genetically variable (Plomin, 1994; Rowe, 1981, 1983). Perhaps this result is not surprising, because children do choose their peers, whereas they cannot choose their family members. Whereas genotype-environment correlations in biologically related families may be of the passive type, peer relations may show the active and reactive types (Plomin, 1994). Adolescents' ratings of positive peer and teacher relationships were moderately heritable (.31 and .38), but parents' ratings of their adolescents' popularity with peers and the delinquent, drug abuse, or college-bound orientation of peers showed more heritability than did parent ratings of the family environment. For separate mother and father ratings, the heritabilities of peer popularity were .62 and .73; for peer college orientation, .73 and .85; for peer delinquency, .70 and .49; and for peer substance abuse, .72 and .74 (Plomin, 1994). Effects of shared environments on adolescents' peer relationships, based on the correlations of genetically unrelated siblings in the same family, were small to moderate (.00 to .42, median = .13).

Plomin (1994) summarized the research on genetic and environmental effects on self-report and observational measures of the family "environment":

> Genetic effects are not just limited to children's perceptions of their family environment. Parents' perceptions of their parenting implicate genetic contributions even in child-based genetic designs (i.e., twins are the children in the family). In child-based genetic designs, genetic effects can be detected only to the extent that parents' perceptions of their parenting reflect genetically influenced characteristics of their children.
>
> Finally, evidence of genetic effects emerges from four observational stud-

ies of parenting and sibling behavior using child-based genetic designs. The results from these observations studies suggest that the genetic contribution to measures of the family environment is not limited to subjective processes involved in questionnaires. Genetic effects appear to be not just in the eye of the beholder but also in the behavior of the individual. (pp. 79–80)

The implication of this rather recent research for studies of family environmental effects on children's personality and intellectual development is profound. In socialization studies, ubiquitous correlations between parent characteristics and features of the parent-provided home with child development have been erroneously explained as a causal effect of home environments on children. In fact, observations from behavior genetic studies, which vary in genetic and environmental relatedness of participants, have shown that the correlation between parental and home characteristics and children's development is not explained primarily by the home environment but instead by genetic resemblance among family members. When only biologically related families have been studied, this genetic effect of parents on children (and siblings on each other) has been misinterpreted, with important misinferences for developmental theory and for intervention efforts to change some parents' childrearing practices.

GENETIC EFFECTS ON INTELLIGENCE: THE LARGER POLITICAL CONTEXT

One cannot ignore the political context for presenting and interpreting research on genetic and environmental variability in intelligence. As has been said so many times, science is not value free, and it operates in a context of disputes about moral/ethical issues of distributive justice and a just society. How unequal should people be in the power and resources they have? Intelligence is pertinent to these disputes, because it directly causes differences in educational achievements, directly and indirectly in occupational achievements, and indirectly in income (Behrman, Hrubeck, Taubman, & Wales, 1980; Fischbein, 1980; Herrnstein, 1973; Herrnstein & Murray, 1994; Jencks, 1979; Scarr & Weinberg, 1994; Scarr & Yee, 1980).

Behavioral scientists of all theoretical persuasions observe that intelligence is closely linked to educational success, which in turn is associated with eventual occupational status, which bears some relationship to earnings. Achievements and socioeconomic rewards are associated with intelligence, which makes some behavioral scientists very uncomfortable with the concept of intelligence itself. The observation of links between intelligence and socioeconomic achievements is not disputed, but the link is ascribed to societal injustice and unequal opportunities for people who come from advantaged versus disadvantaged families. The pervasive correlation between IQ and social class is ascribed to social class differences in opportunities afforded to children during development.

The idea that differences in intelligence are associated with genetic differences is especially distressing to many behavioral scientists, because it implies necessarily that social class differences in children's eventual achievements are also caused, in part, by genetic differences among parents at different social class levels (Herrnstein, 1973). How can children have an equal opportunity to achieve if some are better endowed genetically with intellectual potential? It has been most convenient to deny the possibility and to excoriate those who dared suggest it.

John Rawls (1971) dealt explicitly with the need to compensate for genetic inequalities as well as environmental ones. He argued that distributive justice depends on recognizing individual differences in talents that cause differences in social and economic achievements, and to compensate for them in ways that create a more just society than would occur through unchecked market forces. I agree that this may be the most equitable way to compensate for intellectual differences by detaching, in part, social and economic rewards from the fruits of intellectual differences. Others disagree emphatically with a compensatory view, preferring a libertarian utopia where differentially endowed individuals are left to find their own "valued places" in a vastly unequal society (Herrnstein & Murray, 1994).

Regardless of our political vision of a just society, we cannot make considered judgments about these issues until we are willing to face the observation of genetic variability in intelligence and deal with our values about how much socioeconomic inequality is acceptable in a just society. Then, and only then, can we draw a rational plan for a nation in which we would like to be citizens (Scarr, 1994).

REFERENCES

Bandura, A. (1977). *Social learning theory.* Englewood Cliffs, NJ: Prentice-Hall.
Baumrind, D. (1993). The average expectable environment is not good enough: A response to Scarr. *Child Development, 64,* 1299–1317.
Behrman, J., Hrubeck, Z., Taubman, P., & Wales, T. J. (1980). *Socioeconomic success: A study of the effects of genetic endowments, family environment and schooling.* Amsterdam: North-Holland.
Bouchard, T. J., Jr. (1997). IQ similarity in twins reared apart: Findings and responses to critics. In R. J. Sternberg & E. Grigorenko (Eds.), *Intelligence, heredity, and environment* (pp. 126–160). New York: Cambridge University Press.
Bouchard, T. J., Jr., Lykken, D. T., McGue, M., Segal, N. L, & Tellegen, A. (1990). Sources of human psychological difference: The Minnesota study of twins reared apart. *Science, 250,* 223–228.
Bouchard, T. J., Jr., & McGue, M. (1990). Geneic and rearing environmental influences on adult personality: An analysis of adopted twins reared apart. *Journal of Personality, 58,* 263–292.

Caldwell, B. M., & Bradley, R. H. (1984). *Home observation for the measurement of the environment.* Little Rock: University of Arkansas Press.

Chipuer, H. M., Plomin, R., Pedersen, N. L., McClearn, G. E., & Nesselroade, J. R. (1993). Genetic influence on family environment: The role of personality. *Developmental Psychology, 29,* 110–118.

DeBaryshe, B. D., Patterson, G. R., & Capaldi, D. M. (1993). A performance model for academic achievement in early adolescent boys. *Developmental Psychology, 29,* 795–804.

Fischbein, S. (1980). IQ and social class. *Intelligence, 4,* 51–63.

Guttman, R. (1994, June) *Twin differences in birth weight and later cognitive performance.* Poster presentation at the biennial meeting of the International Society for the Study of Behavioral Development, Amsterdam.

Hawking, S. (1988). *A Brief history of time.* New York: Bantam Books.

Herrnstein, R. (1973). *IQ in the meritocracy.* Boston: Atlantic Monthly Press.

Herrnstein, R., & Murray, C. (1994). *The bell curve.* New York: Free Press.

Hoffman, L. W. (1991). The influence of family environments on personality: Accounting for sibling differences. *Psychological Bulletin, 110,* 187–203.

Jackson, J. (1993). Human behavioral genetics, Scarr's theory, and her views on interventions: A critical review and commentary on their implications for African American children. *Child Development, 64,* 1318–1331.

Jang, K. L. (1993). *A behavioral genetic analysis of personality, personality disorder, the environment, and the search for sources of nonshared environmental influences.* Unpublished doctoral dissertation, University of Western Ontario, London.

Jencks, C. (1979). *Who gets ahead? The determinants of economic success in America.* New York: Basic Books.

Jensen, A. R. (1997). The puzzle of nonshared environment. In R. J. Sternberg & E. Grigorenko (Eds.), *Intelligence: Heredity and environment* (pp. 42–88). New York: Cambridge Universiy Press.

Juel-Nielsen, N. (1965). Individual and environment: A psychiatric-psychological investigation of MZ twins reared apart. *Acta Psychiatrica Scandinavia (Suppl.),* 183.

Kohn, M. L. (1969). *Class and conformity.* Chicago: University of Chicago Press.

Loehlin, J. C., Horn, J. M., & Willerman, L. (1997). Heredity, environment, and IQ in the Texas Adoption Project. In R. J. Sternberg and E. Grigorenko (Eds.), *Intelligence: Heredity and environment* (pp. 105–125). New York: Cambridge Universiy Press.

Loehlin, J. C., Horn, J. M., & Willerman, L. (1989). Modeling IQ change: Evidence from the Texas Adoption Project. *Child Development, 60,* 993–1004.

Maccoby, E. E. (1992). The role of parents in the socialization of children: An historical overview. *Developmental Psychology, 28,* 1006–1017.

McCartney, K., Harris, M. J., & Bernieri, F. (1990). Growing up and growing apart: A developmental meta-analysis of twin studies. *Psycholgical Bulletin, 107,* 226–237.

Moos, R. H., & Moos, B. S. (1981). *Family Environment Scales manual.* Palo Alto, CA: Consulting Psychologists Press.

Pedersen, N. L., Plomin, R., Nesselroade, J. R., & McClearn, G. E. (1992). A quantitative genetic analysis of cognitive abilities during the second half of the lifespan. *Psychological Science, 3,* 346-353.

Plomin, R. (1990). The role of inheritance in behavior. *Science, 248,* 183–188.

Plomin, R. (1994). *Genetics and experience: The interplay between nature and nurture.* Thousand Oaks, CA: Sage.

Plomin, R., & Bergeman, C. S. (1991). The nature of nurture: Perspective and prospective. In R. Plomin & G. E. McClearn (Eds.), *Nature, nurture, and psychology* (pp. 457–493). Washington, DC: American Psychological Association.

Plomin, R., & Daniels, D. (1987). Why are children in the same family so different from one another? *Behavioral and Brain Sciences, 10,* 1–60.

Plomin, R., DeFries, J. C., & McClearn, G. E. (1990). *Behavioral genetics: A primer.* New York: Freeman.

Plomin, R., Loehlin, J. C., & DeFries, J. C. (1985). Genetic and environmental components of "environmental" influences. *Developmental Psychology, 21,* 391–402.

Plomin, R., McClearn, G. E., Pedersen, N. L., Nesselroade, J. R., & Bergeman, C. S. (1988). Genetic influence on childhood family environment perceived retrospectively from the last half of the lifespan. *Developmental Psychology, 24,* 738–745.

Plomin, R., McClearn, G. E., Pedersen, N. L., Nesselroade, J. R., & Bergeman, C. S. (1989). Genetic influences on adults' ratings of their current environment. *Journal of Marriage and the Family, 51,* 791–803.

Plomin, R., & Neiderhiser, J. M. (1992). Genetics and experience. *Current Directions in Psychological Science, 1,* 160–164.

Plomin, R., Reiss, D., Hetherington, E. M., & Howe, G. W. (1994). Nature and nurture: Genetic contributions to measures of the family environment. *Developmental Psychology, 30,* 32–43.

Rawls, J. (1971). *Inequalities and social justice.* Cambridge, MA: Harvard University Press.

Rowe, D. C. (1981). Environmental and genetic influences on dimensions of perceived parenting: A twin study, *Developmental Psychology, 17,* 203–208.

Rowe, D. C. (1983). A biometrical analysis of perceptions of family environment: A study of twin and singleton sibling kinships. *Child Development, 54,* 416–423.

Rowe, D. (1994). *The myth of family influences.* New York: Guilford.

Scarr, S. (1985). Constructing psychology: Making facts and fables for our times. *American Psychologist, 40,* 499–512.

Scarr, S. (1992). Developmental theories for the 1990's: Development and individual differences. *Child Development, 63,* 1–19.

Scarr, S. (1993). Biological and cultural diversity: The legacy of Darwin for development. *Child Development, 64,* 1333–1353.

Scarr, S. (1994). Psychological science in the public arena: Three cases of dubious influence. *Scandinavian Journal of Psychology, 36,* 164–188.

Scarr, S. (1997). Behavior genetic and socialization theories of intelligence: Truce and reconciliation. In R. J. Sternberg & E. Grigorenko (Eds.), *Intelligence: Heredity and environment* (pp. 3–41). New York: Cambridge University Press.

Scarr, S., & McCartney, K. (1983). How people make their own environments: A theory of genotype→environment effects. *Child Development, 54,* 424–435.

Scarr, S., & Weinberg, R. A. (1976). IQ test performance of black children adopted by white families. *American Psychologist, 31,* 726–739.

Scarr, S., & Weinberg, R. A. (1978). The influence of "family background" on intellectual attainment. *American Sociological Review, 43,* 674–692.

Scarr, S., & Weinberg, R. A. (1983). The Minnesota adoption studies: Genetic differences and malleability. *Child Development, 54,* 260–267.

Scarr, S., & Weinberg, R. A. (1994). Educational and occupational achievements of adolescents and young adults in adoptive and biologically-related families. *Behavior Genetics, 24,* 301–325.

Scarr. S., Weinberg, R. A., & Waldman, I. D. (1993). IQ correlations in transracial adoptive families. *Intelligence, 17,* 541–555.

Scarr, S., & Yee, D. (1980). Heritability and educational policy: Genetic and environmental effects on IQ, aptitude, and achievement. *Educational Psychologist, 15,* 1–22.

Shields, J. (1962). *Monozygotic twins brought up apart and brought up together.* London: Oxford University Press.

Teasdale, T. W., & Owen, D. R. (1985). Heredity and familial environment in intelligence and educational level—a sibling study. *Nature, 309,* 620–622.

Thompson, L. A., Detterman, D. K., & Plomin, R. (1993). Cognitive abilities and scholastic achievement: Genetic overlap but environmental differences. *Psychological Science, 3,* 158–165.

Weinberg, R., Scarr, S., & Waldman, I. (1992). The Minnesota transracial adoption study: A follow-up of IQ test performance at adolescence, *Intelligence, 16,* 117–135.

7

Extending *Gf-Gc* Theory Into Practice

Richard W. Woodcock
University of Virginia

The awareness of human intelligence has a long history. From the earliest days on our planet, we have observed the operation of intelligence and have drawn at least two conclusions: First, some people are more intelligent than others; second, each of us is more capable in some ways than we are in others. Some contemporary efforts to describe these individual differences are called "theories of multiple intelligences." Two prominent empirically derived theories are Cattell and Horn's *Gf-Gc* theory (Cattell 1941; Horn 1965, 1985, 1988, 1991, 1994) and Carroll's (1993) three-stratum theory. Stratum 2 of Carroll's theory and the set of broad abilities described by the Cattell-Horn *Gf-Gc* theory are quite similar. Another prominent theory of multiple intelligences, although not empirically derived, is that of Howard Gardner (1983, 1993, 1994).

The purpose of this chapter is not to extend cognitive theory, as such, but instead to nudge current theory further into clinical and research practice. A major aspect of my own work has been the development of test batteries that measure proficiencies across the spectrum of cognitive ability (Woodcock & Johnson, 1977, 1989). That work is not the subject of this chapter; rather, this chapter is directed toward applying modern cognitive theory to the interpretation and use of any collection of cognitive tests. Four topics are addressed:

1. Comments about *Gf-Gc* theory are presented, including information about a proposed "reading-writing" factor.

2. Fifty-three good measures of *Gf-Gc* abilities provided in four major intelligence batteries are identified.

3. Two models of *Gf-Gc* theory are described that are more informative than a simple listing of 8 to 10 broad abilities.

4. Several implications of the previous topics for practice are presented.

Gf-Gc THEORY

The theory of *Gf-Gc* is not described in detail here, and any reader desiring more complete information should refer to Horn (1985, 1988, 1991, 1994). Lists of empirically identified *Gf-Gc* factors include at least eight or nine broad abilities. Table 7.1 lists 10 *Gf-Gc* broad abilities, including a tentative reading-writing factor. The names of the broad abilities presented in Table 7.1 and their notations vary somewhat from writer to writer. Because nine of

TABLE 7.1
Ten *Gf–Gc* Broad Abilities

Name	Symbol	Description
Short-term memory	*Gsm*	Ability to hold information in immediate awareness and then use it within a few seconds.
Verbal-conceptual knowledge	*Gc*	Breadth and depth of knowledge, including verbal communication, information, and reasoning when using previously learned procedures.
Quantitative knowledge	*Gq*	Ability to comprehend quantitative concepts and relationships and to manipulate numerical symbols.
Reading-writing	*Grw*	An ability associated with reading and writing, probably including basic reading and writing skills and the skills required for comprehension/expression. (Not yet well defined in the literature.)
Visuospatial thinking	*Gv*	Spatial orientation and the ability to analyze and synthesize visual stimuli.
Auditory thinking	*Ga*	Ability to analyze and synthesize auditory stimuli.
Long-term storage-retrieval	*Glr*	Ability to store information and retrieve it later through association.
Novel reasoning	*Gf*	Ability to reason, form concepts, and solve problems that often include unfamiliar information or procedures. Manifested in the reorganization, transformation, and extrapolation of information.
Automatic processing speed	*Gs*	Ability to rapidly perform automatic or very simple cognitive tasks.
Correct decision speed	*CDS*	Speediness in finding correct solutions to problems of moderate difficulty.

the broad abilities have an extensive research base, they are not discussed further here. The reading-writing factor that is not well defined in the literature is addressed next.

Reading-Writing

Reading-Writing (*Grw*) is defined in Table 7.1 as "an ability associated with reading and writing, probably including basic reading and writing skills and the skills required for comprehension/expression." This factor (or factors) has been recognized by others, including Carroll (1993), Carroll and Maxwell (1979), Horn (1988), and McGrew, Werder, and Woodcock (1991).

Identification of a *Grw* factor has important practical implications. The addition of this factor to the list of empirically identified abilities essentially completes the set of cognitive and achievement abilities evaluated in a typical comprehensive intellectual and achievement assessment.

Table 7.2 presents an example of exploratory factor analysis results when tests of reading and writing are included with recognized indicators of selected *Gf-Gc* abilities (Woodcock, 1990, 1994). An exploratory procedure was chosen for this purpose because of the limited prior knowledge regarding the factorial structure of the reading and writing tests used as markers in this study. The data selected for this study are drawn from the WJ-R norming sample (Woodcock & Johnson, 1989) and include four measures of reading (Letter-Word Identification, Word Attack, Reading Vocabulary, and Passage Comprehension) and five measures of writing (Punctuation and Capitalization, Spelling, Usage, Writing Fluency, and Writing Samples). These measures span a spectrum from basic skills to the reading and writing of connected text.

Recognizing that the tests of reading and writing might demonstrate a loading on verbal-conceptual knowledge (*Gc*), six measures of *Gc* (Picture Vocabulary, Oral Vocabulary, Listening Comprehension, Science, Social Studies, and Humanities) were included in the set of variables. Because the Writing Fluency test is a highly speeded test, two processing speed (*Gs*) tests (Visual Matching and Crossout) were included as markers for that factor. Two tests of auditory thinking (*Ga*) (Sound Blending and Incomplete Words) were included as markers in case some of the reading or writing tasks require auditory processing ability. Two measures of long-term storage-retrieval (*Glr*) (Memory for Names and Visual-Auditory Learning) were included as a hyperplane based on the assumption that none of the other tests in the study, including the measures of reading and writing, would load on that factor.

The data are based on 3,278 subjects ranging in age from 4 to 89 years who were administered the 21 tests. The effect of age is partialed out to the fourth power. Table 7.2 reports results from a five-factor iterative principle axis solution followed by an oblique promax rotation. Factor loadings, communal-

TABLE 7.2
Identification of a Reading-Writing *Grw* Factor
Following Promax Rotation (N = 3,278, Age = 4 to 89 years)

Test	Factor Loadings					
	Grw	*Gc*	*Gs*	*Glr*	*Ga*	h^2
Writing Samples	.85	—	—	—	—	.62
Letter-Word Identification	.84	—	—	—	—	.80
Word Attack	.82	—	—	—	—	.71
Passage Comprehension	.80	—	—	—	—	.72
Spelling	.77	—	—	—	—	.74
Punctuation and Capitalization	.70	—	—	—	—	.68
Reading Vocabulary	.65	.39	—	—	—	.78
Writing Fluency	.55	—	.31	—	—	.57
Usage	.54	.22	—	—	—	.58
Social Studies	—	.87	—	—	—	.72
Picture Vocabulary	—	.80	—	—	—	.64
Science	—	.79	—	—	—	.67
Oral Vocabulary	—	.74	—	—	—	.74
Humanities	—	.72	—	—	—	.67
Listening Comprehension	—	.71	—	—	—	.61
Visual matching	—	—	.82	—	—	.74
Crossout	—	—	.75	—	—	.61
Memory for names	—	—	—	.72	—	.54
Visual-auditory learning	—	—	—	.66	—	.61
Incomplete Words	—	—	—	—	.54	.43
Sound Blending	.26	—	—	—	.48	.53

Note: Loadings < .20 not reported.
Factor intercorrelations:

Grw	1.00				
Gc	.62	1.00			
Gs	.52	.40	1.00		
Glr	.51	.54	.42	1.00	
Ga	.46	.39	.22	.42	1.00

ity estimates (h^2), and factor intercorrelations are included in Table 7.2. The results from this analysis clearly indicate that all nine reading and writing tests fall onto a common factor labeled here as *Grw* (reading-writing). Table 7.2 indicates further that the six verbal-conceptual and knowledge tests (*Gc*) load onto a single factor. There is a moderate secondary loading on *Gc* for the Reading Vocabulary test, which was expected given its vocabulary content. The two processing speed tests load on the *Gs* factor, and the speeded Writing Fluency test demonstrates a moderate secondary loading on *Gs*. The only major loadings on long-term storage-retrieval (*Glr*) are Memory for Names and Visual-Auditory Learning, two tests known to be markers for that factor (McGrew et al., 1991; Woodcock, 1990, 1994). The two auditory thinking (*Ga*) tests—Sound Blending and Incomplete Words—display primary loadings on that factor, as expected. The Sound Blending test, however, also demonstrates a low secondary loading on the *Grw* factor.

The next step was to determine the effect of extracting more than five factors. The result observed from a six-factor solution was a splintering of the Usage test onto a unique factor for that variable (loading = .63). All other tests retained their previous identities with *Grw, Gc, Gs, Glr,* and *Ga.*

The *Grw* factor appears to represent a common factor underlying both reading and writing. For that reason, it has been named here as a reading-writing factor (*Grw*). Other studies should be conducted to confirm or disconfirm this conclusion.

Good Measures of *Gf-Gc* Abilities

Even if a clinician subscribes to the concept of multiple intelligences, it is not always obvious which of the available tests are good measures of a specific *Gf-Gc* factor. A clinician cannot rely completely on a test author's classification and labeling of tests, even though the test author's intentions may have been honorable. Woodcock (1990) discussed one problem underlying the confusion about what the various tests from different intelligence batteries measure:

> A serious problem exists with many of the factor analytic studies that have been reported on the major cognitive batteries. The variables in those studies routinely have been restricted to only those subtests included within a battery itself. Any single cognitive battery, with the possible exception of the WJ-R, probably does not include enough markers for each embedded factor to allow an appropriate description of the factorial structure of that battery. As a result, factors that are present in a battery are not differentiated or perhaps not even detected. Inappropriate conclusions then may be drawn about the factorial structure of the battery and about the construct validity of the individual subtests. (p. 238)

When appropriate factor analysis studies are completed, useful information emerges about the factor or factors on which the individual tests load. Woodcock (1990) analyzed the data from nine joint factor studies that included the *Kaufman Abilities Battery for Children* (K-ABC), the *Stanford-Binet IV* (SB-IV), the Wechslers (WISC-R, WAIS, WAIS-R), and the *Woodcock-Johnson Psycho-Educational Batteries* (WJ, WJ-R). Fifteen exploratory and confirmatory factor analyses were completed on 68 subtests from these batteries. The display of selected tests by factors in Table 7.3 is primarily based on the information reported in Table 5 of Woodcock (1990).

How can the information in Table 7.3 be used? The most common practice in an intelligence assessment is to administer one particular battery

TABLE 7.3
Good Measures of *Gf-Gc* Factors in Four Cognitive Batteries

Factor	Cognitive Battery			
	WJ-R	Wechslers	SB-IV	K-ABC
Short-term memory (*Gsm*)	(Short-term memory)		(Short-term memory)	(Sequential processing)
	Memory for words	Digit span	Memory for digits	Number recall
	Memory for sentences		Memory for objects	Word order
Verbal-conceptual knowledge (*Gc*)	(Comprehension-knowledge)	(Verbal comprehension)	(Verbal reasoning)	
	Picture vocabulary	Vocabulary	Vocabulary	Riddles
	Listening comprehension	Comprehension	Verbal relations	Faces and places
	Oral vocabulary	Information	Absurdities	
		Similarities	Comprehension	
Quantitative knowledge (*Gq*)	(Quantitative ability)		(Quantitative reasoning)	
	Calculation	Arithmetic	Equation building	Arithmetic
	Applied problems		Number series	
	Quantitative concepts		Quantitative	
Visuospatial thinking (*Gv*)	(Visual processing)	(Perceptual organization)		(Simultaneous processing)
	Visual closure	Object assembly	Pattern analysis	Triangles
	Picture recognition	Block design	Copying	Gestalt closure
		Mazes	Paper folding and cutting	
		Picture completion		
Auditory thinking (*Ga*)	(Auditory processing)			
	Sound blending	(None)	(None)	(None)
	Incomplete words			
	Sound patterns			
Long-term storage-retrieval (*Glr*)	(Long-term retrieval)			
	Delayed-recall —memory for names	(None)	(None)	(None)
	Visual-auditory learning			
	Memory for names			

(Continued)

TABLE 7.3
(Continued)

Factor	WJ-R	Wechslers	SB-IV	K-ABC
	Cognitive Battery			
Novel reasoning (*Gf*)	(Fluid reasoning) Concept formation Analysis-synthesis Spatial relations	(None)	Matrices	(None)
Automatic processing speed (*Gs*)	(Processing speed) Visual matching Cross out	(Processing speed) Coding (digit symbol) Symbol search	(None)	(None)

Note: Battery-specific factor names are in parentheses.

in its entirety. As an alternative to this practice, clinicians should consider the principle of "cross-battery assessment" based on the specific referral question or questions. For example, if an individual is suspected of having a short-term memory problem, Table 7.3 indicates that seven good measures of short-term memory (*Gsm*) are available across the four intelligence batteries. Several of these tests, perhaps even all seven, could be administered to obtain comprehensive information about an individual's performance on this type of task. Two advantages of this approach are that an assortment of related, but not identical, tasks has been administered, and the individual's performance is evaluated by comparison to more than one norming sample.

Additional joint factor analysis studies are needed that include a sufficient breadth and depth of markers to validly describe the construct validity of the subtests in existing cognitive batteries. These studies should include suitable marker variables, such as those identified in Table 7.3. McGhee (1993), for example, reported a joint factor study involving data from the *Differential Ability Scales* (DAS), the *Detroit Tests of Learning Ability-3* (DTLA-3), and marker variables from the WJ-R. Any newly published cognitive battery or revision of an existing battery should provide this type of technical information to potential users.

Beyond knowing which *Gf-Gc* abilities are measured by which tests, how do the several *Gf-Gc* broad abilities coordinate to produce cognitive performance? Can the *Gf-Gc* abilities in Table 7.1 be organized into a more informative structure than a simple list of 10 abilities? Those questions are addressed in the next section.

DYNAMIC MODELS OF *Gf-Gc* THEORY

Two interactive models of *Gf-Gc* theory have been proposed by Woodcock (1993). The first model, called the *Gf-Gc Cognitive Performance Model* (CPM), represents a simple organization of cognitive and noncognitive factors and indicates that cognitive performance is a function of the joint effect of these factors. The second model, which is more complex but also more informative, is called the *Gf-Gc Information Processing Model* (IPM).

Gf-Gc Cognitive Performance Model

The level and quality of an individual's cognitive performance, whether observed during a test or in real life, results from a complex interaction of many components. The various components contributing to cognitive performance may be assigned to four broad categories, differentiated by function:

1. Short-term memory
2. Stores of acquired knowledge
3. Thinking abilities
4. Facilitator-inhibitors

Each of these four categories includes components that contribute in a common way to cognitive performance, but also contribute differently from the common contributions of the other three categories.

Fig. 7.1 illustrates the relationship between the four functional categories and cognitive performance. Note that the term *cognitive performance* is used on the outcome side of the CPM rather than the terms *intelligence* or *cognitive ability*. Intelligence can only be inferred from observations of performance. Furthermore, experienced clinicians know that scores obtained from intelligence tests must often be interpreted with caution because the observed performance may be distorted by individual, environmental, or test situation variables. A brief description of the four-way classification of *Gf-Gc* abilities follows.

Short-Term Memory.   Short-term memory, sometimes called *immediate awareness* in the literature, involves the apprehension and almost immediate use of information. Most available tests of short-term memory measure the span of auditory awareness. This is true of all the short-term memory tests identified in Table 7.3 except SB-IV Memory for Objects.

Stores of Acquired Knowledge.   The second oval in Fig. 7.1 represents the stores of acquired declarative and procedural knowledge. These stores are

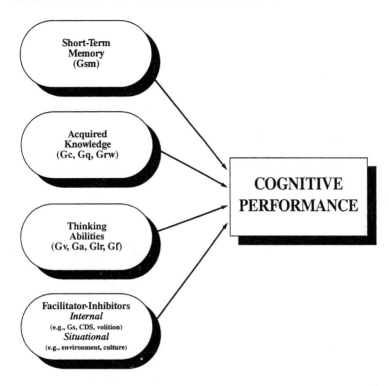

FIG. 7.1. *Gf-Gc* Cognitive performance model.

potentially available for access by short-term memory and subsequent processing. Declarative knowledge is our store of factual knowledge including concepts, rules, and relationships. Procedural knowledge is knowing how to perform processes and routines. Almost everything we do requires a mix of declarative and procedural knowledge. Current *Gf-Gc* research indicates that three psychometrically distinct stores of knowledge probably exist: verbal-conceptual knowledge (*Gc*), quantitative knowledge (*Gq*), and reading-writing knowledge (*Grw*).

Thinking Abilities. Thinking abilities are represented by the third oval in Fig. 7.1. These abilities are probably the core of what many professionals and lay persons mean by "intelligence." Thinking abilities allow an individual to process information that has been placed in short-term memory but cannot be processed automatically. A subject performs very easy cognitive tasks automatically, but must use one or more of the thinking abilities to perform difficult or novel tasks. New learning occurs primarily through the application of relevant thinking abilities. Current *Gf-Gc* research has identified at least four psychometrically distinct thinking abilities: visuospatial thinking

(Gv), auditory thinking (Ga), long-term storage-retrieval (Glr), and novel reasoning (Gf).

Facilitator-Inhibitors.   The last oval in Fig. 7.1 represents the facilitator-inhibitors. These factors modify cognitive performance for better or for worse, often overriding the effects of strengths or weaknesses in the previously described cognitive abilities. The source of some facilitator-inhibitors is internal (e.g., Gs, CDS, health, emotional state, and motivation/volition). The source of other facilitator-inhibitors is situational or environmental (e.g., the presence of visual and auditory distractions, the teaching method, or the tests selected for a cognitive examination).

Cultural diversity is a potential source of variables that may influence an individual's cognitive performance (Nuttall, De Leon, & Valle, 1990). These variables may be internal or situational, and their influences may be positive or negative. Being a member of any classification of cultural subgroup may predispose an individual to certain influences on self-concept, motivation, availability of educational opportunities, or quality of home environment, to name a few.

The organization of the Gf-Gc broad abilities into the Cognitive Performance Model (Fig. 7.1) was the result of a logical effort rather than an empirical process. This hypothesized organization of abilities is testable, and evidence of this organization, if valid, should be observable. Table 7.4 reports the results of one such endeavor. The data were gathered from 1,262 individuals in the WJ-R norming sample who had been administered the 29 tests incorporated in this analysis. These individuals were enrolled in school from kindergarten through college senior. The data analyzed were standard scores based on month of grade placement. The model specified for Table 7.4 was evaluated using the LISREL8 program.

Four of the columns in Table 7.4 represent the four categories of the Cognitive Performance Model. (Automatic processing speed is the only facilitator-inhibitor represented in this data.) Factor loadings for the following 12 measures are reported:

Memory for sentences—a measure of short-term memory (Gsm).

Memory for Words—a second measure of short-term memory (Gsm).

Gc(6)—the average score based on six verbal-conceptual knowledge tests (Picture Vocabulary, Oral Vocabulary, Listening Comprehension, Social Studies, Science, Humanities).

Gq(3)—the average score based on three quantitative knowledge tests (Calculation, Applied Problems, and Quantitative Concepts).

Grw(5)—the average score based on five tests of reading and writing (Letter-Word Identification, Passage Comprehension, Dictation, Proofing, and Writing Samples).

TABLE 7.4
Confirmatory Factor Analysis of the *Gf-Gc*
Cognitive Performance Model (N=1,262, Grades K to 16)

| | Factor Loadings | | | | |
Measure	Short-Term Memory	Stores of Knowledge	Thinking Abilities	Automatic Processing Speed	h²
Memory for sentences	.88	—	—	—	.78
Memory for words	.63	—	—	—	.40
Gc(6)	—	.81	—	—	.66
Gq(3)	—	.80	—	—	.65
Go(5)	—	.84	—	—	.70
Gv(3)	—	—	.55	—	.30
Ga(2)	—	—	.56	—	.32
Sound patterns	—	—	.44	—	.20
Glr(3)	—	—	.59	—	.35
Gf(2)	—	—	.68	—	.46
Visual matching	—	—	—	.80	.64
Crossout	—	—	—	.76	.58

Chi-square with 48 degrees of freedom = 420.

Root mean square error of approximation (RMSEA) = .078 (lower bound = .070, upper bound = .085).

P-value for test of close fit (RMSEA < .05) = .01.

Goodness of fit index (GFI) = 0.95.

$Gv(3)$—the average score based on three tests of visuospatial thinking (Visual Closure, Picture Recognition, and Spatial Relations).

$Ga(2)$—the average score based on two tests of auditory thinking (Sound Blending and Incomplete Words).

Sound Patterns—an additional test of auditory thinking.

$Glr(3)$—the average score based on three tests of long-term storage-retrieval (Memory for Names, Visual-Auditory Learning, and Delayed Recall—Memory for Names).

$Gf(2)$—the average score based on two tests of novel reasoning (Analysis-Synthesis, and Concept Formation).

Visual Matching—a measure of automatic processing speed (Gs).

Crossout—a second measure of automatic processing speed (Gs).

As noted previously, processing speed is the single representative in this dataset for the category of facilitator-inhibitors.

The fit statistics reported in Table 7.4 indicate that there is a reasonable fit of the data to this model (e.g., RMSEA = .078), although not as close as would be desired. Some tests used in the composites are factorially complex measures and, as a result, may not provide ideal data for testing this model. For example, *Ga(2)* produces a modification index suggesting that it should also be freed on the stores of knowledge. The Incomplete Words and Sound Blending tests do require *knowledge* of phonemic relationships and phonic processing. The Sound Patterns test does not and, therefore, may be the better marker for auditory thinking.

Tables 7.5 and 7.6 show two other analyses of the same data analyzed in Table 7.4. Table 7.5 presents the results for a hypothesized single-factor "g" model. The fit statistics indicate a much poorer fit (e.g., RMSEA = .120) when compared to the model tested in Table 7.4. Table 7.6 presents the results obtained after applying two modifications to the model specified in Table 7.4. Both modifications have some substantive justification, particularly the freeing of $Ga(2)$ on the stores of knowledge. The fit statistics for the model in Table 7.6 (e.g., RMSEA = .076) show only a slight improvement over the model evaluated in Table 7.4.

The results reported in Tables 7.4, 7.5, and 7.6 provide some empirical validation of the *Gf-Gc* Cognitive Performance Model. The fit of data to the model might be improved further by selecting variables that are purer measures of the broad factor to which they are assigned. It should be noted, however, that it is the hypothesized organization that is being evaluated, not the factorial structure of a particular battery of tests.

The next section describes an even more informative dynamic model of *Gf-Gc* abilities.

TABLE 7.5
Single-Factor Cognitive Performance Model (N = 1,262, Grades K to 16)

Measure	Factor Loading "g"	h^2
Memory for sentences	.59	.35
Memory for words	.45	.20
Gc(6)	.80	.63
Gq(3)	.79	.63
Go(5)	.83	.69
Gv(3)	.52	.27
Ga(2)	.55	.30
Sound patterns	.43	.18
Glr(3)	.56	.32
Gf(2)	.65	.42
Visual matching	.47	.22
Crossout	.45	.20

Chi-square with 54 degrees of freedom = 1,086
Root mean square error of approximation (RMSEA) = 0.120 (lower bound = .116, upper bound = .131).
P-value for test of close fit (RMSEA < .05) = .01.
Goodness of fit index (GFI) = 0.88.

TABLE 7.6
Confirmatory Factor Analysis of the Cognitive Performance Model With
Two Modifications (N = 1,262, Grades K to 16)

Measure	Factor Loadings				
	Short-Term Memory	Stores of Knowledge	Thinking Abilities	Processing Speed	h^2
Memory for sentences	.88	—	—	—	.78
Memory for words	.63	—	—	—	.40
Gc6)	—	.81	—	—	.66
Gq(3)	—	.80	—	—	.64
Go(5)	—	.84	—	—	.70
Gv(3)	—	—	.44	.20	.33
Ga(2)	—	.36	.20	—	.30
Sound patterns	—	—	.45	—	.20
Glr(3)	—	—	.61	—	.37
Gf(2)	—	—	.70	—	.48
Visual matching	—	—	—	.77	.60
Crossout	—	—	—	.79	.62

Chi-square with 48 degrees of freedom = 383.
Root mean square error of approximation (RMSEA) = .076 (lower bound = .068, upper bound = .085).
P-value for test of close fit (RMSEA < .05) = .01.
Goodness of fit index (GFI) = 0.95.

Gf-Gc Information Processing Model

The model portrayed in Fig. 7.1 organizes cognitive and noncognitive variables into four types of influence on cognitive performance. That model does not suggest how those influences interact in real time to produce cognitive performance. Fig. 7.2, the *Gf-Gc* Information Processing Model, is an extension of the *Gf-Gc* Cognitive Performance Model.

The horizontal dimension of Fig. 7.2 represents a single input-processing-output loop. Note that the sequence of arrows at the bottom of Fig. 7.2 indicates that the loop iterates with the output of one loop being the input for the following loop. Most mental operations require many iterative loops for completion.

The vertical dimension of Fig. 7.2 represents the complexity of processing extending from lower to higher. The complexity of processing increases from the reflexive level through the automatic level and on to the thinking and reasoning levels. A complete sequence of processing begins in the lower left-hand corner with the arrow labeled *physical stimuli* and ends with the two squares on the right side labeled *motor performance* and *cognitive performance.* Physical stimuli may derive from either external or internal sources. The path between physical stimuli and reflex action represents a reflex arc that is activated, for example, if one were to unexpectedly touch a hot object.

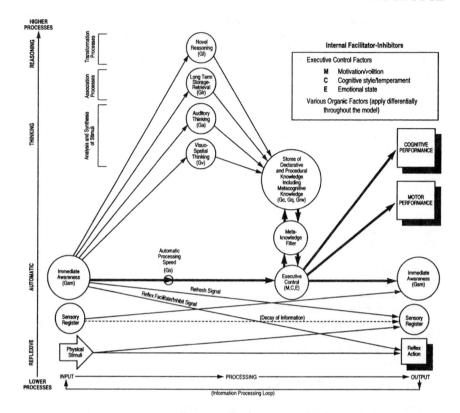

FIG. 7.2.   *Gf-Gc* Information processing model.

The second path from physical stimuli goes to a sensory register in the central nervous system. Information from the sensory register (return now to the input side of Fig. 7.2) is subsequently transmitted to immediate awareness. The span of information that can be held in immediate awareness is measured by tests of short-term memory, *Gsm*.

Executive control, or metacognitive monitoring, operates as the traffic director in this model. It accesses the metaknowledge filter and decides, often imperfectly, whether the needed declarative and/or procedural knowledge is known and available. If not, it generates a strategy for attempting to solve the problem.

What happens, according to this model, if you are asked a simple question such as "How do you spell your name?" The physical stimuli (hearing the question) enter the system and are transmitted to the sensory register and then on to immediate awareness. In turn, the question "How do you spell your name?" is processed by executive control that recognizes, through the metaknowledge filter, that the requested information is known and readily available in your store of acquired knowledge. The spelling of your name is retrieved in a chunk from the appropriate store of declarative knowledge, and your response to the question is represented by the motor and cognitive performance output squares in Fig. 7.2. The entire sequence from hearing the question to spelling your name has taken place at an automatic, or nearly automatic, level without any particular effort other than the willingness to perform the task.

The thicker lines in Fig. 7.2—the paths from immediate awareness through executive control and from stores of knowledge to motor and cognitive performance (and/or immediate awareness)—represent the freeway of cognitive processing. These are the high-speed, relatively simple paths used by tasks that can be performed automatically (or nearly so).

Automatic processing speed, a facilitator-inhibitor, is represented in Fig. 7.2 as a valve in the automatic paths of the model. Tests of *Gs* assess the speed with which simple automatic tasks can be completed.

Suppose the question is changed so that you are asked to spell your name backward. (As a personal introspective experiment, try it.) This information, the question, would proceed from physical stimuli through the sensory register to immediate awareness and to executive control. You have probably never spelled your name backward and, as a consequence, you must think! If you have needed to spell other words backward in the past, you may already have a stored procedure for this task. If so, executive control would relay that known procedure from the procedural knowledge store into immediate awareness along with the question to be answered. If no stored procedure for spelling your name backward is available, executive control works with metacognition to propose a strategy. It is that newly proposed strategy, rather than a previously learned procedure, that is placed in immediate awareness along with the question.

Most people approach the task of spelling their name backward with some strategy for visualizing their name, perhaps as if written on a chalkboard, and then reading off the letter names in reverse order while looking at the visual image in their "mind's eye." Executive control places this strategy into immediate awareness, and mental activity is directed along the path to visual thinking (*Gv*). The new information (letters of your name in reverse) is generated and passes through the knowledge store, leaving an imprint, on the way to cognitive performance and immediate awareness. If this task is practiced enough times, the backward spelling of your name would eventually be stored as a chunk in your store of acquired knowledge and could be retrieved automatically without thinking.

One or more of the four thinking abilities (*Gv, Ga, Glr, Gf*) become involved whenever an answer cannot be retrieved automatically from the stores of knowledge. Most daily cognitive activities are automatic. Spelling your name backward the first few times, however, requires thinking, because the task is novel. Which one or more of the four thinking abilities is called into action depends on the requirements of the task. If the task at hand requires the analysis and synthesis of visual stimuli, then it is primarily visuospatial thinking ability (Gv) that becomes engaged. If a task requires planning and creative problem solving, then novel reasoning (Gf) becomes engaged. The thinking abilities are not hierarchical in the sense that one is more important than, or subsumes, the other. In fact, most cognitive activities probably require the application of several different abilities, to a greater or lesser extent, during the course of completing a task.

A study of the Gf-Gc Information Processing Model suggests at least four implications for instruction and learning:

1. Automatic cognitive performance is constrained by short-term memory (Gsm) and processing speed (Gs).
2. New learning is constrained by the thinking abilities (Gv, Ga, Glr, Gf).
3. All performance (automatic or new learning) is constrained by the stores of knowledge (Gc, Gq, Go).
4. All performance (especially new learning) is constrained by facilitator-inhibitors.

It is generally believed that the capabilities underlying Implications 1 and 2 are not amenable to significant improvements and, if limited in an individual, require compensatory modifications in the environment (e.g., modifying an instructional presentation to accommodate a student's short-term memory deficit). Some writers and researchers are more optimistic, and a number of cognitive training programs are becoming available. On the other hand, the capabilities underlying Implications 3 and 4 are amenable to changes that can result in a significant improvement of cognitive performance. For example, stimulating students' interest in a topic that is to be studied is a well-known strategy for improving the cognitive performance of some learners.

At this time there has been no attempt to validate and revise the Gf-Gc Information Processing Model by testing hypotheses that can be derived from it. For example, hypotheses related to the four implications stated previously could be tested. Furthermore, the function of executive control in the model needs clarification and perhaps simplification. Certain of the functions ascribed in this model to executive control or the metaknowledge filter might be explained alternatively as "transitory applications" of relevant Gf-Gc abilities to a problem. For example, the metacognitive filter function credited with recognizing whether something is known might be more simply modeled as a transitory application of long-term storage-retrieval (Glr) to the problem. Perhaps determining a strategy, such as the one to be followed in spelling one's name backward, could be modeled as a transitory application of novel reasoning (Gf).

The next section presents a practical modification of the *Gf-Gc* Information Processing Model that makes it more useful for clinicians.

Gf-Gc Diagnostic Worksheet

Fig. 7.3 is a modification of the *Gf-Gc* Information Processing Model, and was developed as a diagnostic aid to help clinicians evaluate cognitive and noncognitive information about an individual. The cognitive performance rectangle has been modified to facilitate recording information about the referral question. The facilitator-inhibitors portion of the worksheet draws attention to and provides space for recording relevant information about several noncognitive variables that may be impacting cognitive performance. The letter designation for each type of facilitator-inhibitor also appears at an appropriate location in the model to suggest the impact (negative or positive) of that facilitator-inhibitor. For example, the A for vision/hearing is positioned between the physical stimuli arrow and the left-hand immediate awareness circle in Fig. 7.3. If the subject's vision or hearing is impaired, a minus sign can be placed in the space provided. The other four facilitator-inhibitor codes are found within the executive control circle. Within the circles representing immediate awareness, the thinking abilities, and the stores of acquired knowledge are spaces for recording scores obtained from

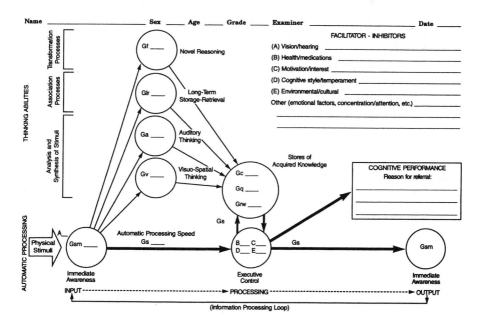

FIG. 7.3. *Gf-Gc* diagnostic worksheet.

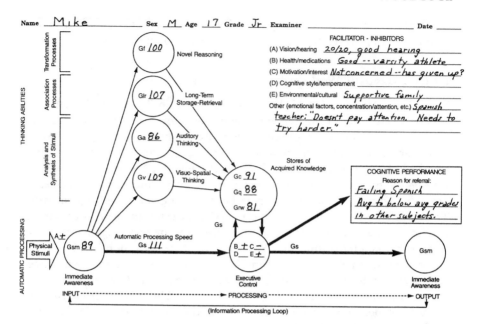

FIG. 7.4. The *Gf-Gc* diagnostic worksheet completed for a 17-year-old male.

the assessment. A space is provided to record the processing speed score (*Gs*) along the broad pathway of automatic processing.

Figure 7.4 presents an example of the *Gf-Gc* Diagnostic Worksheet after relevant information has been recorded for a subject. Mike is a 17-year-old high school junior who is experiencing marked difficulty in his Spanish language class. He was referred to the guidance counselor by his foreign language teacher. Mike's evaluation indicates that his vision and hearing are good and that his health is excellent. In fact, he is a varsity athlete in two sports. Mike does not appear concerned about his problems in the Spanish class and has more or less given up.

An examination of the standard score information in Fig. 7.4 suggests that Mike may have specific weaknesses in auditory thinking (*Ga*) and in short-term memory (*Gsm*). Furthermore, his basic reading and writing skills in English are rather low. (The *Grw* score reported here for Mike is the average of his Letter-Word Identification and Dictation test scores.) Mike's counselor concluded that his foreign language learning problem is probably associated with weaknesses in *Ga, Gsm,* and *Grw.* Lack of motivation is also a possible contributing factor. On further investigation, it was determined that Mike does fairly well in other classes and seems to like school. The Spanish class is the only negative school experience for him. The counselor concluded that Mike's lack of motivation in his Spanish class is probably a secondary effect of his difficulty in performing successfully. As a result of this evaluation, Mike is to be allowed to drop the Spanish course and substitute another class. Furthermore, the school will provide some remedial instruction in basic reading and writing skills, anticipating that improving Mike's ability in this area will enhance his performance in other aspects of the high school curriculum.

SUMMARY AND CONCLUSIONS

This chapter describes several efforts to extend modern cognitive theory into practice. The *Gf-Gc* theory is identified as the major empirical theory of multiple intelligences available today. The *Gf-Gc* Cognitive Performance Model organizes the *Gf-Gc* cognitive factors as well as several noncognitive factors into four functional categories. These categories include short-term memory, stores of acquired knowledge, thinking abilities, and facilitator-inhibitors. An even more explanatory view of intelligence is obtained by combining *Gf-Gc* theory with information processing theory. The *Gf-Gc* Information Processing Model is the result of that effort.

The concept of multiple intelligences can by made more usable for clinicians and researchers in at least two ways:

1. By providing better information about what the available cognitive tests actually measure, irrespective of their published labels.
2. By developing and validating good test batteries that measure multiple intelligences and are informative and practical for the practitioner to use.

Much of current test technology and the practice of assessment lags far behind cognitive science. More test developers and psychologists must change their concepts about the nature of intelligence in order to reduce this lag. It is predicted that cognitive tests of the future will be more complex, not simpler, as conscientious test developers strive to reduce the lag behind cognitive science.

REFERENCES

Carroll, J. B. (1993). *Human cognitive abilities: A survey of factor-analytic studies.* New York: Cambridge University Press.

Carroll, J. B., & Maxwell, S. E. (1979). Individual differences in cognitive abilities. *Annual Review of Psychology, 30,* 603–640.

Cattell, J. B. (1941). Some theoretical issues in adult intelligence testing. *Psychological Bulletin, 38,* 592.

Gardner, H. (1983). *Frames of mind: The theory of multiple intelligences.* New York: Basic.

Gardner, H. (1993). *Multiple intelligences: The theory in practice.* New York: Basic.

Gardner, H. (1994). Multiple intelligences theory. In R. J. Sternberg (Ed.), *Encyclopedia of human intelligence* (pp. 740–742). New York: Macmillan.

Horn, J. L. (1965). *Fluid and crystallized intelligence.* Unpublished doctoral dissertation, University of Illinois, Urbana-Champaign.

Horn, J. L. (1985). Remodeling old models of intelligence. In B. B. Wolman (Ed.), *Handbook of intelligence* (pp. 267–300). New York: Wiley.

Horn, J. L. (1988). Thinking about human abilities. In J. R. Nesselroade & R. B. Cattell (Eds.), *Handbook of multivariate psychology* (rev. ed., pp. 645–865). New York: Academic.

Horn, J. L. (1991). Measurement of intellectual capabilities: A review of theory. In K. S. Mc-Grew, J. K. Werder, & R. W. Woodcock, *WJ-R technical manual* (pp. 197–232). Chicago: Riverside.

Horn, J. L. (1994). Theory of fluid and crystallized intelligence. In R. J. Sternberg (Ed.), *Encyclopedia of human intelligence* (pp. 443–451). New York: Macmillan.

McGhee, R. (1993). Fluid and crystallized intelligence: Confirmatory factor analyses of the Differential Abilities Scale, Detroit Tests of Learning Aptitude-3, and Woodcock-Johnson Psycho-Educational Battery—Revised. *Journal of Psychoeducational Assessment Monograph Series: Advances in Psychoeducational Assessment. Woodcock-Johnson Psycho-Educational Battery—Revised* (pp. 20–38). Brandon, VT: Clinical Psychology Publishing.

McGrew, K. S. (1994a). *Clinical interpretation of the Woodcock-Johnson Tests of Cognitive Ability—Revised.* Boston: Allyn & Bacon.

McGrew, K. S. (1994b). Woodcock-Johnson Tests of Cognitive Ability—Revised. In R. J. Sternberg (Ed.), *Encyclopedia of human intelligence* (pp. 1152–1158). New York: Macmillan.

McGrew, K. S., Werder, J. K., & Woodcock, R. W. (1991). *WJ-R technical manual.* Chicago: Riverside.

Nuttall, E. V., De Leon, B., & Valle, M. (1990). Best practices in considering cultural factors. In A. Thomas & J. Grimes (Eds.), *Best practices in school psychology—II* (pp. 219–233). Washington, DC: National Association of School Psychologists.

Woodcock, R. W. (1990). Theoretical foundations of the WJ-R measures of cognitive ability. *Journal of Psychoeducational Assessment, 8,* 231–258.

Woodcock, R. W. (1993). An information processing view of *Gf–Gc* theory. *Journal of Psychoeducational Assessment Monograph Series: Advances in Psychoeducational Assessment. Woodcock-Johnson Psycho-Educational Battery—Revised* (pp. 80–102). Brandon, VT: Clinical Psychology Publishing.

Woodcock, R. W. (1994). Measures of fluid and crystallized theory of intelligence. In R. J. Sternberg (Ed.), *Encyclopedia of human intelligence* (pp. 452–456). New York: Macmillan.

Woodcock, R. W., & Johnson, M. B. (1977). *Woodcock-Johnson Psycho-Educational Battery.* Chicago: Riverside.

Woodcock, R. W., & Johnson, M. B. (1989). *Woodcock-Johnson Psycho-Educational Battery—Revised.* Chicago: Riverside.

III

POSTER SESSION PAPERS

8

Contemporary Statistical Models for Examining Test Bias

John J. McArdle
University of Virginia

One of the most controversial aspects of research on human cognitive abilities emerges in studies of group differences. Controversy arises whenever group differences are found using psychological measurements, especially when interpretations are made about the likely sources of these differences. The popular terms *test fairness, cultural fairness,* and *test bias* refer to fundamental problems in measuring group differences between majority and minority groups. The controversies surrounding these issues can lead to a variety of social and political problems for both the research and the researcher (e.g., Husén, 1978; Scarr, 1981, 1988; Snyderman & Rothman, 1990).

There are many definitions of test bias and the differences among these definitions remain unclear and are often confused (see Berk, 1982; Bond, 1994; Cole, 1981; Flaugher, 1978; Hartigan, 1990; Linn, 1984; Reynolds & Brown, 1984). But the broad scientific question raised here is a fundamental one: To what degree are the observed group differences reflections of real underlying psychological processes, and to what degree are these difference reflections of the way the psychological tests were constructed? This is a fundamental question in psychological measurement and, because it is directly related to issues of "fairness or unfairness," it is also an issue of major importance in public policy debates.

In 1989 my colleagues and I began examining these questions using several current models of test bias applied to academic data collected on college student-athletes. In this statistical research we focused on a critical question: How can we properly evaluate the fairness or unfairness of new academic rules for initial eligibility to participate in college sports programs? In carrying out this research, we created a set of summary statistics and models which have been considered key evidence in public policy debates (see NCAA, 1991a, 1991b, 1991c, 1992). Selected aspects of these data are presented briefly here. Four kinds of models of test bias are defined and applied to these data, including bias due to (a) sampling, (b) selection, (c) prediction, and (d) measurement. The results of each analyses are summarized, and some limitations and advantages of each approach are discussed.

These contemporary statistical modeling methods offer useful possibilities for the objective scientific research, and scientific objectivity can be critical in many public policy debates. Scientific results are often selectively used by advocates to support a prespecified position, and there is a need to further define the appropriate relationship between the research and the researcher (e.g., Campbell, 1988; Coleman, 1990; Cronbach, 1976; Husén, 1978). One broad goal of this chapter is to encourage more work toward an appropriate balance of both objective and subjective issues.

A Contemporary Model of Test Bias

The term *test bias* is used here to denote a type of modeling analysis. A few simple statistical assumptions form the basis of these analyses:

1. There are *always some differences* between minority and majority groups in some way. The observation of large group differences is typically a necessary but not sufficient condition for test bias.
2. Test bias is reflected in some form of *conditional group difference.* We ask a question such as: For two different individuals in different groups, assuming all else is equal, how large are the differences between their observed scores?
3. A mathematical model can be used to *quantify* the form, direction, and magnitude of these conditional differences. In most models, test bias refers to group differences that remain after other critical predictors are taken into account.
4. A statistical model can be used to *evaluate* the accuracy, precision, or confidence of these quantities. These results can be used to rule out spurious effects due to sample size or sample bias, and allow direct and appropriate comparisons among different research studies.

These kind of assumptions are not novel, but they can have considerable impact in a data analysis approach to understanding test bias issues. For example, we do not try to answer common questions such as: Is test *X* biased against group *B*? This is the kind of "yes or no" question that cannot be dealt with without a variety of ambiguous assumptions about design and inference (e.g., see Cohen, 1994). Instead, we ask: How much, and in what way, is test X biased against group B, and how certain are we about these results? This explicitly means that all tests are biased in some way and the data analysis should be designed to examine the form, direction, magnitude, and accuracy of these biases. This approach allows tests to be "biased" against the larger (majority) groups, although this is unlikely in practice. More critically, this approach allows us to move away from simple yes or no opinions and toward answers for some difficult scientific questions.

Sample Data on Academic and Athletics

Since 1984, the *National Collegiate Athletic Association (NCAA)* Research Committee has been collecting survey information on the academic performances of large samples ($N > 12,000$) of college *student-athletes (SA)*. The NCAA *Academic Performance Study (APS)* data include information on academic performances in high school, such as grades and ACT–SAT test scores; in college, such as grades and matriculation status, and also information about the college, such as average class SAT–ACT and graduation rates. Data from the first 2 years of this study (1984–1985 longitudinal records) were selected for analysis for two reasons—these high-school seniors were admitted to college before the new initial eligibility rules were put into effect, and a 5-year college record is now available. A statistical summary of the available data from the first two years of this study is presented in Table 8.1 (also see McArdle & Hamagami, 1994; NCAA, 1991a, 1991b, 1991c).

These data include approximately 4,500 SA who entered 81 different Division I colleges in 1984 and 1985. For the purposes of the analyses to follow, we eliminated records: (a) having implausible data (2%), (b) with incomplete longitudinal data (23%), (c) non-U.S. citizens (4%), or (d) with missing data on key variables (5%). We also used only records where the race/ethnicity question was answered as either "White Non-Hispanic" or "Black," and this eliminated a small percentage of students (3%) who were either Asian, Native American, or Alaskan Native, Asian or Pacific Islander, or Hispanic. A college graduate was defined here as a student-athlete who graduated from the institution he or she initially attended within five years. We eliminated information from a very small set of SA (< .5%) at 14 colleges where the graduation outcomes were identical for all SA (e.g., no SA within the school graduated). Using these selection criteria, we obtained complete information on 3,224 student-athletes from 68 different colleges.

These selections lead to the statistics for the 1984–1985 freshman student-athletes presented in Table 8.1. Data from the two cohorts are presented separately, and some sampling differences between 1984 and 1985 can be seen here. These cohort sampling differences turn out to be minor in comparison with other group differences. Overall, about 75% of these SA were reported by the college as being White (Caucasian, Non-Hispanic), whereas about 25% were reported by the college as being Black. The overall graduation rates were obtained 5 years later (in 1990 and 1991). On average, the graduation rates are about 50% overall, above 50% for White SA, and closer to 30% for Black SA. Confidence boundaries for these rates are very small, so these group differences are relatively large. This disparity in the graduation rates for White and Black students is not unusual, and matches other national statistics (e.g., Porter, 1990).

Reasons for these group differences in graduation rates are not clear. One possibility raised by previous research is that the White and Black student groups differ in their precollege academic skills. In Table 8.1, the average Core-GPA for all SAs is about 2.9 (on the usual 4-point scale), but this average GPA is closer to 3.0 for White SA and about 2.5 for Black SA. In this same table, the average SAT or ACT scores for all SA is about 870 (on the 1984 SAT 400–1200 scale), but this average is closer to 940 for White SA and about 670 for Black SA. These observed group differences are more than one standard deviation (s.d.) unit in size, but these results are not atypical (see Klitgaard, 1985; Porter, 1990).

TABLE 8.1

A Statistical Summary of the Student-Athlete Data for 1984–1985
Freshman From the NCAA Academic Performance Study (APS)

Student Groups	1984 Freshman		1985 Freshman	
Sample representation:				
Overall SA	1,789	(100.%)	1,658	(100.%)
White SA	1,329	(74.3%)	1,250	(75.4%)
Black SA	460	(25.7%)	408	(24.6%)
Graduation rates (5 years post entry):				
Overall	50.8%	(±2.3)	46.4%	(±2.4)
White SA	58.0%	(±2.6)	51.9%	(±2.8)
Black SA	29.8%	(±4.2)	29.7%	(±4.4)
Entering H.S. core GPA (based on 4-point scale):				
Overall	2.89	(±0.03)	2.83	(±0.03)
White SA	3.05	(±0.03)	2.94	(±0.03)
Black SA	2.43	(±0.05)	2.49	(±0.05)
ACT–SAT Test Scores (Z score in SAT units)				
Overall	881	(±11)	865	(±10)
White SA	955	(±10)	928	(±10)
Black SA	667	(±16)	674	(±18)

Notes: Data extracted from various 1991 NCAA Reports.
Percentages are followed by the approximate 95% margin of error.
Ethnicity determined by questionnaire response of school administrator.
Mean Core GPA and ACT–SAT are followed by 95% confidence interval.

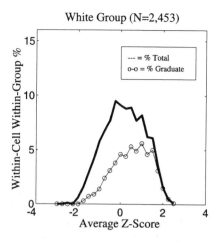
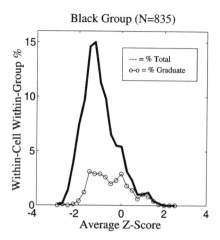

FIG. 8.1. Summary distributions of average Z-scores (GPA and test composite) for White and Black student-athlete groups. Notes: These numerical values are identical to those listed in Table 8.1.

Average Z is formed as a simple average of two precollege variables—the CGPA Z-score and the test Z-score (either SAT or ACT in a Z-score form).

Percentage total is the percentage at or below the current Z-value, based on either $N = 2,453$ (White) or $N = 835$ (Black) enrolled SA. Percentage graduate is a percentage at or below the current Z-value based on $N = 1,282$ (White) or $N = 222$ (Black) graduated SAs.

As a simple summary of more information about high school academic skills, we calculated additional variables: ZTEST indicates a standardized Z-score for SAT, ACT, or both; ZCGPA indicates a Z-score for high school grades in 11 "core" courses; Average is an equally weighted combination of the Z-score forms of both variables. Fig. 8.1 shows the frequency distribution of these average Z-scores separately for the White (75%) and Black (25%) groups. Once again, large differences in these distributions are seen between the White and Black students. The White SA have a symmetric distribution centered around $Z = 0$, whereas the Black SA have a skewed distribution centered just below $Z = -1$. In both groups, the distribution of the SA who graduated shows generally higher average Z scores (for details, see McArdle & Hamagami, 1994).

Evaluating Policy on Academics and Athletics

The substantive basis of this research is based on a contemporary issue in college athletics—the NCAA initial eligibility rule colloquially known as "Prop 48." This rule was named after the number of the legislative proposition at the 1983 NCAA convention and defined minimum academic requirements for high school students who wanted to participate in any NCAA-sanctioned sports in their first year of college. Among these requirements were a high school diploma, at least a 2.0 grade point average based on 11 core courses (e.g., English, Math, Science, etc.), *and* a national achievement test score of either an SAT ≥ 700 or an ACT ≥ 17. These specific cutoff values (of 2.0 and 700 or 17, respectively) were selected by various committees during 1983 using methods that have not been documented. The introduction of this rule in 1983 as an eligibility requirement for all freshman student-athletes generated a great deal of controversy (e.g., Ervin, Saunders & Gillis, 1984; Hargadon, 1984; Jenifer, 1984; Williams, 1983).

Since 1983, a variety of data collected by the NCAA have been used to examine the impact of and potential bias in this rule. The data in Table 8.1 and Fig. 8.1 show at least two key features: (a) there were large differences in the graduation rates between Black and White student-athlete groups, and (b) there were large differences in the initial distributions of high school academic performances between the two groups. The inferences that were quickly made from these data include: (c) the high school academic performances are precursors of the lower graduation rates for the Black students; and, at the same time, (d) the large group differences in the high school national test scores (SAT and ACT; e.g., Fig. 8.1) show primary evidence of test bias against the minority students.

These kinds of data seem to lead to inconsistent statements about the adequacy of the Prop 48 policy. However, researchers with statistical training will recognize that inferences (c) and (d) do not follow from results (a) and (b). At very least, inferences about the individual level effects cannot be assured on the basis of aggregate data. Such simplistic and improper inferences are instances of the well known *aggregation or ecological fallacy* (e.g., Goodman, 1953, 1959; Lohmöller & Falter, 1986; Robinson, 1950). Unfortunately, these inferences appear in published newspaper articles and other public forums, and even in reports of otherwise well-designed scientific research. This leads us to a key question: Are there any appropriate ways to understand these kinds of data? The remainder of this chapter explicates some contemporary modeling analyses designed to deal with this intriguing question.

MODELING SAMPLING BIAS

Defining Sampling Bias

The first models presented here are based on one of the most familiar questions about group differences: Do groups appear to differ because of the sampling conditions of the study? This is an initial question in most any research study, and we use it here as a relatively simple starting point for defining our methodology.

The first question in the public debate around such issues is generally: Is the study sample representative of the population of interest? Although this is often phrased as a question about proportionality and sizes of groups, we can write this in a more formal fashion as

$$\Pi = Probability\ [Included\ in\ the\ Sample\ |\ Population] \qquad (1)$$

where Π indicates the probability of an individual (or other unit) being selected for participation in the study sample given that the person is a member of the population of interest. Using this notation, we can further define

$$Bias\{Sampling\} = \mathcal{F}\{\Pi^{(a)} - \Pi^{(b)}\} \qquad (2)$$
$$= \mathcal{F}\{\Delta\Pi\},$$

where the superscripts a and b indicate membership in two different groups, and the $\mathcal{F}$ indicates some quantifiable function of the difference ($\Delta\Pi$) between the two probabilities. Here it is important to note that Π is the probability of inclusion in the sample *within* each group and not the simple proportion of persons of each group included. Thus, to the degree that groups $\Pi^{(a)} \neq \Pi^{(b)}$ (or $\Delta\Pi \neq 0$), then the sampling procedure for the study can be said to be biased with respect to these groups. If the group excluded from the study at a higher rate also happens to be a minority group, then the study design itself reflects a sampling bias against the minority group. The direction, size, and precision of this function need to be quantified before we can evaluate these kind of impacts.

Sampling Bias Results

At the initiation of the NCAA-APS survey, 301 Division I colleges were randomly stratified into one of five cohorts for sampling, and the first two cohorts included 55 colleges sampled in 1984 and 55 different colleges sampled in 1985. Members of each of these 110 colleges were contacted, and 82 (74.5%) completed at least some parts of the survey. All student-athletes within each school were reported on for as long as they remained at the school. Fig. 8.2 is a display of the frequency of different levels of ACT or SAT scores for the individual student-athletes (Student Test) compared to the average ACT or SAT scores for the students at the school they entered (School Test). These data show a broad positive relationship at the extremes of the two scores, but only a small relationship in the middle ranges. Unfortunately, this potentially informative result is limited by our sampling of schools. That is, before any inference to the general population is made, we must first examine selection bias at the school level.

The sampling question of initial interest here is a comparison of schools that participated in the 1984–1985 APS sample versus all other NCAA Division-I colleges. A summary of the statistical information from eight univariate comparisons is presented in Table 8.2. Each comparison was based on either an independent groups t-test (ANOVA for continuous variables), an x^2 test (logit for categorical variables), or a more complex univariate model. For example, the variable "Percentage of Minority Students" within each school is listed as 20.7% in the 1984–1985 sample (82 schools) and 21.7% among the other schools (220 schools). The percentages for each school were transformed to a more symmetric distribution (using a logit equation), the two groups were compared using a t-test, and the results show no accurate differences between groups (i.e., no test was significant at the $\alpha = .05$ test level). Among 15 college-level variables studied (including the 8 listed in Table 8.2), only three variables showed statistical differences between the participating and nonparticipating schools: The APS schools include schools with a larger number of undergraduates, full-time faculty, and athletic scholarships.

Two more elaborate multivariate model of sampling differences were also used to examine sampling bias. The first was based on a discriminant analysis model in which the 15 variables from each college were treated as a vector. Under the assumption of equal within-group covariance matrices, this test of the equality of mean vectors (centroids) is equivalent to a Hotelling's

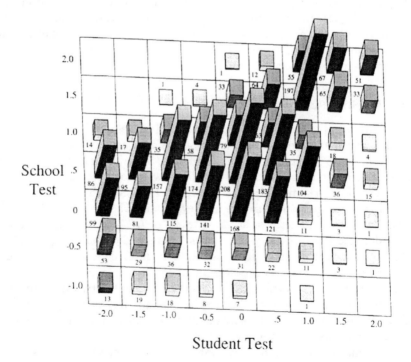

FIG. 8.2. Bivariate frequency distribution of the SAT for the student-athletes, and the average SAT scores for the entering class of the colleges they attended.

TABLE 8.2
A Statistical Summary of the NCAA College Data
for Sampling Bias Analysis

College Variables	APS 1984–1985 Sample N ≈ 81 Colleges Mean (s.d.)		Other Division I Sample N ≈ 220 Colleges Mean (s.d.)	
Number undergraduates	12,724	(7,865)	10,635	(7,572)
Graduation rate	53.7%	(19.7)	52.6%	(19.9)
Percentage minority	20.7%	(18.4)	21.7%	(22.8)
Percentage private	24.7%	(43.4)	36.2%	(48.2)
Student/faculty ratio	12.6%	(4.8)	12.9	(5.2)
Total cost	$12,956	(5,127)	$13,465	(5,158)
Student body H.S. GPA	3.10	(0.27)	3.09	(0.28)
Student body ACT-SAT Z	0.61	(.060)	0.57	(0.60)

Notes: Data extracted from 1993 CEEB Undergraduate Institutions database
Accuracy of group differences discussed in text.

T^2 or two-group MANOVA with 15 variables. The overall multivariate test (Wilk's $\Lambda = .08$) suggested the group differences hypothesis was not accurate (at the $\alpha = .05$ test level), and no further follow-up tests were conducted. A relaxation of the within-group covariance assumption did not alter this result. The second multivariate model of group differences was based on a logit regression model (Hosmer & Lemeshow, 1989; McArdle & Hamagami, 1994). In these models, the outcome was a binary variable (1 = included, 0 = not included), and 15 predictors were used. In theory, these logit models produce equivalent results to the discriminant analysis models in cases where the outcome proportions are equal. Thus, and not surprisingly, these models also failed to distinguish any notable predictors of the sample differences.

Limitations of Sampling Bias Analyses

The statistical models used previously deal with only one kind of question, but they illustrate several key points. These comparisons require independent groups, so the group comparisons are made between the study sample and the population minus the sample. The results here show that the initial sampling bias is relatively small, and the only differences found here come because fewer private schools agreed to participate in the first 2 years of the survey (for more details, see McArdle & Hamagami, 1994; NCAA, 1992).

This example also illustrates how we deal with group comparisons of more complex forms. That is, we did not find any sizable group differences here, so we assume that the first group of colleges are a random sample of all colleges of interest (i.e., NCAA Division I schools). Because there are no sampling differences, we do not need to make any further statistical adjustments or corrections (e.g., using weighted data, etc.). At the same time, we also recognize some limitations of this approach. Lack of differences may come about because the number of sampling units used is so small ($N = 301$), leading to low statistical power, and possibly because we have only examined a few highly correlated variables. The differences observed are not large enough, given the background variation of these variables, to make a reasonably accurate statement about these group differences. Thus, and in contrast to more typical statements about statistical significance, we say that our analyses have *not accurately (n.a.)* determined any group differences.

MODELING SELECTION BIAS

Defining Selection Bias

The next models presented here are based on one of the most familiar questions about group differences: Does the use of a test score for selection result in unfairly favoring one group over another? This is a central question in personnel selection, entry to clinical services, admissions to special jobs programs, and admission to higher education. It is also a key question in the public debate around such issues.

Terms such as *unfair* or *biased* are not easy terms to define, because they are used in many different ways. However, if we try to relate these terms to the initial selection question raised earlier, we can make a formal statement of fairness: For all persons in all groups who reach the same criterion, the rule should make the same selection decision. To the degree that this does not happen the rule is deemed unfair. More formally, we can write

$$\Pi_c = Probability[Selection \mid Criterion = True] \qquad (3)$$

so Π_c indicates the probability of an individual being selected by some test given that the criterion is true. Using this notation, we can define

$$Bias\{Selection\} = \mathcal{F}\{\Pi_c^{(a)} - \Pi_c^{(b)}\} \qquad (4)$$
$$= \mathcal{F}\{\Delta\Pi_c\},$$

where, as in equation (2), the superscripts a and b indicate membership in two different groups, and the $\mathcal{F}$ indicates some quantifiable function of the difference $\Delta\Pi_c$} between the group probabilities. This equation goes one step beyond the previous sampling bias model, because here we assume we have identified the same kind of individual (i.e., *Criterion = True*) in different groups (a and b), and an unbiased selection mechanism should lead to the same decision for both persons. To the degree the same decision rate does not occur ($\Pi_c^{(a)} \neq \Pi_c^{(b)}$ or $\Delta\Pi_c \neq 0$), then the selection procedure using this test is unfair. If the group that is excluded at a higher rate also happens to be a minority group, then the use of the test for this purpose leads to selection bias against the minority group. Once again, the direction, size, and accuracy of these statements need to be calculated before we can evaluate these kind of impacts.

Decision Theory Methods

Particularly good technical discussions of selection bias can be found in research on *decision theory analysis*. Detailed overviews can be found in the work of Wiggins (1973), Swets (1988), and Lindley (1985), and specific examples on college admissions are discussed in the work of Gross and Su (1975), Breland and Ironson (1976), Cronbach (1976), Linn (1976), Novick and Peterson (1976), Sawyer, Cole, and Cole (1976), Peterson and Novick (1976), and Crouse and Trusheim (1988).

One way to apply these decision theory methods to the NCAA questions is based on a retrospective examination of the data. We can compare the observed academic status of the individual, as a success or nonsuccess, with the theoretical declaration of a specific eligibility rule, as eligible or not eligible. This classical approach leads us to four key classifications of students labeled in Table 8.3A as true negatives, false negatives, false positives, and true positives. For example, true negatives are persons who would have been declared not eligible by the specific rule and in fact did not succeed by some academic criterion (e.g., graduation). In contrast, false negatives are persons who would have been declared not eligible by the specific rule but in fact did succeed by the same academic criterion.

We further expand this analysis by adding a separate category for two student-athlete groups, White SA and Black SA, as defined in Table 8.3B. This leads to four kinds of eligibility decisions that turn out to be correct predictions of later graduation status, labeled *decision benefits*. This also leads to four kinds of incorrect eligibility decisions, labeled *decision costs*. The comparison of costs versus benefits is a key issue in the comparison of different rules.

The costs and benefits can be calculated from any data that are observed without censoring. From the NCAA data presented earlier, we can create a wide variety of frequency tables (as in Table 8.3) for a large number of different cutoff scores. This procedure yields different estimates of each of the eight cells for each cutoff. As an illustration here, Fig. 8.3 is a plot of the eight observed cell frequencies of Table 8.3B (labeled $B1$ to $B4$, and $C1$ to $C4$) as a function of the use of a cutoff score on the composite variable (the average Z) defined earlier.

If we wish to make a rational and objective decision that is in some sense both fair and optimal for these data, we need a strategy for *weighting the costs against benefits*. In most decision models the outcomes are not all of equal importance, and the choice of a utility structure (or a payoff matrix)

TABLE 8.3
Overview of Decision Tables for Selection Bias Models

A. Standard decision table

Observed Outcome (from Actual Data)

		Nonsuccess	*Success*	*Total*
Expected by Eligibility Rule	Not eligible	True Negative (TN): not eligible and did not succeed	False Negative (FN): not eligible but did succeed	TN + FN: Number declared not eligible
	Eligible	False Positive (FP): eligible but did not succeed	True Positive (TP): eligible and did succeed	FP + TP: Number declared eligible
	Total	TN + FP: Number of nonsuccesses	FN + TP: Number of successes	TN + FN + FP + TP: Total number of persons

B. Decision table including group differences

Observed Outcome

		White		*Black*		*Total*
		Nonsuccess	*Success*	*Nonsuccess*	*Success*	
Expected by Eligibility Rule	Not eligible	Benefit(1)	Cost(2)	Benefit(3)	Cost(4)	Frequency (NE)
	Eligible	Cost(1)	Benefit(2)	Cost(3)	Benefit(4)	Frequency (E)
	Total	Frequency (WNS)	Frequency (WS)	Frequency (BNS)	Frequency (BS)	Frequency (N)

C. An example of a MIXED-weight utility structure (from Gross & Su, 1975)

Observed Outcome

		White		*Black*	
		Nonsuccess	*Success*	*Nonsuccess*	*Success*
Expected by Eligibility Rule	Not eligible	+1	−3	+1	−5
	Eligible	−1	+2	−1	+3

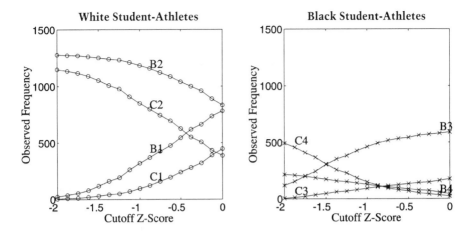

FIG. 8.3. Costs (C) and benefits (B) components for different cutoffs using the average Z-score as an initial eligibility rule (see Table 8.3 and text for description).

becomes important (Lindley, 1985). Any utility weight W is defined here as a real number (e.g., 1, 2, −1, −3, 15.5, etc.) assigned to each of the outcomes presented earlier. The overall *expected utility* (*EU*) for any cutpoint (or threshold t) can then be formed as the sum of the products of these frequencies and weights (i.e., $EU(t) = \Sigma_{i=1}^{8} [F_i(t) \times W_i]$ and the cutoff score (t) with a *maximum EU* can be selected as the best rule for the state goals.

An example of the some utility weights are taken from Gross and Su (1976) and defined in Table 8.3C. This set of utilities is unbalanced with respect to both false negatives and true positives, and with respect to the weights assigned to majority and minority groups. The false negatives count the most (−3 and −5), but the true positives are also important (+2 and +3). Also, the black (minority) group counts more in both cases (e.g., −5 and +3 for Black SA versus −3 and +2 for White SA). The unique parts of this table are not based in the absolute values of the numbers, but are a function of the ratios of the numbers used within the four columns (McArdle, Hamagami, & Paskus, 1994).

Selection Bias Results

In the selection bias analysis that follows, we try to address two key questions about the previous student-athlete data: Is the current cutoff score biased, and what alternative cutoff score should be used? In previous reports we used a variety of decision theory models and analyses to examine the test-score and grade-score cutoffs (but see McArdle, Hamagami, & Paskus, 1994; NCAA, 1991b, 1991c). A selected set of these results are presented here.

Table 8.4 shows the potential effects of three possible initial eligibility

TABLE 8.4
Projected Outcomes of NCAA
Initial Eligibility Rules for Selection Bias Models
(Percentages with one-year projected samples size in parentheses).

| | Alternative Eligibility Rules | | | | | |
| | Pre-86 | | Prop 48 | | Index II | |
Projected Outcomes	%	(N)	%	(N)	%	(N)
A: Declared Ineligible						
Overall	0.0	(0)	27.0	(3,400)	19.6	(2,470)
White	0.0	(0)	13.6	(1,290)	8.7	(820)
Black	0.0	(0)	66.2	(2,090)	52.2	(1,640)
White-Black Difference	0.0	(0)	-52.6	(-800)	-43.5	(-820)
B: False Negatives						
Overall	0.0	(0)	6.4	(810)	3.8	(480)
White	0.0	(0)	3.9	(370)	2.1	(200)
Black	0.0	(0)	13.5	(420)	8.8	(280)
White-Black Difference	0.0	(0)	-9.6	(-50)	-6.8	(-80)
C: False Positives						
Overall	54.3	(6,840)	29.7	(3,740)	35.1	(4,420)
White	44.5	(4,210)	34.1	(3,220)	37.9	(3,580)
Black	70.0	(2,210)	16.6	(520)	26.7	(840)
White-Black Difference	-25.5	(2,000)	17.4	(2,700)	11.2	(2,740)
D: Graduates (if eligible)						
Overall	45.7	(6,190)	59.0	(7,430)	56.4	(7,110)
White	55.5	(5,240)	60.2	(5,690)	58.5	(5,560)
Black	30.0	(950)	49.8	(1,570)	44.3	(1,400)
White–Black Difference	25.5	(4,290)	10.4	(4,120)	14.2	(4,160)

Notes: Pre-86 = 1989–1990 final graduation rates without censoring.

Prop 48 = Censoring with h.s. core-GPA = 2.0 and SAT =700 or ACT = 17.

Index II = Compensatory rule set at $Z \approx -1.2$ (e.g., core = 2.40 and test = 650/16).

All cell entries are calculated using just-cited formulas and then rounded.

1984–1985 freshman student-athletes $N = 3,417$ from $C = 82$ colleges (see NCAA Report #91–01; Presented Feb. 1991, Feb. 1994; McArdle & Hamagami, 1994).

Sample size projections based on 1984–1985 yearly population of $N = 12,600$ total, 9,450 White; and 3,150 Black student-athletes.

rules where college graduation is the academic outcome. The rule in the first column of Table 8.4 is labeled *Pre-86* because here we show the basic outcomes before the new rules were put into effect (in 1986). All SA in the 1984–1985 data were declared eligible, so the corresponding ineligibility row in Table 8.4 is empty. These specific percentages of Table 8.4 can also be used to make numerical projections of the number of student-athletes nationwide each year (based on about 12,600 SA in about 300 Division I colleges). Under the Pre-86 rule, about 54.3% (or 6,840 SA nationwide) were declared as eligible but did not graduate (false positives), whereas about 45.7% (5,760

SA), were both eligible and graduates (true positives in this case). Also, 55.5% of the White SA were graduates, whereas about 30.0% of the Black SA were graduates.

The second rule is labeled *Prop 48*, because here we show several outcomes that might have occurred if the current NCAA eligibility rule had been adopted 2 years earlier (in 1984) and no individual had changed his or her behavior. Under this new rule, 27% (3,410) of the 1984–1985 SA would have been declared as ineligible. Although it is not clear in this table, about 95% of these ineligibles would have been the result of a "lower than minimum" SAT or ACT score. This result is most dramatic for Black SA, of whom 66.2% (2,090) would have been declared ineligible, whereas only 13.6% (1,290) of White SA would have been declared ineligible. The differences in the within-group percentages (−52.6%) and projected frequencies (−800) clearly show a differential impact on the Black group.

A different selection impact is seen in the four rows under false negatives (FN). These entries describe the number of graduates who would have been declared as ineligible by the rule. These are the raw cell percentages (from Table 8.3) and not the alternative FN rates (i.e., FN / [FN + TN]) used in other applications of decision theory. These percentages show that when Prop 48 criteria are applied to the 1984–1985 classes, 6.4% (or 810) of all graduates would have been declared ineligible. The corresponding outcomes for the Black student-athletes (13.5%, 420 SA) are clearly larger than for the White student-athletes (3.9%, 370 SA). The White–Black difference (−9.6%, −50 SA) is again disproportional and, by standard statistical conventions, this effect is considered accurate (i.e., the 95% confidence boundaries of the proportions do not overlap).

The last two sets of rows of the Prop 48 column tell a slightly different story that also needs to be considered. Here, we see the false positive (FP) rates (29.7%T, 34.1%W, and 16.6%B) are much smaller than the corresponding rates in the *Pre-86* columns (54.3%T, 44.5%W, and 70.0%B). This implies that the Prop 48 rule is more accurate at identifying the nongraduates and declaring them as ineligible. This identification of false positives leads to an increased graduation rate for those that would be admitted; overall from 45.7% to 59.0%, for White SA from 55.5% to 60.2%, and for Black SA from 30.0% to 49.8%. This increase in the graduation rates for eligible students is naturally considered a benefit, and it is an indirect result of selecting out those SA with lower test scores (see Fig. 8.1).

The third rule in Table 8.4 is labeled *Index II* and this is (a) based on a cutoff on the equally weighted average Z-score and (b) uses a cutting score of $Z = -1.2$. This kind of combination is often termed an "indexing" rule, and this specific cutoff is one of several cutoffs defined in previous reports (see NCAA 1991c). Using an Index II rule, the overall number declared ineligible is substantially lower (19.6%, 2,470 SA) and the White–Black difference is smaller (−43.5%, −820 SA). The false negative percentage is also low-

ered to 3.8% (480 SA), so 2.6% (330 SA) more graduates would be declared -
eligible under this rule compared with Prop 48. The White–Black false negative difference is also lowered (from −9.6% to −6.8%), so these unintended
impacts are decreased in both groups. In contrast, the false positive percentages of Index II are higher than are those in Prop 48, and this leads to slightly
decreased graduation rates. The Index II graduation rates (56.4%T, 58.5%W,
and 44.3%B) are projected to be much higher than the pre-86, but are projected to be slightly lower than those found with the Prop 48 rule.

Using the previous logic of expected utilities, we can compare the projected impacts of these rules against one another in a more formal fashion.
To illustrate this point, we separately multiply the implied frequencies in
Table 8.4 by the utility weights in Table 8.3C and obtain three separate estimates of the expected utility for each rule: EU(Pre-86) = 1875 or 72.5%,
EU(Prop 48) = 1892 or 72.6%, and EU(Index II) = 2084 or 74.1%. All three options are very close, but the Index II achieves the highest EU, so it can be
considered the best choice of the three options by less than 2%.

This approach also provides a formal way to a search for an objectively defined optimal cutoff score. In this kind of a search, we select a variable and
a utility structure and examine the EU over a reasonable range of cutoff
scores. To illustrate this procedure, we now use the Average Z-score variable
described in Fig. 8.1. As it turns out, the data presented in Fig. 8.3 are quite
informative because they can be used to calculate EU for any clearly defined
utility structure.

In the first plot of Fig. 8.4A we illustrate the EU score as a function of different cutoff values on the Average Z variable with Mixed weights (Table
8.3C). The 72.5% value can be found as the Y-axis when the X-axis is $Z = -1$.
The overall function plotted increases gradually from $Z = -2$ to about $Z =
-1.2$, and then declines rapidly as it approaches $Z = 0$. This value of $Z = -1.2$
yields an $EU\% = 74\%$, and this is how we selected the Index II rule. Fig. 8.4B
represents the same EU function plotted against the number of persons declared ineligible by the rule. The question asked here is slightly different:
Given a prespecified number of persons declared ineligible, which rule is
best? Here, the peak score of $EU\% = 74\%$ occurs at an ineligibility rate of
26% (this is comparable to the $Z = -1.2$). This percentage ineligible scaling is
displayed here because it allows us to compare the results across variables
with different scales.

There are a new set of statistical problems using explicit utilities. The
dashed lines of Figs. 8.4A and 8.4B are "bootstrapped" estimates of the 99%
confidence boundary around these choice points. The 99% confidence boundary shows that differences of about 2% are statistically accurate differences
(at the $\alpha < .01$ test level). This means, for example, the EU at $Z = -1.5$ is not
accurately different from the EU for a $Z = -1.0$ cutoff score, but both are accurately different from, say, the EU for a higher $Z = -.5$ cutoff. The confi-

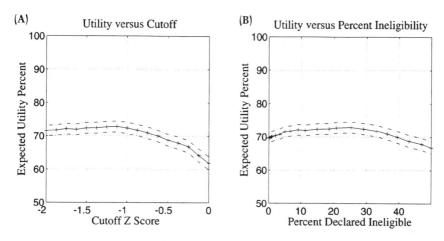

FIG. 8.4.   The expected utility (*EU*) functions for the average *Z*-score cutoffs and the mixed group weights (dashed lines indicate 99% confidence boundary based on bootstrap estimates; see Table 8.3B).

dence boundary in Fig. 8.4B suggests a comparable *EU* can be obtained at any ineligibility rate between 20% and 30%. Thus, many cutoff decisions in this range have a relatively large margin of error.

Limitations of Selection Bias Analyses

In the course of this work we have examined many different kinds of rules and sets of utility weights (see NCAA, 1991b, 1991c), and this selection bias analysis can be criticized on a number of grounds. The projected impacts for rules such as Prop 48 and Index II are based on the critical assumption that no distribution changes will occur as a result of the rule implementation, for either the students or the schools. It is thought by some that increases in academic performances would naturally occur, as students work harder to reach the minimum scores required to play. If so, these projected outcomes are based on a "worst case scenario." However, it is also possible that the raising of the minimum scores will create more academic pressures for lower-scoring students, and this might lead to more failures as "self-fulfilling prophecies." Unfortunately, the exact balance of positive and negative changes due to these rules changes is unknown, because the persons who were not eligible were no longer measured. The "static" projections of Table 8.4 represent only one kind of empirical evidence that can be considered.

The differential impacts among the minority and majority graduates is a selection bias, because we assume that the students in each group reached an equivalent criterion. That is, if "graduation from any college" is considered an equivalent criterion, then the false negatives are clearly mistakes (or costs) that do not coincide with the stated intent of any rule. Because we are now talking about students who have an equivalent outcome (i.e., graduation), the large White–Black false negative difference (–9.6) in Prop 48 represents the size of the selection bias against the minority group. However, which criteria should be used remains an open question. For example, if the pre-86 requirements of "graduating from high school with at least a 2.0 overall GPA" were considered sufficient evidence of group equality, then the large overall selection impact (–52.6) would be considered a selection bias. However, this latter selection impact is not usually considered as a selection bias but simply a reflection of the large group differences in the high school academic scores (see Fig. 8.1).

The complexities of selection bias analyses illustrate some essential tensions found in trying to create a fair decision rule: As the cutoff scores become increasingly stringent, the number of false negative mistakes (or costs) also increase, but the number of false positive mistakes (also a cost) decrease. The issues of selection bias due to Prop 48 cannot be fully examined without some deeper understanding of the costs, especially the large minority selection biases, compared to the benefits, including increased graduation rates. In theory, if we do choose the mixed utility structure (Table 8.3C), then a new rule such as Index II would be a better choice than the Prop 48 rule. The subjective definition of utilities remains among our most complex problems.

MODELING PREDICTION BIAS

Defining Prediction Bias

Additional features of the broad test bias questions surround the choice of the basic variables used in making the rules. In evaluating these variables, we often create a slightly different conditional group difference question: Does the predictor X have equally good validity for groups A and B, or does X exhibit "differential validity" for the prediction of Y across groups A and B? In more formal terms, we rewrite this question as: For persons with the same X score but in different groups A and B, do the validity equations make systematically different predictions $\hat{Y}^{(a)}$ and $\hat{Y}^{(b)}$?

A great deal of technical work has gone into clarifying the precise meaning of prediction bias in the historical context of linear regression analysis (e.g., Cleary, 1968; Linn & Werts, 1971; Thorndike, 1971), and some details are worth illustrating. Here we write a standard regression model for subject n on outcome Y as

$$Y_n = I + S \cdot X_n + E_n$$
$$= \hat{Y}_n + E_n \tag{5}$$

where X is the observed predictor variable, I is the intercept in the equation (the expected score on Y when X is zero), S is the slope in the equation (the expected change in Y for a one-unit change in X), and E is a random error or residual score that is not directly observed (usually assumed to be normally distributed with variance U^2 and mean zero). $\hat{Y}$ is the predicted value of Y for a particular score on X. For simplicity, let us assume the error scores are uncorrelated with the predictor variables within both groups, and we further assume some persons have the same X score but are members of two independent groups (A and B). In this case, we can write

$$
\begin{aligned}
Bias(Prediction) &= \mathcal{F}\{[\hat{Y}^{(a)}|X] - [\hat{Y}^{(b)}|X]\} \text{ or} \qquad (6)\\
&= \mathcal{F}\{(I^{(a)} + S^{(a)} \cdot X) - (I^{(b)} + S^{(b)} \cdot X)\}\\
&= \mathcal{F}\{(I^{(a)} - I^{(b)}) + (S^{(a)} - S^{(b)}) \cdot X\}\\
&= \mathcal{F}\{\Delta I + \Delta S \cdot X\}
\end{aligned}
$$

where the conditional group differences in intercepts (ΔI) and slopes (ΔS) are accumulated over both groups. Now it is clear that important differences will exist when (a) the slopes are different ($S^{(a)} \neq S^{(b)}$), (b) the intercepts are different ($I^{(a)} \neq I^{(b)}$), or (c) both intercepts and slopes are different.

This model is formally equivalent to a statement that says, "If person n in group A and person m in group B have exactly the same score on X, then how much of a difference do we predict about $\hat{Y}_n^{(a)}$ and $\hat{Y}_m^{(b)}$?" If we collect data from a reasonably large sample size and use standard regression procedures, we are not likely to accept the null hypothesis of strict equality of intercepts or slopes (see Cohen, 1994). On the other hand, with increasingly large sample sizes we can achieve increasingly accurate calculations of the size of the differences between groups in intercepts and slopes, and expected predictions. The latter approach is demonstrated in analyses to follow.

Logit Regression Methods

One popular statistical model used to compare group differences conditional on another variable is the well-known analysis of covariance (ANCOVA) model (Cohen & Cohen, 1985). In this model we use standard multiple regression techniques to create coefficients to represent the group average and group differences in I and S. In this context, we ask the group difference question as if a variety of correlated background variables were being held constant. This ANCOVA regression model is well known, and it has been used in many studies of prediction bias (e.g. Cleary, 1968; Goldberger, 1984; Hartigan, 1990; Hartigan & Wigdor, 1989; Humphreys, 1986; Hunter & Schmidt, 1978; Hunter, Schmidt, & Hunter, 1979).

In many analyses of academic performance, the variables are assumed to be continuously distributed and the ANCOVA model can be fitted using ordinary regression techniques. However, in Table 8.1 we defined college grad-

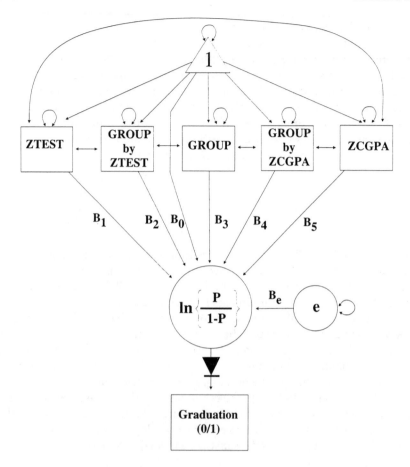

FIG. 8.5A.   A graphic description of the logit regression analysis model for prediction bias.

uation as a binary outcome (i.e., either "yes" or "no"). It is well known that
binary measurement creates some problems for standard parametric statistics such as linear regression. In order to deal with these statistical issues we
used a *logistic* or *logit regression model* to predict graduation rates from the
independent variables (for more details, see Hosmer & Lemeshow, 1989; Mc-
Ardle & Hamagami, 1994).

The logit model with group differences is presented in a general ANCOVA
fashion as a path diagram in Fig. 8.5. In this path diagram, squares are used to
represent observed or measured variables including Group effects (dummy
coded), scores on Tests and Grades, and the interaction of Group by Tests
and Group by Grades. Circles are used to represent unobserved or latent
variables, and we use a circle here to represent the transformation of the bi-

nary variable into the log odds. One-headed arrows are used to represent regression coefficients, and two-headed arrows are used to represent estimated correlation or variance terms. The unit constant is included (as a triangle) to include all means (M_k) and intercepts (I). More details on these kinds of path diagrams are given by McArdle and Boker (1991). A similar model is described for item bias by several other authors (e.g., Swaminathan & Rogers, 1990).

Prediction Bias Results

The logit model of Fig. 8.5A was fitted to the student-athlete data of Table 8.1, and some summary results are presented in Table 8.5A. Here, we only included SA with complete data on at least one predictor, and this led to an overall sample size of $N = 3,288$ (and altered the overall graduation rate to 45.7%).

The first model fitted (labeled 0 in Table 8.5) is a baseline model where only a unit constant is fitted. The logit coefficient estimate of $B_0 = -.171$ was transformed into a probability $\pi_0 = 45.7$, and this is the baseline graduation rate (see Table 8.1). The next model (1) adds group information and yields coefficients $B_0 = .091$ and $B_g = -1.106$: The transformed probabilities of $\pi_0 = 53.8$ reflects the White group rate, and the $\pi_g = -25.7$ reflects the overall difference between the White and Black group rates. This group difference parameter is "accurately" larger than zero, and the inclusion of group membership adds 3.8% to the overall fit of the model. (More specifically, the inclusion of Group has decreased the size of the baseline likelihood ratio by $LIP = 3.8\%$; see McArdle & Hamagami, 1994).

The second model adds individual information about high school grades to the prediction of graduation rate, and the fit is increased by 11.1%. The logit probability $\pi_0 = 51.4$ indicates an expected graduation rate of 51.4% for students with a high school Core-GPA $Z = 0$ (at about GPA = 3.00 in raw units), and the $\pi_c = 16.5$ indicates a change of 16.5% up or down for each one Z-score unit change in Core-GPA (in raw units, up from a 3.0 to a 3.5, or down from 3.0 to 2.5). The third model adds individual information about ACT or SAT test score to the prediction of graduation rate, and the fit is increased by 13.9%. Here, $\pi_0 = 48.1$ is the expected graduation rate for students with a Test $Z = 0$ (about SAT = 900 or ACT = 21 in raw units), and the $\pi_t = 21.8$ indicates a change up or down for each one Z-score unit change in Test (in raw units, up from a 900 to an 1100, or down from 900 to 700). The final model shows that the prediction of Graduation from the Average Z-score yielded the best improvement in fit (of 15.0%) for any single predictor.

The other models of Table 8.5A use two or more predictor variables. The fifth uses both Core-GPA and Test information and obtains a larger effect for the Test variable, and a slightly improved fit of 15.4%. This improvement in fit is better than using either variable alone (Model 2 or Model 3), but it is not substantially better than using the Average Z (Model 4). Models 6 and 7 add Group information together with the Core-GPA and Test scores. The sixth model yields accurate coefficients for Core-GPA and Test scores, but the Group coefficient is not accurate, and only a small amount (0.1%) is gained in fit. The final model goes one step further and adds Group-by-Core

TABLE 8.5
Selected Logit Regression Results for APS Prediction Bias Models

A: Logit models results from overall 1984–1985 sample ($N = 3,288$)

Logit Model	Rate of Change Parameter Estimates						
	Intercept π_0	Group π_g	Z-CGPA π_c	Z-TEST π_t	G × ZC π_{gc}	G × ZT π_{gt}	Fit Index LIP
0. Baseline	45.7*	—	—	—	—	—	0.0%
1. Group	52.3*	−27.7*	—	—	—	—	3.8%
2. Core GPA	51.4	—	16.5*	—	—	—	11.1%
3. Test	48.1*	—	—	21.8*	—	—	13.9%
4. Average	51.1	—	11.2	11.2*	—	—	15.0%
5. Core, Test	50.3	—	8.4*	16.2*	—	—	15.4%
6. Group, Core, Test	49.9	4.0	7.6*	16.7*	—	—	15.5%
7. Interactions	49.9	4.0	7.6*	16.7*	4.7	−1.1	15.5%

B: Logit models fitted to separate student-athlete groups

Logit Model	Rate of Change Parameter Estimates			
	Intercept π_0	ZCGPA π_c	ZTEST π_t	Fit Index LIP
0. Overall	50.3	8.4*	16.2*	15.4%
1. White SA	49.9	11.8*	15.2*	12.7%
2. Black SA	53.9	7.6*	16.7*	12.0%
3. White male revenue	55.2*	6.9*	14.4*	16.0%
4. White male nonrevenue	39.5*	6.9*	22.3*	22.9%
5. White females	54.5*	5.9*	16.4*	13.2%
6. Black male revenue	54.2*	11.3*	15.7*	16.2%
7. Black male nonrevenue	51.7*	6.2*	25.5*	22.8%
8. Black females	51.0*	14.0*	8.0*	8.9%

Notes: NCAA data with $N = 3,288$ with complete data on at least Z-test or ZCGPA variable.
Maximum-likelihood estimates from SAS PROC LOGISTIC program.
Parameters π are probabilities estimated from B weights.
The intercept π_0 is the expected base rate when all other predictor variables are zero.
The other π_k are the expected rate of change for a one-unit change in the independent predictor from the base rate (at the zero point on X).
Asterisks indicate accurate parameter (with $t \geq 1.96$).
The *LIP* is the percentage of change in the likelihood from the baseline model.

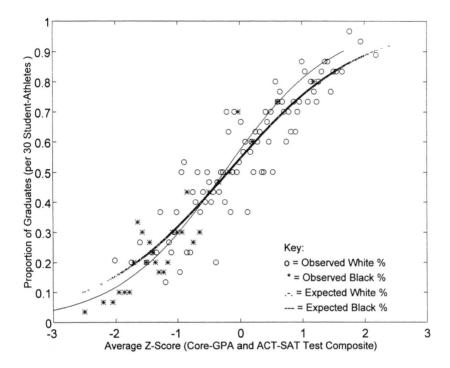

FIG. 8.5B. A graphic description of the logit regression analysis model for prediction bias.

and Group-by-Test interactions; the new coefficients are not accurate and the overall fit is not altered. Thus, we conclude Model 4 is the best model for these data.

The results of model 4 are displayed in Fig. 8.5B. Here, the average Z-scores are plotted on the X-axis, and the probability of college graduation is plotted on the Y-axis. This plot included information about both groups, including selected graduation rates, the mean scores (connected lines), and the predicted values at all points. These increasing probability functions show a small but reliable gain in the probability of graduation rate with small increases in the Average Z. These equations show some differences favoring Whites at the lower end and favoring Blacks at the upper end. Near the means these differences are trivial, and this is one explanation for the lack of accurate group differences in Core-GPA slopes.

These results can be interpreted to mean that the Core-GPA and Test scores are useful predictors and there is little evidence for different validity equations for different groups. That is, there are large graduation rate differences between the racial groups, but these are largely predictable from the previous differences in Core-GPA and Test scores. Using this approach, there are large between-group prediction differences, but there is also almost no prediction bias for either variable.

To investigate this issue in more detail, the equations of Table 8.5B give results for the Core-GPA and Test score logit model fitted to the separate groups of student-athletes listed in Table 8.1. This is done to examine the possibility that we have ignored some important heterogeneity in these groups. These results show all coefficients are significant in all groups, but there are slight differences in the relative impact of Core-GPA and Test scores in the separate groups. There are also notable differences in fit between the males and females, and between the male revenue (i.e., basketball and football players), and nonrevenue groups (i.e., other sports). The previous aggregation of SA into only two groups may not be appropriate in all cases, so these differences are potentially useful in further studies on these effects.

Limitations of Prediction Bias Models

Our main results show that both high school core grades and SAT or ACT test scores are accurate predictors of college graduation up to 5 years later. The test score variable was slightly stronger than the high school grades variable, but both were considered better than either one alone, and the average (or equally weighted) score is the single-best individual predictor. These results mimic previous prediction models of first-year grades (e.g., Willingham, Lewis, Morgan, & Ramist, 1990).

The lack of an accurate prediction bias between groups can be interpreted to mean that the large initial group differences in the high school academic variables parallel the subsequent group differences in college graduation. A variety of more complex group models and multilevel logit regression models have been used to deal with the wide range of differences among colleges (for details, see McArdle & Hamagami, 1994), but these results on prediction bias remain much the same.

Whenever we cannot accurately quantify prediction bias, a few methodological limitations should be considered:

- The same bias may exist in the predictor and the criterion, and this would lead to a failure to detect group differences in these equations.
- There may be different forms of bias in the criterion itself across groups, and these biases might tend to cancel.
- The inclusion of additional variables may dramatically change this prediction bias interpretation.
- It is possible that the binary variables do not yield enough precision of measurement to detect small group differences, and larger samples may be needed.
- Other forms of test bias, including sampling, selection, or measurement bias, may still exist, even if there is no prediction bias.

MODELING MEASUREMENT BIAS

Defining Measurement Bias

In a fourth set of analyses we deal with a potentially more fundamental question about group differences: When we administer the same test material in similar situations, are we measuring the same constructs in all groups? In more formal terms, this question leads to a basic unfairness question: For persons in different groups but with equal *underlying or latent ability*, does the use of the specific test favor one person over another? This is a measurement question about the functional equality of latent constructs, true scores, or common factors, which, by definition, are not directly observed (see Thissen, Steinberg, and Warner, 1988, 1993). Perhaps it is not surprising that this is a question that is often asked on a theoretic basis but seldom answered on an empirical basis.

One possible resolution of this question has been examined using a linear factor analysis model with multiple groups. Assume that V, W, X, and Y are a set of four independently observed variables. We write a factor analytic model for the observed scores for subject n as

$$V_n = I_v + L_v \cdot C_n + U_{vn},$$
$$W_n = I_w + L_w \cdot C_n + U_{wn},$$
$$X_n = I_x + L_x \cdot C_n + U_{xn},$$
$$Y_n = I_y + L_y \cdot C_n + U_{yn},$$

(7)

where the C is a unobserved common factor score and the U_k is an unobserved unique factor score for the k–th variable. In this representation, the parameters I_k are intercepts for each variable, and the L_k are factor loadings (or slopes) for the regression of the observed scores W, X, Y, and Z on the common factor scores C. For simplicity, we assume that the unique factors are uncorrelated with the common factors within all groups. Then for persons with the same latent score C in two independent groups A and B we can write

$$Bias\{Measurement\} = \mathcal{F}\{\sum_{k=1}^{4} [(I_k + L_k \cdot C)^{(a)} - (I_k + L_k \cdot C)^{(b)}]\}$$

(8)

$$= \mathcal{F}\{\sum_{k=1}^{4} [(I_k^{(a)} + L_k^{(a)} \cdot C) - (I_k^{(b)} + L_k^{(b)} \cdot C)]\}$$

$$= \mathcal{F}\{\sum_{k=1}^{4} [(I_k^{(a)} - I_k^{(b)}) + (L_k^{(a)} - L_k^{(b)}) \cdot C]\}$$

$$= \mathcal{F}\{\sum_{k=1}^{4} [\Delta I_k + \Delta L_k \cdot C]\}$$

where the conditional group differences in intercepts (ΔI_k) and loadings (ΔL_k) are accumulated over all observed variables into vectors ($\Delta I + \Delta L$). This measurement bias equation is now quite similar to the previous prediction bias model equation, except here the predictor variable C is unobserved.

The questions here are based on the equality of the factor loadings L_k over groups. That is, we are interested in asking: What is the loss in fit if we assume the factor loading for each variable is identical over groups? More formally, we can write $L_k^{(a)} = L_k^{(b)}$ for all k variables, as an initial test of the hypothesis of *factor invariance*. The loss of fit due to this kind of parameter invariance is a first index of measurement bias. A second and stronger form of factorial invariance involves the means and intercepts. Here we are interested in asking questions such as: What is the loss in fit if we assume the means in the first group are the same as the means in the second group except for deviations due to the common factor? On a formal basis, we write constraints on the observed group means (M_k) such as: $M_k^{(a)} = I_k^{(a)}$ and $M_k^{(b)} = I_k^{(b)} + L_k \cdot M_c^{(b)}$. Here, the parameter $M_c^{(b)}$ represents the mean differences in the common factor scores in the second group relative to the first group (for details, see Horn & McArdle, 1992; McArdle & Cattell, 1994; McArdle & Nesselroade, 1995).

Structural Factor Analysis Methods

Latent variable *structural equation modeling (SEM)* has been used by many researchers to deal with basic questions about group differences. In a technical sense, the multiple group ANCOVA regression model presented earlier can easily be represented using standard SEM techniques (Jöreskog & Sörbom, 1979, 1993). Newer SEM programs also allow the direct representation of multiple independent groups, and this approach has certain advantages here (Horn & McArdle, 1980; McArdle, 1994; Sörbom, 1974, 1978). This MG-SEM also makes it relatively easy to examine another assumption of the standard ANCOVA model—the equality of the variances of the error (E) around the two regression lines (i.e., $U_a^2 \neq U_b^2$). Incidentally, this last feature of the prediction model has been used as evidence for prediction bias (e.g., Hartigan & Wigdor, 1989).

Another benefit of this general MG-SEM approach is that allows us to use latent variables to account for patterns of incomplete or missing data (for a review, see Little & Rubin, 1987; McArdle, 1994). Fig. 8.6A is a path diagram of four different structural regression models for the prediction of graduation from the ZTEST and ZCGPA. (For simplicity, now, we do not deal with the logit form of the rate variable.) In the first model, all independent variables are measured (squares) and only the residual variable (E) is unobserved (circle). In the second model, all model parameters are the same, but the ZTEST is now unobserved as well. This is a model for a subset of the data where, say, the ACT or SAT tests were either not taken or not reported. In the third model, the ZCGPA is not observed (not reported) and is considered as a la-

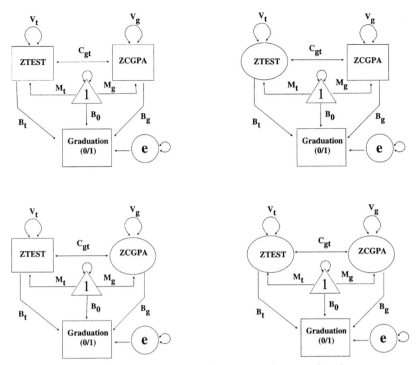

FIG. 8.6A.   A graphic description of multiple groups with incomplete data.

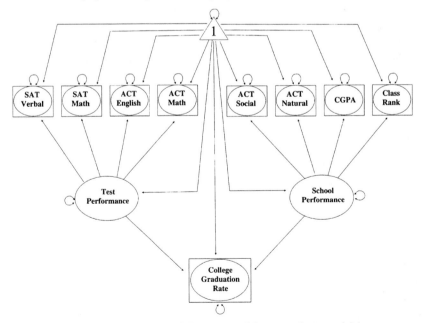

FIG. 8.6B.   A graphic description of the structural factor analysis model for measurement bias.

tent variable. In the fourth model, both the ZCGPA and the ZTEST are missing and are considered as latent variables. When this kind of model is used for both Black and White groups, we have eight independent groups and two models to consider.

The traditional factor analysis model includes many indicators of each factor. This approach has been used to examine factorial invariance over groups by a variety of researchers (see Horn & McArdle, 1980, 1992; Jöreskog & Sörbom, 1979; McArdle & Cattell, 1994; McDonald, 1985; Meredith, 1965, 1990, 1993; Rock, Werts, & Flaugher, 1978). In this SEM approach, measurement bias has been tested by fitting equality or invariance constraints in a structural model and examining the relative change in the goodness-of-fit due to these restrictions (see Browne & Cudeck, 1993; Saris & Sattora, 1993). These same principles have been applied in the context of measurement bias (see Hoetler, 1983; McFatter, 1987; Meredith & Millsap, 1992; Millsap & Everson, 1991, 1993; Millsap & Meredith, 1994; Muthén & Lehman, 1985; Tracey & Sedlacek, 1987).

Measurement Bias Results

The multivariate data available from the NCAA Academic Performance Survey allows only a limited study of measurement bias. A theoretical model for the available NCAA data is presented in Fig. 8.6B. This model includes two common factors labeled Test Performance and School Performance. This is not an arbitrary model, but it is implied by the combined use of tests and grades in the initial eligibility rules. As before, the constant (triangle) is included to allow for hypotheses about the intercept and factor mean differences. The representation of circles within squares indicates that these specific variables may (square) or may not (circle) be measured in any of the eight groups in this problem. (Incidentally, this graphic device can be seen as the result of holding together eight overheads with similar parameters but with different patterns of circles and squares.)

We next created a multivariate array of academic data on grades and test scores, including nine variables: the SAT Verbal and Math subtests; the ACT English, Math, Social Studies, and Natural Sciences subtests; the high school core GPA and class rank; and college graduation (yes or no). We found that the largest pattern of missing data occurred in the SAT and ACT scores and not in the GPA reported. This is not too surprising, because in 1984–1985 minimum scores on these tests were not explicitly required by the NCAA. The pattern of missingness for eight groups is listed in Table 8.6A. This table is also broken down into White and Black SA groups. Although very few students took both tests, the SAT scores were reported by a larger percentage of White SA (54%), and no scores are reported for a larger percentage of Black SA (10%).

Table 8.6B shows the results from three versions of this model fitted to eight independent group mean and covariance matrices. In all cases, the first common factor was identified by forcing the loadings for the SAT-Verbal to unity, the second common factor was identified by forcing the loadings for the Core-GPA to unity, and all other parameters are ratios of these loadings. In the first model we assume *total invariance* of all parameters across all

TABLE 8.6
Structural Factor Analysis Modeling Results
for Measurement Bias Models

A: Available (and missing) data patterns on test score variables $(N = 3,278)$
Patterns of Available Data

Group	No Test	ACT Only	SAT Only	Both Tests
Overall	143	1243	1684	208
	(1.0%)	(37.9%)	(51.4%)	(6.3%)
White (W)	64	887	1310	186
	(1.0%)	(36.2%)	(53.5%)	(7.6%)
Black (B)	79	356	374	22
	(10.1%)	(43.8%)	(45.0%)	(2.6%)

B: Parameter estimates for three latent variable models based on multivariate means and covariances of eight complete and incomplete data groups (see A)

	Total Invariance				Metric Invariance				Configural Invariance			
	Test		Grade		Test		Grade		Test		Grade	
	W	B	W	B	W	B	W	B	W	B	W	B
Parameters												
Factor Means	.0 =	.0 =	.0 =	.0 =	.0 =	−1.31	.0 =	−1.01	.0 =	.0 =	.0 =	.0 =
Factor Devs.	.95	.95	1.18	1.18	.79	.72	1.34	.94	.78	.77	1.09	.93
Factor Corr	.71	.71			.67	.53			.69	.55		
Loadings												
GRAD	.16	.16	.08	.08	.15	.15	.08	.08	.17	.15	.08	.10
SAT V	1.0 =	1.0 =	—	—	1.0 =	1.0 =	—	—	1.0 =	1.0 =	—	—
SAT M	1.22	1.22	—	—	1.22	1.22	—	—	1.29	1.02	—	—
ACT V	.52	.52	—	—	.51	.52	—	—	.49	.55	—	—
ACT M	.73	.73	—	—	.72	.72	—	—	.74	.58	—	—
ACT S	.64	.64	—	—	.63	.63	—	—	.64	.66	—	—
ACT N	.61	.61	—	—	.59	.59	—	—	.59	.57	—	—
Core-GPA	—	—	1.0 =	1.0 =	—	—	1.0 =	1.0 =	—	—	1.0 =	1.0 =
HSRANK	.75	.75	—	—	.75	.75	—	—	.85	.72	—	—
Fit Indices												
LRT/DF	2151 / 207				940 / 202				726 / 177			
dLRT/dDF	—				1211 / 5				214 / 25			
RMSEA (−,+)	.054 (.051,.056)				.033 (.031,.036)				.031 (.028,.034)			

eight groups and yield a relatively poor fit (LRT = 2,151 on DF = 207 with $RMSEA$ = .054). This model seems to show reasonable parameter values, except that the SAT-Math tends to dominate the Test factor more than expected by chance.

In a second model of *metric invariance*, only the factor loadings and variable intercepts are required to be invariant across the White and Black groups. (For estimation purposes, this model does require invariance of all parameters for the four incomplete data groups within each racial group.) This model yields a reasonably good fit for this large sample size (LRT = 940 on DF = 202, so $RMSEA$ = .033). A substantial improvement in fit relative to the total invariance model ($dLRT$ = 1211 on dDF = 5) is achieved because latent group mean and covariance differences are allowed. Here, all mean differences between groups are required to be patterned in accordance with the invariant factor loadings, and these means are estimated to be lower on both common factors for the Black group (M_{c1} = −1.3, and M_{c2} = −1.0). The factor variances and covariances are different as well.

The third model of *configural invariance* relaxes the strict invariance assumptions across the White and Black groups. Again, this model requires invariance of all parameters across the incomplete data groups within each racial group. This model yields another improvement in overall fit (LRT = 726 on DF = 177, $RMSEA$ = .031) and an improvement over the metric model ($dLRT$ = 214 on dDF = 25). This model allows the factor loadings to be different, but only the SAT-Math loading appears much smaller within the Black group. Although not listed here, there are clear group differences in the variable intercepts (I_k) that do not follow the same factor pattern. The metric model fits the data, and the configural model is close (i.e., within the same $RMSEA$ confidence interval), but the magnitude of this improvement may still be meaningful. This raises the possibility that different constructs are being measured in each group, and this issue needs to be explored in any further use of the overall multifactor model.

Another alternative model was fitted—a simple one-factor model for all variables. This academic performance factor model fit these data very poorly: The total (LRT = 3960 on DF = 209), metric (LRT = 2877 on DF = 207), and configural (LRT = 2363 on DF = 182) all represented much worse fits than the two factor alternatives based on Fig. 8.6B. When dealing with White-Black differences on these academic variables, it is fairly obvious that a "Spearman's g" hypothesis is *not* an adequate starting model (compare Horn, 1988, chap. 4, this volume; Humphreys, 1985; Jensen, 1980, 1985; Johnson & Nagoshi, 1985; Jones, 1985).

Limitations of Measurement Bias Models

This structural equation approach to measurement bias allows the quantification of group difference questions about latent variables. Some of these questions reflect the qualitative nature of the group differences as well. These models provide estimates of various parameters of test validity that are difficult if not impossible to obtain using other techniques. Our main results are limited by the initial selection of measured variables, and the resulting measurement model comparisons are not as precise as possible. The White-Black differences in response patterns seen earlier may be related to the overall interpretation of the latent variable model. More detail is needed about the reasons why data are missing for the Black SA. These design problems are not likely to be solved by more advanced data analyses.

The model results listed earlier use all the available data and can be considered optimal statistical estimates (see Little & Rubin, 1987). However, in other advanced models we have considered each pattern of missing data as an independent group and fit a multiple group SEM (as in McArdle, 1994). In these analyses, the changes in the estimated parameters were related to the patterns of missing data to evaluate various questions of whether these data were *missing at random*. In most cases the parameters exhibited only small changes in values, and these changes were not related to group differences in the missing data.

Even with these methodological problems we can easily conclude that achievement comparisons of black and white groups should not be based on single tests or measurements. This is not a new result (e.g., Cattell & Butcher, 1968; Husén, 1978; Pascarella & Terenzini, 1991), but it is another way to argue that a single factor model is hopelessly inadequate for most measurements of human cognitive abilities (for references, see Carroll, 1993; Horn, 1988; McArdle, 1994; Woodcock, 1990). Again, and at very least, this study of group differences in latent academic achievement variables can tell us about theoretical models, such as g, that are very far away from adequate internal measurement validity (see Horn, chap. 4, this volume; Snow, chap. 5, this volume). In this way the group differences questions lead to more general answers about the validity of the psychological constructs.

DISCUSSION

Methodological Issues

Four statistical methods were used to illustrate some contemporary approaches to the analysis of test bias questions. These illustrations included analyses of: *sampling* bias using standard statistical tests, *selection* bias using decision theory analyses, *prediction* bias using logit regression models, and *measurement* bias using structural equation modeling. Selected numerical examples from the NCAA-APS data were used to illustrate each analysis.

In broader terms, the contemporary statistical models we have used here can be related to more classical issues of *construct validity* (e.g., Cronbach & Meehl, 1959). These concepts include: sampling bias as a form of *ecological* validity, selection bias as a form of *discriminant* validity, prediction bias as a form of *external* validity, and measurement bias as a form of *internal* validity (see McArdle, 1994; McArdle & Prescott, 1992; Shepard, Camilli, & Averill, 1981). The kind of models used to address these issues are relatively complex, but they all have some technical and conceptual benefits for the kinds of test-bias problems discussed.

Lay persons and scientists alike seem keen to make statements such as, "There are no differences between groups." However, from a purely methodological perspective we must recognize that there are always some differences between groups. This linguistic problem is easy to ignore when we are dealing with random samples (as in the first illustration), but it can have serious consequences in the substantive group difference questions (in the other examples). To follow this lead, and avoid unwanted surplus meaning, a shift was also made here away from using the term *significant* and toward a new use of the older term *accurate*. This change in the use of the statistical language of uncertainty is not new, and it has been long criticized for being less definitive than is required for critical public policy issues. Changes in our language can help set the stage for more appropriate substantive inferences in this context of test bias, and these changes may be needed.

Substantive Issues

The substantive problems discussed in this research are timely for several reasons. Specifically, the colleges of the NCAA are currently engaged in heated debates on issues of eligibility and academic performances. These questions concern appropriate use of information from high school transcripts and from standardized test scores. The unclear and competing goals of some initial eligibility rules reflect some of the struggles and tensions between groups in college sports. Of course, these are not necessarily issues of race alone; the initial racial differences in high school academic achievements are likely to be the outcome of a much more complex set of sociopsychological group and individual differences that we have not measured here (e.g., Betancourt & Lopez, 1993; Crouse & Trusheim, 1988; Hargadon, 1984; Hartigan, 1990; Jones, 1991, Williams, 1983). Improved measurement of academic attainments and predictors may provide a useful starting point toward improved measurement of the high school and college experiences needed for a successful adult life in an increasingly complex culture.

The graduation rates observed before 1984 were studied by others, and these data, to some degree, led to the Prop 48 legislation. However, this may be another example of an unfortunate lack of appropriate statistical inference. As it turns out, although the average graduation rates of student-athletes is slightly lower than those of other students at the same schools, the average graduation rates *within* both Black and White SA groups are *higher* than those for other students within these same ethnic groups. This result comes about because the overall student-athlete population includes a higher proportion of minority students (30%) than does the typical student body (10%). Any inferences about generally poor academic performance by individual student-athletes need to be tempered with these facts and statisitcal issues (e.g., "Simpson's Paradox").

The decision theory analysis presented here highlights two key public policy problems. First, the data may not be accurate enough (e.g., due to small sample sizes, large measurement errors) to assist in the required decision. This means that the policymakers, whether they wish to or not, need to agree on specific standards for data accuracy and outcomes. Second, policymakers, whether they wish to or not, need to agree on a specific utility structure for different outcomes. The choice of such goals is often a subjective process that leads to large differences in utilities among decision makers. If selection bias against the minority group graduates is important in this decision, then the utility weights need to be constructed to highlight these mistakes. Of course, creating the appropriate utility structure is not easy. After decades of research on this general topic, Cronbach (1975) labeled this utility problem as "the Achilles heel of decision theory." Nevertheless, the quantitative mixture of some generally agreed-upon criteria, some reliably observed data, and some clearly defined goals, remain the critical components in the choice of a fair and unbiased selection test.

Personal Issues

I end this chapter on a more subjective note. I believe there is a great opportunity to use formal statistical models to help clarify public policy debates, but there is also a great danger of miscommunication, confusion, and misinterpretation due to the advanced nature of some statistical models. Thus, there is ever increasing work for "methodological epistimologists" (Campbell, 1988).

I also believe there exists much confusion and even misuses of test bias models by many people doing research and teaching in the field of human cognitive abilities. I initially believed that this confusion was a by-product of the lack of advanced statistical training obtained at the graduate level. But I have come to understand that there is a strong emotional factor that relates to the content of the result—that is, the adequacy of the methodology is often evaluated simply by the desirability of the results it produces.

Part of this confusion is likely due to the great emotional content concerning historical work on the Black-White differences in tests of cognitive ability (Betancourt & Lopez, 1993. Within many groups there may be mistrust

(Betancourt & Lopez, 1993; Fancher, 1985; Gould, 1981; Jones, 1991) because psychological tests (a) have been used to suppress opportunities for the
underprivileged, (b) ignore other important individual and cultural attrib-
utes, and (c) have been promoted as measures of "innate" ability implying
(d) further learning is not possible. The genetic selection arguments (i.e., eugenics) argued by some well-known scientists (e.g., Cattell, chap. 2, this volume; Jensen, 1985) have not been based on reliable data and, in any case, are
not related to these Black-White group differences at all. That is, there is not
a single credible genetic study that shows (a) the genes that are related to
"physical differences between the races" are in any way related to (b) the
genes supposedly forming the polygenic characteristics known as "cognitive
ability." Researchers invested in improvements in quantitative methods
would be wise to recognize the long history of confusion created by previous
theories and modelers (for review, see Gould, 1981; Scarr, 1988).

I also recognize that a statistical methodology should not be chosen because it produces a predefined and "acceptable" result. One philosophy
about statistical models of test bias seems to be "If I agree with the result
then I agree with the model!" This kind of "advocacy" can be dangerous
even if it is well motivated. There are some important guidelines to follow
here:

> The appropriate role of the educator in the decision-making process is pri-
> marily to provide information and expert [judgments] and thereby to help
> broaden the base upon which decisions are made by those who, in a repre-
> sentative democratic system, have been elected to make these decisions. If
> the educator is a researcher, it is even more important that he should play
> his role according to the rules and confine it to professional performance as
> long as he wears his researcher's hat. Let me hasten to add that the educator,
> whether a teacher or a researcher, is obviously entitled as a private person to
> advance opinions or make political statements. Equally self-evidently, how-
> ever, he should try to keep these personal statements clearly separate from
> the generalizations drawn from his scholarly inquiries. The nature of the re-
> search can easily affect the relationship between the researchers and the pol-
> icymaker. . . . (Husén, 1978, pp. 576)

I have used this contemporary statistical approach to deal with some of
these science-advocacy issues. Other kinds of test bias analyses can also be
used to help tease apart some of the most interesting parameters related to
group differences, fairness, and equity, and these need to be further extended
in both practical and theoretical applications. Researchers who take on these
tasks need to be extremely sensitive to both the previous history and the current confusion about test bias by both highly trained researchers and lay-
persons alike. Possibly this work must be done by researchers who have "a
strong political stomach" (Eleanor Cherminski, personal communication,

May 1, 1993). I hope these contemporary studies of test bias can contribute in some useful way to the national debate over these intriguing contemporary questions.

ACKNOWLEDGMENTS

This chapter was originally presented on September 24, 1994, Charlottesville, VA. Requests for copies should be sent to John J. McArdle, Jefferson Psychometric Laboratory, Department of Psychology, University of Virginia, Charlottesville, VA 22963. This research would not have been possible without many friends and colleagues, especially Steve Boker, Aki Hamagami, John Horn, Ron Johnson, John Nesselroade, Bill Meredith, and Tom Paskus. I am also grateful to the members of the Research Staff and Research Committee of the National Collegiate Athletic Association; especially I thank my friends and colleagues Ursula R. Walsh, Todd A. Petr, Daniel T. Dutcher, and Nancy L. Mitchell, for their public support of this research. All data presented here were used by special permission of the NCAA Research Committee (approved July 1994).

REFERENCES

Berk, R. A. (Ed.). (1982). *Handbook of methods for detecting test bias.* Baltimore, MD: Johns Hopkins Press.
Betancourt, H., & Lopez, S. R. (1993). The study of culture, ethnicity, and race in American psychology. *American Psychologist, 48*(6), 629–637.
Bond, L. (1994, July). Bias in standardized testing and performance assessment: The quest for a fair test. *Federation News*, p. 8.
Breland, H. M., & Ironson, G. H. (1976). Defunis reconsidered: A comparative analysis of alternative admission strategies. *Journal of Educational Measurement, 13*(1), 89–99.
Browne, M., & Cudeck, R. (1993). Alternative ways of assessing model fit. In K. Bollen & S. Long (Eds.), *Testing structural equation models* (pp. 136–162). Beverly Hills, CA: Sage.
Campbell, D. T. (1988). *Methodology and epistemology for social sciences. Selected papers.* Chicago: University of Chicago Press.
Carroll, J. B. (1993). *Human cognitive abilities: A survey of factor-analytic studies.* New York: Cambridge University Press.
Cattell, R. B., & Butcher, H. J. (1968). *The prediction of achievement and creativity.* New York: Bobbs-Merrill.
Cleary, T. A. (1968). Test bias: Prediction of grades of negro and white students in integrated colleges. *Journal of Educational Measurement, 5*(2), 115–124.
Cohen J. (1994). The earth is round, $p < .05$. *American Psychologist, 49*(12), 997–1003.
Cohen, J., & Cohen, P. (1985). *Multiple regression/correlation for the behavioral sciences.* Hillsdale, NJ: Lawrence Erlbaum Associates.
Cole, N. S. (1981). Bias in testing. *American Psychologist, 36*, 1067–1077.
Coleman, J. S. (1990). *Equality and achievement in education.* Boulder, CO: Westview.

Cronbach, L. J. (1976). Equity in selection—where psychometrics and political philosophy meet. *Journal of Educational Measurement, 13*(1), 31–41.

Cronbach, L. J., & Meehl, P. (1955). Construct validity in psychological tests. *Psychological Bulletin, 52,* 281–302.

Crouse, J., & Trusheim, D. (1988). *The case against the SAT.* Chicago: University of Chicago Press.

Ervin, L., Saunders, S. A., & Gillis, H. L. (1984). The right direction but short of the mark: The NCAA's Proposal 48. A comment. *The College Board Review, 131,* 15–19.

Flaugher, R. L. (1978). The many definitions of test bias. *American Psychologist, 1,* 671–679.

Goldberger, A. S. (1984). Reverse regression and salary discrimination. *Journal of Human Resources, 19,* 293–318.

Goodman, L. (1953). Ecological regression and the behavior of individuals. *American Journal of Sociology, 18,* 663–664.

Goodman, L. (1959). Some alternatives to ecological correlation. *Journal of Sociology, 64,* 610–625.

Gould, S. J. (1981). *The mismeasure of man.* New York: Norton.

Gross, A. L., & Su, W. (1975). Defining a "fair" or "unbiased" selection model: A question of utilities. *Journal of Applied Psychology, 60*(3), 345–351.

Hargadon, F. A. (1984). Responding to charges of test misuse in higher education. In C. W. Daves (Ed.), *The use and misuse of tests* (pp. 69–89). San Francisco: Jossey-Bass.

Hartigan, J. A. (1990). Adjustments of minority group test scores used in employment referrals. *Chance: New Directions for Statistics and Computing, 3*(3), 38–44.

Hartigan, J. A., & Wigdor, A. K. (1989). *Fairness in employment testing: Validity generalization, minority issues, and the general aptitude test battery.* Washington, DC: National Academy Press.

Hoelter, J. N. (1983). Factorial invariance and self-esteem: Reassessing race and sex differences. *Social Forces, 61*(3), 834–846.

Horn, J. L. (1988). Thinking about human abilities. In J. R. Nesselroade & R. B. Cattell (Eds.), The *handbook of multivariate experimental psychology, volume 2* (pp. 645–686). New York, Plenum.

Horn, J. L., & McArdle, J. J. (1980). Perspectives on mathematical and statistical model building (MASMOB) in aging research. In L. W. Poon (Ed.), *Aging in the 1980s: Contemporary perspectives.* Washington, DC: American Psychological Association.

Horn, J. L., & McArdle, J. J. (1992). A practical and theoretical guide to measurement invariance in aging research. *Experimental Aging Research, 18*(1), 117–144.

Hosmer, D. W., & Lemeshow, S. (1989). *Applied logistic regression.* New York: Wiley.

Humphreys, L. G. (1985). Race differences and the Spearman hypothesis. *Intelligence, 9,* 275–283.

Humphreys, L. G. (1986). An analysis and evaluation of test and item bias in the prediction context. *Psychological Bulletin, 71,* 327–333.

Hunter, J. E., & Schmidt, F. L. (1978). Differential and single-group validity of employment tests by race: A critical analysis of three recent studies. *Journal of Applied Psychology, 63*(1), 1–11.

Hunter, J. E., Schmidt, F. L., & Hunter, R. (1979). Differential validity of employment tests by race: A comprehensive review and analysis. *Psychological Bulletin, 86,* 721–735.

Husén, T. (1978). Educational research and educational reform: A case study of Sweden. In P. Suppes (Ed.), *Impact of research on education* (pp. 523–579). Washington, DC: National Academy of Education.

Jenifer, F. G. (1984). How test results affect college admissions of minorities. In C. W. Daves (Ed.), *The use and misuse of tests* (pp. 90–105). San Francisco: Jossey-Bass.

Jensen, A. R. (1980). *Bias in mental testing.* New York: Free Press.

Jensen, A. R. (1985). The nature of the black–white difference on various psychometric tests: Spearman's hypothesis (with open peer commentary). *The Behavioral and Brain Sciences, 8,* 192–263.

Johnson, R. C., & Nagoshi, C. T. (1985). Do we know enough about g to be able to speak of black–white differences. *The Behavioral and Brain Sciences, 8,* 232–234.

Jones, J. M. (1991). Psychological models of race: What have they been and what should they be? In L. Garnets, J. Jones, D. Kimmel, S. Sue, & C. Tavris (Eds.), *Psychological perspectives on human diversity in America* (pp. 7–46). Washington, DC: American Psychological Association.

Jones, L. V. (1985). Golly g: Interpreting Spearman's general factor. *The Behavioral and Brain Sciences, 8,* 228.

Jöreskog, K. G., & Sörbom, D. (1979). *Advances in factor analysis and structural equation models.* Cambridge, MA: Abt.

Jöreskog, K. G., & Sörbom, D. (1993). *LISREL VII: A guide to the program and applications.* Chicago: SPSS.

Klitgaard, R. E. (1985). *Choosing elites.* New York: Basic.

Lindley, D. V. (1985). *Making decisions. Volume II.* London: Wiley.

Linn, R. L. (1976). In search of fair selection procedures. *Journal of Educational Measurement, 13*(1), 53–58.

Linn, R. L. (1984). Selection bias: Multiple meanings. *Journal of Educational Measurement, 21,* 33–47.

Linn, R. L., & Werts, C. E. (1971). Considerations for studies of test bias. *Journal of Educational Measurement, 8,* 1–4.

Little, R. T. A., & Rubin, D. B. (1987). *Statistical analysis with missing data.* New York: Wiley.

Lohmöller, J.-B., & Falter, F. (1986). Some further aspects of ecological regression analysis. *Quality and Quantity, 20,* 109–125.

McArdle, J. J. (1994). Structural factor analysis experiments with incomplete data. *Multivariate Behavioral Research, 29*(4), 409–454.

McArdle, J. J., & Boker, S. M. (1991). *RAMpath: Automatic path diagram software.* Hillsdale, NJ: Lawrence Erlbaum Associates.

McArdle, J. J., & Cattell, R. B. (1995). Structural equation models of factorial invariance in parallel proportional profiles and oblique confactor problems. *Multivariate Behavioral Research, 29*(1), 61–101.

McArdle, J. J., & Hamagami, F. (1994). Logit and multilevel logit modeling studies of college graduation for 1984–85 freshman student-athletes. *The Journal of the American Statistical Association, 89*(427), 1107–1123.

McArdle, J. J., Hamagami, F., & Paskus, T. S. (1994). *Decision theory modeling studies of college admission and graduation for 1984–85 freshman student-athletes.* Unpublished manuscript, Department of Psychology, University of Virginia.

McArdle, J. J., & Nesselroade, J. R. (1995). Structuring data to study development and change. In S. H. Cohen & H. W. Reese (Eds.), *Life-span developmental psychology: Methodological innovations* (pp. 223–267). Hillsdale, NJ: Lawrence Erlbaum Associates.

McArdle, J. J. & Prescott, C. A. (1992). Age-based construct validation using structural equation modeling. *Experimental Aging Research, 18*(3), 87–115.

McFatter, R. M. (1987). Use of latent variable models for detecting discrimination in salaries. *Psychological Bulletin, 101,* 120–125.

Meredith, W. (1965). A method for studying differences between groups. *Psychometrika, 30*(1), 15–29.

Meredith, W. (1990, November). *Factorial invariance from a measurement perspective.*

Presidential address at the Annual Meetings of the Society for Multivariate Experimental Psychology. Providence, RI.

Meredith, W. (1993). Measurement invariance, factor analysis, and factorial invariance. *Psychometrika*.

Meredith, W., & Millsap, R. E. (1992). On the misuse of manifest variables in the detection of measurement bias. *Psychometrika*, *57*, 289–311.

Millsap, R. E., & Everson, H. (1991). Confirmatory measurement model comparisons using latent means. *Multivariate Behavioral Research*, *26*(3), 479–498.

Millsap, R. E., & Everson, H. (1993). Methodology review: Statistical approaches for assessing measurement bias. *Applied Psychological Measurement*, *17*, 297–344.

Millsap, R. E., & Meredith, W. (1994). Statistical evidence in salary discrimination studies: Nonparameteric inferential conditions. *Multivariate Behavioral Research*, *29*, 339–364.

Muthén, B., & Lehman, J. (1985). Multiple group IRT modeling: Applications to item bias analysis. *Journal of Educational Statistics*, *10*, 133–142.

National Collegiate Athletic Association. (1991a). *A statistical analysis of the predictions of graduation rates for college student-athletes* (NCAA Research Report #91–02). Overland Park, KS: Author.

National Collegiate Athletic Association. (1991b). *A graphic display of initial-eligibility rules applied to 1984 and 1985 freshman student-athletes* (NCAA Research Report #91–04). Overland Park, KS: Author.

National Collegiate Athletic Association. (1991c). *A decision-theory analysis of initial-eligibility rules applied to 1984 and 1985 freshman student-athletes* (NCAA Research Report #91–05). Overland Park, KS: Author.

National Collegiate Athletic Association. (1992). *A statistical comparison of the college graduation of freshman student-athletes before and after proposition 48* (NCAA Research Report #92–02). Overland Park, KS: Author.

Novick, M. R., & Peterson, N. S. (1976). Towards equalizing educational and employment opportunity. *Journal of Educational Measurement*, *13*(1), 77–88.

Pascarella, E. T., & Terenzini, P. T. (1991). *How college affects students*. San Francisco: Jossey-Bass.

Peterson, N. S., & Novick, M. R. (1976). An evaluation of some models for cultural-fair selection. *Journal of Educational Measurement*, *13*(1), 3–29.

Porter, A. M. (1990). *Undergraduate completion and persistence at four-year colleges and universities*. Washington, DC: National Institute of Independent Colleges and Universities.

Reynolds, C. R., & Brown, R. T. (1984). *Perspectives on bias in mental testing*. New York: Plenum.

Robinson, W. S. (1950). Ecological correlations and the behavior of individuals. *American Sociological Review*, *15*, 351–357.

Rock, D. A, Werts, C. E., & Flaugher, R. L. (1978). The use of analysis of covariance structures for comparing psychometric properties of multiple variables across populations. *Multivariate Behavioral Research*, *13*, 408–413.

Saris, W. E., & Satorra, A. (1993). Power evaluations in structural equation models. In K. Bollen & S. Long (Eds.), *Testing structural equation models* (pp. 181–204). Beverly Hills, CA: Sage.

Sawyer, R. L., Cole, N. S., & Cole, J. W. L. (1976). Utilities and the issue of fairness in a decision theoretic model for selection. *Journal of Educational Measurement*, *13*(1), 59–76.

Scarr, S. (1981). *I. Q., race, social class and individual differences: New studies of old problems*. Hillsdale, NJ: Lawrence Erlbaum Associates.

Scarr, S. (1988). Race and gender as psychological variables: Social and ethical issues. *American Psychologist*, *43*(1), 56–59.

Shepard, L. A., Camilli, G., & Averill, M. (1981). Comparison of six procedures for detecting test item bias using both internal and external ability criteria. *Journal of Educational Statistics, 6*, 317–375.

Snyderman, M., & Rothman, S. (1990). *The IQ controversy, the media and public policy.* New Brunswick, NJ: Transaction.

Sörbom, D. (1974). A general method for studying differences in factor means and factor structure between groups. *British Journal of Mathematical and Statistical Psychology, 27*, 229–239.

Swaminathan, H., & Rogers, H. J. (1990). Detecting differential item functioning using logistic regression procedures. *Journal of Educational Measurement, 27*(4), 361–370.

Swets, J. A. (1988). Measuring the accuracy of diagnostic systems. *Science, 240*, 1285–1293.

Thorndike, R. L. (1971). Concepts of culture-fairness. *Journal of Educational Measurement, 8*, 63–70.

Thissen, D., Steinberg, L., & Wainer, H. (1988). Use of item response theory in the study of group differences in trace lines. In H. Wainer & H. I. Braun (Eds.), *Test Validity* (pp. 147–169). Hillsdale, NJ: Lawrence Erlbaum Associates.

Thissen, D., Steinberg, L., & Wainer, H. (1993). Detection of differential item functioning using the parameters of item response models. In P. W. Holland & H. Wainer (Eds.), *Differential item functioning* (pp. 67–113). Hillsdale, NJ: Lawrence Erlbaum Associates.

Tracey, T. J., & Sedlacek, W. E. (1987). A comparison of white and black student academic success using noncognitive variables: A LISREL analysis. *Research in Higher Education, 27*(4), 333–348.

Wiggins, J. S. (1973). *Personality and prediction: Principles of personality assessment.* Reading, MA: Addison-Wesley.

Williams, J. (1983). The impact of Rule 48 upon the black student athlete: A comment. *The Journal of Negro Education, 52*, 362–373.

Willingham, W. W., Lewis, C., Morgan, R., & Ramist, L. (1990). *Predicting college grades: An analysis of institutional trends over two decades.* New York: College Entrance Examination Board.

Woodcock, R. W. (1990). Theoretical foundations of the WJ-R measures of cognitive ability. *Journal of Psycho-Educational Assessment, 8*, 231–258.

9

Interbattery Convergent Measurement Models Applied to the WAIS and WJ-R

Steven H. Aggen
Department of Psychology
University of Virginia

The *Wechsler Adult Intelligence Scale* (WAIS) is one of the more widely used instruments for assessing adult human intelligence (Kaufman, 1990; Matarazzo, 1972; Wechsler, 1941). Since its introduction in 1939, the Wechsler Bellevue and later revisions to the WAIS (Wechsler, 1955) and WAIS-R (Wechsler, 1981) have been the focus of a considerable amount of adult intelligence measurement research (Botwinick, 1977; Guertin, Ladd, Frank, Rabin, & Hiester, 1971; Matarazzo, 1972, 1980). Although numerous factor analytic studies on the WAIS are available in the literature, there still remain questions about what abilities are actually measured by the subscales (Horn & McArdle, 1980; McArdle & Horn, 1989).

From a structural measurement standpoint, empirical measurement research on the WAIS has not culminated in a clear understanding of the number or types of abilities involved in response patterns to WAIS subscale items. Some of this measurement ambiguity may be due to the way in which the WAIS was developed. The multiple criteria used for selecting items to be included in the battery are not easily integrated under any well-articulated theory of human cognitive abilities. As a result, psychometric research has produced only a "fuzzy" architecture of the structure of intellectual abilities measured in the WAIS.

Although a number of issues related to the measurement properties of the WAIS subscales have not been satisfactorily resolved, this has not impeded applied research or deterred its use in basic investigations aimed at establishing a science of human cognition (Horn, 1988). Given the extensive use of the instrument and these equivocal measurement findings, additional psychometric research on the measurement characteristics of the WAIS is still needed.

McArdle and Horn (1989) reported large-sample results based on structural analyses of the WAIS using age as a principle organizing dimension. Models including age relationships arranged in accordance with several prominent theories about intellectual functioning were used to evaluate hypotheses about the measurement characteristics of the WAIS. These models required that expectations about the covariation among the WAIS subscales account for theory-derived constraints as well as patterned age relationships. Although a simple structure interpretation for the WAIS was not supported, model results suggested a complex WAIS measurement structure that was more consistent with a Gf-Gc interpretation. Adopting simple structure may not always serve as the best criteria when investigating measurement structures (McArdle & Cattell, 1994).

One caveat of these findings, and one that continues to be a concern for adult intellectual measurement research using the WAIS, is that most analyses conducted on the WAIS subscales are confined to the subscales themselves. Because of their complex measurement properties and narrow breadth of measurement, internal consistency results based on the WAIS subscales alone may be limited in clarifying questions about ability measurement structure. A number of researchers have expressed concern about the restricted number of markers available in any single battery for adequately measuring and investigating the array of human abilities (Carroll, 1993; Woodcock, 1990).

Test batteries constructed under different psychometric theories provide an opportunity for extending construct validity research (McArdle & Prescott, 1992). Woodcock (1990) conducted a comparative factor analytic study on data from several widely used intellectual assessment batteries. Data from the 1977 *Woodcock-Johnson Psycho-Educational Battery* (WJ) and 1989 *Woodcock-Johnson Psycho-Educational Battery—Revised* (WJ-R) norming samples, as well as concurrent validity data from three other batteries (i.e., the WISC-R, K-ABC, and the fourth edition of the Stanford-Binet) were examined. The multiple battery data were factor analyzed to investigate common structures across batteries using a Gf-Gc organization. The WJ-R cognitive measures were found to be a good empirical representation of the theory of fluid and crystallized intelligence (Cattell, 1940; Horn, 1991).

Of the 15 independent exploratory and confirmatory factor solutions obtained from the nine datasets, median factor loadings for the Wechsler subscales on eight of the WJ-R Gf-Gc factors were reported. The information, comprehension, similarities, and vocabulary WAIS subscales all showed strong loadings on the comprehension/knowledge (Gc) factor as measured in the WJ-R. Median loadings were .67 for information, .60 for similarities, .81 for vocabulary, and .69 for comprehension.

The present study extends the scope of the measurement framework for investigating structural properties of the WAIS subscales. Because a verbal factor is consistently reported in many of the factor analytic studies performed on the WAIS, we use it here as the focus of our convergent measurement models.

The structural modeling techniques used here integrate: interbattery measurement models, patterns of age relations, selection effects, and incomplete data structures (McArdle, 1994b). The verbal WAIS subscales are examined individually and collectively to evaluate their measurement characteristics. Scales from the WJ-R Tests of Cognitive Abilities are used as an external reference of ability measurement to isolate components of measurement variance in the WAIS subscales (Woodcock & Mather, 1989).

METHODS

Three independent samples were used here. Sample 1 consisted of N = 178 National Growth and Change Study (NGCS) (McArdle, 1994a) subjects who were administered all 11 WAIS subscales and selected WJ-R cognitive scales. NGCS subjects were selected from the national norming sample of the WJ-R N = 6,359 (McGrew, Werder, & Woodcock, 1990; Woodcock & Johnson, 1989). Test scores for the 178 subjects were gathered at two separate measurement occasions. In 1993, N = 123 subjects were administered the multiple battery measures and in 1994, N = 55 additional subjects were tested. This sample is referred to as the "linking" sample because subjects have test scores on both batteries.

The second sample came from a large WAIS databank compiled by McArdle and Horn (1989). This sample included N = 1,500 adults over the age of 18 who participated in the 1955 standardization of the WAIS (Wechsler, 1955). Subject weights were calculated from U.S. Census data to make statistical adjustments in accord with current national demographic information (see McArdle & Horn, 1989).

A third sample of N = 2,234 adults was obtained from the WJ-R norming sample (McGrew et al., 1990). The WJ-R norming sample is a nationally representative sample gathered using a random stratified sampling design for 10 individual and demographic variables (Woodcock & Mather, 1989). Subjects in the norming sample ranged in age between 24 months and 95 years of age. Only adults were retained for these analyses.

These last two large samples have representative test score information on the WAIS and WJ-R, respectively. They are used to anchor the intrabattery measurement models adjusting for any sampling fluctuations that might be present in the smaller linking sample. These samples are referred to as the "reference" samples.

Interbattery measurement models are applied to the WAIS information, comprehension, similarities, and vocabulary subscales. Of course, the WAIS-R Verbal Scale also includes the Arithmetic and Digit Span tests. Therefore, the WAIS-R Verbal Scale may be even more complex than the factor examined here. Because the WAIS subscales have different scoring systems, all scales were converted to a common metric. Each subject's total raw score was converted to a percentage correct form. This rescaling puts all subscales on a 0 to 100 metric while retaining the original variable distributions and correlations (see McArdle, 1988; McArdle & Horn, 1989).

Eight WJ-R measures were used to indicate four different broad abilities: comprehension-knowledge, fluid reasoning, long-term storage and retrieval, and short-term memory. The WJ-R tests were selected because the scales theoretically yield interval-level measurement (see Wright & Stone, 1979). The WJ-R *W-score* metric is used for calculating all summary statistics.

Table 9.1 gives descriptive summaries for the WAIS and WJ-R variables in each of the samples. The Gc, Gf, Glr, and Gsm labels denote composite variables used as proxies for the WJ-R ability factors. Each composite is an average of the two WJ-R scales used to measure the factors. Table 9.1 also shows the incomplete data pattern structure across the samples.

Fig. 9.1 gives descriptive summaries for the WAIS verbal subscales and WJ-R composites. A 95% confidence boundary is included to indicate where the bulk of the data points fall, as well as a linear regression line. Data points located outside the ellipsoid suggest possible outliers; outliers may be leverage points or influential observations that disproportionately affect the estimated regression coefficient (see Belsley, Kuh, & Welsch, 1980).

MODELS

A series of path and latent variable models (McDonald, 1985) were developed to test hypotheses about the measurement properties of the verbal subscales of the WAIS. Both univariate and multivariate interbattery models were fit to multiple sample data. Multiple-group models were used to stabilize intrabattery measurement structures, and to estimate and interpret components of WAIS measurement variance. A priori hypotheses based on results reported by Woodcock (1990) were evaluated using a confirmatory approach. Complete technical details are not presented here (but computer program scripts can be obtained from the author).

Parameter value estimates and standard errors were obtained using LISREL 8 (Jöreskog & Sörbom, 1993). All models are expressed in RAM notation and fit to cross-product information (McArdle & McDonald, 1984). Maxi-

TABLE 9.1

Summary Statistics for the NGCS Linking Sample (1993, 1994),
the 1955 WAIS Standardization Sample, and the WJ-R Norming Sample

Name	IN	CO	SI	VO	Gc	Gf	Glr	Gsm	Age[1]	Age[2]	Age[3]
National Growth and Change Samples (1993, 1994), $N = 178$											
Mean	66.42	73.34	62.70	73.98	543.51	508.27	498.47	510.36	0.37	4.69	5.52
Standard	14.43	12.71	18.14	13.93	16.91	20.77	14.81	17.52	2.14	4.50	21.77
IN	1.00										
CO	.56	1.00									
SI	.45	.30	1.00								
VO	.69	.57	.46	1.00							
Gc	.66	.44	.54	.71	1.00						
Gf	.39	.31	.55	.23	.56	1.00					
Glr	.26	.25	.55	.19	.52	.78	1.00				
Gsm	.28	.25	.32	.35	.55	.59	.57	1.00			
Age[1]	.02	.05	−.39	.16	−.32	−.68	−.71	−.50	1.00		
Age[2]	−.20	−.27	−.25	−.08	−.50	−.45	−.38	−.43	.39	1.00	
Age[3]	.04	.03	−.31	.18	−.41	−.65	−.67	−.54	.87	.65	1.00
1955 WAIS standardization sample, $N = 1,500$											
Mean	53.27	59.70	48.57	52.89	—	—	—	—	−1.32	3.61	−9.11
Standard	19.94	15.74	22.28	21.52	—	—	—	—	1.37	3.59	11.62
IN	1.00										
CO	.72	1.00									
SI	.71	.66	1.00								
VO	.83	.75	.73	1.00							
Gc	—	—	—	—	—						
Gf	—	—	—	—	—	—					
Glr	—	—	—	—	—	—	—				
Gsm	—	—	—	—	—	—	—	—			
Age[1]	.00	−.03	−.15	.06	—	—	—	—	1.00		
Age[2]	−.03	−.01	.10	−.09	—	—	—	—	−.89	1.00	
Age[3]	.04	.01	−.09	.10	—	—	—	—	.88	−.99	1.00
WJ-R Norming Sample, $N = 2,254$											
Mean	—	—	—	—	536.45	508.67	499.95	512.71	−1.42	5.72	−11.44
Standard	—	—	—	—	20.54	19.50	13.83	19.24	1.92	3.75	17.15
IN	—										
CO	—	—									
SI	—	—	—								
VO	—	—	—	—							
Gc	—	—	—	—	1.00						
Gf	—	—	—	—	0.59	1.00					
Glr	—	—	—	—	0.52	0.72	1.00				
Gsm	—	—	—	—	0.57	0.56	0.53	1.00			
Age[1]	—	—	—	—	−.16	−.54	−.55	−.37	1.00		
Age[2]	—	—	—	—	−.15	.11	.16	.03	−.46	1.00	
Age[3]	—	—	—	—	−.11	−.47	−.50	−.33	.93	−.50	1.00

Notes:—indicates unavailable data. Age is centered at 50.

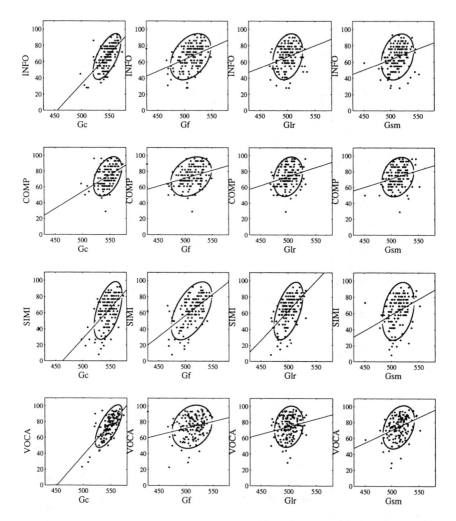

FIG. 9.1.   Bivariate scatter plots of the WAIS verbal subscales and WJ-R factor composite variables with 95% confidence ellipsoids and linear regressions added.

mum likelihood is used to minimize the fit function. The likelihood ratio test (LRT), under specific distributional assumptions, may be evaluated as a chi-square variate with degrees of freedom (df) determined by the number of model parameters to be estimated. The root mean squared error of approximation (RMSEA; Browne & Cudeck, 1993; Steiger, 1990) is also reported to quantify the probability of "close fit" [P(close)].

Fig. 9.2 presents a path model illustrating the univariate interbattery measurement model following diagraming conventions suggested by Mc-Ardle and Boker (1991). Mean and intercept terms are important in these multiple-group models to handle selection effects (see McArdle, 1988). The complete model imposes a structural organization on the observed covariation among the WAIS, WJ-R composites, and age variables.

The model in Fig. 9.2 is used to organize the information, comprehension, similarities, and vocabulary subscales as direct outcomes of the WJ-R composite variables. This model permits the decomposition of the measurement

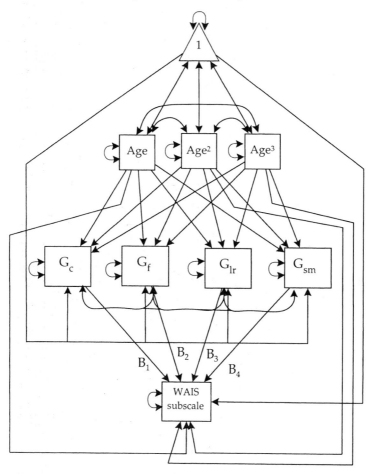

FIG. 9.2.   Single-group interbattery convergent measurement model isolating components of variance in the separate verbal subscales of the WAIS, using composite variables of factors measured in the WJ-R. Note: a somewhat unusual notation in this model is the double-head symmetric arrows connecting the triangle and age variables. These are read as the covariance between age and a constant vector of ones. When using cross-products, these are the mean of each age variable. The slings attached to the age variable are no longer variance terms but rather mean cross-products.

variance of each WAIS subscale using the WJ-R composites and age variables. Background correlations among the WJ-R composites and age polynomials are allowed to be estimated from the data. The differences between this model and a series of separate multiple regressions is that all WJ-R composite predictors are statistically "adjusted" for the linear, quadratic, and cubic effects of age and a maximum likelihood, rather than a least squares algorithm being used to estimate parameter values.

Fig. 9.3 presents a multiple-group version of the model presented in Fig. 9.2. The same structural parameters of Model 2 are fit, but this model brings in the reference samples. To symbolize incomplete data structures, nodes or pseudovariables are used (Horn & McArdle, 1980; Jöreskog & Sörbom, 1988;

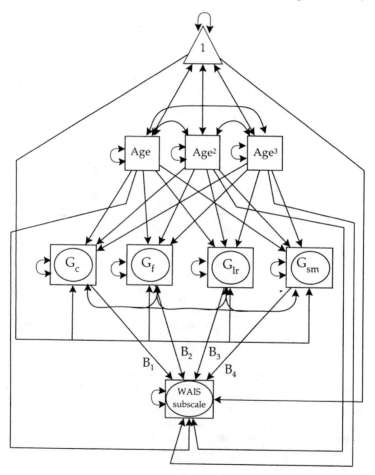

FIG. 9.3.   Multiple-group interbattery convergent measurement model, with incomplete patterns of variable information.

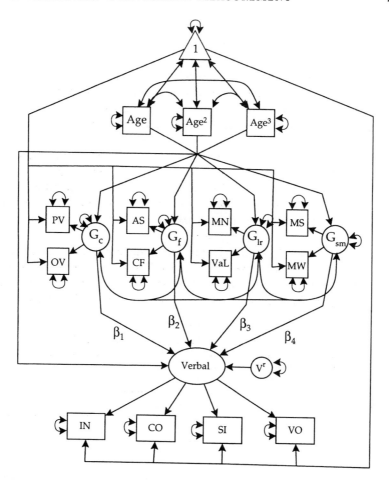

FIG 9.4.   Latent variable interbattery convergent measurement model, using factors from the WJ-R to isolate components of measurable variance in the WAIS verbal factor.

Rindskopf, 1984). Nodes indicate whether variables are present or absent in the data.

Fig. 9.4 shows the full latent variable multiple-group model. Multiple-group notation is suppressed here for clarity. This complete multivariate latent interbattery measurement model gives estimates of the measurement variance components of the WJ-R abilities on the WAIS verbal factor scores. The factor model is used to determine the communalities of the WAIS and WJ-R measured variables, and to examine the structure of the interbattery regressions. This model gives a direct evaluation of the variance structure of the WAIS verbal factor in terms of the WJ-R ability factors.

RESULTS

Univariate results are given in Table 9.2. Models are listed across the columns, and each row displays information about a model parameter. Each model parameter has two entries. The first column is the maximum likelihood estimate for the parameter, and the second column indicates whether the estimate is significant.

Cubic age effects for all four WAIS subscales in the unrestricted and restricted models are significant. Some care is needed when interpreting age polynomial estimates. Because the cubic age parameter is significantly different from zero given that all lower order terms are estimated, on statistical grounds, a complex curvilinear interpretation of age relationships among the WAIS verbal subscales is retained.

The labels B_{gc}, B_{gf}, B_{glr}, and B_{gsm} denote parameter estimates for the direct effect of the WJ-R ability composites on the WAIS subscales. Because cross-product information is used, parameter estimates are unstandardized and can be interpreted as the percentage correct unit change in a WAIS verbal

TABLE 9.2
Univariate Results for Interbattery Regressions of the Four
WAIS Verbal Subscales Onto Composite Variables Representing
Four WJ-R Factors (Single-Group Model Using Complete Data
From the NGCS Linking Sample; See Fig. 9.2)

| | \multicolumn{8}{c}{Models} | | | | | | | |
| | \multicolumn{2}{c}{IN} | | \multicolumn{2}{c}{CO} | | \multicolumn{2}{c}{SI} | | \multicolumn{2}{c}{VO} |
Par	U	R	U	R	U	R	U	R
B_0	−35.6 *	−29.3 *	−23.1 *	−10.1 *	−35.1 *	−23.8 *	−44.2 *	−35.5 *
B_{age1}	−.07	−.20 *	.06	−.11	−.29 *	−.48 *	.04	−.04
B_{age2}	−.04	−.05	−.11	−.10 *	−.02	−.01	.01	.01
B_{age3}	.05 *	.05 *	.04 *	.04 *	.04 *	.03 *	.04 *	.04 *
B_{Gc}	5.6 *	6.6 *	1.7 *	3.3 *	4.3 *	5.5 *	6.8 *	7.9 *
B_{Gf}	2.5 *	= 0	1.6 *	= 0	1.9 *	= 0	.21	= 0
B_{Glr}	.11	= 0	2.1 *	= 0	3.5 *	=0	.96	= 0
B_{Gsm}	−.21	= 0	.51	= 0	−1.5 *	= 0	1.7 *	=0
dLRT	0	22	0	23	0	22	0	30
ddf	0	3	0	3	0	3	0	3
RMSEA	—	.190	—	.196	—	.190	—	.227
95 CI	—	.11–.28	—	.11–.29	—	.11–.28	—	.14–.32
$P_{perfect}$	—	.00	—	.00	—	.00	—	.00
P_{close}	—	.00	—	.00	—	.00	—	.00

Notes: U = Unrestricted model, R = Restricted model, * = Parameter estimate significant, $p < .05$.

subscale for every unit change in the WJ-R composite, holding constant all other variables.

The WJ-R comprehension-knowledge (B_{gc}) ability factor had the largest effect on the WAIS subscales. The effect of B_{gc} is enhanced in all cases when other parameters are forced to zero. However, there is evidence from these unrestricted models that other WJ-R abilities have nonzero effects on the WAIS subscale variance. The reasoning (B_{gf}) parameter estimate is significant in the information, comprehension, and similarities models. Long-term storage and retrieval (B_{glr}) is significant in the comprehension and similarities models, as is short-term memory (B_{gsm}) for similarities and vocabulary.

The results show the differences (dLRT) between the restricted and the unrestricted models are all significant (e.g., $dLRT(3) = 30$ for vocabulary). These differences are based on the three degrees of freedom gained by forcing B_{gf}, B_{glr}, and B_{gsm} to zero. The restricted model does a poorer job of accounting for the data. These results are consistent with the interpretation that the WAIS subscales are complex and do not represent unidimensional measurement properties.

Results for univariate multiple-group models are given in Table 9.3. These results are used to verify findings obtained in the single-group models. Metric invariance is forced on all one-headed arrows across groups (Horn & Mc-Ardle, 1992; Meredith 1964), whereas all background covariances are allowed to be estimated from the data. These invariance constraints adjust parameter estimates for sampling fluctuations that might be present in the smaller linking sample.

Almost all estimates show a higher unit change for the WAIS subscales given a unit change in the WJ-R composites. The pattern of regression coefficients is similar to the univariate single-group results, except for the vocabulary subscale. The vocabulary subscale now has significant parameter estimates on all four WJ-R ability composites. The vocabulary model produced the poorest fit for both the restricted and unrestricted models LRT(18) = 277 and LRT(18) = 310. The RMSEA is .06 with a p(close) = .007. The restricted similarities model produced the largest LRT difference (dLRT(3) = 40). In the comprehension model, the Gc component is now the largest but both Gf and Glr have nontrivial effects.

Complete results for the multivariate latent single-group models are shown in Table 9.4. Common factors of the WJ-R are now directly estimated. Columns two through six give results for placing different restrictions on the model. Age effects are not altered much when different restrictions on the interbattery structural regressions are imposed.

Three WJ-R factors had significant effects in the model. Comprehension/knowledge again showed the strongest relationship with the WAIS verbal factor in all models. Removing this relationship results in a dLRT = 50. The "No Gf" model showed a smaller but statistically significant difference

TABLE 9.3

Univariate Results for Interbattery Regressions of the Four
WAIS Verbal Subscales Onto Composite Variables Representing
Four WJ-R Factors (Multiple-Group Model Using Linking Sample
and Reference Sample Data; See Fig. 9.3)

	Models							
	IN		*CO*		*SI*		*VO*	
Par	U	R	U	R	U	R	U	R
B_0	−45.5 *	−39.4 *	−41.3 *	−27.7 *	−57.3 *	−42.7 *	−61.1 *	−49.4 *
B_{age1}	.19 *	.05	.32 *	.09	.07	−.17 *	.30 *	.16 *
B_{age2}	.07 *	−.08 *	.08 *	.08 *	.09 *	.11 *	.09 *	.09 *
B_{age3}	.02 *	.02 *	.01 *	.01 *	.02 *	.02 *	.03 *	.03 *
B_{Gc}	6.5 *	8.3 *	3.5 *	6.38 *	5.9 *	8.8 *	8.2 *	20.3 *
B_{Gf}	3.2 *	= 0	3.0 *	= 0	3.4 *	= 0	1.2 *	=0
B_{Glr}	.31	= 0	2.5 *	= 0	4.78 *	= 0	1.9 *	= 0
B_{Gsm}	−.43	= 0	.27	= 0	−2.1 *	= 0	1.4 *	= 0
LRT_t (df)	159 (18)	191 (21)	192 (18)	225 (21)	172 (18)	212 (21)	277 (18)	310 (21)
LRT_{g1}	139 [88]	170 [89]	176 [92]	210 [93]	154 [89]	192 [91]	228 [82]	263 [85]
LRT_{g2}	11 [7]	12 [6]	9 [5]	9 [4]	10 [6]	11 [5]	33 [12]	31 [10]
LRT_{g3}	8 [5]	9 [5]	7 [3]	7 [3]	8 [5]	9 [4]	16 [6]	16 [5]
dLRT (ddf)	—	33 (3)	—	33 (3)	—	40 (3)	—	33 (3)
RMSEA	.04	.04	.05	.05	.05	.05	.06	.06
95% CI	.04–.05	.04–.05	.04–.06	.04–.06	.04–.05	.04–.05	.05–.07	.05–.07
$P_{perfect}$	.00	.00	.00	.00	.00	.00	.00	.00
P_{close}	.96	.95	.66	.66	.88	.80	.01	.01

Notes: U = Unrestricted model, R = Restricted model, [ ] = Percentage of total c^2, * = Parameter estimate significant, $p < .05$.

(dLRT(1) = 6). The last model, labeled "Only Gc," forces all but the comprehension/knowledge parameter to be zero and yields a dLRT(3) = 28. In summary, these results suggest that although Gc accounts for the largest portion of variance in the WAIS verbal factor, it is not the only WJ-R ability sharing consistent measurement variance with the WAIS verbal factor.

Multiple-group latent variable model results are given in Table 9.5. The multiple-group models provide a clearer resolution of the relationships between the WAIS and WJ-R factors, but do not alter the overall interpretation. The largest portion of measurement variance in the WAIS verbal factor is accounted for by Gc ($B_{gc} = 1.84$, $t = 11.9$). Fluid reasoning is still a significant predictor of measurement variance in the WAIS verbal factor, as indicated by the fit (dLRT(1) = 4, p(close) = .955). These multiple group results also provide information about the proportions of misfit contributed by each sample.

TABLE 9.4

Latent Variable Multivariate Model Results for the Direct Regression of the Verbal Factor Measured by the WAIS Subscales on Selected Ability Factors Measured in the WJ-R (Single-Group Model)

Par	Full Model		No G_f		No G_{lr}, G_{sm}		No G_c		Only G_c	
B_{age1}	−.23	*	−.23	*	−.24	*	−.24		−.23	*
B_{age2}	−.15	*	−.15	*	−.15	*	−.15	*	−.15	*
B_{age3}	.04	*	.05	*	.05	*	.05		.05	*
β_{gc}	.71	*	.72	*	.76	*	= 0		1.15	*
β_{gf}	.33	*	= 0		.51	*	1.0	*	= 0	
β_{glr}	.12		.34	*	= 0		1.24	*	= 0	
β_{gsm}	.20	*	.35	*	= 0		1.40	*	= 0	
λ_{pv}	= 1		= 1		= 1		= 1		= 1	
λ_{ov}	.51	*	.52	*	.51	*	.64	*	.62	*
λ_{as}	= 1		= 1		= 1		= 1		= 1	
λ_{cf}	1.12	*	1.11	*	1.11	*	1.12	*	1.12	*
λ_{mn}	= 1		= 1		= 1		= 1		= 1	
λ_{val}	1.24	*	1.23	*	1.23	*	1.24	*	1.21	*
λ_{ms}	= 1		= 1		= 1		= 1		= 1	
λ_{mw}	.96	*	.99	*	.91	*	.90	*	.88	*
λ_{in}	.99	*	.98	*	1.01	*	1.01	*	.97	*·
λ_{co}	.66	*	.65	*	.68	*	.67	*	.66	*
λ_{si}	.72	*	.71	*	.75	*	.76	*	.73	*
λ_{vo}	= 1		= 1		= 1		= 1		= 1	
ε_{in}	.59	*	.61	*	.56	*	.57	*	.63	*
ε_{co}	.96	*	.97	*	.94	*	.95	*	.96	*
ε_{si}	2.50	*	2.50	*	2.50	*	2.40	*	2.50	*
ε_{vo}	.45	*	.42	*	.47	*	.46	*	.39	*
LRT_t (df)	439 (66)		445 (67)		443 (68)		489 (67)		467 (69)	
dLRT (ddf)	—		6 (1)		4 (2)		50 (1)		28 (3)	
RMSEA	.18		.18		.18		.19		.18	
95% CI	.16–.20		.16–.20		.15–.20		.17–.21		.16–.20	
$P_{perfect}$	.00		.00		.00		.00		.00	
P_{close}	.00		.00		.00		.00		.00	

Notes: B = unstandardized regression weight, β = standardized regression weight, λ = factor loading, ε = uniqueness, U = unrestricted model, R = restricted model, * = parameter significant, $p < .05$.

TABLE 9.5

Latent Variable Multivariate Model Results Examining
the Direct Relationships Between the Verbal Factor Marked
by the WAIS Subscales and the Selected Ability Factors
from the WJ-R Tests of Cogntitive Ability (Three-Group Model)

Par	Full Model	No G_f	No G_{lr}, G_{sm}	No G_c	Only G_c
B_{age1}	−.31 *	−.31 *	−.31 *	−.31	−.29 *
B_{age2}	−.04 *	−.04 *	−.03 *	−.05 *	−.03 *
B_{age3}	.04 *	.04 *	.04 *	.04	.04 *
β_{Gc}	1.8 *	2.0 *	2.0 *	= 0	2.0 *
β_{Gf}	.75 *	= 0	.26 *	7.0 *	= 0
β_{Glr}	−.25	.25 *	= 0	−.17	= 0
β_{Gsm}	−.20 *	−.03	= 0	.17	= 0
λ_{pv}	= 1	= 1	= 1	= 1	= 1
λ_{ov}	1.01 *	1.01 *	1.10 *	1.01 *	1.01 *
λ_{as}	= 1	= 1	= 1	= 1	= 1
λ_{cf}	1.11 *	1.10 *	1.10 *	1.10 *	1.10 *
λ_{mn}	= 1	= 1	= 1	= 1	= 1
λ_{val}	1.34 *	1.34 *	1.34 *	1.34 *	1.34 *
λ_{ms}	= 1	= 1	= 1	= 1	= 1
λ_{mw}	1.10 *	1.10 *	1.11 *	1.11 *	1.10 *
λ_{in}	.87 *	.87 *	.87 *	.87 *	.87 *
λ_{co}	.64 *	.64 *	.64 *	.64 *	.64 *
λ_{si}	.87 *	.87 *	.86 *	.86 *	.86 *
λ_{vo}	= 1	= 1	= 1	= 1	= 1
ε_{in}	.82 *	.82 *	.82 *	.82 *	.82 *
ε_{co}	.83 *	.83 *	.83 *	.83 *	.983 *
ε_{si}	1.85 *	1.85 *	1.85 *	1.85 *	1.85 *
ε_{vo}	.64 *	.64 *	.64 *	.64 *	.64 *
LRT_t (df)	1397 (140)	1401 (141)	1400 (142)	1425 (141)	1405 (143)
LRT_{g1}	830 [59]	841 [59]	835 [60]	835 [59]	832 [59]
LRT_{g2}	178 [13]	192 [14]	175 [13]	195 [14]	183 [13]
LRT_{g3}	388 [28]	389 [27]	380 [27]	394 [27]	389 [28]
dLRT (ddf)	—	4 (1)	3 (2)	28 (1)	8 (3)
RMSEA	.05	.05	.05	.05	.05
95% CI	.04–.05	.04–.05	.04–.05	.04–.05	.04–.05
$P_{perfect}$	.00	.00	.00	.00	.00
P_{close}	.94	.96	.97	.91	.97

Notes: B = unstandardized regression weight, β = standardized weight, λ = factor loading, ε = uniqueness, [ ] = percentage of total χ^2, * = parameter estimate significant, $p < .05$.

DISCUSSION

The measurement literature on the WAIS has not supported a classical simple structure interpretation. Factors extracted are often difficult to interpret, because of sparse and muddled markings within the WAIS subscales. Some of this ambiguity may be attributed to the lack of a clearly specified structural theory about the abilities measured in the WAIS. Of the abilities measured in the WAIS, the verbal factor has consistently surfaced as being the most robust.

To further investigate the ability measurement structure of the WAIS information, comprehension, similarities, and vocabulary subscales, a series of interbattery convergent measurement models were proposed. The models tested both convergent and discriminant measurement hypotheses. Selected ability measures from the WJ-R served as cross-battery sources for decomposing components of measurement variance in the WAIS subscales.

Univariate results suggest that each of the WAIS subscales is a complex mixture of different abilities as measured in the WJ-R. Comprehension and similarities showed the most measurement diversity. Comprehension had significant components of variance for Gc, Gf, and Glr, whereas similarities displayed nontrivial components for all four broad abilities. In the multiple-group models correcting for selection effects, the WAIS vocabulary subscale had significant portions of measurement variance accounted for by all four WJ-R composites. This is a particularly noteworthy result, because vocabulary is often considered to be a central marker of the verbal/comprehension ability and general intelligence.

The verbal factor defined by the information, comprehension, similarities, and vocabulary WAIS subscales (but not including the Arithmetic and Digit Span subtests) was closely aligned with the comprehension-knowledge (Gc) factor of the WJ-R. Although Gc was clearly the most predominant predictor of measurement variance, a nontrivial fluid reasoning component was also evident.

The subscales were also found to have complex age patterns. Cubic age polynomials were retained for all WAIS subscales. These nonlinear age relations are consistent with the finding that the WAIS subscales measure a mixture of different abilities. The factors, Gc, Gf, Glr, and Gsm are characterized by different life-span developmental trajectories. When combined in various proportions, complicated age patterns can result (Horn & Cattell, 1966). The nonlinear age relations may be attributed to the WAIS subscales having both Gc and Gf measurement variance. These interbattery results suggest the WAIS verbal subscales to be more complex than previously thought.

Although these interbattery results can be compared to the confirmatory factor models reported by Woodcock (1990), the latent interbattery structural regression analyses reported here are conceptually different from those used by Woodcock. The restrictive interbattery models isolate and separate common portions of the WJ-R measures, whereas the factor comparisons used by Woodcock did not. The regression of the WAIS verbal factor onto the WJ-R ability factors provides direct estimates of the measurement variance in the WAIS accounted for by the WJ-R abilities. Also, age effects, mean structures, and selection effects are not directly dealt with in the Woodcock analyses.

These findings offer further support for a Gf-Gc interpretation of the WAIS, but also suggest additional complexity in the interpretation of the WAIS verbal factor (Horn & McArdle, 1980; McArdle, 1989). Although the WAIS verbal factor was closely aligned with the WJ-R comprehension-knowledge factor, a reliable Gf component was also retained. This result suggests that the subscales are measuring aspects of intellectual functioning other than those attributable to acculturation. For example, successfully answering items on the similarities subscale may depend on more than word recognition and understanding; the ability to extract relationships and form concepts may also be involved. The mixture of WJ-R abilities found for the WAIS subscales make sense if the items included in the subscales are examined closely. With more difficult items, subjects may be invoking new strategies based on reorganizing of their thinking.

In sum, WAIS subscales were examined at both the univariate and multivariate levels, and the results were complex. Nevertheless, the modeling strategy used here demonstrates how *intrabattery* simple structure construct validation can be supplemented by using multiple-group *interbattery* structural regression models.

AUTHOR'S NOTE

The author is indebted to Jack McArdle for his ideas about the methodological techniques discussed in this research, and to Richard Woodcock for his comments and suggestions. This chapter is based on a poster session presented at the conference of the same name as this text at the University of Virginia, Charlottesville, VA, September 22–24, 1994.

REFERENCES

Belsley, D. A., Kuh, E., & Welsch, R. E. (1980). *Regression diagnostics*. New York: Wiley.
Botwinick, J. (1977). *Intellectual abilities*. In J. E. Birren & K. W. Schaie (Eds.), *Handbook of the psychology of aging* (pp. 580–605). New York: Van Nostrand Reinhold.
Browne, M. W., & Cudeck, R. (1993). Alternative ways of assessing model fit. In K. A. Bollen

& J. S. Long (Eds.), *Testing structural equation models* (pp. 136–162). Newbury Park, CA: Sage.

Carroll, J. B. (1993). *Human cognitive abilities: A survey of factor analytic studies.* New York: Cambridge University Press.

Cattell, R. B. (1940). A culture-free intelligence test I. *Journal of Educational Psychology, 31*(3), 161–179.

Guertin, W. H., Ladd, C. E., Frank, G. H., Rabin, A. I., & Hiester, D. S. (1971). Research with the Wechsler Intelligence Scales for Adults: 1965–1970. *The Psychological Record, 21*, 289–339.

Horn, J. L. (1988). Thinking about human abilities. In J. R. Nesselroade & R. B. Cattell (Eds.), *Handbook of multivariate psychology* (rev. ed., pp. 645–865). New York: Academic Press.

Horn, J. L. (1991). Measurement of intellectual capacities: A review of theory. In K. S. McGrew, J. K. Werder, & R. W. Woodcock (Eds.), *WJ-R technical manual* (pp. 197–232). Chicago: Riverside.

Horn, J. L., & Cattell, R. B. (1966). Refinement and test of the theory of fluid and crystallized general intelligence. *Journal of Educational Psychology, 57*(5), 253–270.

Horn, J. L., & McArdle, J. J. (1980). Perspectives on mathematical/statistical model building (MASMOB) in research on aging. In L. W. Poon (Ed.), *Aging in the 1980's: Selected contemporary issues in the psychology of aging* (pp. 503–541). Washington, DC: American Psychological Association.

Horn, J. L., & McArdle, J. J. (1992). A practical and theoretical guide to measurement invariance in aging research. *Experimental Aging Research, 18*(3), 117–144.

Jöreskog, K. G., & Sörbom, D. (1988). *LISREL 7: A guide to the program and applications.* Chicago: SPSS.

Jöreskog, K. G., & Sörbom, D. (1993). *LISREL 8 users guide.* Chicago: Scientific Software.

Kaufman, A. S. (1990). *Assessing adolescent and adult intelligence.* Boston: Allyn & Bacon.

Matarazzo, J. D. (1972). *Wechsler's measurement and appraisal of adult intelligence* (5th ed.). Baltimore, MD: Williams & Wilkins.

Matarazzo, J. D. (1980). *Wechsler's measurement and appraisal of adult intelligence.* New York: Oxford University Press.

McArdle, J. J. (1988). Dynamic but structural equation modeling of repeated measures data. In J. R. Nesselroade & R. B. Cattell (Eds.), *Handbook of multivariate experimental psychology* (2nd ed., pp. 561–614). New York: Plenum.

McArdle, J. J. (1989). A structural modeling experiment with multiple growth functions. In R. Kanfer, P. L. Ackerman, & R. Cudeck (Eds.), *Abilities, motivation, and methodology: The Minnesota symposium on learning and individual differences* (pp. 71–117). Hillsdale, NJ: Lawrence Erlbaum Associates.

McArdle, J. J. (1994a). *Growth curves of adult intelligence from convergence data.* National Institute of Aging grant application, University of Virginia.

McArdle, J. J. (1994b). Structural factor analysis experiments with incomplete data. *Multivariate Behavioral Research, 29*(4), 409–454.

McArdle, J. J., & Boker, S. M. (1991). *RAMpath: Path diagram software.* Hillsdale, NJ: Lawrence Erlbaum Associates.

McArdle, J. J., & Cattell, R. B. (1994). Structural equation models of factorial invariance in parallel proportional profiles and oblique confactor problems. *Multivariate Behavioral Research, 29*(1), 63–113.

McArdle, J. J., & Horn, J. L. (1989). *A mega analysis of aging and the WAIS: Structural modeling of intellectual abilities organized by age trends.* Unpublished manuscript, University of Virginia.

McArdle, J. J., & McDonald, R. P. (1984). Some algebraic properties of the reticular action model for moment structures. *British Journal of Mathematical and Statistical Psychology, 37*, 234–251.

McArdle, J. J., & Prescott, C. A. (1992). Age-based construct validation using structural equation modeling. *Experimental Aging Research, 18*(3), 87–115.

McDonald, R. P. (1985). *Factor analysis and related methods.* Hillsdale, NJ: Lawrence Erlbaum Associates.

McGrew, K. S., Werder, J., & Woodcock, R. W. (1990). *WJ-R technical manual.* Allen, TX: DLM Teaching Resources.

Meredith, W. (1964). Notes on factorial invariance. *Psychometrika, 29*(2), 177–185.

Rindskopf, D. (1984). Using phantom and imaginary latent variables to parameterize constraints in linear structural models. *Psychometrika, 49*(1), 37–47.

Steiger, J. H. (1990). Structural model evaluation and modification: An interval estimation approach. *Multivariate Behavioral Research, 25*(2), 173–180.

Wechsler, D. (1941). *The measurement of adult intelligence* (2nd ed.). New York: Williams & Wilkins.

Wechsler, D. (1955). *WAIS manual: Wechsler adult intelligence scale.* New York: Psychological Corporation.

Wechsler, D. (1981). *WAIS-R: Wechsler adult intelligence scale—Revised.* New York: Harcourt, Brace, Jovanovich.

Woodcock, R. W. (1990). Theoretical foundations of the WJ-R measures of cognitive ability. *Journal of Psvchoeducational Assessment, 8*, 231–258.

Woodcock, R. W., & Johnson, M. B. (1989). *Woodcock-Johnson psycho-educational battery —Revised.* Allen, TX: DLM Teaching Resources.

Woodcock, R. W., & Mather, N. (1989). *WJ-R tests of cognitive ability standard and supplemental batteries: Examiner's manual.* Chicago, IL: Riverside.

Wright, B. D., & Stone, M. H. (1979). *Best test design.* Chicago: MESA Press.

10

A Psychotelemetry Experiment in Fluid Intelligence

Steven M. Boker
University of Notre Dame

John J. McArdle
The University of Virginia

Collecting individually administered mental ability tests is often a long and tedious task. Data are often collected on readily available volunteer samples of persons, such as college students, hospital patients, or elderly persons. It is extremely difficult to measure individuals who are middle-aged, occupationally successful, or otherwise actively engaged in work or social events. It follows that subject selection biases are a persistent problem (e.g. Berk, 1983; Heckman & Robb 1986).

Specific kinds of measurement bias are created due to difficulties in testing. Some logistic problems can be managed with tests having multiple-choice formats, or with time-limited tests, but such problems are exacerbated in difficult tasks of mental power. Difficult tasks are precisely the kind needed to measure individual differences in the cognitive abilities, such as the cognitive ability termed *general fluid intelligence* (g_f; after Horn, 1988; Horn & Cattell, 1982). By definition, g_f requires "the adduction of relationships which are not previously defined by the culture." (Horn, 1988, p. 660). There is growing evidence that computer-assisted testing procedures may be helpful in these kinds of psychometric measurements (Embretson, 1992).

Over the past 2 decades, the computer network now known as the Internet has exhibited remarkable growth (Krol, 1992). The Internet connects computers used by researchers, government installations, and technical businesses around the world. The experiment we describe here makes use of the Internet by using electronic mail (e-mail) to facilitate electronic transfer of our testing program and the data generated by a subject's interaction with the program. This means that the subject can participate in a psychometric experiment at a location convenient to him or her, without the need for a researcher to be physically present.

One premise of this experiment is that a large proportion of individuals using the Internet are the kinds of people who are not typically sampled in standard psychological research: successful, active, and middle-aged. It is further supposed that individuals using the Internet would be attracted by the novelty of participating in a new type of experiment using Internet technology. Some empirical data suggested that such an effect due to self-selection in computerized surveys might be observed (Synodinos, Papacostas, & Okimoto, 1994; Walsh, Kiesler, Sproull & Hesse, 1992).

We propose the general term *psychotelemetry* to refer to the remote collection of psychometric data. This choice of terminology follows the accepted use of *biotelemetry*, which refers to the remote collection of biometric data. In this pilot experiment we examined the possibility of testing individuals remotely, using a computer testing program called PsyLog (Boker & McArdle, 1982, 1992). The responses to individuals on a set of power letter series items (after Horn, 1988) were collected and analyzed using several forms of data analyses to examine the individual response patterns and their relation to age.

METHODS

Subject Participation

Participation in this pilot experiment was requested by posting a news item on a NeXT computer user's newsgroup (comp.sys.next.misc) of the Usenet News. The Usenet News is an electronic information forum that is similar to a computer bulletin board and is available to users of the Internet (Krol, 1992). To the estimated 40,000 readers of this newsgroup, we sent out a "request for testing." We received e-mail replies from $N = 170$ individuals. The testing program was mailed to all persons and data from $N = 47$ individual NeXT users were received (a response rate of 27%). In all, a period of 10 days elapsed from the date of original call for volunteers to the date when the last set of data were received.

Subjects represented an unusually narrow set of selection criteria, because in order to participate they needed to: use a NeXT computer, which was directly connected to the Internet; be active readers of the Usenet news; be willing to volunteer for an experiment in measurement of abilities; and be persistent enough to finish the test in spite of minor technical difficulties with the program that presented the experiment.

A number of problems prevented willing volunteers from being able to participate. Some volunteers were not directly connected to the Internet. Roughly 30 volunteers (30/170) were prevented from participating by their employers, who felt that their volunteers' participation might occur during working hours. Anecdotally we also know that, due to unforeseen and unknown circumstances, an unknown number of volunteers were simply unable to run the software that presented the experiment. These problems are likely to be encountered in future psychotelemetric experiments.

Computer Software

We used a version of the PsyLog software (Boker & McArdle, 1992) to present the experiment and collect the data. PsyLog is software that was written specifically for the automatic presentation of psychometric instruments and the automatic collection and archiving of the resulting data. PsyLog reads a command file containing the psychometric instrument and then presents to the subject a series of computer screens, one at a time. The subject is asked to respond to these screens, and PsyLog stores the responses into a subject record within the software. This subject record is then either (a) stored to disk if PsyLog is being used on a machine located at the experimenter's facility, or (b) automatically returned electronically via e-mail to the experimenter if PsyLog is being used at a remote location.

In this experiment, we distributed the PsyLog program to each volunteer subject electronically via e-mail over the Internet. All subjects then ran the program on their local computer. Once the instrument had been completed, the subject was informed that the experiment was over, and was asked to give consent for the data to be used. If the subject responded positively, the results were automatically e-mailed back to our laboratory for aggregation into a central database. In order to preserve the privacy of a subject, the Psy-Log program encrypted the subject's record before e-mailing the result of the experiment.

One advantage of computer-presented testing is that response time data can be gathered for each item in the experiment (Rafaeli & Tractinsky, 1991). With millisecond accuracy, PsyLog captures the stimulus presentation time and response time (relative to the beginning of the experiment) of every event that occurs during the process of the experiment. This data presented us with the opportunity of an item-level analysis of the response time data.

A Fluid Intelligence Scale

The specific battery we presented here included a subset of items previously used in our studies of fluid intelligence g_f (see Horn, 1988; Horn & Cattell, 1966, 1982). The power letter series task we used was developed by John L.

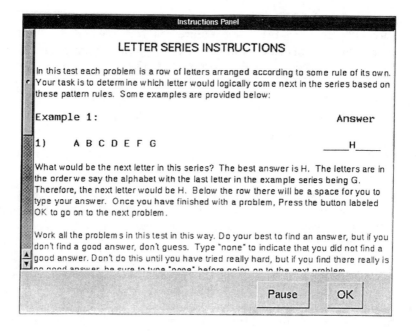

FIG. 10.1.   The panel that presented the instructions to the subject.

Horn for use in research studies of aging. In this task, subjects were required to examine a series of 5 to 10 letters and then enter the next best letter in the sequence. The subjects were told to take their time, answer each item in order, and use a "no-answer" option if they thought there was no best letter. The panel that presented the instructions to the subjects is shown in Fig. 10.1.

In earlier experiments (see Horn 1988), 3 practice items were self-administered and then 35 items were ordered into 7 sets of 5 items. Each of the 5 items was placed in theoretically increasing levels of difficulty, so a subject would get a few easy items, then some very hard items, and then go back to some easy items. This ordering was designed to have individuals continue to work on several items at their highest possible level without complete frustration. This electronic administration followed the same exact format. The overall battery presented by PsyLog included:

1. A short introduction to the project.
2. A brief set of demographic questions.
3. A 38-item power letter series task of g_f (3 practice items).
4. A comparable 38-item power number series task of g_f (3 practice items).
5. An informed consent agreement.
6. A debriefing statement.

The exact keystroke responses and the time-of-response data were stored in individual data files. No data were e-mailed unless the subject responded positively to the informed consent agreement.

Planned Statistical Data Analyses

In our initial planning we had hoped to analyze the pattern of correct and incorrect responses for the e-mail subjects, relate these patterns to the age of the subjects, and compare these responses to the three other groups listed earlier. However, the great majority of the e-mail subjects responded correctly to all the items, so these comparisons will not be pursued further here. The response time Rt to each response (correct or incorrect) was available for all e-mail subjects, and it is the main dependent variable used here.

In a first set of analyses, we describe the "within-subjects" variation in individual response times. There are a wide variety of ways to describe response time functions (see Cerella, 1990; Link, 1992; Luce, 1986), but we only use a simple polynomial approach here. In this case, we write

$$Rt_{i,n} = \sum_{p=0}^{P} (\beta_{p,n} W_i^p) + \varepsilon_{i,n} \text{ and} \tag{1}$$

where, for each individual n, $Rt_{i,n}$ is the response time (in seconds) to item i, $\beta_{p,n}$ is the pth polynomial regression coefficient, W_i is the pth power of the item's W-scale score, and $\varepsilon_{i,n}$ is a random error component. We fit these first-level models using standard least squares regression.

In a second set of analyses, we examine the "between-subject" differences associated with age. Here, we write another polynomial model as

$$\beta_{p,n} = \sum_{q=0}^{Q} (\gamma_q Age_n^q) + v_{p,n} \tag{2}$$

where $\beta_{p,n}$ is the individual regression coefficient for individual n, Age_n^q is the qth power of the self-reported age of the n subject, γ_q is the qth regression coefficient for the polynomial prediction of the individual regression parameter, and $v_{p,n}$ is the corresponding error component. We also fit these second-level models using least squares regression.

In a third set of analyses, we present a more formal simultaneous equations model of both analyses described previously. We fit this model using a variation on the multilevel model approach (as in Aitken & Longford, 1986; Bock, 1989; Bryk & Raudenbush, 1993; Goldstein & McDonald, 1988; Raudenbush, 1988). This kind of simultaneous equations model introduces latent variables at different levels; we fit these models using several new but available computer programs such as ML3 (Prosser, Rabash, & Goldstein, 1991) and VARCLUS (Longford, 1987). In these models we assume that (a) the $\varepsilon_{i,n}$ is normally distributed with mean zero and constant variance so that $\varepsilon_i \sim N(0, \Sigma_{i,i})$ and (b) the $v_{k,n}$ is normally distributed with mean zero and constant variance so that $v_p \sim N(0, \Omega_{p,p})$ (see Braun in Bock, 1989). Maximum-likelihood estimates and standard errors are calculated for all model parameters, and goodness of fit can be assessed with a likelihood ratio test statistic.

In all statistical analyses to follow, we evaluate significance at the standard $\alpha = .05$ test, and we also assume that a change in variance explained of over 5% is noteworthy.

RESULTS

Initial Data Summary

The first column in Table 10.1 lists the demographic and psychometric characteristics of the current sample. We obtained $N = 46$ valid responses from e-mail subjects. These subjects reported a mean age of 29.6 (sd = 6.8), and most were male ($N = 44$ or 93.5%). The next three columns of Table 10.1 give a summary of three recent studies using this power letter series task administered using the standard paper-and-pencil booklets. This table also includes data from several other groups: UVa college students, UVa aging subjects, and USC aging subjects.

In Table 10.1 we also present a new scaling of the power letter series task. All data in this table are presented in a special transformation of the Rasch ability scale termed the "W-scale" (see Woodcock, 1978, 1990). The W ability scale uses a log(9) transformation of a Rasch raw-ability scale (including additive and multiplicative constants). This is theoretically an equal interval metric, and is important for further change interpretation.

The specific W values presented here were calculated by aggregating the information from the correct and incorrect response patterns across all items and groups listed previously (using the BIGSTEPS program by Wright & Linacre, 1992). This analysis suggested that the 35 items had estimated W scales that ranged from a low of 470 (Item 3) to a high of 543 (Item 8). Table 10.1 shows the first four moments of these W scores for all four groups. Using this scaling, we find that the e-mail subjects are far superior and much narrower in correct/incorrect letter series performance. The UVa aging subjects have the lowest W scores (W mean = 504) with the largest range (W sd = 15), and the e-mail subjects have the highest W scores (W mean = 534) with the smallest range (W sd = 7).

TABLE 10.1
Some Demographic Characteristics of Several Studies
on Power Letter Series

	Telemetry Subjects	UVa College Subjects	UVa Aging Subjects	USC Aging Subjects
Experimental Design				
Location	NeXT e-mail	Virginia	San Francisco	Los Angeles
Time limits	None	30 min.	30 min.	30 min.
Sample size	46	258	46	367
Mean age	29.6	18.9	65.7	67.0
(sd Age)	(6.8)	(1.5)	(1.3)	(13.6)
Percent male	93.5%	42.6%	39.1%	47.4%
Power letter series W-Scale				
Mean	534.1	524.1	504.2	507.1
(SD)	(7.4)	(8.2)	(15.0)	(14.0)
Skewness	.41	−1.23	−.38	.35
Kurtosis	−1.63	4.66	−.12	−.60

Note: The first column lists results from the current psychotelemetry experiment. The second column lists results from an independent study of college students at the University of Virginia. these students were volunteers who took a group-administered paper-and-pencil version of the power letter series task and were given participation credit for Introductory Psychology. The third column lists results from an independent study of cognitive aging. These subjects were individually measured on the power letter series task in their home or office as part of an ongoing longitudinal study of aging (by the second author). The fourth column lists results from an independent study of cognitive aging done by researchers at the University of Southern California. These subjects took a group-administered paper-and-pencil version of the power letter series task as part of an ongoing longitudinal study of aging (by Jennie Noll & John Horn).

·In the scaling, the constant of 500 for each scale is arbitrarily centered at the mean of scores (usually for the fifth grade), but any changes from this constant are not arbitrary for any grade or any scale. For example, a change in 10 units on the W-scale means that a person can now perform with 75% success those tasks that were formerly performed with 50% success, and this is the same interpretation at any initial starting score.

Analysis 1: Individual Regression Components

Fig. 10.2A is a plot of the data obtained from a randomly selected subject. These data points (circles) show the response time (in seconds) as a function of the theoretical difficulty level (in W units) of the 38 individual items. The location of these data on the x-axis is fixed by our experimental design, but the Rt was limited only by the subjects willingness to continue to work toward an answer. For this specific subject, the average Rt recorded was just under 60 seconds, and the subject clearly responded quicker to the easier items (under 500). The solid line is the fitted line from a quadratic polynomial model (equation [1], with $P = 2$). This single curve was estimated with $\beta_0 = 6.4 \times 10^{-2}$, the estimated Rt for an item with $W = 500$, $\beta_1 = -2.5 \times 10^{-3}$, the

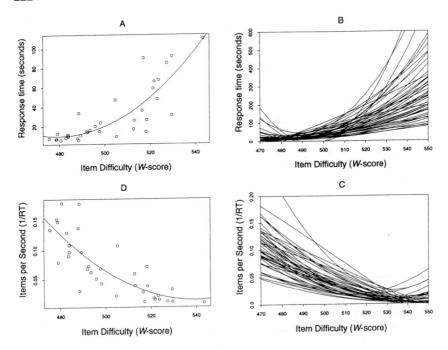

FIG. 10.2.   A. Response time as a quadratic function of item difficulty level for Subject 1.
B. Response time quadratic functions for all subjects. C. Response speed as a quadratic
function of item difficulty level for Subject 1. D. Response speed quadratic functions for all
subjects.

linear change in the Rt for a one unit change in Item W, $\beta_2 = 3.2 \times 10^{-5}$, the
quadratic change in the Rt for a one-unit change in Item W. This polynomial
curve captures approximately $R^2 = 50\%$ of the variance in the Rt scores for
this individual.

Polynomial regression models were fit to the Rt of each subject. In sequence, we fitted separate models to each subject:

1. A linear model produced an average $R^2 = 45\%$ (sd = 1%).
2. A quadratic model produced an average $R^2 = 50\%$ (sd = 2%).
3. A cubic model produced an average $R^2 = 52\%$ (sd = 2%).

Because the change to a cubic model was relatively small, we selected the
quadratic model for all further analysis.

Fig. 10.2B is a plot of the estimated quadratic curves for all $N = 47$ subjects. The similarity of these curves is notable—all subjects start out with
very short Rt and then proceed to require longer time to complete the more
difficult items (i.e., over $W = 500$). Notice that the items in these plots are ordered with respect to difficulty rather than in order of presentation. One subject seemed to be an outlier, because this subject's mean Rt was greater than

three minutes per item (on debriefing, this subject volunteered that a household emergency had occurred in the middle of the test). The other $N = 46$
subjects were used for all further analyses.

Fig. 10.2C is a plot of the same data for the first subject, with the recipro-
cal of Rt as the y-axis (see Tukey, 1977). This transformation of the Rt variable has the substantive interpretation of "items per second," and it may
have a more symmetric distribution. This figure shows decreasing scores as
a function of item difficulty. Fig. 10.2D is a plot of the quadratic curves for
all subjects using the this inverse Rt as the dependent variable. As it turns
out, this inverse Rt has good behavior in all further regression analyses, and
it could be used in place of the simple Rt fitted earlier.

Analysis 2: Age-Response Time Component Regressions

In our second set of analyses, we examined the systematic variation in the
individual Rt parameters as a function of the subjects' age.

Fig. 10.3A is a plot of the individual intercept parameters as a function of
self-reported age. The average $\beta_{0,n}$ here is approximately 60 seconds. The qua-

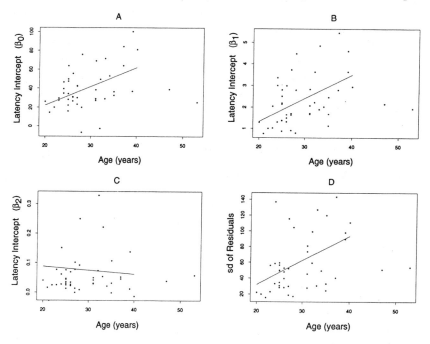

FIG. 10.3.   A. Response time intercepts (β_0) as a function of age. $R^2 = .225$ (.001). B. Response time slopes (β_1) as a function of age. $R^2 = .239$ (.0001). C. Response time curvatures
(β_2) as a function of age. $R^2 = .011$ (.51). D. Standard deviation of residuals as a function of
age. $R^2 = .197$ (.003).

dratic age polynomial curve plotted in this figure accounts for about 21% of the total variance. These intercept terms show a systematic increase with increasing age, followed by a rapid decline for the two oldest subjects. Because this variable represents the speed of response, the average Rt to all items appears to be increasing with age. That is, except for the two oldest subjects, we find a general slowing with increasing age (up to age 40).

Fig. 10.3B is a plot of the individual slope parameters as a function of self-reported age. The average $\beta_{1,n}$ here is approximately 3 seconds per W-unit change. The quadratic age polynomial curve plotted in this figure also accounts for about 21% of the total variance. Again, these slopes show a systematic increase with increasing age, followed by a rapid decline for the two oldest subjects. Because this variable represents the changing speed of response to more difficult items, we see progressive slowing of response to more difficult items. That is, except for the two oldest subjects, we find another kind of general slowing with increasing age (up to age 40).

Fig. 10.3C is a plot of the individual curvature parameters as a function of self-reported age. The average $\beta_{2,n}$ here is approximately .1 seconds per W-unit change. The quadratic age polynomial curve plotted in this figure also accounts for only 5% of the total variance. Here we find great variation in some of these younger subjects, and the overall age pattern is not very clear.

Fig. 10.3D is a plot of the individual error parameters as a function of self-reported age. The average $\beta_{e,n}$ here is approximately 60 seconds per W-unit change. The quadratic age polynomial curve plotted in this figure accounts for about 18% of the total variance. Again, these error terms show some increase with increasing age, but there is little evidence for a systematic effect.

Analysis 3: Multilevel Response Time Models

In order to examine the statistical characteristics of this model, we also calculated several simultaneous equation versions of the previous analyses fitted by the ML3 computer program (Prosser et al., 1991). Table 10.2 presents results from four "multilevel models" applied to the Rt from these psychotelemetry data.

The first column (Model 0) gives results for the fit of a standard two-level (i.e., 1 within and 1 between) variance components model of the raw scores on Rt. This model includes significant components for the intercept or grand mean (60.8), the within-persons or Level 1 variance (8963), and the between-person or Level 2 variance (535). The overall fit is given by the log likelihood (of $-2LL = 20,417$), and this is used as a standard of comparison for the other three models.

The second column (Model 1) lists parameters for a multilevel model where we have added a quadratic model to the within-person variance terms. All three fixed parameters are significant ($\beta_0 = 39.9$, $\beta_1 = 2.34$, $\beta_2 = .056$), and

TABLE 10.2
Multilevel Modeling Results From the Psychotelemetry Experiment

Model Parameter	Model 0: Baseline	Model 1: Quadratic Rt	Model 2: Linear Age	Model 3: Quadratic Age
First-level regression parameters				
$\beta_0 = 1 \to Rt$	60.8*	39.9*	11.2*	−85.1*
$\beta_1 = W \to Rt$		2.34*	1.09*	−5.23*
$\beta_2 = W^2 \to Rt$		.056*	.056*	−.13*
First-level variance parameters				
$\sigma_0 = \varepsilon \leftrightarrow \varepsilon$	8693*	4612*	4612*	4612*
Second-level regression parameters				
$\gamma_{0,1} = Age \to \beta_0$			.97*	6.97*
$\gamma_{1,1} = Age \to \beta_1$			.042*	6.43*
$\gamma_{2,1} = Age \to \beta_2$			.000	.01
Second-level curvature parameters				
$\gamma_{0,2} = Age^2 \to \beta_0$				−.09*
$\gamma_{1,2} = Age^2 \to \beta_1$				−.005*
$\gamma_{2,2} = Age^2 \to \beta_2$				−.0001*
Second-level variance parameters				
$\sigma_1 = \zeta_1 \leftrightarrow \zeta_1$	535*	141*	101*	66.1
$\sigma_2 = \zeta_2 \leftrightarrow \zeta_2$		1.04*	.92*	.78*
$\sigma_3 = \zeta_3 \leftrightarrow \zeta_3$		.002*	.002*	.002*
Second-level covariance parameters				
$\sigma_{1,2} = \zeta_1 \leftrightarrow \zeta_2$			11.7*	7.27*
$\sigma_{1,3} = \zeta_1 \leftrightarrow \zeta_3$			.32*	.23
$\sigma_{2,3} = \zeta_2 \leftrightarrow \zeta_3$			.05*	.05*
Overall goodness-of-fit parameters				
$-2lnL$ = likelihood	20417	19317	19311	19303
$\chi^2 = \delta - 2lnL$	0	1100	1094	1087
N_{par} = number of parameters	3	7	13	16
df = degrees of freedom	0	4	7	10

Note: $N = 46$; Asterisk indicates a parameter that is at least 1.96 times as large as its standard error (i.e., $p < .05$).

the random (within-person) error variance is reduced by about 50% (to 4612). Each of these three parameters has significant between-persons (Level 2) variance also ($\sigma_1 = 141$, $\sigma_2 = 1.04$, $\sigma_3 = .002$). This model changes the overall likelihood (to $-2LL = 19.317$), yielding a significant improvement in fit of $dLRT = 1100$ for four extra parameters.

The third column (Model 2) lists results where we added three terms to allow for the correlation of the three first-order terms (σ_1, σ_2, etc.), and three parameters where we estimated the linear effects of age (between persons) on the three quadratic model parameters (within persons). These results show significant effects for all parameters except the linear effect of age on the β_2 curvature, but the net improvement in fit ($dLRT = 6$ on $dDF = 3$) is small but significant.

The fourth column (Model 3) lists results where a quadratic model for between-group ages was fitted. Here, we find the addition of a significant quadratic age effect for β_0 and β_1, with an important reduction in second level error variance. In contrast to Model 2, this model shows a nonsignificant improvement in fit ($dLRT = 3$ on $dDF = 3$). Thus, Model 2 is chosen here as the best model.

In summary, these multilevel models suggest that (a) about 47% of the variance at the first level can be explained by the quadratic model, and (b) that a much smaller amount (1% to 30%) of the variance between people in these correlated coefficients can be explained by quadratic age effects. However, the changes in overall fit are not large, and we expect other between-persons effects to be likely. The simultaneous multilevel models are consistent with the separate analyses of Figs. 10.2 and 10.3.

GENERAL DISCUSSION

This research initially demonstrates that psychotelemetry—the remote collection of psychometric information—is both possible and practical. The potential benefits of psychotelemetric measurement include rapid automated gathering of large samples, measurement of populations that have been traditionally difficult to sample, and the inclusion of response time data along with the item answers. Another benefit of psychotelemetric measurement is that instruments can be administered extremely quickly over a wide geographic area. This experiment gathered data from individuals in widely scattered locations around the United States, and the time from the call for participation until the beginning of analysis was relatively short (10 days).

The substantive results of this experiment are informative as well. Initially, we found that subjects who are willing to participate in this kind of an experiment were high scorers but varied in a great deal in age (and presumably other demographic characteristics). This meant we could not obtain useful data on correct/incorrect response patterns as we had hoped; but, thanks to our data collection recordings, we could obtain accurate information on response times (Rt) for correct answers. These Rt data proved to be highly related to the pattern of difficulty levels of the items for most subjects. Using a quadratic model, we were able to reliably recast the repeated scores for each individual Rt into an individual response function, and this function showed differences in the way that different persons slow down with difficult items. Furthermore, the demographic age variable was linearly related to the intercept and slope of this function; that is, the older the age, the longer the Rt and the more peaked the slope. Taken together, these results both between and within individuals are consistent with a great deal of previous research in cognitive aging (Horn, 1988; Hoyer & Rybash, 1994; Salthouse, 1988, 1991a, 1991b).

Psychotelemetry is feasible and has benefits not afforded by traditional methods, and other researchers are likely to attempt psychotelemetric experiments. It is therefore particularly important that the unanticipated problems that were encountered with this experiment be clearly stated, so that they can be successfully avoided by others.

Because the subject may be using an arbitrary computer hardware and software environment, the psychotelemetry software must be thoroughly tested for compatibility with the widest available range of hardware before it is used in the field. Problems with the first version of our software made it impossible for some people to finish the test. We cannot overstress the importance of this point; if the successful completion of the experiment covaries with the psychometric variables in question, a potentially serious selection bias will be introduced into the data.

Our debriefings allowed subjects to enter comments, and these showed that a few people attempted to use the program in unanticipated ways. The instructions must be made exceptionally precise and clear to the widest possible range of subjects. Because a psychotelemetric instrument by definition must be self-administered by the subject, there must be tight software controls restricting the subject's behavior to the range of experimental interest. This problem is difficult, but is not insoluble. Careful instrument and software design can overcome the problem of self-administration.

The physical environment of the subject is not as well controlled during psychotelemetry as it would be in a laboratory experiment. Arbitrary distractors may occur during the presentation of the instrument. A concerted effort to control or at least measure these distractors should be made, and debriefing should include an opportunity for the subject to relate unusual circumstances during testing. For example, the debriefing data for this experiment revealed that the one outlier was caused by an unavoidable household emergency that occurred during the administration of the test. These kinds of problems are likely to occur in any experiment, but they may be special threats to the validity and reliability of psychotelemetric data.

Overall, this experiment effectively demonstrated the feasibility of psychotelemetric measurement. The future of this form of data collection seems to be extremely promising. As the Internet grows and more individuals have access to its services, the potential subject pool will grow proportionately. The development of the World Wide Web also has potential for gathering psychotelemetric data quickly and efficiently. Further experiments along these lines are being planned.

ACKNOWLEDGMENTS

This research was supported by Grant #AG-7407 from the National Institute of Aging and the Center for Developmental and Health Research Methodology. Parts of these data were collected and analyzed by several members of the Jefferson Psychometric Lab, including Steve Aggen, Aki Hamagami, Patricia Hulick, and Thomas Mulligan. Preliminary results of this study were presented to the 1993 meeting of the Society for Multivariate Experimental Psychology, and we would like to thank the members for their constructive criticism. We also thank John L. Horn, Richard Woodcock, and John R. Nesselroade for their helpful comments. Reprints can be obtained from the authors at the Department of Psychology, University of Notre Dame, Notre Dame, IN 46556.

REFERENCES

Aitken, M., & Longford, N. (1986). Statistical modelling issues in school effectiveness studies. *Journal of the Royal Statistical Society, 149*, 1–43.

Berk, R. (1983). An introduction to sample selection bias in sociological data. *American Sociological Review, 48*, 386–398.

Bock, R. D. (1989). *Multilevel analysis of educational data.* New York: Academic.

Boker, S. M., & McArdle, J. J. (1982). *Psylog: Software for psychometric testing.* Unpublished software.

Boker, S. M., & McArdle, J. J. (1992). *PsyLog: Software for psychometric measurement.* Unpublished software.

Bryk, A. S., & Raudenbush, S. W. (1993). *Hierarchical linear models: Applications and data analysis methods.* Newbury Park, CA: Sage.

Cattell, R. B. (1971). *Abilities: Their structure, growth and action.* Boston: Houghton-Mifflin.

Cerella, J. (1990). Aging and information-processing rate. In J. E. Birren Schaie, K. W. S. Schaie (Eds.), *Handbook of the psychology of aging: Third edition* (pp. 201–221). San Diego: Academic.

Embretson, S. E. (1992). Computerized adaptive testing: Its potential substantive contributions to psychological research and assessment. *Current Directions in Psychological Science, 1*(4), 129–131.

Goldstein, H., & McDonald, R. P. (1988). A general model for the analysis of multilevel data. *Psychometrika, 53*, 455–467.

Heckman, J., & Robb, R. (1986). Alternative methods for solving the problem of selection bias in evaluating the impact of treatments on outcomes. In H. Wainer (Ed.), *Drawing inferences from self-selected samples* (pp. 63–107). New York: Springer.

Horn, J. L. (1988). Thinking about human abilities. In J. R. Nesselroade & R. B. S. Cattell (Eds.), *The handbook of multivariate experimental psychology* (Vol. 2, pp. 645–685). New York: Plenum.

Horn, J. L., & Cattell, R. B. (1966). Refinement and test of the theory of fluid and crystallized intelligence. *Journal of Educational Psychology, 57*, 253–270.

Horn, J. L., & Cattell, R. B. (1982). Whimsey and misunderstandings of Gf-Gc theory. *Psychological Bulletin, 91,* 623–633.

Hoyer, W., & Rybash, J. (1994). Characterizing adult cognitive development. *Journal of Adult Development, 1*(1), 7–12.

Krol, E. (1992). *The whole internet catalog & user's guide.* Sebastopol, CA: O'Reilly and Associates.

Link, S. W. (1992). *The wave theory of difference and Similarity.* Hillsdale, NJ: Lawrence Erlbaum Associates.

Longford, N. (1987). A fast scoring algorithm for maximum likelihood estimation in unbalanced mixed models with nested effects. *Biometrika, 74,* 812–827.

Luce, R. D. (1986). *Response times: Their role in inferring elementary mental organization.* Cambridge, England: Cambridge University Press.

Prosser, R., Rabash, J., & Goldstein, H. (1991). *ML3: Software for three-level analysis user's guide for V.2.* London: Institute of Education.

Rafaeli, S., & Tractinsky, N. (1991). Time in computerized tests: A multitrait, multimethod investigation of general knowledge and mathematical reasoning on-line examinations. *Computers in Human Behavior, 7*(3), 215–225.

Raudenbush, S. (1988). Educational applications of hierarchical linear models: A review. *Journal of Educational Statistics, 13,* 85–118.

Salthouse, T. (1988). Utilization of path-analytic procedures to investigate the role of processing resources in cognitive aging. *Pychology and Aging, 3*(2), 158–166.

Salthouse, T. (1991a). Mediation of adult age differences in cognition by reductions in working memory and speed of processing. *Psychological Science, 2*(3), 179–183.

Salthouse, T. (1991b). *Theoretical perspectives on cognitive aging.* Hillsdale, NJ: Lawrence Erlbaum Associates.

Synodinos, N. E., Papacostas, C. S., & Okimoto, G. M. (1994). Computer-administered versus paper-and-pencil surveys and the effect of sample selection. *Behavior Research Methods, Instrumentation & Computers, 26*(4), 395–401.

Tukey, J. W. (1977). *Exploratory data analysis.* Reading, MA: Addison-Wesley.

Walsh, J. P., Kiesler, S., Sproull, L. S., & Hesse, B. W. (1992). Self-selected and randomly selected respondents in a computer network survey. *Public Opinion Quarterly, 56*(2), 241–244.

Woodcock, R. W. (1978). *Development and standardization of the Woodcock-Johnson psycho-educational battery.* Hingham, MA: Teaching Resources Corp.

Woodcock, R. W. (1990). Theoretical foundation of the WJ-R measures of cognitive ability. *Journal of Psychoeducational Assessment, 8,* 231–258.

Wright, B. D., & Linacre, J. M. (1992). *BIGSTEPS: Rasch analysis for all two-facet models.* Chicago: MESA Press.

11

A Developmental-Based Item Factor Analysis

Fumiaki Hamagami
University of Virginia

Human beings are distinguished from other primates and mammals by highly developed cognitive abilities, such as the acquisition of symbolic languages and formal reasoning ability. Much research has been devoted to understanding human intelligence better (Guilford, 1967; Guttman, 1965; Spearman, 1904; Thurstone, 1932, 1947; Woodcock, 1990). A prominent theory of cognitive ability was developed by Cattell (1963), who proposed a dichotomy of cognitive ability. Horn and Cattell (1966; Horn, 1978, 1988) proposed acquired knowledge and information as *crystallized ability* and abstract reasoning as *fluid ability.*

Cognitive ability is neither static nor invariable. Just as human bodies display variability in size and shape, individuals manifest differences in cognitive abilities. The developmental dynamics and individual differences of cognitive ability have captured the interest of methodologists. Corballis and Traub (1970) and Nesselroade (1972) introduced a longitudinal factor analysis technique for analyzing such data (see also Olsson & Bergman, 1977). Following Guttman (1954), Jöreskog (1970), Jöreskog and Söbom (1979), and others have described change in terms of simplex and autoregressive structures. Hertzog and Nesselroade (1987) examined these issues, and McArdle and Nesselroade (1994) combined both autoregressive structure and difference score factor models to study developmental change.

This research discussed in this chapter applies a developmental method by McArdle and Nesselroade to item factor analysis of cognitive abilities. The study focuses on the concept of *Gf-Gc ability.* The major interest is in developmental aspects of these two cognitive ability between adolescence and early adulthood age. The model consists of two cognitive stimuli (crystallized ability and fluid ability) and several cognitive binary responses selected from the Revised Stanford-Binet Intelligence Scale (Terman & Merrill, 1937). To achieve this goal, we avail of some recent techniques of the structural equation model (Christoffersson, 1975; McDonald, 1985; Muthén, 1978; Parry & McArdle, 1991). The factor model is based on multivariate binary responses. The use of linear factor model techniques inevitably violates fundamental assumptions of linearity and multivariate normality tied with continuous variable factor models. Item response factor models require nonlinear structural equation modeling.

METHODS

Subjects

Katherine P. Bradway (1944, 1945a, 1945b) originally collected a set of cognitive ability data in 1941. Of 213 children who participated in the standardization of the Revised Stanford-Binet Intelligence Scale, 111 subjects were retested in 1941 and 1956. These 111 subjects, measured at ages 14 and 28, comprise the current sample. In 1941, subjects ranged in age from 12 to 17.5 (mean = 13.6 and s.d. = 1.5). In 1956, subjects were 27 to 32.5 (mean = 29.5 and s.d. = 1.6). The average education reported was 15.6 years (s.d. = 2.6) at the 1956 testing.

Variables

Ten binary test items were selected from Form L of the Revised Stanford-Binet Scale (Terman & Merill, 1937). Table 11.1 describes the selected items. The scale consists of 20 different age levels. With each increment of an age level, a degree of difficulty also increases. Each age level contains several different test items, plus one alternate. The complete test consists of 129 items. Each of 129 items was subjectively classified into one of three categories: (a) a crystallized (Gc) ability item, (b) a fluid (Gf) ability item, and (c) a short-term acquisition and retrieval (SAR) item. For example, one test item, induction, was categorized as a fluid item because it requires a reasoning independent of prior learning or information. In contrast, vocabulary was classified as a crystallized item because knowledge of words depends on previous learning. The basal age level of the test administration in 1956 was the year-level 14, just prior to average adult level. Five items were selected to represent crystallized ability and five items represented fluid ability. SAR items were not included in the analysis. Subjects' responses to 10 items were coded either 1 (pass) or 0 (fail). Table 11.2 shows descriptive statistics

TABLE 11.1
Classification and Description of Selected Items
From Revised Stanford-Binet Scales

Items	Year Level	Theoretical Classification	Description
1. Induction	XIV-2	Fluid	Ask testees to identify the number of holes in folded papers
2. Codes	AA-2	Fluid	Ask testees to solve some cryptic codes
3. Find reasons	SAII-2	Fluid	Ask testees to provide some reasons for questions
4. Paper cut	SAIII-4	Fluid	Ask testees to draw figures of unfolded papers with parts cut out
5. Reasoning	SAIII-5	Fluid	Ask testees to use mathematical concept of number series
6. Vocabulary	AA-1	Crystallized	Ask testees to define up to 20 words
7. Abstract word	AA-3	Crystallized	Ask testees to describe difference in meaning of two abstract words
8. Similarity	SAI-6	Crystallized	Ask testees to describe essential similarity among general items
9. Proverb	SAII-4	Crystallized	Ask testees to tell what proverbs mean
10. Analogy	SAIII-3	Crystallized	Ask testees to provide antonyms as opposite analogy

on these items. Table 11.3A shows within-occasion tetrachoric correlations and difference score correlations among Stanford-Binet items. Table 11.3B shows tetrachoric correlations among items between Occasions 1 and 2.

Item Level Factor Models

Alternative factor models were tested using mean and covariance information simultaneously (Muthen & Christoffersson, 1981). Alternative models are:

1. The null model, where no covariances among items are expected.
2. The general factor model, where a unitary factor underlies measurements.
3. The *Gc* factor model, where only the *Gc* factor explains all covariances among items.
4. The *Gf* factor model.
5. The orthogonal *Gf-Gf* model, where no covariances are expected between *Gf* items and *Gc* items.

6. The oblique *Gf-Gf* model, where covariances are expected between the *Gf* factor and the *Gc* factor.

7. The full two-factor model, where all factor indeterminacy is eliminated.

The LISREL7 (Jöreskog & Söbom, 1988) and LISCOMP (Muthen, 1987) are employed to estimate structural parameters.

TABLE 11.2
Summary Statistics of Selected Stanford-Binet Items

Variables	Proportion of Pass	Standard Deviation	Threshold Values (Z)
Adolescent Age:			
(1) Induction	.62	.49	−.30
(2) Codes	.37	.48	.30
(3) Find reason	.16	.37	.98
(4) Paper cut	.14	.35	1.06
(5) Reasoning	.05	.22	1.60
(6) Vocabulary	.59	.49	−.25
(7) Abstract word	.49	.50	.00
(8) Similarity	.33	.47	.42
(9) Proverb	.07	.26	1.46
(10) Analogy	.11	.31	1.23
Adult age:			
(1) Induction	.93	.26	−1.46
(2) Codes	.71	.46	−.55
(3) Find reason	.46	.50	.09
(4) Paper cut	.22	.41	.78
(5) Reasoning	.26	.41	.66
(6) Vocabulary	.98	.13	−2.09
(7) Abstract word	.92	.38	−1.39
(8) Similarity	.83	·.38	−.94
(9) Proverb	.44	.50	.16
(10) Analogy	.49	.50	.02
Difference score:			
(1) Δ Induction	.31	.48	—
(2) Δ Codes	.33	.62	—
(3) Δ Find Reason	.30	.51	—
(4) Δ Paper Cut	.08	.48	—
(5) Δ Reasoning	.21	.45	—
(6) Δ Vocabulary	.39	.49	—
(7) Δ Abstract Word	.42	.51	—
(8) Δ Similarity	.50	.58	—
(9) Δ Proverb	.37	.55	—
(10) Δ Analogy	.38	.55	—

Note: Threshold values denotes a normal score equivalent for proportion of correct responses.

TABLE 11.3A
Tetrachoric Correlation Coefficients Among Selected Stanford-Binet
Intelligence Scales Items for the Adolescent Group and Adult Ages
Measured Two Different Occasions ($N = 111$)

Variables	(1)	(2)	(3)	(4)	(5)	(6)	(7)	(8)	(9)	(10)
Adolescent age:										
(1) Induction	1.000									
(2) Codes	.315	1.000								
(3) Find reason	.400	.376	1.000							
(4) Paper cut	.616	.192	.201	1.000						
(5) Reasoning	.309	−.064	.484	.687	1.000					
(6) Vocabulary	.524	.644	.216	.494	.087	1.000				
(7) Abstract word	.615	.615	.462	.504	.209	.853	1.000			
(8) Similarity	.403	.426	.533	.364	.406	.685	.669	1.000		
(9) Proverb	.540	.477	.517	.207	.535	.557	.645	.055	1.000	
(10) Analogy	−.053	.294	.184	.620	.412	.549	.245	.247	.500	1.000
Adult Age:										
(1) Induction	1.000									
(2) Codes	.443	1.000								
(3) Find reason	.119	.189	1.000							
(4) Paper cut	.353	.286	.144	1.000						
(5) Reasoning	.402	.463	.213	.341	1.000					
(6) Vocabulary	.594	.471	.231	−.043	.006	1.000				
(7) Abstract word	.132	.764	.528	.385	.281	.760	1.000			
(8) Similarity	.497	.570	.439	.291	.520	.609	.693	1.000		
(9) Proverb	.260	.268	.327	.195	.266	.204	.310	.400	1.000	
(10) Analogy	−.012	.499	.335	.323	.299	.257	.555	.477	.520	1.000
Difference scores:										
(1) Δ Induction	1.000									
(2) Δ Codes	−.010	1.000								
(3) Δ Find reason	−.041	.028	1.000							
(4) Δ Paper cut	.139	−.111	.060	1.000						
(5) Δ Reasoning	−.170	.076	−.033	.099	1.000					
(6) Δ Vocabulary	.263	.169	−.028	.074	−.120	1.000				
(7) Δ Abstract word	.279	.180	.001	.170	−.068	.498	1.000			
(8) Δ Similarity	.102	.291	−.011	.001	−.083	.212	.323	1.000		
(9) Δ Proverb	.049	.167	.185	.036	.128	.037	.084	.131	1.000	
(10) Δ Analogy	−.029	.157	.206	.169	.156	−.076	−.088	.005	.309	1.000

Nonlinear Structural Equation Models for Change

The primary focus is on a developmental aspect of the factor models. A path diagram in Fig. 11.1 depicts a generic longitudinal factor analysis model for the binary items. There are six different parameter types in this analysis. They are factor loading (λ), factor variance (Φ_{Gc} and Φ_{Gf}), factor covariance ($\Phi_{Gc,Gf}$), factor means (α_{Gc} and α_{Gf}), factor regression parameters (β), and item thresholds (τ).

TABLE 11.3B
Tetrachoric Correlations Among Repeated Measure Items Selected From Stanford-Binet Intelligence Scales

	(1)	(2)	(3)	(4)	(5)	(6)	(7)	(8)	(9)	(10)	(11)	(12)
Percent correct	.618	.600	.500	.336	.164	.055	.927	.982	.918	.827	.464	.255
Z-value extrapolation	-.301	-.253	.000	.422	.980	1.602	-1.456	-2.093	-1.393	-.943	.091	.660
Tetrachoric correlation:												
(1) Induction 14	1.00											
(2) Vocabulary 14	.425	1.00										
(3) Abstract words 14	.615	.853	1.00									
(4) Similarity 14	.403	.685	.669	1.00								
(5) Find reason 14	.400	.216	.462	.533	1.00							
(6) Reasoning 14	.309	.087	.209	.406	.484	1.00						
(7) Induction 30	.644	-.034	.337	-.055	.088	-.036	1.00					
(8) Vocabulary 30	.379	.361	.266	.101	-.126	-.398	.594	1.00				
(9) Abstract words 30	.237	.660	.564	.388	.126	-.005	.132	.760	1.00			
(10) Similarity 30	.495	.467	.312	.139	.370	.205	.497	.609	.693	1.00		
(11) Find reason 30	.325	.201	.417	.526	.601	.607	.119	.231	.528	.439	1.00	
(12) Reasoning 30	.517	.314	.282	.530	.256	.514	.402	.006	.281	.520	.213	1.00

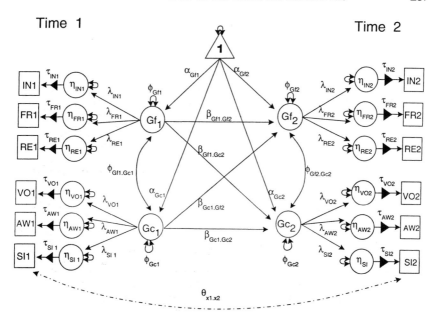

FIG. 11.1.   Longitudinal item factor analysis for LISCOMP estimation.

Six items (induction, find reason, reasoning, vocabulary, abstract words, and similarity) were selected to investigate the systematic relationship between earlier measurement of latent traits and the later measurement using several alternative forms of longitudinal factor model (McArdle & Nesselroade, 1988), including longitudinal increases of factor scores. We also tested longitudinal change in factor variance and covariance and autocorrelated uniqueness across occasions. Finally, we tested the longitudinal invariant nature of factor patterns. We examined if these selected items could measure the identical latent cognitive ability across different occasions.

Fig. 11.2 describes a longitudinal factor model using difference scores. A factor at Time 1 is derived from observed binary variables, as in the previous longitudinal factor model. However, a factor at Time 2 is not indicated by observed binary variables at Time 2. The latent variable at Time 2 is based on difference scores between Time 1 and Time 2. Thus, this model structures a growth factor at Time 2, where a factor is indicated by change scores from Time 1 and Time 2. Parameters at Time 2, therefore, are psychometric values of a developmental change. They are mean of change factors ($\alpha_{\Delta Gf}$, and $\alpha_{\Delta Gc}$), variance of change factors ($\Phi_{\Delta Gf}$, and $\Phi_{\Delta Gc}$), covariance of change factors ($\Phi_{\Delta Gf, \Delta Gc}$), loadings of change factors ($\lambda_{\Delta y}$), a regression weight from Time 1 factor scores to difference factors ($\beta_{\Delta Gc, Gc1}$, $\beta_{\Delta Gc, Gf1}$, $\beta_{\Delta Gf, Gc1}$, and $\beta_{\Delta Gf, Gf1}$), and correlated uniqueness between Time 1 variables and difference scores ($\theta_{x1, \Delta x}$). Analyses of the change models were performed based on three Gc

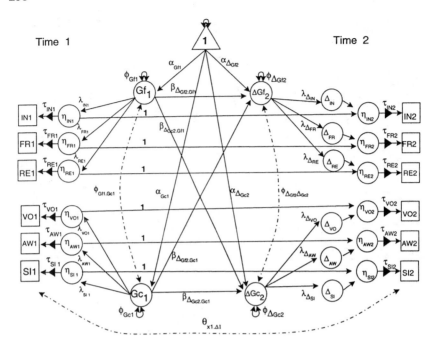

FIG. 11.2.   Item factor analysis using difference scores for LISCOMP.

items and three Gf items from each occasion due to some limitation in programming imposed by the LISCOMP program.

RESULTS

Multiple-Group Item Factor Model

The results of multiple group item factor models are presented in Table 11.4.
The general factor invariance model with the tetrachoric LISREL approach
fitted the data well ($\chi^2_{TL} = 110$, df = 90, $p < .90$). Likewise, the oblique factor
model invariance model equally fitted the data well ($\chi^2_{TL} = 110$, df = 89, $p <
.75$). When any model imposed parameter constraints of null correlations
among items, the model fit deteriorates. These results suggest that selected
Stanford-Binet items at least allow measurement of common latent factor
for both adolescent age and adult age. It is interesting to note that, even on
the item level, selected items seemed to capture some of the essence of Gc
and Gf ability.

When the LISCOMP GLS method is applied, LISCOMP computes the full

TABLE 11.4
Summary of Simultaneous Confirmatory Item Factor Models
for Multiple-Group Estimation

Models	Age Different Model					Two-Age Invariant Model				
	RMSR	dRMSR	LRT	df	dLRT	RMSR	dRMSR	LRT	df	dLRT
Tetrachoric correlation and RAM parameterization:										
Null model	.37	—	332	90	—	.37	—	332	100	—
Unitary factor	.12	.25	103	70	219	.14	.23	110*	90	222
Gc factor	.30	.07	219	80	113	.30	.07	223	95	109
Gf factor	.34	.03	278	80	54	.34	.03	283	95	49
Orthogonal	.27	.10	165	70	167	.27	.10	174	90	158
Oblique	.12	.25	102	68	230	.14	.23	110*	89	222
Full 2k	.27	.10	86	56	247	.23	.14	100*	83	232
LISCOMP parameterization:										
Null model	.47	—	3675	90	—	.55	—	3765	100	—
Unitary factor	.32	.15	1533	70	1142	.45	.10	2113	90	1652
Gc factor	.42	.05	2736	80	939	.52	.03	2758	95	1007
Gf factor	.45	.02	3096	80	569	.54	.01	3266	95	499
Orthogonal	.40	.07	2086	70	1589	.51	.04	2233	90	1532
Oblique	.31	.16	1480	68	1295	.47	.08	1937	89	1828
Full 2k	.32	.15	1215	56	2480	.44	.11	1947	83	1818

Note: RMSR is an abbreviation for root mean square residuals.
* indicates that a p level of goodness of fit exceeds .05 alpha level. For LISCOMP estimation, default weights did not allow continuation of iterative procedures; thus, we applied a ridge procedure to the weight matrix. LRT and RMSR reflect this weight matrix transformation.

large-sample weight matrix by inverting the sample covariance matrix for the vector of sample statistics, divided by the total sample size. The vector of sample statistics includes the first-order proportion, the second-order sample proportion, the sample tetrachoric correlation, and standard deviation of the sample tetrachoric correlation. With a small sample size, as in the present case, the default full weight matrix was usually not positive definite. Because the matrices of both age groups were singular, a ridge method was employed to circumvent the singularity. A constant was added to the main diagonal elements of the sample tetrachoric matrix, so LISCOMP could proceed to estimate the specified parameters. The results were based on these modified matrices.

The LISCOMP method generated similar results. However, there was a distinguishable feature where χ^2 values were inflated. This occurred because the ridge methods were employed in computing the weight matrix. In other words, a constant was added to each main diagonal element of the sample tetrachoric correlation matrix. The pattern of fit improvement concurred with that observed in the LISREL invariance analyses. The general factor invariance model explained more interitem covariances over the null model $(\Delta\chi^2_{TC} = 1652, \Delta df = 10, p < .0001)$. The oblique invariance factor model improved the fit as well $(\Delta\chi^2_{TC} = 1828, \Delta df = 12, p < .0001)$. The fit improvement from the orthogonal invariance model to the oblique invariance model was significant $(\Delta\chi^2_{TC} = 296, \Delta df = 2, p < .0001)$. The hypothesis of an orthogonal Gf-Gc factor model was rejected in favor of the oblique relationship. The hypothesis that Gc alone would explain the given covariances among test items was a bad idea. The hypothesis that only the fluid factor would account for interitem correlation information was also not tenable.

Longitudinal Factor Analysis Model

Because the Gf-Gc model was of primary interest, several alternative Gf-Gc factor invariance models were analyzed. The orthogonal factor model did not fit data $(\chi^2 = 1118, df = 62)$. Allowing the Time 2 factor scores to regress on the Time 1 factor scores improved the model fit $(\Delta\chi^2 = 732, \Delta df = 6)$ over the orthogonal factor model. Allowing factor variance to vary over time improved the model fit $(\Delta\chi^2 = 832, \Delta df = 8)$ over the orthogonal Gc-Gf model. When autocorrelations among uniqueness are added, the model indicates a better fit $(\Delta\chi^2 = 64, \Delta df = 6)$ than the unequal factor variance model. When equality constraints were imposed on factor variance across time, the model fit significantly became worse $(\Delta\chi^2 = 45, \Delta df = 0)$ over the autocorrelated uniqueness model. When equality constraints were imposed on item thresholds over age, the model fit worsened $(\Delta\chi^2 = 47, \Delta df = 0)$ over the autocorrelated uniqueness model. When factor means were allowed to vary, the model fit marginally improved $(\Delta\chi^2 = 9, \Delta df = 4)$ over the autocorrelated uniqueness model. When factor patterns were allowed to vary, the model fit significantly improved $(\Delta\chi^2 = 89, \Delta df = 4)$ over the different factor mean model.

Table 11.5 summarizes parameter estimates for the alternative longitudinal models of the Gc-Gf factor structure. Time 1 factor scores have a positive impact on the Time 2 factor scores. It seems that both Gc ability and Gf ability do not stop growing at age 14. The Gc ability at age 14 has the greater impact on Gf at age 30 than on Gc at age 30. Similarly, the Gf ability at age 14 has a greater effect on Gc at age 30 than on Gf at age 30. Threshold estimates indicate that subjects have responded correctly to more items at age 30 than at age 14. A difference in factor patterns across time suggests that, for adolescents, induction and vocabulary were the strongest measures of Gf and Gc scores, respectively. In contrast, for adults, the strongest indicators were find reason and abstract word, with effects of other items present. A size of factor variance is smaller at the adult age than at the adolescent. Similarly, a within-time Gc-Gf correlation is smaller at the adult age than at the adolescent.

TABLE 11.5
Summary of Parameter Estimates of Longitudinal Item Factor Model for
Six Items Selected From Stanford-Binet Intelligence Scale by LISCOMP

Parameter	Orthogonal Model		Oblique Model		Factor Variance		Correlated Unique	
	T1	T2	T1	T2	T1	T2	T1	T2
Factor loading:								
λ_{IN}	1.00	1.00	1.00	1.00	1.00	1.00	1.00	1.00
λ_{FR}	.64	.64	.66	.66	.66	.66	.69	.69
λ_{RE}	.92	.92	.41	.41	.60	.60	.60	.60
λ_{VO}	1.00	1.00	1.00	1.00	1.00	1.00	1.00	1.00
λ_{AW}	.46	.46	.54	.54	.97	.97	.60	.60
λ_{SI}	.45	.45	.82	.82	.89	.89	1.06	1.06
Item thresholds:								
τ_{IN}	-.85	-1.46	*-.13	-1.46	*-.15	-1.46	-.26	-1.46
τ_{FR}	.96	.21	1.04	.21	.91	.21	.80	.21
τ_{RE}	1.72	.66	1.24	.66	1.54	.66	1.65	.66
τ_{VO}	-.13	-2.09	-.44	-2.09	-.48	-2.09	-.39	-2.09
τ_{AW}	*.40	-.55	*-.05	-.55	* .16	-.55	* .08	-.55
τ_{SI}	.49	-1.39	.31	-1.39	.35	-1.39	.47	-1.39
Autocorrelation across occasions:								
θ_{IN}	—	—	—	—	—	—	* .27	—
θ_{FR}	—	—	—	—	—	—	* .05	—
θ_{RE}	—	—	—	—	—	—	.36	—
θ_{VO}	—	—	—	—	—	—	* .03	—
θ_{AW}	—	—	—	—	—	—	.26	—
θ_{SI}	—	—	—	—	—	—	-.56	—
Factor regression:								
$\beta_{Gc1\text{-}Gc2}$	—	—	.48	—	.29	—	.37	—
$\beta_{Gc1\text{-}Gf2}$	—	—	*.13	—	*-.02	—	.16	—
$\beta_{Gf1\text{-}Gc2}$	—	—	*.00	—	-.10	—	*-.08	—
$\beta_{Gf1\text{-}Gf2}$	—	—	.48	—	.71	—	* .14	—
Factor variance-covariance:								
ϕ_{GcGf}	.00	.00	.67	1.09	.53	.15	.55	.31
ϕ_{Gc}	1.00	1.00	1.00	1.00	1.00	* .24	1.00	* .02
ϕ_{Gf}	1.00	1.00	1.00	1.00	1.00	-.40	1.00	.35
Factor means:								
α_{Gf}	—	—	—	—	—	—	—	—
α_{Gc}	—	—	—	—	—	—	—	—
Scaling distribution parameters:								
δ_{IN}	1.00	1.12	1.00	.42	1.00	.61	1.00	.79
δ_{FR}	1.00	.64	1.00	.89	1.00	1.39	1.00	1.62
δ_{RE}	1.00	-.29	1.00	.97	1.00	1.15	1.00	1.11
δ_{VO}	1.00	1.01	1.00	.88	1.00	1.04	1.00	1.06
δ_{AW}	1.00	2.64	1.00	2.19	1.00	2.93	1.00	2.80
δ_{SI}	1.00	1.02	1.00	.76	1.00	.84	1.00	.84
Fit index:								
χ^2	1117		386		287		223	
df	62		56		54		48	

(Continued)

TABLE 11.5
(Continued)

Parameter	Factor Mean		Unequal Loading		Equal Variance		Equal Threshold	
	T1	T2	T1	T2	T1	T2	T1	T2
Factor loading:								
λ_{IN}	1.00	1.00	1.00	1.00	1.00	1.00	1.00	1.00
λ_{FR}	.67	.67	.68	.79	.84	.84	.87	.87
λ_{RE}	.60	.60	.38	.86	.72	.72	.58	.58
λ_{VO}	1.00	1.00	1.00	1.00	1.00	1.00	1.00	1.00
λ_{AW}	.63	.63	.93	.49	.35	.35	.96	.96
λ_{SI}	1.03	1.03	.79	1.99	1.19	1.19	.77	.77
Item thresholds:								
τ_{IN}	-.29	-1.46	-.29	-1.46	-.29	-1.46	-.64	-.64
τ_{FR}	.79	.21	.86	.21	1.09	.21	.41	.41
τ_{RE}	1.69	.66	1.55	.66	1.52	1.55	1.35	1.35
τ_{VO}	-.37	-2.09	-.32	-2.09	-.30	-.32	-.29	-.29
τ_{AW}	.07	-.55	*-.12	-.55	*-.08	-.55	-.22	-.22
τ_{SI}	.50	-1.39	.39	-1.39	-.37	-1.39	-.08	-.08
Autocorrelation across occasions:								
θ_{IN}	.37	—	.39	—	* .22	—	.32	—
θ_{FR}	.07	—	.19	—	* .06	—	.26	—
θ_{RE}	* .37	—	* .14	—	.50	—	* .31	—
θ_{VO}	* .06	—	*-.14	—	*-.18	—	-.07	—
θ_{AW}	.25	—	.17	—	.33	—	.09	—
θ_{SI}	-.45	—	-.61	—	-.59	—	-.08	—
Factor regression:								
$\beta_{Gc1-Gc2}$	* .34	—	.18	—	.67	—	.06	—
$\beta_{Gc1-Gf2}$	.21	—	* .16	—	* .15	—	* .03	—
$\beta_{Gf1-Gc2}$	*-.05	—	* .11	—	*-.15	—	*-.00	—
$\beta_{Gf1-Gf2}$	* .09	—	* .19	—	*-.18	—	-.20	—
Factor variance-covariance:								
ϕ_{GcGf}	.55	.28	.67	.16	.43	.66	.54	.04
ϕ_{Gc}	1.00	* .09	1.00	* .03	.60	.60	1.00	*-.16
ϕ_{Gf}	1.00	.33	1.00	.28	.74	.74	1.00	.01
Factor means:								
α_{Gf}	@0	* .19	@0	.15	—	—	—	—
α_{Gc}	@0	.08	@0	*-.05	—	—	—	—
Scaling distribution parameters:								
δ_{IN}	1.00	@ .79	1.00	@ .79	1.00	.71	1.00	1.35
δ_{FR}	1.00	@1.06	1.00	@1.06	1.00	1.01	1.00	7.33
δ_{RE}	1.00	@2.80	1.00	@2.80	1.00	2.92	1.00	7.96
δ_{VO}	1.00	@ .84	1.00	@ .84	1.00	.66	1.00	9.02
δ_{AW}	1.00	@1.62	1.00	@1.62	1.00	.87	1.00	1.13
δ_{SI}	1.00	@1.11	1.00	@1.11	1.00	.85	1.00	.54
Fit index:								
χ^2	212		124		267		259	
df	52		48		48		48	

Note: @ denotes that parameters are fixed at a value.
* indicates that a parameter estimate is not statistically significant at $\alpha = .05$.

Difference Score Factor Analysis Model

A series of difference score factor models (McArdle & Nesselroade, 1994; Nesselroade & Bartsch, 1977) were fit to the same data. Table 11.6 summarizes these results. Results were paralleled to those obtained in the longitudinal factor models. The orthogonal factor model over time was rejected (χ^2 = 658, df = 60). Factor variances at age 14 are different from those of difference scores at age 30 ($\Delta\chi^2$ = 32, Δdf = 2). The initial uniqueness scores covary with the later uniqueness scores ($\Delta\chi^2$ = 274, Δdf = 6). Factor scores at age 14 influenced factor scores of difference scores at age 30 ($\Delta\chi^2$ = 272, Δdf = 4). Expected item thresholds changed over time (χ^2 = 652, df = 6). Factor means grew from age 14 to age 30 ($\Delta\chi^2$ = 334, Δdf = 6). When uniqueness autocorrelation, factor regression, and different factor variances were simultaneously estimated, the model fit improved ($\Delta\chi^2$ = 436, Δdf = 12). When factor means were allowed to vary, the model fit further improved ($\Delta\chi^2$ = 446, Δdf = 8). When factor loadings were allowed to vary over time, the model fit further improved ($\Delta\chi^2$ = 535, Δdf = 12).

DISCUSSION

The primary focus of this research was to investigate the new approach for the longitudinal factor model and the difference score factor model for binary items. Through them, identification of both construct growth and construct change became easier. The longitudinal factor analysis was congruent with findings of the difference score factor model. Models that account for covariances among the crystallized items and fluid items are found to fit data better than do the others. The general factor model and oblique Gf-Gc model were equally tenable in this sense.

Results support that the factor variance at age 14 is larger than the difference scores factor variance at age 30. Results also indicate that the Gc factor was correlated with the Gf factor within time across time. However, the within-time Gc-Gf correlation decreased at age 30 in comparison with that at age 14. Results also showed uniqueness scores to be correlated over time, so specific factors may be important as well. Results also indicated quantitative changes in abilities over time, as shown in a change in factor means and expected item threshold values. As a whole, subjects at age 30 are better able to solve Stanford-Binet items than they are at age 14. That is to say, selected items from the Stanford-Binet Test seemed easier for subjects at age 30 than at 14. Furthermore, factor scores at age 14 positively influenced growth of factor scores at age 30. Results suggest that the factor pattern at age 14 was different from the factor pattern on item difference scores at age 30. This leads to a conclusion that there seems to be some qualitative shift in abilities between age 14 and age 30.

TABLE 11.6
Summary of Alternative Longitudinal Item Difference Score Factor Models

Alternative Models	Factor Regression β	Factor Variance ϕ_{var}	Autoreg Across Age $\theta_{e1,e2}$	Factor Covariance ϕ_{cov}	Factor Loading λ	Factor Mean α	Scaling Parameter Δ	Threshold Parameter τ	Model Fit χ^2	df
Orthogonal	Fixed 0	Fixed 1	Fixed 0	Differ	Equal	Fixed 0	Differ	Differ	658	60
Variance	Fixed 0	Differ	Fixed 0	Differ	Equal	Fixed 0	Differ	Differ	626	58
Autoregression	Fixed 0	Fixed 1	Estimated	Differ	Equal	Fixed 0	Differ	Differ	384	54
Factor regression	Estimated	Fixed 1	Fixed 0	Differ	Equal	Fixed 0	Differ	Differ	386	56
Threshold	Estimated	Differ	Fixed 0	Differ	Equal	Fixed 0	Differ	Equal	652	54
Regress + variance	Estimated	Differ	Fixed 0	Differ	Equal	Fixed 0	Differ	Differ	286	54
Autoreg + variance	Fixed 0	Differ	Estimated	Differ	Equal	Fixed 0	Differ	Differ	347	52
Auto + regression	Estimated	Fixed 1	Estimated	Differ	Equal	Fixed 0	Differ	Differ	314	50
Auto + regression + variance	Estimated	Differ	Estimated	Differ	Equal	Fixed 0	Differ	Differ	222	48
Factor mean	Estimated	Fixed 1	Estimated	Differ	Equal	Estimated	Differ	Differ	324	54
Mean + variance	Estimated	Differ	Estimated	Differ	Equal	Estimated	Differ	Differ	212	52
Unequal loading	Estimated	Differ	Estimated	Differ	Differ	Estimated	Differ	Differ	123	48

Note: "Fixed 0" means that parameters are fixed at 0.
"Fixed 1" means that parameters are fixed at 1.
"Differ" means that parameters are estimated independently across age.
"Equal" means that parameters are equated across age.
"Estimated" means that parameters are estimated.

This research illustrates a psychometric method to deal with a longitudinal data consisting of binary items. Using this method, it is possible to test the Gf-Gc theory using the Stanford-Binet Scale Test at the item level. Using both the longitudinal factor model and the difference score factor model, we can test both qualitative and quantitative change and growth in cognitive ability. These results clearly showed that cognitive ability is multifaceted and differentiated into secondary components (i.e., *Gf* and *Gc*). The Stanford-Binet items seem to be able to identify these two different latent constructs without a systematic test bias in at least adolescent age and adult age groups. However, results of the cognitive model should not be considered as conclusive due to the small sample size and the small number of binary items in the model.

In summary, McArdle and Nesselroade (1994) demonstrated how to model the longitudinal data, and this chapter extends such an approach to the longitudinal item data (see also Horn & McArdle, 1992). The longitudinal item factor model is useful to investigate growth of any latent trait on the item level. This model approach could help understand not only what each test item measures on the item level, but also invariance structure of *multidimensional* traits across occasions as well as qualitative shifts of these traits.

AUTHOR'S NOTE

This research has been supported by grants from the National Institute on Aging (AG07137).

REFERENCES

Bradway, K. P. (1944). IQ constancy on the revised Stanford-Binet from the preschool to the junior high school level. *Journal of Genetic Psychology, 65,* 197–217.

Bradway, K. P. (1945a). Predictive value of Stanford-Binet preschool items. *Journal of Educational Psychology, 36,* 1–16.

Bradway, K. P. (1945b). An experimental study of factors associated with Stanford-Binet IQ changes from the preschool to the junior high school. *Journal of Genetic Psychology, 66,* 107–128.

Cattell, R. B. (1963). The theory of fluid and crystallized general intelligence: A crucial experiment. *Journal of Educational Psychology, 54,* 1–22.

Christoffersson, A. (1975). Factor analysis of dichotomous variables. *Psychometrika, 40,* 5–22.

Corballis, M. C., & Traub, R. E. (1970). Longitudinal factor analysis. *Psychometrika, 35,* 79–98.

Guilford, J. P. (1967). *The nature of human intelligence.* New York: McGraw-Hill.

Guttman, L. (1954). A new approach to factor analysis: The radex. In P. F. Lazarsfeld (Ed.), *Mathematical thinking in the social sciences* (pp. 258–348). Glencoe, IL: Free Press.

Guttman, L. (1965). A facet definition of intelligence. *Scripta Hierosolymitana, 14,* 166–181.

Hertzog, C. & Nesselroade, J.R. (1987). Beyond autoregressive models: Some implications of the trait–state distinction for the structural modeling of developmental change. *Child Development, 58,* 93–109.

Horn, J. L. (1978). Human ability systems. In P. B. Baltes (Ed.), *Life-span development and behavior: Vol I* (pp. 211–256). New York: Academic.

Horn J. L. (1988). Thinking about human abilities. In J. R. Nesselroade & R. B. Cattell (Eds.), *Handbook of multivariate experimental psychology, Volume 2* (pp. 645–685). New York: Plenum.

Horn, J. L., & Cattell, R. B. (1966). Refinement and test of the theory of fluid and crystallized intelligence. *Journal of Educational Psychology, 57,* 253–270.

Horn, J. L., & McArdle, J. J. (1992). A practical and theoretical guide to measurement invariance in aging research. *Experimental Aging Research, 18,* 117–144.

Jöreskog, K. G. (1970). Estimation and testing of simplex models. *British Journal of Mathematical and Statistical Psychology, 23,* 121–146.

Jöreskog, K. G., & Söbom, D. (1979). *Advances in factor analysis and structural equation models.* Cambridge, MA: Abt.

Jöreskog, K. G., & Söbom, D. (1988). *LISREL7: A guide to the program and applications.* Chicago, IL: SPSS.

McArdle, J. J., & Nesselroade, J. R. (1994). Using multivariate data to structure developmental change. In H. Reese & S. Cohen (Eds.), *Life-span developmental psychology* (pp. 223–267). Hillsdale, NJ: Lawrence Erlbaum Associates.

McDonald, R. P. (1985). *Factor analysis and related methods.* Hillsdale, NJ: Lawrence Erlbaum Associates.

Muthen, B. (1978). Contributions to factor analysis of dichotomous variables. *Psychometrika, 43,* 551–560.

Muthén, B. O. (1987). *LISCOMP: Analysis of linear structural equations with a comprehensive measurement model.* Mooresville, IN: Scientific Software.

Muthén, B. O., & Christoffersson, A. (1981). Simultaneous factor analysis of dichotomous variables in several groups. *Psychometrika, 46,* 485–500.

Nesselroade, J. R. (1972). Note on the longitudinal factor analysis model. *Psychometrika, 37,* 187–191.

Nesselroade, J. R., & Bartsch, T. W. (1977). Multivariate perspectives on the construct validity of the trait–state distinction. In R. B. Cattell & R. M. Dreger (Eds.), *Handbook of modern personality theory* (pp. 221–238). Washington, DC: Hemisphere.

Olsson, L., & Bergman, A. (1977). A longitudinal factor model for studying change in abilities. *Multivariate Behavioral Research, 12,* 221–241.

Parry, C. & McArdle, J. J. (1991). An applied comparison of methods for least squares factor analysis of dichotomous variables. *Applied Psychological Measurement, 15*(1), 35–46.

Spearman, C. (1904). General intelligence, objectively determined and measured. *American Journal of Psychology, 15,* 201–293.

Terman, L. M., & Merrill, M. A. (1937). *Stanford-Binet intelligence scale.* Cambridge, MA: Riverside.

Thurstone, L. L. (1932). *Theory of multiple factors.* Ann Arbor, MI: Edwards.

Thurstone, L. L. (1947). *Multiple factor analysis.* Chicago: University of Chicago Press.

Woodcock, R. W. (1990). Theoretical foundations of the WJR measures of cognitive ability. *Journal of Psychoeducational Assessment, 8,* 231–258.

12

A Structural Factor Analysis of Gender and Age Differences in Cognitive Ability

Patricia A. Hulick
University of Virginia

The measurement of human abilities and the question of the existence of gender differences remain two of the more controversial topics in psychology. Studied in combination, they lead to complex discussions about how best to assess ability, and how males and females differ in ability. Questions such as "Do females have more verbal ability than males?" or "Do males have more quantitative ability than females?" provoke many reactions, because the answers may have broad-ranging implications. Consequently, it is important to gain a more complete understanding of the ways in which males and females may differ in cognitive patterns, and how best to measure such differences.

The psychological literature includes a wide variety of different findings of gender differences in cognitive abilities. The immense amount of research has been consolidated and summarized in the form of meta-analyses and comprehensive reviews (e.g., Feingold, 1988, 1992; Halpern, 1992; Hyde, 1981; Hyde, Fennema, & Lamon, 1990; Hyde & Linn, 1988; Maccoby, 1966; Maccoby & Jacklin, 1974). But these summaries often contradict each other. These inconsistencies may be the result of heterogeneity across age groups, heterogeneity of specific abilities assessed, and differences in individual tests used to measure each ability. Like physical abilities, cognitive abilities do not remain constant throughout life. Horn's (1988) work indicates that abilities grow differentially across the life span. It seems reasonable to consider the existence of interactive effects as well (e.g., ability by age by gender).

Holding features of the research design constant may not necessarily lead to consistent findings. Perhaps the problem is the strategy used to investigate gender differences in ability. Research has focused primarily on either mean differences, variability differences, or differences in correlations. Earlier research concentrated on only one aspect, often inadvertently assuming equivalence of other structural characteristics. When these assumptions are violated, they may lead to incongruent findings.

Structural equation modeling techniques have been utilized to provide comprehensive examinations of group differences in a variety of domains (e.g., Gustafsson, 1984; Hertzog & Schaie, 1986; Horn & McArdle, 1992; Marsh & Grayson, 1990; McArdle, 1994; McArdle & Cattell, 1994; McArdle & Prescott; 1992; McGaw & Jöreskog, 1971; Pike, 1991; Turban, Sanders, & Osburn, 1989). Hertzog and Carter (1982) used these methods to demonstrate the similarity of male and female intellectual structures.

The present study is designed to use structural modeling techniques to examine comprehensively the gender and age differences in cognitive ability structures as measured by the *Woodcock-Johnson Psycho-Educational Battery—Revised* (WJ-R; see Table 12.1). This approach is utilized to ascertain both the nature (qualitative) and the magnitude (quantitative) of the differences and to test consecutive hypotheses. The primary questions of interest are: What is the nature of gender differences in several broad and reliable cognitive abilities in (a) the mean levels, (b) the variability, (c) the covariances, (d) the unique variances, and (e) the factor patterns?

METHODS

Participants

The sample used in this study is a subset of the WJ-R norming sample. The original sample consisted of $N = 6,359$ subjects from more than 100 U.S. communities; subjects were randomly selected using a stratified sampling design that controlled for 10 specific community and subject variables. Using this design enabled a representative sample of the U.S. population to be obtained (see McGrew, Werder, & Woodcock, 1991; Woodcock, 1990; Woodcock & Johnson, 1989, 1990).

Inclusion requirements for the present study were (a) complete data for the 18 WJ-R subtests of interest, (b) race classification as either White or Black, (c) complete information regarding educational level, and (d) age requirements implicit in (a) (i.e., some subtests are not suitable for very young children). A subset of this sample was used for analysis in this study, whereas the remaining data were reserved for future analyses (e.g., cross-validation). The sample for the present study was further classified according to age and gender. There are N = 1,351 subjects in the child/adolescent sample (younger than 18 years of age), with N = 688 males and N = 663 females. There are N = 1,249 subjects in the adult sample (18 years of age and older), with N = 618 males and N = 631 females.

Variables

The WJ-R battery "is a wide-range comprehensive set of individually administered tests for measuring cognitive ability, scholastic aptitude, and achievement" (Woodcock, 1990, p. 231). The W-scores on 18 of the WJ-R subjects were selected to represent eight hypothesized cognitive abilities (see Table 12.1).

Procedure: Models and Hypotheses

Structural equation modeling (SEM) techniques (e.g., the LISREL computer program by Jöreskog & Sörbom, 1988; see also Loehlin, 1987; McDonald, 1985) are used to test the hypotheses. In Fig. 12.1, separate but identical hypothetical factor models are included for males and females. Each broad ability factor is represented by two WJ-R subtests, and has a mean (factor mean, labeled FM) and a variance (factor variance, labeled FV). Each subtest also

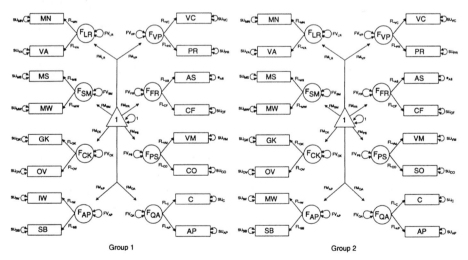

FIG. 12.1. Two-group model used to examine gender and age differences in the hypothetical structure of cognitive abilities, as measured by the WJ-R (adapted from Woodcock, 1990). (Note: Covariances/correlations between each pair of abilities are assumed to exist, although they are not pictured here. Subtest means exist as well, but they also are not pictured here.)

TABLE 12.1
The Broad Cognitive Abilities Examined in the Present Study
and the WJ-R Subtests That Are Used as Indicators of These Abilities

Cognitive Ability WJ-R Subtest	Description
Long-term Retrieval (LT)	Storage and retrieval of information over extended periods of time
Memory for Names (MN)	Learn and recall the names of newly introduced space creatures
Visual-Auditory Learning (VA)	Read a passage composed of newly learned symbol-word assocations
Short-Term Memory (SM)	Acquisition and use of information within a short period of time
Memory for Sentences (MS)	Recite words, phrases, and sentences that have just been auditorally presented
Memory for Words (MW)	Recite groups of unrelated words that have just been auditorally presented
Comprehension-Knowledge (CK)	General breadth and depth of knowledge
Oral Vocabulary (OV)	Identify synonyms and antonyms of several words
General Knowledge (GK)	Answer questions in the areas of science, social studies, and humanities
Auditory Processing (AP)	Comprehension and synthesis of auditory patterns
Incomplete Words (IW)	Name complete words that have been presented auditorally without one or more of its phonemes
Sound Blending (SB)	Name complete words that have been presented auditorally as individual syllables or phonemes
Visual Processing (VP)	Perception and thought with visual patterns and spatial configurations
Visual Closure (VC)	Identify pictures that have been altered in some way
Picture Recognition (PR)	Identify previously seen pictures among a larger set of pictures
Fluid Reasoning (FR)	Capability to reason in novel situations
Analysis-Synthesis (AS)	Complete a logic puzzle given a set of rules to follow
Concept Formation (CF)	State rule for colored geometric figures when shown instances and noninstances of the concept
Processing Speed (PS)	Performance of clerical tasks at a rapid pace.
Visual Matching (VM)	Circle the two identical numbers in a row of six numbers
Cross-Out (CO)	Mark five drawings in a row that are the same as the first drawing in the row
Quantitative Ability (QA)	Capability to understand and use mathematical concepts and symbols
Calculation (C)	Perform mathematical calculations
Applied Problems (AP)	Solve practical mathematical problems

Adapted from Woodcock (1990); Woodcock and Johnson (1989, 1990).

has a unique variance that represents the portion of the test not in common with other tests of the same factor (subtest uniqueness, or SU). The factor loadings (labeled FL) provide an index of relatedness of each subtest to other subtests that represent the same factor. Correlations are assumed to exist between broad abilities as well (FC).

To test the equivalence of particular parameters across gender, the respective parameters are first constrained to be equal, and the fit of the model to the data is examined. Next, the respective parameters in each group are freed to vary across groups, and the fit of the new model to the data is examined. The two model fits are then compared. The changes are studied in an "all," "some," and "none" fashion to investigate the pervasiveness of the difference (e.g., If males have a higher level of cognitive ability than do females, do they have higher levels on all cognitive abilities or just certain abilities?) For clarification, the first set of analyses is detailed next.

The initial set of analyses provides a test of the theory that males and females do not have equivalent mean levels of cognitive abilities. Initially *all* of the cognitive ability factor means are constrained to be equal for males and females (Model 0 in Table 12.2A). Then only *some* of the factor means are constrained to be equal across gender (Model 1 in Table 12.2A), whereas others are allowed to vary. Quantitative ability, fluid reasoning, processing speed, and visual processing parameters were selected to vary for the partial invariant models, whereas long-term memory, short-term memory, crystallized ability, and auditory processing parameters remained invariant in these same models. This selection was based on the notion that the first four abilities are more often studied in gender difference research than are the last four. (For consistency, this same set was utilized for the partial invariant models of age differences.) Finally, *none* of the factor means are constrained to be equal across sex (Model 2 in Table 12.2A). The fit of the three models are compared to determine which provides the most parsimonious fit to the data, and thus, the extent and pervasiveness of mean differences in the eight hypothesized broad abilities.

Four additional hypotheses are tested using this sequential approach. These models include equality of factor variances and covariances, subtest variances, and measurement (i.e., factor loadings). The three "subhypotheses" of all, some, or no differences are tested for each structural hypothesis. The structural characteristics are examined in a fully nested sequence such that once a parameter is freed to vary across groups, it remains variant when subsequent hypotheses are tested.

A comparative approach is used to assess model fit. Rather than determining if a given model provides a good fit to the data, the emphasis is on determining whether or not a given model provides a significantly better fit to the data than another model (e.g, $\Delta\chi^2$, *LIP*). The fit indexes are outlined in Table 12.3.

RESULTS

A summary of overall goodness-of-fit measures and an overview of differences of fit indexes for alternative models of gender and age differences in cognitive abilities are provided in Tables 12.2A, 12,2B, 12.4A, and 12.4B. Due to the parallel nature of gender differences across age groups, fit indexes for only the child/adolescent sample are provided.

Gender Differences

There are small but consistent patterns worth noting. Partial invariance models produce better fits to the data than do the respective invariant mod-

TABLE 12.2A
Goodness-of-Fit Measures for Alternative Models
of Gender Differences in the Child/Adolescent Sample

Model	Level of Invariance	χ^2	df	RMSEA	p_{exact}	p_{close}
0. Null Hypothesis	Full Invariance	732	228	.04	.00	1.00
1. Factor Mean	Partial Invariant	649	224	.04	.00	1.00
2. Factor Mean	Full Variant	628	220	.04	.00	1.00
3. Factor Variance	Partial Invariant	618	216	.04	.00	1.00
4. Factor Variance	Full Variant	617	212	.04	.00	1.00
5. Factor Covariance	Partial Invariant	587	190	.04	.00	1.00
6. Factor Covariance	Full Variant	574	184	.04	.00	1.00
7. Subtest Uniqueness	Partial Invariant	558	176	.04	.00	1.00
8. Subtest Uniqueness	Full Variant	552	168	.04	.00	1.00
9. Factor Loading	Partial Invariant	536	164	.04	.00	1.00
10. Factor Loading	Full Variant	530	160	.04	.00	1.00

TABLE 12.2B
Summary of Differences-of-Fit Indexes for Alternative Models
of Gender Differences in the Child/Adolescent Sample

Comparison	Hypothesis Tested	$\Delta\chi^2$	Δdf	LIP	DIP
0 – 1	Gender differences in some factor means?	83	4	11%	3%
0 – 2	Gender differences in all factor means?	104	8	14%	2%
0 – 3	Gender differences in some factor variances?	114	12	16%	1%
0 – 4	Gender differences in all factor variances?	115	16	16%	1%
0 – 5	Gender differences in some factor correlations?	145	38	20%	1%
0 – 6	Gender differences in all factor correlations?	158	44	22%	1%
0 – 7	Gender differences in some subtest variances?	174	52	24%	0%
0 – 8	Gender differences in all subtest variances?	180	60	25%	0%
0 – 9	Gender differences in some factor loadings?	196	64	27%	0%
0 – 10	Gender differences in all factor loadings?	202	68	28%	0%

TABLE 12.3
Fit Indexes Used to Assess Model Fit

Fit Index	Interpretation
χ^2, df, p(exact)	The likelihood ratio, degrees of freedom, and associated probability level typically used for structural equation modeling hypothesis testing (Jöreskog & Sörbom, 1988)
RMSEA	Root mean square error of approximation; average difference between observed and expected covariances (Browne & Cudeck, 1993)
p(close)	Measure of the probability that the residuals are nearly zero (in conjunction with the RMSEA; Browne & Cudeck, 1993)
LIP	Likelihood improvement percentage; percentage of improvement gained in the model of interest over a baseline model $(1 - \text{model } \chi^2 / \text{baseline } \chi^2)$ (McArdle, 1988; McArdle & Prescott, 1992)
DIP	Degree of freedom improvement percentage; average percentage of improvement over the baseline gained for each degree of freedom utilized to obtain the fit (McArdle, 1988; McArdle & Prescott, 1992)
Modified Information Criteria (Empirical Penalty Line)	This requires plotting the likelihood ratio (χ^2) as a function of the degrees of freedom for each model. Then a regression line is fit through the origin of $\chi^2 = 0$ and $df = 0$; this is referred to as an empirical "penalty line." Models that are above this line have a relatively higher χ^2 value given the respective df, and models below the line have a relatively lower χ^2 for the respective df. This method moves away from relying on tests of statistical significance and simply compares the effect of one set of changes to another to determine which model generally leads to a better fit of the data (McArdle, 1988; McArdle & Prescott, 1992).

els, whereas fully variant models generally do nothing to further improve the fit. The parameters of some, but not all, of the ability measures are different for males and females.

There are small quantitative (mean) and qualitative (variance, covariance, uniqueness, and factor loading) differences in performance. The partial invariant and fully variant factor mean models provide improved fits to the data, but at different costs. The fully variant model provides an improved model fit in both age groups, but the estimated factor mean differences for six of the eight abilities are not statistically different from zero. Young females exhibit higher levels of auditory processing and processing speed skills. Adult females exhibit a higher level of visual processing, whereas adult males exhibit a higher level of quantitative ability. The evidence suggests

TABLE 12.4A
Goodness-of-Fit Measures for Alternative Models of Age Differences

Model	Level of Invariance	χ^2	df	RMSEA	p_{exact}	p_{close}
0. Null Hypothesis	Full Invariance	4492	228	.09	.00	.00
1. Factor Mean	Partial Invariant	4443	224	.09	.00	.00
2. Factor Mean	Full Variant	2668	220	.07	.00	.00
3. Factor Variance	Partial Invariant	2571	216	.07	.00	.00
4. Factor Variance	Full Variant	2492	212	.06	.00	.00
5. Factor Covariance	Partial Invariant	1893	190	.06	.00	.00
6. Factor Covariance	Full Variant	1557	184	.05	.00	.01
7. Subtest Uniqueness	Partial Invariant	1468	176	.05	.00	.03
8. Subtest Uniqueness	Full Variant	1264	168	.05	.00	.41
9. Factor Loading	Partial Invariant	1130	164	.05	.00	.95
10. Factor Loading	Full Variant	1076	160	.05	.00	.98

TABLE 12.4B
Summary of Differences-of-Fit Indexes
for Alternative Models of Age Differences

Comparison	Hypothesis Tested	$\Delta\chi^2$	Δdf	LIP	DIP
0 – 1	Age differences in some factor means?	49	4	1%	0%
0 – 2	Age differences in all factor means?	1824	8	41%	5%
0 – 3	Age differences in some factor variances?	1921	12	43%	4%
0 – 4	Age differences in all factor variances?	2000	16	45%	3%
0 – 5	Age differences in some factor correlations?	2599	38	58%	2%
0 – 6	Age differences in all factor correlations?	2935	44	65%	1%
0 – 7	Age differences in some subtest variances?	3024	52	67%	1%
0 – 8	Age differences in all subtest variances?	3228	60	72%	1%
0 – 9	Age differences in some factor loadings?	3362	64	75%	1%
0 – 10	Age differences in all factor loadings?	3416	68	76%	1%

that the mean level of performance is different for males and females on some, but not all, abilities.

Better fits to the data are obtained as the qualitative parameters are sequentially freed to vary across gender. The improvement in model fit gained when all of the parameter constraints are relaxed is approximately twice as great as the improvement in fit obtained when only the quantitative parameters are not constrained to be equal across gender. The total improvement may seem large, yet each parameter change provides only a small improvement. There is a large fit improvement only when all of the parameter changes are simultaneously taken into account. The individual qualitative changes are minimal.

The penalty line in Fig. 12.2 shows that that no one model fits the data much better than the others. The only models that yield lower χ^2 values than expected, given the df, are those that relax the constraint of all or some

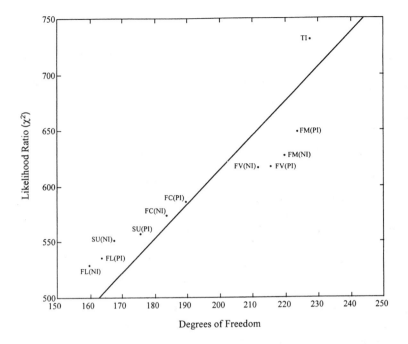

FIG. 12.2.   Goodness-of-fit alternative models for gender differences in children/adolescents.

factor means and factor variances. This is consistent with the findings cited earlier. The largest fit improvement due to one structural change is achieved when some of the factor means are not constrained to be equal across groups, *LIP* = 11% (see Table 12.2B). Each subsequent change is small by comparison to this initial relaxed parameter constraint. Simultaneous consideration of the various fit indexes suggests that there is insufficient evidence for measurement bias or variability differences between males and females. The broad abilities are not differentially related for males and females either. The only gender difference is the mean level of performance, and this difference does not pervade all abilities.

Age Differences

There is evidence for both quantitative and qualitative differences in cognitive abilities as a function of age. The pattern of differences between partial invariance models and fully variant models falls into three groups: large, moderate, and minimal differences.

Complete invariant and partial invariant models for the factor means do not differ. There is great improvement in model fit obtained in the fully vari-

ant factor mean model. This is strong evidence for mean differences on all of
the abilities.

Evidence for qualitative differences are small by comparison. Factor variability and subtest uniqueness partial invariance models produce small but
consistently better fits to the data than do total invariance models. The fully
variant models further improve the fit by approximately the same amount.
These qualitative differences exist to the same extent for all abilities, but are
minimal.

The partial invariant factor loading model is much more of a likely fit to
the data than is the complete invariant factor loading model. The difference
in improved model fit seems small, but it is important to be cautious about
this finding, because nonequivalence of these parameters suggests that clus-
ters of subtests do not measure the same ability for the two age groups.
Other comparisons are irrelevant if different constructs exist across groups.

There is one qualitative difference of moderate size. Both factor covari-
ability partial invariant and fully variant models improve the fit to the data.
The way in which the factors are related may be different for children/ado-
lescents than for adults. These differences pervade all abilities. One should
be cautious to make inferences involving multiple abilities if they are differentially related. For example, a verbal-performance discrepancy score is often used to determine strengths and weaknesses of an individual. The discrepancy measure will not carry the same meaning across groups if the two
abilities are differentially related across groups. The single quantitative difference produces as much improvement in fit as do all of the qualitative differences combined. This suggests that the largest cognitive ability difference
between children/adolescents and adults is a mean difference in performance. The qualitative differences are small, but should not be considered
negligible and unimportant. The evidence suggests that different factors may
be measured, and that factors may be differentially related across age groups.

It is evident in Fig. 12.3 that no one model fits the data much better than
other models. There is a group of models that seems to fit somewhat better
than most of the others. Models that allow differences in factor covariances,
subtest uniquenesses, and factor loadings across age yielded the lowest χ^2
values than expected, given the df. The variant subtest uniqueness and factor loading models are the best-fitting models using this decision method,
and this is consistent with the conclusions based on the previous fit statistics.

DISCUSSION

Much past research indicates that there are several gender differences in cognitive abilities. This study indicated that the gender differences are minimal
at best. The quantitative differences are small and do not pervade all abili-

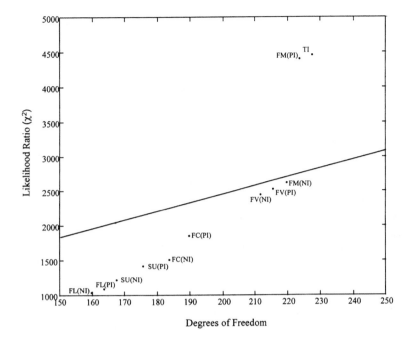

FIG. 12.3.   Goodness-of-fit alternative models for age differences.

ties. Young females exhibited higher levels of auditory processing and processing speed, whereas young males and young females performed equiva-
lently on the remaining six abilities. Adult females exhibit higher levels
of visual processing, whereas adult males exhibit higher levels of quantitative ability; no mean differences are exhibited on the remaining six abilities
within the adult sample. There are not qualitative differences between young
males and females or between adult males and females.

There are several differences *between* age groups. Adults exhibit higher
levels of all measured cognitive abilities. The relationship between some
abilities (visual processing, fluid reasoning, processing speed, and quantitative ability) may be different across age groups, and some combinations of
subtests may be differentially related across age groups (visual closure and
picture recognition, analysis-synthesis and concept formation, cross-out
and visual matching, calculation and applied problems).

Remaining Questions and Future Research

Of primary concern is to understand why there are so many contradictory
findings in this area of research. If the origin of the inconsistencies can be

ascertained, then this knowledge may be used to reduce or eliminate the incongruent findings.

Effect Size

The proportion of variance in ability measures accounted for by gender in previous work was calculated to gain a better understanding of the actual magnitude of the differences shown in earlier research. In many cases the effect size is small. This proportion[1] ranged from $\eta^2 = .00$ to $\eta^2 = .36$. It typically was not greater than $\eta^2 = .05$. The results of the present study do not necessarily differ from results of previous research. The difference is the emphasis of small effects. In the present study, the small effects were manifested as small changes in model fits.

Selection Effects

The inconsistencies may be the result of sample characteristics. We must be aware of who the participants are in each study before making comparisons. There are a wide range of ability levels, and results are largely dependent on the segment of the population being studied. For instance, much of the cognitive ability gender difference controversy has focused on achievement measures such as the SAT. The key issue often overlooked is that individuals who take admissions examinations are a specific subgroup of the population. It has been suggested that individuals who actually take such tests have more aptitude than do individuals who do not take these types of tests. Individuals who take admissions tests represent a segment of the population that has an above-average chance of succeeding in higher education. Differences between males and females who belong to such subgroups may not be representative of the differences in the general population (see Berk, 1983). Recall that the current sample is a subset of the WJ-R norming sample and is deemed to be representative of the U.S. population as a whole.

---

[1]The following formula was used to calculate η^2:

$$\eta_2 = \frac{F_{effect} * (df_{effect})}{F_{effect} * (df_{effect}) + df_{error}}$$

If the F-statistic was not included in the publication, t^2 was used ($F = t^2$ when $df_{effect} = 1$).
If no test statistic was included in the publication, but group means and standard deviations were, then the following calucation was used to compute t^2 and subsequently F:

$$t^2 = \frac{M_1 - M_2}{\sqrt{\frac{\sigma_1^2}{N_1} + \frac{\sigma_2^2}{N_2}}}$$

where M_1 and M_2 are the means for the two groups, σ_1^2 and σ_2^2 are the variances for the two groups, and N_1 and N_2 represent the number of subjects in each group. See Rosenthal and Rosnow (1991).

Inclusion of Additional Variables

The empirical suggestion that age should be taken into account leads to the idea that additional variables should be considered as well. One possibility is education. Students within each grade level are typically close in age, but there are often exceptions (e.g., adults who return to college later in life). It should not be assumed that an individual of a given age has necessarily completed a particular amount of schooling.

Researchers have also suggested that race may play a role (e.g., Jensen, 1980). An interaction between race and gender may exist as well. For instance, Jensen (1988) concluded that males were more variable than females on measures of math concepts and applications, but this finding was based on samples of White children; no differences were found within a Black sample.

A Developmental Approach

The lack of consistent findings in earlier research may be due to the absence of a developmental approach to understanding gender differences in cognitive abilities. There may be differential intellectual growth patterns for males and females (Cattell, 1987; Fairweather, 1976; Feingold, 1992; Maccoby, 1966; Maccoby & Jacklin, 1974), just as there are differential physical growth patterns between them.

Investigation of these data led to the conclusion that cognitive ability differences may be more a function of age than gender. Age analyses indicated that there are several quantitative differences between the two age groups, and there may be some qualitative differences as well. The results are consistent with Horn's (1988) findings that different abilities change in different ways across the life span. A more complete developmental approach (e.g., using Piaget's four stages of cognitive development as more in-depth age classifications) is needed to provide a better understanding of cognitive ability growth as a function of age.

SUMMARY

The focus of this research was to examine the structure and measurement of human cognitive abilities as a function of gender and age. Although there is strong evidence for measurement validity across gender, males and females exhibited mean differences in performance on some of the measures. There appear to be several quantitative differences as a function of age, but these may not be interpretable because there is reason to question the measurement validity across the two age groups.

What the present study did not address was the structure and measurement of abilities as measured by the numerous other ability measures currently available, nor does this study address other validity issues. The measurement structure of the WJ-R is similar across gender, but this does not imply that other forms of bias would not result from using such test batteries (e.g., predictive validity), if studied.

REFERENCES

Berk, R. A. (1983). An introduction to sample selection bias in sociological data. *American Sociological Review, 48*(3), 386–398.

Browne, M. W., & Cudeck, R. (1993). Alternative ways of assessing model fit. In K. A. Bollen & J. S. Long (Eds.), *Testing structural equation models* (pp. 136–162). Newbury Park, CA: Sage.

Cattell, R. B. (1987). The natural history of ability: Distribution and relation to sex and age. In R. B. Cattell (Ed.), *Intelligence: Its structure, growth, and action* (pp. 153–211). New York: North-Holland.

Fairweather, H. (1976). Sex differences in cognition. *Cognition, 4*, 231–280.

Feingold, A. (1988). Cognitive gender differences are disappearing. *American Psychologist, 43*(2), 95–103.

Feingold, A. (1992). Sex differences in variability in intellectual abilities: A new look at an old controversy. *Review of Educational Research, 62*(1), 61–84.

Gustafsson, J. (1984). A unifying model for the structure of intellectual abilities. *Intelligence, 8*, 179–203.

Halpern, D. F. (1992). *Sex differences in cognitive abilities.* Hillsdale, NJ: Lawrence Erlbaum Associates.

Hertzog, C., & Carter, L. (1982). Sex differences in the structure of intelligence: A confirmatory factor analysis. *Intelligence, 6*, 287–303.

Hertzog, C., & Schaie, K. W. (1986). Stability and change in adult intelligence: 1. Analysis of longitudinal covariance structures. *Psychology and Aging, 1*(2), 159–171.

Horn, J. (1988). Thinking about human abilities. In J. R. Nesselroade & R. B. Cattell (Eds.), *Handbook of multivariate experimental psychology* (pp. 645–685). New York: Plenum.

Horn, J. L., & McArdle, J. J. (1992). A practical and theoretical guide to measurement invariance in aging research. *Experimental Aging Research, 18*(3), 117–144.

Hyde, J. S. (1981). How large are cognitive gender differences? A meta-analysis using w^2 and d. *American Psychologist, 36*(8), 892–901.

Hyde, J. S., Fennema, E., & Lamon, S. J. (1990). Gender differences in mathematics performance: A meta-analysis. *Psychological Bulletin, 107*(2), 139–155.

Hyde, J. S., & Linn, M. C. (1988). Gender differences in verbal ability: A meta-analysis. *Psychological Bulletin, 104*(1), 53–69.

Jensen, A. R. (1980). *Bias in mental testing.* New York: Free Press.

Jensen, A. R. (1988). Sex differences in arithmetic computation and reasoning in prepubertal boys and girls. *Behavioral and Brain Sciences, 11*(2), 198–199.

Jöreskog, K. G., & Sörbom, D. (1988). *LISREL VII: A guide to the program and applications.* Chicago: SPSS.

Loehlin, J. C. (1987). *Latent variable models: An introduction to factor, path, and structural analysis.* Hillsdale, NJ: Lawrence Erlbaum Associates.

Maccoby, E. E. (1966). *The development of sex differences.* Stanford, CA: Stanford University Press.

Maccoby, E. E., & Jacklin, C. N. (1974). *The psychology of sex differences.* Stanford, CA: Stanford University Press.

Marsh, H. W., & Grayson, D. (1990). Public/Catholic differences in the high school and beyond data: A multigroup structural equation modeling approach to testing mean differences. *Journal of Educational Studies, 15*(3), 199–235.

McArdle, J. J. (1988). Dynamic but structural equation modeling of repeated measures data. In J. R. Nesselroade & R. B. Cattell (Eds.), *The handbook of multivariate experimental psychology, Volume 2* (pp. 561–614). New York: Plenum.

McArdle, J. J. (1994). Structural factor analysis experiments with incomplete data. *Multivariate Behavioral Research, 29*(4), 409–454.

McArdle, J. J., & Cattell, R. B. (1994). Structural equation models of factorial invariance in parallel proportional profiles and oblique confactor problems. *Multivariate Behavioral Research, 29*(1), 63–113.

McArdle, J. J., & Prescott, C. A. (1992). Age-based construct validation using structural equation modeling. *Experimental Aging Research, 18*(3), 87–115.

McDonald, R. P. (1985). *Factor analysis and related methods.* Hillsdale, NJ: Lawrence Erlbaum Associates.

McGaw, B., & Jöreskog, K. G. (1971). Factorial invariance of ability measures in groups differing in intelligence and socioeconomic status. *British Journal of Statistical Psychology, 24,* 154–168.

McGrew, K. S., Werder, J. K., & Woodcock, R. W. (1991). *WJ-R technical manual.* Allen, TX: DLM.

Pike, G. R. (1991). Using structural equation models with latent variables to study student growth and development. *Research in Higher Education, 32*(5), 499–524.

Rosenthal, R., & Rosnow, R. L. (1991). *Essentials of behavioral research: Methods and data analysis.* New York: McGraw-Hill.

Turban, D. B., Sanders, P. A., Francis, D. J., & Osburn, H. G. (1989). Construct equivalence as an approach to replacing validated cognitive ability selection tests. *Journal of Applied Psychology, 74*(1), 62–71.

Woodcock, R. W. (1990). Theoretical foundation of the WJ-R measures of cognitive abilities. *Journal of Psychoeducational Assessment, 8,* 231–258.

Woodcock, R. W., & Johnson, M. B. (1989). *Woodcock-Johnson Psycho-Educational Battery—Revised.* Allen, TX: DLM.

Woodcock, R. W., & Johnson, M. B. (1990). *Woodcock-Johnson Psycho-Educational Battery—Revised.* Allen, TX: DLM.

13

Age Differences
in Processes of Fluid and
Crystallized Intelligence

Jennie G. Noll
John L. Horn
University of Southern California

This study was designed to provide information about how complex cognitive capabilities can be described in terms of more elementary cognitive processes. The theory on which the study was based was described in some detail earlier in this book (see Horn, chap. 4, this volume). Several forms of intelligence are recognized in that theory. Particular interest in the present study is focused on two of these intelligences—crystallized intelligence (Gc) and fluid intelligence (Gf).

The factor Gc is characterized by knowledge and reasoning that is learned under the conditions of acculturation—through the everyday infusions of the mass media and learning of the kind promoted in school courses, home childrearing, vocational training, and commonly used self-help programs. In contrast, Gf is characterized by reasoning under novel conditions—that is, reasoning with problems of a kind that ordinarily are not met or emphasized in acculturation. Of particular interest are findings indicating that these two forms of intelligence have quite different relationships to age through the adulthood period of development. On the average (over many individuals) Gf declines with age, whereas in the same samples of subjects the averages for Gc increase. The question is why: What are the factors that lead one of these forms of intelligence to decrease and the other to increase? The approach adopted in this attempt to help answer this question is one of determining the extent to which elementary cognitive processes can account for the decrease in Gf and/or the increase in Gc.

Using mathematical/statistical part correlation techniques to effect controls, Horn, Donaldson, and Engstrom (1981) found that an elementary process of concentration (CON) described some of the aging decline of Gf. In particular, in a unit of IQ in which Gf declined approximately 3.75 points per decade from near 20 years of age through near 60 years of age, CON reduced the decline of Gf by about 1.3 IQ units to a decline of approximately 2.44 points per decade. Horn et al. also found that estimates of short-term apprehension/retrieval (SAR) and cognitive speed (Gs) independently accounted for statistically significant portions of the decline of Gf, a finding that was replicated with other estimates of SAR and Gs in a study reported by Salthouse (1993). Neither Horn et al. nor Salthouse reported how, if at all, the SAR, Gs, and/or CON process indicators accounted for age-related improvements in Gc.

Horn (1982) reported that if Gf were controlled in Gc, there was an increase with age of an additional 1.2 units of IQ per decade over a period from the early 20s to the early 60s. This finding has two important implications for the rationale of the present study. First, it indicates that Gf is contained in Gc, and there produces a declining influence in what is otherwise a function that improves with age. This suggests that Gf is a confound in Gc. This is expected, of course, because it is unlikely that any estimate of Gf can be completely devoid of the acculturational influences that characterize Gc. To remove this confound would be to estimate a more nearly pure measure of Gc, and thus provide a basis for estimating its improvement through the adulthood period of development.

Second, the finding of Horn (1982) suggests that processes of Gf—such as those of concentration, cognitive speed, and short-term apprehension and retrieval—may be largely responsible for the improvement in Gc realized through control with Gf. It is worthwhile to determine if this is the case for particular process indicators, because if it is not, then it is to be expected that other processes of Gf are responsible for improvement in Gc effected by Gf control. Research might then be more pointedly directed at identifying these other processes.

To provide information of relevance for answering these general questions the present study was directed, first, at replicating previous findings indicating that the decline of Gf can be accounted for in part by declines in CON, SAR and Gs; and, second, describing the extent to which, if at all, these process indicators account for age-related improvements in Gc independent of their association with Gf. In addition, analyses were directed at describing the extent of Gf decline with age when the measurement overlap (putative confound) of Gc is statistically controlled.

PROCEDURES

Estimates of Gf, Gc, and three process indicators—CON, SAR, and Gs—
were obtained in 577 adults. Part correlation analyses (Horn et al., 1981)
were effected to describe age differences in these measures.

Drawing the Sample of Subjects

Through the summer and fall of 1994 and 1995, adults residing in Los Angeles County were tested in groups of four to eight people to obtain a total
sample of $N = 577$ subjects. The age range in the sample was 22 to 92 years
(mean = 58.42, sd = 16.30). Females constituted 55.5% of the sample; 88.2%
were White; 5.1% were Hispanic; 3.4% were Black; 2.1.% were Asian; and
1.2% were of other ethnicity. Mean family income before taxes was a
bracket (supplied in the questionnaire) of $40,000–$49,000. Mean level of
formal education also was for a bracket, this labeled "some college." Current employment was largely either white collar (30.1%), retired (40.2%), or
"homemaker" (25.7%). The remainder of the sample was unemployed
(2.1%) or reported other forms of work (1.9%).

Obtaining Estimates of Gf and Gc Abilities

The following tests, found in previous research to be salient markers for either the Gf or Gc common factors (see Horn, chap. 4, this volume), were
used to obtain estimates of Gf and Gc.

To Estimate Fluid Reasoning (Gf)

1. *Power Letter Series (PLS).*   This 38-item test requires subjects to detect
a series in a string of letters and choose a letter that continues the series. In
the instructions and examples introducing the test, subjects are taught that
some problems have no good solution. This is done by introducing trial
questions in which there is no solution. Subjects are advised that when a
problem of this kind is encountered in the test, they should select a "no answer" (NA) option and move on to the next item. Thus, the subject learns
that if after working on a problem for a reasonable amount of time no good
answer can be found, then the problem may be one for which there is no solution. This enables the person to abandon a problem that has a good solution when that solution is beyond the person's level of comprehension. This
condition, plus the fact that the subjects must produce an answer—not select an answer from among several choices—decreases the likelihood that
subjects will guess or can guess a correct answer. These testing conditions

also discourage perseveration on particular items at the expense of attempting others.

In the test itself, three items at a very low level of difficulty are presented first to provide a warmup. These items are followed by seven sets of five items, one item from each of five levels of difficulty arranged in order from "most simple" to "most difficult." Subjects were given 20 minutes to work on the test. They were told that it was not necessary to finish all items, but to do their best on the items attempted.

Although the test was timed, the measure obtained with it is not. Within each set of five items ordered according to difficulty, score is the sum of difficulty weights (1, 2, 3, 4, or 5) for each item correct. For example, the score for one who got all items correct within a particular set of five items would be $1 + 2 + 3 + 4 + 5 = 15$. This score is summed over the sets completed (prorated for sets partially completed) and divided by the number of completed sets to obtain the measure. The maximum score attainable is thus 15, and this score can be obtained by completing as little as one set. Scores can range from 0 (incorrect answers at all levels of difficulty) to 15 (correct answers for items at all levels). The measure thus is an indication of the level of difficulty successfully resolved, not the number of problems solved within a time limit.

2. Common Word Analogies (CWA).   This provided a verbal test estimate of Gf, important because the Gf-Gc distinction has been referred to as if it represented a nonverbal-verbal distinction. But Gf is indicated by reasoning within verbal tasks, as well as within spatial and auditory materials. CWA requires subjects to figure out the relationship between two common words and choose a word from a list of common words that represents an analogous relationship for a third word. For example:

> SOON is to NEVER as NEAR is to (choose one word from the following list):
> NOWHERE   FAR AWAY   DISTANT   SOMEWHERE   HERE

Given that the meanings of the words in each item are known to the respondent, the task is one of reasoning to determine the relationship among the meanings. The time limits were sufficient to enable all subjects to complete this 15-item test. Subjects were encouraged to choose a "no answer" option if there appeared to be no reasonable choice for completion of the analogy. Possible scores range from 0 (none correct) to 15 (all correct).

To Estimate Crystallized Knowledge (Gc)

1. Basic Vocabulary (VOC1).   In each of 15 items, subjects indicated in a set of five words the one word that was most nearly synonymous with a target word.

2. Intermediate Vocabulary (VOC2). As in VOC1, subjects selected the word most nearly synonymous with a target word from among a set of five choices. There were 15 such items.

In both VOC1 and VOC2, subjects were given time to attempt all items. Possible scores on each of the two tests range from 0 to 15.

3. Esoteric Analogies (ESA). This test is comparable in form to the common word analogies measure of Gf, but understanding the relationships among concepts in esoteric analogies requires advanced knowledge, as acquired through the acculturation that characterizes Gc. For example, to solve the analogy

GUSTATORY is to TASTE as OLFACTORY is to:
    SMELL   TOUCH   FEEL   HEAR   BALANCE

one needs to have acquired meanings for the words *gustatory* and *olfactory,* terms that are acquired through advanced acculturation. There were 15 such items. Scores thus can range from 0 to 15. Subjects were encouraged to select a "no answer" option, rather than skip the item or guess, if there appeared to be no good solution.

Obtaining Estimates of Process Variables

To Estimate Concentration (CON)

Slow Tracing. In this test, subjects are asked to trace an irregular line as slowly as possible while keeping their pencil moving at all times. Two instructional trials of the task are given. On the first instructional trial, the administrator very deliberately watches a stopwatch tick down long after all subjects have completed tracing the line. With emphasis, the administrator then asks subjects to trace a new line *as slowly as possible.* Again, the administrator does not call time until a minute after all subjects have completed tracing the (rather short) line, and again it is emphasized that the task is to trace *as slowly as possible.* These instructions encourage subjects to try to trace very slowly. It is readily seen on subsequent trials that, indeed, subjects try very hard to trace very slowly. Score is the shortness of the line traced.

Two trials beyond the instruction trials were given in the present testing to obtain the measure and provide a basis for estimating reliability. The traced line on each trial was measured in centimeters, the two lengths were added and the sum was subtracted from 100 to provide the measure. Thus, the smaller the number of centimeters, the larger the score. Large score indicates slowness. Slowness indicates concentration. The two-trial reliability of the measure was .87.

To Estimate Short-term Apprehension Retrieval (SAR)

Memory for Paired Associates (MPA).   Subjects were given 3 minutes to study 21 pictures each paired with a two-digit number. They were then given a page containing only the pictures and allowed 2 minutes to recall the numbers that had been paired with the pictures. Score was count of the number correct pairings. Possible scores range from 0 to 21.

To Estimate Cognitive Speed (Gs)

Speeded Letters Comparison (SLC).   This task requires subjects indicate whether sets of letters are the same or different. The following are two examples of such sets:

		Same	Different
almpq	almpp	____	____
tfstd	tfstd	____	____

The comparison sets were arranged in columns. The subjects moved down the columns, making same/different judgments as quickly as possible. Score is the number of correct comparisons in a 30-second trial. Possible scores range from 0 to 25 (number of comparisons on the page).

METHODS OF ANALYSIS

The part of a target measure linearly estimated with (predicted by) a control variable was first calculated. This was subtracted from the obtained target to obtain a residual measure from which all that could be estimated with the control variable had been removed (partialed out). That residual was correlated with age. The difference between this correlation for the residual and the age correlation for the unresidualized target was calculated to estimate the extent to which the control variable was involved in (accounted for by) the target's correlation with age. (Technical details and examples of how these analyses were performed can be obtained from the authors.)

To provide an indication that the control variable has a significant (different from zero) effect, the significance of the difference between the multiple correlation before control and after control can be calculated. The R-square change assesses the extent to which the addition of each subsequent component adds significantly to the multiple correlation.

For purposes of communicating results in graphic presentations, correlations and part correlations were converted to regression coefficients expressed in IQ units with the standard deviation for the ability set to 15. IQ units are familiar, and differences between correlations and part correlations expressed in these units illustrate how control of processes affects relationships between variables.

Conversion to IQ units can be illustrated concretely in the present sample with the PLS estimate of Gf. The zero-order correlation of PLS with age is $-.469$. The standard deviation for age is 16.30. Using the abbreviations A = Age and Gf = PLS, the regression of Gf on age when the sigma for Gf is set to 15 is simply: $B(Gf,A) = -.469 * (15 / 16.3) * A = -.431 * A$. The slope, $-.431$, indicates the amount of change of Gf in IQ units for a unit of (year of) age. Ten years of age would thus yield 4.31 IQ units of decline in Gf.

RESULTS

Descriptive Findings

Groupings by 10 years of age were formed through the range from 36 to 75 years of age; those below age 35 years and above age 75 years were grouped to specify the two extremes. Table 13.1A provides descriptive information for these groupings for all the ability measures.

For the Gf indicators and processes labeled *power letter series (PLS)*, *memory for paired associates (MPA)*, *slow tracing concentration (CON)*, and *speeded letter comparison (SLC)*, there was monotonic decrease in the means for the groupings from youngest to the oldest persons. A linear function with negative slope was found to fit the relationship to age: A quadratic parameter was not needed. For CWA estimate of Gf, the averages increased from the young age grouping to the 46–55 age grouping, then decreased monotonically. A quadratic parameter was needed to describe this relationship.

For the indicators of the Gc-maintained abilities—basic vocabulary (VOC1), advanced vocabulary (VOC2), and esoteric word analogies (ESA)— the means increased with age up to the 56–65 age grouping, decreased for this age group, and increased from this point onward. The trend was thus generally monotonic. A linear function with positive slope provided a fit for the relationships for these variables with age. The standard deviations varied somewhat from one age grouping to another for the indicators of both the vulnerable and maintained abilities, but the variations were not monotonic with age. A basis for interpreting these variations was not determined.

The intercorrelations among the ability measures were generally positive (Table 13.1B). All the vulnerable abilities had significant negative correlations with age (i.e., all the correlations were significantly different from zero). The two vocabulary indicators of Gc had significant positive correlations with age. The correlation of age with esoteric analogies and all the correlations between gender and the ability measures were not significantly different from zero.

TABLE 13.1A
Means and Standard Deviations for Standardized (Mean = 0, sd = 1)
Cognitive Variables Across Several Age Groups

	Age Group					
	22–35 N = 61 $\bar{X}$(std)	36–45 N = 90 $\bar{X}$(std)	46–55 N = 101 $\bar{X}$(std)	56–65 N = 88 $\bar{X}$(std)	66–75 N = 150 $\bar{X}$(std)	76–92 N = 87 $\bar{X}$(std)
1. Power letter series	.73(.96)	.53(1.02)	.24(.89)	−.03(.96)	−.43(.81)	−.56(.78)
2. Common analogies	.07(.91)	.36(.97)	.34(.80)	−.02(1.03)	−.34(1.03)	−.22(.98)
3. Esoteric analogies	−.59(1.09)	.15(1.03)	.31(.92)	−.10(1.03)	−.12(.92)	.19(.90)
4. Basic vocabulary	−.74(.89)	−.04(.90)	.07(.80)	−.21(.89)	.06(1.11)	.57(.93)
5. Intermediate vocabulary	−.55(.99)	.00(1.07)	.16(.94)	−.17(.88)	.01(1.01)	.35(.93)
6. Memory for paired associates	.77(1.07)	.38(1.07)	.30(1.08)	.11(.80)	−.38(.61)	−.72(.77)
7. Slow tracing	.68(.82)	.41(.86)	.38(.89)	.20(.72)	−.36(.86)	−.92(.97)
8. Speeded letter comparison	.95(.80)	.67(.91)	.43(.90)	−.11(.60)	−.51(.67)	−.84(.90)

Note: Cognitive variables standardized (mean = 0, std = 1) across the entire sample
(N=577) before age groups were formed.

TABLE 13.1B
Zero-Order Correlations Between the Eight Cognitive Ability Variables
of Table 13.1A: Correlations With Age and Gender Also Shown (N = 577)

	1	2	3	4	5	6	7	8
1	1.000							
2	.601[†]	1.000						
3	.341[†]	.511[†]	1.000					
4	.221[†]	.410[†]	.641[†]	1.000				
5	.288[†]	.430[†]	.661[†]	.720[†]	1.000			
6	.449[†]	.331[†]	.230[†]	.072	.141[†]	1.000		
7	.405[†]	.262[†]	.091	−.071	.030	.379[†]	1.000	
8	.468[†]	.300[†]	.130[*]	−.061	.068	.406[†]	.360[†]	1.000
Age	−.469[†]	−.231[†]	.071	.251[†]	.156[†]	−.469[†]	−.497[†]	−.629[†]
Gender	.001	.002	.026	.072	.061	.001	.082	.020

Note: Male = 1, Female = 2 for the variable gender.
[*] = Significant at $p < .05$.
[†] = Significant at $p < .01$.

Measurement Considerations

In previous factor analytic studies (Horn, chap. 4, this volume; Boker & Mc-Ardle, chap. 10, this volume), power letter series, relative to other markers of Gf, was found to most purely indicate the factor and the correlates of the factor. Common word analogies, on the other hand, although indicating the Gf factor, also related to the Gc. These results are seen in the present study.

The average PLS correlation with other Gf indicators and processes (CWA, MPA, CON, SLC) is .48; the average PLS correlation with Gc indicators (ESA, VOC1, VOC2) is .28: The difference between a correlation of .48 and one of .28 is significantly different from zero at the .01 level. Conversely, the averages of the correlations of CWA with indicators of Gf and Gc are .37 and .45, respectively, and a difference between a correlation of .37 and one of .45 is not significantly different from zero in the sample at hand.

Common factor estimates of Gf and Gc typically correlate about .30. The correlations here for the PLS estimate of Gf with the markers for Gc are .34, .22, and .29. The correlations of the CWA estimate of Gf with these Gc markers, on the other hand, are .51, .41, and .43—larger correlations, indicating greater contamination of Gc in the measurement of Gf with CWA than with PLS. To use CWA alone to measure Gf or to include it in a linear composite with PLS for this estimation would be to obtain estimates that are tipped toward measuring Gc as well as Gf.

CWA and PLS were thus analyzed separately to provide estimates of Gf relationships to age and to the estimates of processes. In some of the analyses, estimates of Gc were partialed out of Gf estimators to provide purified indications of the relationships for fluid ability.

Just as the CWA measure of Gf is contaminated with Gc to a larger extent than PLS is contaminated, so the ESA measure of Gc is contaminated with Gf to a larger extent than VOC1 and VOC2. This can be seen in the patterns of correlations of age and the estimates of Gf for ESA as compared to VOC1 and VOC2. The VOC1 and VOC2 estimates of Gc correlate .251 and .156, respectively, with age, but ESA correlates only .071. VOC1 and VOC2 correlate .221 and .288, respectively, with PLS: ESA correlates .341. Thus, the ESA estimate of Gc can be seen to involve a larger element of Gf than do the other estimates of Gc. The results suggest, also, that VOC2 involves a larger element of Gf than does VOC1. Thus, to combine the three measures in a single estimate of Gc would contaminate the composite Gc with different portions of Gf. It is best, therefore, to analyze the Gc estimates separately.

The vocabulary estimates of Gc were designed to represent two levels of frequency of use—basic vocabulary (VOC1) and intermediate vocabulary (VOC2). The distribution for VOC1 was found to be skewed: Many subjects gave correct responses to all or almost all items. The distribution for VOC2 was nearly symmetrical, suggesting that VOC2 would provide the better es-

TABLE 13.2

Effects of Partialing Out Cognitive Processes on the Correlations Between Age and Indicators of Gf Based on Power Letter Series (PLS) and Gc Based on an Intermediate Vocabulary Test

| | Results for Gf Models | | | | | | Results for Gc Models | | |
	PLS Alone 1	PLS: VOC2 Out 2	PLS: ESA Out 3	PLS: VOC2 + VOC1 Out 4	PLS: VOC2 + ESA Out 5	PLS: VOC2 + VOC1 + ESA Out 6	VOC2 Alone 7	VOC2: PLS Out 8	VOC2: PLS + CWA Out 9
Base models:									
Correlation with Age	-.469	-.531*	-.524*	-.540*	-.539	-.538	.156	.281*	.291
IQ Units	-4.31	-4.88	-4.82	-4.97	-4.96	-4.95	1.43	2.58	2.68
Reduced models:									
MPA out	-.299†	-.365†	-.372†	-.379†	-.388†	-.377†	.203†	.302†	.296†
CON out	-.291†	-.358†	-.356†	-.337†	-.371†	-.361†	.171†	.251†	.256†
SLC out	-.210†	-.268†	-.274†	-.280†	-.289†	-.281†	.198†	.255†	.245†
MPA + CON out	-.201†	-.273†	-.282†	-.286†	-.279†	-.287†	.201	.269†	.261†
MPA + SLC out	-.142†	-.206†	-.220†	-.221†	-.235†	-.227†	.220†	.268†	.250†
CON + SLC out	-.131†	-.190†	-.199†	-.202†	-.213†	-.206†	.200	.263	.223
MPA + CON + SLC out	-.090†	-.155†	-.171†	-.169†	-.185†	-.178†	.213†	.248†	.230†

* = Significant R^2 change at the .05 level from the R^2 of the previous base model, in which the effect is nested. Example: The R^2 for PLS:VOC2 + VOC1 is significantly greater than the R^2 for the model PLS:VOC2 at $p < .05$.

† = Significant R^2 change from the previous model, in which the effect is nested at $p < .05$. Example: the R^2 for the model in which MPA is partialed out is significantly greater than the R^2 for the model PLS alone; the R^2 for the model where MPA + CON are partialed out from PLS alone is significantly greater than the model where MPA or CON are partialed out separately from PLS alone.

CON = concentration; CWA = common word analogies; ESA = esoteric word analogies; MPA = memory for paired associates; PLS = power letter series; SLC = speeded letter comparison; VOC1 = basic vocabulary; VOC2 = intermediate vocabulary.

timate of Gc. But the correlation with age was found to be larger for VOC1 than for VOC2, suggesting that VOC1 might be the better estimator of Gc. Results from the part correlational analyses described in the following sections speak to the question of which vocabulary measure best indicates Gc.

Partitioning Age Differences in Estimates of Gf and Gc

Analyses were first directed at describing effects for obtained measures and then at describing effects for measures purged of a confound of one form of intelligence (e.g., Gc) in the other (e.g., Gf). In the first kind of analysis, cognitive processes represented by MPA, CON, and SLC were parted from PLS and CWA estimates of Gf, the resulting residuals were correlated with age, these correlations were subtracted from corresponding the zero-order correlations, and it was determined whether or not a null correlation was contained within two confidence intervals for the residual correlation. The second form of analysis was the same, except an estimate of Gc contamination in the measurement of Gf was partialed out prior to the previously described analyses. Similarly, the analyses for Gc were the same except the partialing-out was from estimates of Gc. Summaries of results from these analyses are provided in Table 13.2.

Age Differences for Estimates of Gf

Cognitive processes represented by MPA, CON, and SLC were partialed out from PLS and CWA estimates of Gf, the resulting residuals were correlated with age, and these correlations were compared by subtraction with corresponding zero-order correlations. Estimates of Gc contamination in the measurement of Gf were partialed out, and the correlations with age for this refined residual were obtained and compared with the zero-order correlations.

The correlations and part correlations for the PLS estimate of Gf are provided in the first six columns of Table 13.2. The columns of the table contain process correlations for different purifications in the estimate of Gf. The first column is for PLS estimate alone. The second column is for a Gf estimate refined by removal of variance shared with the nonskewed, intermediate vocabulary (VOC2) estimate of Gc. The third column is for a Gf estimate refined by removal of variance shared with the ESA estimate of Gc. The remaining columns are for Gf estimates refined by removal of combinations of VOC1, VOC2, and ESA. The stars in the row marked "Base Models" in Table 13.2 indicate whether or not removal of an estimate of Gc contamination from Gf results in a significant shift in the age correlation. It can be seen that removal of either VOC1, VOC2, or ESA alone, or removal of the combined effect of VOC1 and VOC2 , produces a significant shift. The skewed VOC1 estimator of Gc adds to the VOC2 estimator in assessment of the Gc contamination of Gf. Further combinations with ESA do not produce significant shifts.

The rows of the table contain—for each of the column models—the age-Gf correlations and part correlations for each removal of a cognitive process involved in the activation of Gf. In the first column of the table it can be seen that the correlation of age with the PLS alone estimate of Gf is −.469 (corresponding to approximately 4.31 IQ point per decade decline); when the estimate of a short-term memory process (MPA) is removed, the correlation drops to −.299 (2.75 IQ points per decade decline). This reduction is significant at the .05 level. Thus, some of the age-related decline of Gf (approximately 1.56 IQ points per decade) can be accounted for by a process of short-term apprehension and recall. These results are presented in Fig. 13.1A.

Entries in the remaining rows of the first column of Table 13.2 show that some of the age-related decline of Gf is associated with processes of concentration and cognitive speed, each considered alone and in combination with the other process indicators. With both MPA and CON removed, the correlation is −.201, which is significantly smaller (absolute value) than the −.299

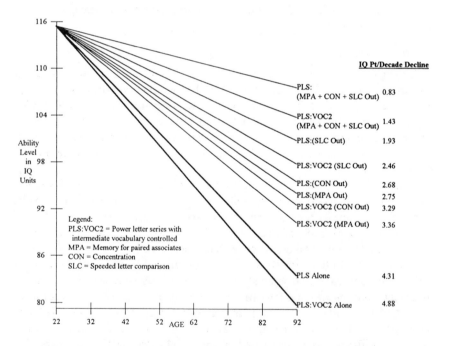

FIG. 13.1A. The effect of removing the variance of memory for paired associates (MPA), concentration (CON), and speeded letter comparison (SLC) from the age-related decline of power letter series alone (PLS alone) and with intermediate vocabulary controlled (PLS: VOC2).

that results when MPA alone is removed, and it is smaller than the −.291 that results when CON alone is removed. Partialing out both MPA and CON, or both MPA and SCL, or both CON and SLC, results in age-correlations that are significantly smaller than the correlation resulting when one or the other of these processes is removed. Removing the influences associated with all three processes results in a correlation (−.09) that is significantly smaller than the correlations resulting when any two processes are removed. It can be seen that in all the columns, removal of the indicators of processes from each of the different estimates of fluid reasoning produces a significant shift in the age correlation. The age correlations in the last row of the table are significantly different from zero in all columns for which an estimate of Gc was used to refine the measure of Gf. As is clearly depicted in Fig. 13.1A, all but .83 IQ points per decade decline can be accounted for by these processes.

The results of Table 13.2 thus indicate that fluid reasoning involves a capacity for concentration, a capacity for apprehending and retaining information over short periods of time, and a capacity for thinking quickly. Measurement of these processes, and indeed the processes themselves, may overlap (e.g., short-term apprehension itself involves some concentration). But each process measure is sufficiently independent of the others to indicate a separate feature of fluid reasoning and its age-related decline: Separate processes thus are parts of the kind of loss of fluid reasoning that occurs with advancing age in adulthood. If contamination due to Gc in this measurement of Gf is removed, decline of Gf is still indicated after all the decline associated with the three process variables has been removed. There is a 1.43 IQ point per decade decline for PLS (VOC2 removed) after the processes are removed (see Fig. 13.1A).

For the CWA estimator of Gf, the results that are in the same form as just described in Table 13.2 for the PLS estimator, but are not shown due to space constraints. The correlation of the CWA estimate alone with age is −.231. This corresponds to 2.12 IQ units of decline per decade. When estimates of the concentration, short-term memory, and cognitive speed processes are removed in this Gf estimator, the indications of aging decline practically disappear, resulting in a slightly positive (.047) relationship to age. This finding suggests that all that is left in CWA after Gf processes are removed is a small component of crystallized knowledge.

However, the CWA estimate of Gf can be purified by removing the VOC1, VOC2, or ESA estimators of Gc, or further by removing the contaminant estimated by both VOC1 and VOC2. The three process variables, each considered alone and in combination with the others, produce a significant change in the correlation between age and the CWA estimate of Gf. Even after all the effects associated with process estimators have been removed, there remains a small (but statistically significant) negative correlation between age and the CWA estimate of Gf. These results are essentially the same as indicated for the PLS estimator of Gf.

Thus, although PLS is a better measure of fluid intelligence than is CWA — it is less contaminated with crystallized intelligence — the results obtained with these two estimates of Gf are consistent in indicating that concentration, short-term apprehension and recall, and cognitive speed are elements of Gf that decline with age. The results from analyzing these two estimates of Gf are also consistent in suggesting that there is a part of Gf, and age-related decline of Gf, that is not represented by the three processes. At least, there is a part not estimated with the measures used in this study to measure concentration, short-term apprehension and recall, and cognitive speed. A portion of fluid ability decline with age remains to be accounted for after these processes are partialed out. Other operational definitions of processes are needed to help us understand this remaining portion of fluid intelligence decline.

Age Differences for Estimates of Gc

The results for these analyses are summarized in columns 7, 8, and 9 of Table 13.2. The columns represent different purifications in estimation of Gc; the rows represent removal of different processes and combinations of processes.

It can be seen that the correlation of age with the VOC2 estimates of Gc is .156, corresponding to 1.43 points of IQ increase per 10-year period (see Fig. 13.1B). With the PLS estimate of Gf contamination removed, this correlation becomes .281, corresponding to an IQ increases of 2.58 IQ points over a 10-year period. These results are highly similar for the VOC1 and ESA estimates of Gc (results not shown). The skewed basic vocabulary measure (VOC1) has the larger relationship to age, both before and after removal of Gf contamination. Removal of the Gf contaminant has the largest effect (.071 to .248) on the ESA estimate of Gc, and the smallest effect (.251 to .371) on the VOC1 estimate. For each of the estimates of Gc, CWA does not further estimate the Gf contamination estimated with PLS alone.

Looking down column 7 for the VOC2 estimate of Gc (Table 13.2), it can be seen that removal of the estimators of short-term memory, cognitive speed, and concentration processes, each alone, significantly increases the correlation between age and Gc. These processes of Gf contaminate the measure of Gc, just as does Gf itself (estimated with PLS). With these contaminants removed, the positive correlations of the Gc estimates with age increase from that of the age-VOC2 Alone correlation.

Given that the process measures represent parts of Gf that contaminate measurement of Gc, then if these contaminants are removed, the positive correlation of crystallized intelligence with age should increase, as it does. But if the Gc estimate were already purified by removal of contamination

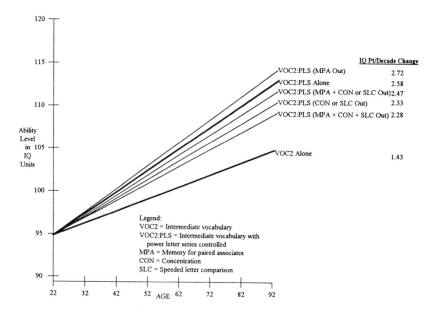

FIG. 13.1B. The effect of removing the variance of memory for paired associates (MPA), concentration (CON), and speeded letter comparison (SLC) from the age-related enhancement of intermediate vocabulary when power letter series is controlled (VOC2:PLS).

with Gf, then the effects of again removing such contamination with the measures of Gf should be damped. This is the effect seen in columns 8 and 9 of Table 13.2. These columns contain estimates of Gc in which the PLS and CWA estimate of Gf contaminants were first removed before removing the effect of the process variables. The results indicate that for all the analyses in which processes were removed from the Gc estimates purged of Gf variance, MPA is the only process variable that results in increased performance when removed from the age-ability correlation. Removing the contamination associated with the PLS estimate of Gf from the VOC2 estimate of Gc increases the age correlation to .281 (or 2.58 IQ points per decade increase; see Fig. 13.1B), as noted previously, which then is significantly increased to .302 (or 2.72 IQ points per decade increase) when MPA is removed. The correlation does not further increase, however, with removal of CON, or SLC, or both. The results are essentially the same for the ESA estimate of Gc that is purified by removal of PLS, but not for the VOC1 estimate of Gc.

There is thus evidence that in short-term memory there is a process in addition to those of Gf that contaminates the highly difficult measure of Gc. This contaminant may reflect the fact that the long-term storage of crystallized knowledge is, in its origins, functionally linked to short-term memory. Short-term memory is a necessary condition for long-term storage: Consolidation in short-term memory is necessary to make information retainable in long-term memory (Bower, 1975; Broadbent, 1966).

SUMMARY OF FINDINGS

Measured under conditions in which speed of response is minimized (power letter series; PLS), the decline of fluid intelligence (Gf) over a span from 22 to 92 years of age is approximately linear and about 4 IQ points for each 10-year period of development. Measured with common word analogies (CWA)—a test that also measures crystallized intelligence (Gc) as well as Gf—the decline of Gf is about 2 IQ unites per decade. Purged of Gc, the decline estimated with PLS is about 5 units of IQ per decade; estimated with CWA, the decline is about 4 IQ units per decade.

Cognitive speed, concentration, and short-term memory are processes of fluid intelligence that decline with age in adulthood. If the amount of Gf decline associated with these processes is removed in the PLS estimate of Gf, the remaining decline is about 1 IQ unit per decade in the raw measure and about 1.5 IQ units in measures purged of Gc confound. For the CWA estimate of Gf, the corresponding estimates are .5 and 1.0 IQ units of decline per 10-year period of development.

The results thus indicate that fluid reasoning involves a capacity for concentration, a capacity for apprehending and retaining information over short periods of time, and a capacity for thinking quickly even in measures that do not reward speed of response. When there is damage to any one of these processes, very likely the entire system is affected. Fallible measurement of these processes overlap—indeed, the processes themselves may overlap in function. For example, short-term apprehension involves concentration. But each process can be measured with sufficient independence to indicate separate components of fluid intelligence and its age-related decline. The separate process measurements thus provide indications of the kind of factors involved in reasoning and the kind of losses that occur with increasing probability into adulthood.

The results also indicate that, particularly after contamination of Gc in the measurement of Gf is considered, there is decline of Gf that is not indicated by the processes sampled in this study. Other processes must be involved.

In the same sample of people in which average decline of Gf is indicated, there is indication of increase in crystallized intelligence. For a basic vocabulary (VOC1) estimate of Gc, this increase is about 2 IQ units per 10-year period of development. Purged of a measurement confound estimated with the PLS estimate of Gf, the increase is approximately 3.4 IQ units per decade. Additionally purged of a confound estimated with the short-term apprehension (MPA) process of Gf, the increase in Gc over the adulthood years is approximately 3.6 IQ units per decade. For intermediate vocabulary (VOC2) and esoteric analogies (ESA) estimates of Gc, the age increases are initially smaller than for the VOC1 estimate. When purged of confounds associated with estimates of Gf and the MPA component of Gf, the increases for the VOC2 and ESA estimates of Gc are approximately 3 and 2.8 IQ units, respectively, for a 10-year period.

Short-term apprehension is a process in addition to those of Gf that contaminates reasoning and high-difficulty measures of Gc (i.e., ESA and VOC2), but can have little effect in prevalent, low-difficulty elements of acculturation (VOC1). The Gf and MPA contaminants may reflect, in part, the use of Gf reasoning in the Gc measures, and, in part, the fact that the long-term storage of crystallized knowledge is, in its origins, functionally linked to short-term memory. Short-term memory is a necessary condition for long-term storage: consolidation in short-term memory is necessary to make information retainable in long-term memory (Bower, 1975; Broadbent, 1966).

The pattern of correlations thus suggests the following conclusions:

1. Basic vocabulary, relative to intermediate vocabulary and esoteric analogies, is the better indicator of the part of crystallized knowledge that increases with age in adulthood: The zero-order and part correlations for VOC1 are notably larger than the comparable correlations for VOC2 and ESA.

2. In the Gc estimates obtained with intermediate vocabulary and esoteric analogies, short-term apprehension indicates a confound that is not fully represented in the power letter series measure of Gf: With PLS removed, removal of MPA further increases the correlations between age and the residual VOC2 and ESA estimates of Gc. The VOC2 and ESA expressions of Gc thus appear to depend on short-term apprehension, a process of Gf. The part of Gf that is not represented by concentration and cognitive speed thus appears to be the principal confound of Gf in the measurement of Gc.

3. This is not true for the basic vocabulary (VOC1) estimate of Gc.

Estimates of Gf decline and Gc increase in this study are similar to the comparable estimates obtained in previous studies in which the range of age was considerably smaller than in this study (Hofer, 1994; Horn et al., 1981; Horn & Donaldson, 1980). The findings are, in this sense, consistent with the findings of previous research.

The results also are consistent with previous findings in suggesting that after controlling Gf for linear effects associated with fallible estimates of concentration, cognitive speed, and short-term apprehension, an aspect of Gf remains that is negatively related to age. Depending on which indicator of Gf is analyzed, this reliable residual is estimated to be 1 to 1.4 IQ units of decline for 10-year periods. It is reasonable to suppose that this residual process involves comprehension of relationships and understanding of implications (i.e., the eduction of relations and correlates; Spearman, 1923). Further research is needed to isolate such components.

The results also indicate that fallible estimates of Gc probably involve some aspects of Gf and the processes that characterize Gf. These confounds are seen particularly in relatively difficult vocabulary and analogies estimates of Gc and MPA, although some confound of Gf is seen also in a basic vocabulary estimate of Gc. Put more bluntly, with less interpretation, the results suggests that estimates of Gc improvement with age will be relatively large for measures that minimize any need to apprehend and hold information in immediate awareness and to reason with novel problems.

In general, this evidence suggests that separate causal factors operate through development to affect somewhat separate cognitive processes and produce individual differences in separate vulnerable and maintained abilities. Further evidence is needed to elucidate the nature of these causal factors.

An important proviso should accompany the interpretations offered here for the results obtained in this study. In the analyses and interpretations of this study it is assumed that the correlation between Gf and Gc represents overlap in measurement. But the positive correlation between Gf and Gc may result because Gf and Gc stem from the same influences, as well as because there is overlap (confound) in the operations of measurement of the two. To the extent that the Gf-Gc correlation for the fallible measures represents influences intrinsic to the development of both Gf and Gc, these influences are removed by the partialing out procedures of our analyses. If Gf and Gc stem from the same influences—say, g—then even under the most ideal circumstances of measurement and subject sampling the two would be positively correlated—due to g. To treat all common factor variance, including that of common factor g, as measurement contamination is to overestimate the measurement confound. In the present study there was no way to independently estimate the g and measurement confound, so there was no way to accurately assess the extent to which control for confounding produced overcontrol that suppressed the influence of g (if there were such influence).

AUTHOR'S NOTE

This research was supported by the National Institute on Aging Grants R01 AG09936 and T32 AG00156. Thanks are due also for the editorial suggestions of Jack McArdle and Richard Woodcock.

REFERENCES

Bower, G. H. (1975). Mental imagery and associative learning. In L. W. Gregg (Ed.), *Cognition in learning and memory* (pp. 213–228). New York: Wiley.

Broadbent, D. E. (1966). The well ordered mind. *American Educational Research Journal, 3*, 281–295.

Hofer, S. M. (1994). *On the structure of personality and the relationship of personality to fluid and crystalized intelligence in adulthood.* Unpublished doctoral dissertation, University of Southern California, Los Angeles.

Horn, J. L. (1982). The aging of human abilities. In B. B. Wolman (Ed.), *Handbook of developmental psychology* (pp. 847–870). New York: Prentice-Hall.

Horn, J. L., & Donaldson, G. (1980). Cognitive development in adulthood. In O. G. Brim & J. Kagen (Eds.), *Constancy and change in human development* (pp. 445–529). Cambridge, MA: Harvard University Press.

Horn, J. L., Donaldson, G., & Engstrom, R. (1981). Application, memory, and fluid intelligence decline in adulthood. *Research on Aging, 3*, 23–84.

Salthouse, T. A. (1993). Speed mediation of adult age differences in cognition. *Developmental Psychology, 29*(4), 722–738.

Spearman, C. (1923). *The nature of "intelligence" and the principles of cognition.* London: Macmillan.

14

Decision Validity Methods Applied to Cognitive Assessments of Brain Disorder

Thomas S. Paskus
University of Virginia

Cutting scores on any diagnostic instrument should be evaluated in terms of the relative frequencies and costs/benefits of resulting decision outcomes (Cronbach & Gleser, 1965; Meehl & Rosen, 1955). The *decision validity* (Paskus, 1993; Paskus & McArdle, 1996) of a diagnostic test can be defined as the discriminative accuracy of the cutting score employed, as evaluated within or across tests for a particular set of testing circumstances. Fig. 14.1 displays two hypothetical populations and the resulting decision outcomes after a cutting score is chosen on some indicator. The criterion-positive population represents those persons experiencing some disease, disorder, or condition of interest, and the criterion-negative population depicts everyone else tested. Typically, any chosen cutting score will result in some correct and incorrect diagnoses for each population. Finding an optimal cutting score involves mathematically reweighting the population distributions by the costs/benefits, locating the cut producing an acceptable distribution of decision outcomes, and comparing the result to the accuracy obtainable using other indicator variables. In the present study, this logic was applied to the detection of brain disorder using various cognitive ability composites.

Although brain disorders typically result in behavioral deficits of intellect, emotionality, and self-control, cognitive deficits have been a primary focus of neuropsychological assessment, in part because they are easier to evaluate in typical examination settings than are deficits in emotion or control (Lezak, 1995). Wechsler's intelligence scales (W-B, WAIS, WAIS-R) have historically been at the core of these examinations (Lezak, 1995). A promi-

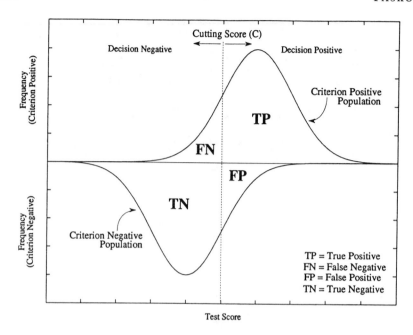

FIG. 14.1.   Criterion-based decision analysis representation.

nent Wechsler indicator has been the difference between verbal IQ (VIQ) and performance IQ (PIQ), concomitant to the belief that performance abilities are more susceptible to many forms and locations of brain disorder than are verbal abilities (Wechsler, 1958).

Although some studies have shown the verbal-performance difference to be useful in differentiating diffuse, right-hemisphere, and left-hemisphere damage from each other and from normal brain functioning (e.g., Reitan, 1955; Russell, 1979), the diagnostic effectiveness of VIQ-PIQ has been questioned. For instance, there seems to be no neuroanatomical relationship between VIQ and PIQ (Lezak, 1995), VIQ-PIQ effects are not unique to brain disorders (Frank, 1983; Wechsler, 1958), and VIQ-PIQ differences may have different meaning as a function of full-scale IQ (FSIQ), gender, and age (Lezak, 1995; Wechsler, 1958).

The standard criterion for diagnosing brain damage has been a VIQ-PIQ difference of 10 to 15 points (although VIQ-PIQ discrepancies ranging from 8 to 25 points have been proposed as cutting scores; see Frank, 1983). This standard appears to originate from Wechsler's definition of abnormality based on the variance among normal individuals in his standardization samples and not on empirical brain damage research (Wechsler, 1958). The individual subtest scores that determine VIQ and PIQ tend to be affected quite differently by brain damage, even within the verbal and performance groupings. A number of studies have reported that digit symbol is greatly affected by any form of damage (see Brooks, 1989; Frank, 1983; Lezak, 1995; Russell, 1972). Other performance subtest scores (block design, picture arrangement, and object assembly) usually decrease to some degree as well, but picture completion seems relatively resilient to any type of brain damage (Lezak, 1995). Among the verbal subtests, only vocabulary, information, and comprehension tend to remain stable following damage (Lezak, 1995). The similarities test is usually somewhat sensitive to brain damage (Brooks, 1989; Lezak, 1995), whereas arithmetic and digit span have proven to be ambiguous and unpredictable depending on the nature of the damage (Lezak, 1995). Because the verbal-performance difference (and its standard diagnostic cut score) has been widely used but often criticized, this study examined its potential efficacy compared to several other Wechsler subtest composites.

METHODS

Subjects

The sample examined was a subset of the sample collected and described by Whiddon (1977). The subjects referred to as brain disordered ($N = 134$) were an aggregate of male patients from two southern Veterans Administration hospitals who were diagnosed with what was called Organic Brain Syndrome (OBS) at the time (mean age = 45 years; mean FSIQ = 84; Whiddon, 1977). Forty-eight of the patients had OBS diagnoses associated with some form of chronic organicity (e.g., neural degenerative diseases). Of the remaining 86 brain-disordered subjects, 43 possessed damage to the right side of the brain and 43 had left-side damage. In the present study, *brain disorder* was defined as a dichotomous variable; type of brain damage was not considered.

The normal comparison group consisted of 128 male subjects (mean age = 31 years; mean FSIQ = 84; Whiddon, 1977) who had been solicited to take the Wechsler Adult Intelligence Scale (WAIS) for an advanced graduate-level course at a southern university on WAIS administration and interpretation. Subjects were chosen from a larger pool by a random stratified sampling procedure to match the full-scale WAIS score distribution of the brain-disordered group. Because this resulted in a non-brain-damaged sample with lower than average FSIQ, they have been referred to as a "low-normal" comparison group.

Variables

The data published in Whiddon's (1977) manuscript included the scaled scores from the 11 subtests of the WAIS. Subject age and education level

TABLE 14.1
Comparison of Scaled WAIS Subtest Scores for Criterion Groups

| WAIS Subtest | Criterion Group | | | | Within-Group Correlations | | | | | | | | | | |
| | Low Normal | | Brain Disorder | | Low Normal = Below | | | | | | Brain Disorder = Above | | | | |
	Mean	(sd)	Mean	(sd)	I	C	A	S	D	V	DS	PC	BD	PA	OA
Information (I)	7.38	(3.04)	8.49	(3.31)	—	.74	.68	.71	.63	.78	.24	.53	.16	.22	.15
Comprehension (C)	7.86	(3.77)	8.49	(3.92)	.78	—	.58	.73	.54	.70	.25	.48	.18	.17	.21
Arithmetic (A)	6.91	(3.16)	7.12	(3.42)	.74	.70	—	.53	.66	.59	.40	.54	.31	.28	.23
Similarities (S)	7.09	(3.43)	7.87	(3.98)	.72	.71	.63	—	.61	.77	.39	.44	.23	.27	.21
Digit span (D)	7.10	(2.87)	7.12	(3.70)	.46	.46	.48	.45	—	.57	.37	.40	.17	.18	.19
Vocabulary (V)	6.78	(3.32)	8.19	(3.46)	.80	.78	.73	.69	.45	—	.23	.40	.14	.19	.13
Digit symbol (DS)	6.66	(3.22)	4.59	(3.35)	.61	.60	.56	.68	.41	.55	—	.51	.57	.57	.53
Picture completion (PC)	7.41	(3.00)	7.43	(3.38)	.49	.51	.39	.46	.26	.40	.58	—	.48	.62	.53
Block design (BD)	6.81	(2.79)	6.25	(3.66)	.44	.49	.35	.48	.30	.50	.64	.61	—	.55	.67
Picture arrangement (PA)	7.48	(2.74)	6.16	(3.12)	.60	.63	.54	.55	.44	.57	.66	.64	.65	—	.59
Object assembly (OA)	6.66	(2.85)	6.29	(3.81)	.37	.52	.34	.51	.33	.47	.59	.45	.72	.53	—

Notes: Low normal $N = 128$; brain disorder $N = 134$.
Verbal Subtests: I, C, A, S, D, V; Performance subtests: DS, PC, BD, PA, OA.

were discussed by Whiddon (1977), but were not contained in the published dataset. Table 14.1 presents a comparison of subtest scores for both groups. The low-normal subjects had higher mean scores on several subtests traditionally associated with the performance factor, notably digit symbol and picture arrangement. The brain-disordered subjects, however, had substantially higher scores on all of the verbal subtests except for arithmetic and digit span. Because the groups were matched on full-scale IQ scores, if brain-disordered subjects collectively possessed deficits in some abilities, higher scores would necessarily be seen in one or more other abilities.

Decision validity was assessed for four different WAIS predictor variables. The first was simply the digit symbol (DS) scaled score. This individual subtest score was chosen as a predictor because it had the largest between-groups mean difference of any of the subtests, and it is generally most affected by brain disorder. The second predictor variable was the difference between overall verbal and performance scores. Note that these verbal and performance scores were sums of scaled subtest scores and were not identical to Wechsler's VIQ and PIQ. Scores were left in this metric because subject age was not available for calculating VIQ and PIQ.

The third predictor variable was a linear composite in which subtest scores were weighted by the parameter estimates obtained from a logit regression predicting presence of brain disorder from all 11 WAIS subtests. For ease of interpretation, logit composites were converted to probability values. The fourth predictor variable was a simplified linear combination derived from the results of the logit regression. Two verbal subtests—information (I) and vocabulary (V)—and two performance subtests—digit symbol (DS) and picture arrangement (PA)—exhibited stronger predictive ability than other subtests, and were used to create a "salient logit" composite labeled IV-DsPa. These four subtests were not weighted by their logit parameter estimates; the composite was created simply by summing vocabulary and information and subtracting digit symbol and picture arrangement scaled scores [e.g., IV-DsPa = (I + V) − (DS + PA)].

Assessment of Decision Validity

Optimum cutting scores on each predictor variable for a given set of utilities (costs/benefits) were assessed in the present study using methods similar to those employed by McArdle and Hamagami (1991). Using an iterative procedure, successive cutting scores were defined across the full range of data (20 to 50 different cuts made, depending on the range of the predictor variable), and costs/benefits were applied as weights to the resulting decision outcome frequencies at each cutting score. The sum of weighted frequencies represented the overall utility of a particular cutting score. By plotting overall utility for all values of the predictor, the appropriateness of a potential cutting score could be assessed quite readily in relation to other potential cuts on that predictor variable. These comparisons were enhanced by converting total utility for a given threshold to *expected-utility percent* (EUP; McArdle & Hamagami, 1991), essentially a weighted form of the decision accuracy statistic. Comparisons of overall utility for a predictor score across different sets of utilities were not appropriate using either of these utility metrics, because both confound weighted accuracy with effective sample size. However, between-test accuracy comparisons within a given set of utility weights could be made for specific cutting scores.

A simple bootstrap procedure was performed to estimate the potential effects of sampling error on expected-utility percent across all possible cutting scores for each predictor. This method entailed creating 100 random samples of 262 subjects each (same N as in the original sample), with replacement from the original sample. Utility curves were calculated for each predictor using each of the 100 samples. The number of resamplings was chosen based on research showing that 100 is typically sufficient for estimating standard error (Stine, 1990). These 100 curves were then used to calculate a mean curve that closely approximates the original full sample utility curve, and to calculate a standard error estimate around each successive cutting score. These standard error estimates were then used to compute approximate 95% confidence boundaries around the mean utility curves.

Utility Structures

Decision validity was assessed for each of the four composite predictor scores using four different utility structures, relative costs, and benefits associated with each decision outcome. The utilities examined (Fig. 14.2) were not based on monetary units, but instead were weights meant to represent importance relative to the other decision outcomes. The choice of utility structure should be dictated by how the test will be used. These particular utility structures were chosen to reflect potential neuropsychological testing situations.

As shown in Fig. 14.2, Utility Structure A was equivalent to the weights implicit when the overall decision accuracy statistic is used to judge the discriminative ability of a variable at a particular cutting score (Gross & Su, 1975); all decision outcomes were weighted equally. That is, errors associated with misdiagnosing somebody with brain disorder (false negative; FN) were treated as being equally costly as misdiagnosing somebody without brain disorder (false positive; FP). The benefits of correct diagnoses—true positives (TP) and true negatives (TN)—were considered of the same magnitude as the costs of misdiagnosis.

Utility Structure B was taken from Tsujimoto and Berger (1988), who used such a structure in the prediction of child abuse. These weights implied a high benefit associated with correctly detecting brain damage (TP), a high

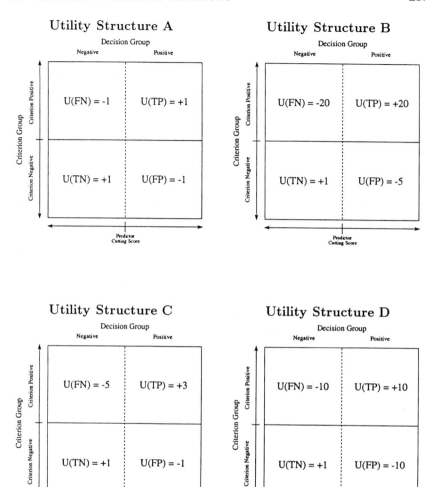

FIG. 14.2.   Utility structures.

cost incurred by missing brain disorder (FN), and a moderate cost of misdiagnosing somebody without brain disorder (FP). Overall, this utility structure gave special emphasis to correctly identifying the criterion-positive (brain-disordered) group.

Utility Structure C was described by Gross and Su (1975) in a paper on "fair" personnel selection. As in Structure B, the criterion-positive group was overweighted. However, undetected brain disorder (FN) was weighted more heavily than any other decision outcome. False positives were no longer considered very costly (e.g., perhaps there is little additional cost involved to either party in running more tests). Utility Structure D reflected a scenario mentioned in Tsujimoto and Berger (1988) and quantified here. These weights implied that misdiagnosing a normal person (FP) was just as costly as missing a person with damage (FN).

RESULTS

The brain-disordered and low-normal samples overlapped substantially on all four WAIS composites, as displayed in Fig. 14.3. Thus, no measure was able to approach perfect group differentiation. However, as shown in Table 14.2, decision validity was effected by composite choice and applied costs/benefits. For example, when employing Utility Structure A, the logit and salient logit composites were markedly better discrimination indexes (77.2%

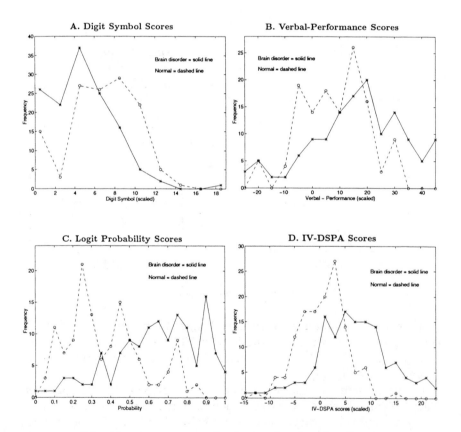

FIG. 14.3.   Criterion-group distributions for selected predictors.

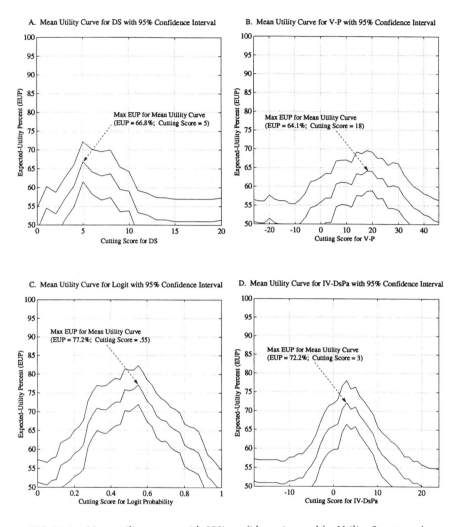

FIG. 14.4.   Mean utility curves with 95% confidence interval for Utility Structure A.

and 72.2% weighted accuracy, respectively) than were digit symbol (66.8%) or V-P (64.1%) at their respective optimal cutting scores. However, for Utility Structures B and C, overweighting criterion-positive decision outcomes (TP and FN) to such an extent resulted in essentially no differential predictive ability; classifying all subjects as brain disordered resulted in the highest (and equivalent) levels of accuracy for each composite. This result is also displayed graphically for Utility Structures A (Fig. 14.4) and C (Fig. 14.5). The middle curve on each plot represents mean EUP at each possible index cutting score. The outer curves are the bootstrapped 95% confidence inter-

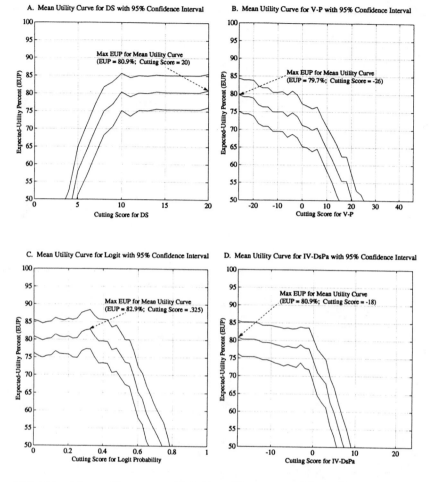

FIG. 14.5. Mean utility curves with 95% confidence interval for Utility Structure C.

vals around the EUP curve. Decision validity is evaluated at the peak value of each EUP curve along with the corresponding confidence interval at the optimal cutting score. It can also be seen from Table 14.2 and Figs. 14.4 and 14.5 that optimal cutting scores for each composite varied over a wide range as a function of the costs/benefits of decision outcomes.

The decision validity of the verbal-performance difference was essentially equivalent to that of the other composites for Utility Structures B and C. However, when employing Utility Structures A and D, the optimal cutting score for both the logit and salient logit (IV-DsPa) composites led to better differentiation than the optimal V-P cut. In fact, digit symbol scores alone discriminated as well as V-P for each set of costs/benefits examined.

TABLE 14.2
Results of Decision Validity Bootstrap Procedure
for Four Utility Structures

Utility Structure	TP	FN	FP	TN	Composite	Optimal Cutting Score	Maximum Expected Utility %	Max EUP 95% CI
A	+1	−1	−1	+1	DS	5	66.8	(61.5–72.1)
					V-P	18	64.1	(58.7–69.5)
					Logit	.550	77.2	(72.0–82.4)
					IV-DsPa	3	72.2	(66.4–78.0)
B	+20	−20	−5	+1	DS	20	87.7	(81.3–94.1)
					V-P	−26	86.4	(80.1–92.7)
					Logit	.000	87.7	(81.3–94.1)
					IV-DsPa	−18	87.7	(81.3–94.1)
C	+3	−5	−1	+1	DS	20	80.9	(76.2–85.6)
					V-P	−26	79.7	(75.0–84.4)
					Logit	.325	82.9	(77.3–88.5)
					IV-DsPa	−18	80.9	(76.2–85.6)
D	+10	−10	−10	+1	DS	10	69.5	(62.6–76.4)
					V-P	6	65.5	(58.7–72.3)
					Logit	.325	76.9	(69.9–83.9)
					IV-DsPa	−1	71.4	(64.2–78.6)

Notes: Expected utility percentage (EUP) = $100 * \dfrac{U_{total} - U_{min}}{U_{max} - U_{min}}$ where

$U_{total} = (U_{TP} * F_{TP}) + (U_{FN} * F_{FN}) + (U_{FP} * F_{FP}) + (U_{TN} * F_{TN})$,
$U_{min} = (U_{FN} * F_{CP}) + (U_{FP} * F_{CN})$, and
$U_{max} = (U_{TP} * F_{CP}) + (U_{TN} * F_{CN})$.

DISCUSSION

For a cutting-score-based decision to be valid, not only should the cutting score be optimal for a given test, but it should also be as accurate as optimal cutting scores on any other available index. The decision validity methods used here indicate that the WAIS verbal-performance difference was not optimal in the assessment of brain damage when compared to several other WAIS indicators. This result was consistent across different utility structures representative of different testing situations that might be encountered in neuropsychology. Although all WAIS predictors showed some ability to differentiate brain disorder from normal functioning, these results lend credence to the contention that tests of cognitive ability cannot attain the same level of accuracy as can other currently available diagnostic tools (e.g., CT scan; Lezak, 1995).

Correct choice of cutting score for any given test can have a substantial impact on that instrument's usefulness. Although a particular predictor value may prove most effective for some testing situations, this application clearly shows that optimal cuts are not stable across situation. For example, Wechsler's 10-point VIQ-PIQ cut translates to between about 15 and 32 points in the metric used in this study (Wechsler, 1955). For Utility Structure A, the optimal V-P cut falls within this range. For other costs/benefits, this was not the case, and 10 points likely would not be optimal for Utility Structure A if the brain-disorder base rate was different in our study. This pitfall has been long recognized (Meehl & Rosen, 1955), but too often test users blindly apply cutting scores without knowledge of their efficacy in the applied setting.

One typical approach to choosing a test instrument and cutting score has been to choose a predictor based on a high correlation with the criterion, and then pick a normative cut. This approach effectively specifies distributional form and implicitly chooses a utility structure for the user that may lead to suboptimal decisions (Paskus & McArdle, 1996). Another common method of test evaluation (e.g., Kessel & Zimmerman, 1993) is to compare tests using point estimators that implicitly assume a set of utilities (e.g., sensitivity, specificity, unweighted decision accuracy) without considering how the tests will be used or whether the cutting scores examined are even optimal within the test. Neither of these methods guarantees optimal discrimination. If point prediction is going to be used in decision making, then decision methods should employ a logic that accounts explicitly for within- and between-test characteristics as they vary across assessment context.

AUTHOR'S NOTE

This chapter was derived from a predissertation research project submitted in partial fulfillment of Master of Arts requirements, University of Virginia, May 1993. Correspondence should be addressed to Thomas S. Paskus, Department of Psychology, Gilmer Hall, University of Virginia, Charlottesville, VA 22903 (e-mail: paskus@Virginia.edu). Thanks to John McArdle, John Nesselroade, and Richard Woodcock for their insight and comments on the manuscript, and to Fumiaki Hamagami for generously sharing his technical and programming expertise.

REFERENCES

Brooks, N. (1989). Closed head trauma: Assessing the common cognitive problems. In M. D. Lezak (Ed.), *Assessment of the behavioral consequences of head trauma* (pp. 61–85). New York: Alan R. Liss.

Cronbach, L. J., & Gleser, G. C. (1965). *Psychological tests and personnel decisions.* Urbana: University of Illinois Press.

Frank, G. (1983). The Wechsler enterprise. New York: Pergamon.

Gross, A. L., & Su, W. (1975). Defining a "fair" or "unbiased" selection model: A question of utilities. *Journal of Applied Psychology, 60,* 345–351.

Kessel, J. B., & Zimmerman, M. (1993). Reporting errors in studies of the diagnostic performance of self-administered questionnaires: Extent of the problem, recommendations for standardized presentation of results, and implications for the peer review process. *Psychological Assessment, 5,* 395–399.

Lezak, M. D. (1995). *Neuropsychological assessment* (3rd ed.). New York: Oxford University Press.

McArdle, J. J., & Hamagami, F. (1991). *A decision theory analysis of initial eligibility rules applied to 1984 and 1985 freshman student-athletes* (NCAA Research Report Number 91–05). Overland Park, KS: National Collegiate Athletic Association.

Meehl, P. E., & Rosen, A. (1955). Antecedent probability and the efficiency of psychometric signs, patterns, or cutting scores. *Psychological Bulletin, 52,* 194–216.

Paskus, T. S. (1993). *A study of decision validity methods applied to the assessment of brain disorders with the WAIS.* Unpublished master's thesis, University of Virginia, Charlottesville.

Paskus, T. S., & McArdle, J. J. (1996). *Determining the implied relative importance of dichotomous outcomes from previous decisions.* Manuscript submitted for publication.

Reitan, R. (1955). Certain differential effects of left and right cerebral lesions in human adults. *Journal of Comparative and Physiological Psychology, 48,* 474–477.

Russell, E. W. (1972). WAIS factor analysis with brain-damaged subjects using criterion measures. *Journal of Consulting and Clinical Psychology, 39,* 133–139.

Russell, E. W. (1979). Three patterns of brain damage on the WAIS. *Journal of Clinical Psychology, 35,* 611–620.

Stine, R. (1990). An introduction to bootstrap methods: examples and ideas. In J. Fox & J. S. Long (Eds.), *Modern methods of data analysis* (pp. 325–373). Newbury Park, CA: Sage.

Tsujimoto, R. N., & Berger, D. E. (1988). Predicting/preventing child abuse: Value of utility maximizing cutting scores. *Child Abuse and Neglect, 12,* 397–408.

Wechsler, D. (1955). *WAIS manual: Wechsler adult intelligence scale.* New York: The Psychological Corporation.

Wechsler, D. (1958). *The measurement and appraisal of adult intelligence* (4th ed.). Baltimore: Williams & Wilkins.

Whiddon, M. F. (1977). *Identification and validation of a subtest pattern on the Wechsler adult intelligence scale that will separate brain damaged, schizophrenic, and normal subjects by means of a discriminant function analysis* (University Microfilms International No. 78–2942).

IV

DISCUSSIONS

15

Discussions of
Human Cognitive Abilities
Conference Papers[1]

DISCUSSION FOLLOWING THE TALK
BY JOHN B. CARROLL

Dick Snow: Are there any questions or comments about Dr. Carroll's talk from the members of the audience?

John Horn: This is not so much a question, as a comment, on your last remark on the kind of evidence that has suggested that predictions, that the so called *g* factor which is, which is really not, varies quite differently from one prediction setting to another is not the same factor as is being used, you understand, in the surveys of these predictions. The thing that doesn't seem to be sufficiently recognized in previous research is that the criteria that are being used are themselves not multifactorial. They are not attempting in those studies to predict the varied behavior that, in fact, the predictors could predict if the criteria would be fair to represent that. They are often based on ratings, often based on very global kinds of observations by these raters; the raters are not trained to be observant; there is much halo going on in them. It is just absurd to expect that the multifactor conception that we know to be necessary to explain behavior would be well mirrored in these kinds of criteria. That is my principle argument with the Schmid-Leiman procedure, and I know you don't neglect this problem.

John Carroll: I can only agree with you very much. I would certainly want to put all those ideas into a proposal to serve in any validity study. I did a lot of validity studies in the second language field and I was able to get ratings

---

[1] These discussion were transcribed from original videotapes of the HCA meeting, and reviewed and edited for clarity only by the book editors. We apologize in advance for any words or phrases that were misunderstood and incorrectly transcribed.

and different kinds of criteria and what it seemed to me was that some cases there were divergent validities depending upon the criteria you used. And for that reason I felt that it was necessary to assume different dimensions that were being used in the validity studies, but I never tried to make a survey. I have no idea what kind of surveys, let us say, Ed Fleishman used in developing his standards of abilities.

John Horn: I think your point is good—when people do go to the trouble to get differential criteria they find differential predictions.

Earl Hunt: If I could follow up on what is going to be a major limitation in the field of ability studies. Lets take an example, probably the best ability study that I know of, and this is the Army Project A, a very extensive study. Even that was a one-shot test of the individuals at time of training, most of them relatively new to their field. The Army is an organization that has no union so it has more structure over its personnel than practically anybody else, because most of the time, thankfully, the Army has no mission. Therefore people can be taken away for the purpose of the testing, can be taken away from productive work for the purpose of testing. I'm raising all these issues very seriously about the limitations of which the methodologies can contribute because they assume a fairly static picture of the abilities acquired, and the impracticality in any real world sense in doing this sort of testing that will be required. That doesn't mean the problem doesn't exist, it just means I haven't the faintest idea how it can be solved.

John Horn: Incidentally, I think words like "monumental" and "landmark" are very aptly used to describe your work.

Discussion Following the Talk by Raymond B. Cattell

John Horn: Does anyone have questions for Dr. Cattell?

John Carroll: I would just like to point out that you said that you talked about my being uncomfortable with hierarchical factor analysis. But I would point out that actually I re-analyzed most of these studies so that I did confirm your fluid and crystallized intelligence in those cases.

Raymond Cattell: Yes. Well, when we were talking this morning, I felt that you were embarrassed by having to organize a lot of studies, many of which have not reached decent simple structure.

John Carroll: That's right.

Raymond Cattell: So a blurring affect. Well there is a problem in higher order factors that you have to determine the angles between the lower orders really exactly or else you've got chaos, and I'm actually a bit of a critic on this but I'm afraid that three out of four factor analyses that I see published have not been simple structure. I can take the data and rotate perhaps ten times or a dozen times more and reach a better hyperplane count. And so we need an advance in factor analytic techniques before we can be sure of the form of the higher order factors.

Jack McArdle: Can I ask a question now? I refer to the dysgenic trends you just displayed. There is a concern by many of us that some of the data that you have presented on dysgenic trends are based on very old data. Aren't these all kind of old studies? Also, I am thinking of this as a prediction study and I wonder if your predictions have come to be true? As I understand it, the predictions about lowering IQ for the group were not realized in the 1930s when you conducted your own longitudinal studies in those same places. So my question now is do you have any new data, or do you suggest that there are any new data during the last 50 years that suggests the dysgenic trends that you predicted have actually come about?

Raymond Cattell: Oh no, that would take another 7,000 persons, and I'm not about to take on this kind of study, not at my age anyway. But Vining, a University of Pennsylvania population statistician, has repeated these studies just about 4 years ago in America, and basically has come out with just the same rate of decline in IQ as I did. That is, one point of IQ decline per ten years. And so I think the problems you're meeting nowadays is crime, and poorer education performance, and so on, seems to me are not worth tackling individually because they are all parts of one of the same thing—basically, a decline in intelligence and the shortening of the reproduction level, particularly the 120 to 150. I bet if we took a count in this room we would find we are not reproducing our numbers.

Sandra Scarr: I am not familiar with the data that you presented here, but Sheldon Reed and his colleagues at the University of Minnesota published a paper by Reed & Reed. They took a whole cohort, a population sample that was quite a good sample at that time. They looked, not at parents, only because when you look at family size we're looking at people who have at least one child, but if you look at the whole population, there are many people in the lowest IQ groups who do not reproduce at all. Though those who do may have larger than average family sizes, in fact, they found that reproduction was not unequally distributed in the lower because of almost a universal reproduction of people of higher than average intelligence.

Raymond Cattell: Well, I predicted the calculation of one point of IQ per decade, and this was a very loose calculation I made in those days. Vining was more sophisticated and he allowed for the couples who don't reproduce at all and the differential death rate of intelligence, but he still came out with much the same results. However, there is data by a New Zealander called Flynn that you might know of but that claims to be no change in retesting over the last 20 years for school children. And this is sometimes been call "Cattell's Paradox"—in spite of everything pointing to a decline there is no decline.

Sandra Scarr: On the contrary, scores have gone up. Secularly, Flynn reports that scores go up secularly across time, which is contrary to what you said.

Herb Eber: Yes, I agree, there is at least some data that the IQs have gone up.

Raymond Cattell: Yes, but mostly we depend upon g_c tests.

John Horn: Flynn makes the case more on the basis of the Raven's matrices.

Herb Eber: I don't find that surprising because I also know that children of parents who come here from other cultures are enormously taller. The age of first menstrual period has gone down by 4 years in the last 100 years in this country. The age of puberty for boys similarly. Many of our current problems may, in fact, relate to that more than they do to some other factors.

Raymond Cattell: Yes, it would take a much more sophisticated recent study that Jack McArdle was asking for just now. We can't take this evidence as final and I agree there are so many factors in it. There is the differential death rate, which to some extent corrects the differential growth rate, and no one has tested the differential death rate to my knowledge. It's too late for me to test it.

Robert Thorndike: I also think it is worth commenting on the Reed & Reed study. It was important in number of ways.

Steve Aggen: I'd like to ask a different kind of question now. Do people attribute increases in violence to lower intelligence? Do you feel that we have enough evidence to make that jump right now? From what you know given the current state of research on intelligence or on g, do we know enough about g to take that as a causal force related to changes in or increases in violence in our society? I don't know, but I think there is still a lot of research that needs to be done to clarify that issue.

John Horn: Let me rephrase the question slightly—Is there a correlation between intellectual capability and crime? Is there enough evidence to make that statement that you did make as a matter of fact.

Raymond Cattell: Intellectual ability at what level? The imbecile level?

John Horn: Well it's a complex question. Is there a relationship between intelligence, and crime? And if so, which crime? And so on.

Robert Thorndike: I think we need to insert an intermediate variable here. There is clearly a negative relationship between socioeconomic status and intelligence. People with high SES categories generally score higher on intelligence tests than people with low SES categories. The same thing is true of crime rates and SES. People with low SES categories have a much higher rate of crime than the people with high SES categories. The false inferences are about what's doing what, and here it starts to gets very tenuous.

Sandra Scarr: Now it's time to defend Professor Cattell. Actually, I think that Richard Herrnstein and Charles Murray in their book *The Bell Curve* come out very strongly and show that partialling out social class, if anything, increases the relationship between intelligence and social pathology if you take out social class. They take intelligence measures as given in the literature, so we're not arguing fluid or crystallized intelligence here. They show quite powerful relationships including crime and delinquency of all kinds, welfare dependency. Those observations I think are indisputable. What they mean is another question. And what we ought to do about them is another whole set of questions.

Robert Thorndike: Maybe we shouldn't be partialling out SES, but using both of the variables as predictors?

Sandra Scarr: Right, you can't explain intelligence away with social class as a mediating or intervening variable.

Lee Willerman: Just one point about intelligence which may come as no surprise. I think that the overall correlation between criminality and IQ is really a product of two different IQ distributions. One of which has to do with adolescence criminality, which is rather short-lived, and does not persist into adulthood. The second distribution, which is about 17 points lower in IQ than controls, are kids that not only have low IQ but have a variety of real psychological deficits, many of which they had at an early age, like hyperactivity and conduct disorder in children.

In a longitudinal study in New Zealand researchers have shown an interesting finding about the overall IQ and crime correlation. In contrast to other studies which have found an 8-point IQ difference generally, this longitudinal study found that there are two groups of children—one where there is childhood difference in crime but shows no difference in IQ. In this first group, these crimes are largely adolescent types of crimes. In a second group, some of which are serious, the much more serious are persistent into adulthood.

Herb Eber: Let us emphasize that when you talk about crime you have to remember you're talking about unsuccessful criminals.

Lee Willerman: No, the self-report studies, which include people who have not been caught, have shown the correlations are unchanged. Getting caught is largely a function of frequency of offense.

Raymond Cattell: Well one thing we tend to overlook is the 20% of environmental influence, even on g_f. I think we've all been tending to think of that as schooling differences. Recently, evidence is that doesn't matter much, rather it's things like fevers, and blows on the head, and nutrition. A recent study shows IQ going up about 3 or 4 points in a group that was undernourished to begin with. In an average population no, but in a group that is being very poorly fed or short on vitamins or the rest of it, you can raise IQ that way by 2 or 3 points anyway.

Barry Mehler: Dr. Cattell, you said that much of mankind is obsolete and we need to breed for a larger brain size. I wonder if you could suggest how that might be achieved.

John Horn: How would you make brains larger? You would like to see mankind, humankind improve with a larger brains. How would you go about making brains larger?

Raymond Cattell: There is nothing but Darwin at the moment—natural selection. So we have to encourage natural selection. We could encourage mutations perhaps.

Roderick McDonald: As an extremely patriotic expatriate of Australia, I naturally think the increase in crime in the USA is an American cultural phenomena, not necessary in other parts of the world. And this makes me also think the remark you made also about differences in abilities, specifically in Negro men and Negro women versus the rest of the cultures that this result was also an American phenomena. In particular, I would focus on the question of self esteem in males and females on parity in a society of African states versus growing up in, say, the Carribean. I would want to know a great deal about their cultural background before I have any sense of what race and class we are defining.

John Horn: I think the main point of the question can be restated as, "are there data showing different intellectual levels in male and female African Americans based only on studies in America?" Was it African-American or was it Black?

Raymond Cattell: Yes, these studies were done in America.

Roderick McDonald: So, these studies were specifically cultural to me, and this does not generalize to, say, the Carribean where many successful people, the Prime Ministers, members of the Supreme Court, and so on, are all Black.

John Horn: So Rod's suggestion is that it is a peculiarly American type of phenomenon.

Raymond Cattell: Yes, I think it is. And it might arise from the fact the intelligence of the female is more important for survival of the children than the intelligence of the father, so you get more selection going on among the women than among the men.

Discussion Following the Talk by Dr. Evegny Sokolov

Steve Porges: Are there any questions for Dr. Sokolov?

Raymond Cattell: Has anyone found neurological locations in the visual area for these four sensitivities?

Evegny Sokolov: The visual system can be regarded as several layers of informational transformations. So, at the receptor level we have horizontal cells where a kind of reorganization takes place. In bipolar cells that is the area where normalization takes place. In the visual cortex we have a set of selected neurons, this was mainly done at London University, and we have shown that in additional visual system D4 there are neurons selectively tuned to different colors, including purple, where no specific wave lengths exist. So it means that in the visual cortex we have a real set of selected neurons. More difficult is to evaluate the process of transformation of plastic changes in output command neurons We have studied command neurons mainly in a primitive animals, but now it is possible to study command neurons in fish because in this animal there exists very big neurons that are responsible for the defense response of the fish. I hope that we can reach these output systems.

Sandra Scarr: I find it surprising that the visual system in fish can be so similar to the visual system in primates. This suggests from an evolutionary point of view that the color vision is a very old, old, system shared by most of the living world or at least the non-protoazoic living world. Are we expecting in snails to find very similar kinds of neurons and similar organization?

Evegny Sokolov: We have to distinguish two problems. One is a number of different pigments participating in particular color visual system, and the other problem is the hierarchical organization of the information processing. For example, in men we can find people with the absence of red pigment. But we have studied such people, and still we have a spherical surface. So it means that after the receptors we have the same stage of organization of the red. From point of view of pigment, the visual system is very flexible.

For example, the snail has only one pigment, but still in the snail with one pigment we can find two types of fibers coming from the retina of this animal. One type of fiber is excited by light and the other type is inhibited. So the principles are very basic, I believe, and I agree it is a very old system in this sense. On the other hand, the variability of pigments reached in human beings, genetic changes can change this. By the way it's a very interesting problem finding the relationship between genes and color vision because now it is very well known that with red, blue, and green pigments, their variability is multiplied. So this is a very promising area of research.

Steven Boker: One color that we have a subjective experience about that I don't see when I look at your chart is the color brown. Would you say something more about this?

Evegny Sokolov: We have studied color vision using color display and on the color display we can generate on a single page only stimuli having no additional darkness. To generate darkness you need to introduce induction fields, and we can generate brown and all kinds of dark red or dark blue. Using this induction field, under usual experience we see this as the pigment colors, because of the presence of the contrast. They are not presented perhaps here in this form, but we have used special experiments studying how this space is modified. We have tried to see whether by induction fields we can get a five-dimensional space, or still four-dimensional space. If it is four-dimensions, then additional portions of the sphere are now included. So new types of neurons are involved.

Final Discussion on the
"Future Work on Human Cognitive Abilities"

Jack McArdle: To begin this final session I would like to first offer the conference speakers an opportunity to say a few more words about any topic they find relevant to the issues raised at this meeting. But I would ask that they also tell us a bit about what they think is most important for future work on these questions. After these initial statements, we will open up the discussion for additional questions or statements from other members of the audience.

John Carroll: It occurs to me that when I wrote my book, there were a lot of questions that remained unanswered that I couldn't answer from the literature. Spotted throughout the book are various suggestions about what we need to know. I am interested in the basic science aspects of this, because we have got to have the basic science answers we need to know. We need to have it adequately spelled out because if we don't, then people are going to have doubts, be skeptical, among other things, or just come out with wrong answers.

As I say, I wanted to emphasize the basic science aspects of this. For example, in my book I tried to make the claim we have not adequately dealt with the "speed-level" problem, as I call it—some people call it the "speed-power" problem. Actually, in one time in my life I was closely associated with Brett Baxter, who pointed out that power dealt with the mixture of speed and level. Well anyway, read my book for the definitions of speed and power and what we need to know more clearly, whether these are speeded aspects of performance or more related to level of difficulty that can be mastered. These issues are in respect to a whole series of abilities in the stratum, first-order factors, second-order factors, and g. We need more information now about the relevance of these elementary cognitive processes so-called, which are often speeded and mark the various neuro-physiological measures which have been proposed along the lines of Anthony Vernon's recent book about the speed of mental processing. We need to get basic science aspects of the speed-level problem problem solved with respect to the relevance of g, the relevance of these elementary cognitive processes, speed, accuracy, levels, with respect to g. So those are some of the things I brought up in my book.

A comment about what Sandra Scarr said in her paper that is very interesting. A lot of people have been making models, and everything seems to fit or not fit depending upon what you've got in the model. And I keep thinking about how this is relevant to my own situation. I don't know that I'm particularly bright, but Leona Tyler did give me the Stanford-Binet when I was a graduate student and I did get the top level score for an adult, so that must mean something. But I don't feel I'm terribly bright. There are lots of people around who seem more creative, more elegant in their thinking, than I am. I had a very ordinary background. I was the first member of my family to go to college. The only explanation I have for my own brightness is that I started out being very curious about everything. My family gave me 25 cents for the *Book of Knowledge*, and I used to read that avidly. Then later I used to like to go to the library. What effect did that have on me? I don't think anything that my parents did for me, other than give me that *Book of Knowledge*, had anything to do with the development of my intelligence. Maybe there is a genetic component there but I would have no way of evaluating it, because I don't know their backgrounds.

But people have got to work on this problem. And it can't be done with respect to just a single model. There has got to be a merging aspects of the behavioral genetic aspects and the socialization aspects. The most interesting thing I have read recently, at least, is the work of Steven Ceci. He does present a model which seems to me to be suitably balanced between the genetic and socialized aspects of development. Well that's all I have to say for now.

Raymond Cattell: The only thing that I found disappointing is the building of necessarily rickety theory on the basis of factor analysis that is published prematurely without being checked. There is no doubt in my mind that we have a plague of poor factor analyses—that is to say, factor analyses that are not rotated definitely to simple structure, to a significant simple structure. I can understand this because you get very weary in long factor analysis. It reminds me of the early attempts to find the North Pole. There were many attempts before people got there, but they all thought they got there. We need a better instruction at the undergraduate and graduate levels about what is to be done. And I'm even going to be critical of John Horn on one thing, and that is that he used Equamax rotation program. Well firstly, no automatic rotation program takes us to simple structure. And secondly, Equamax equalizes the size of all the factors. Well that is an assumption, that is a meta-theory, and if the factors are actually different, you will not find them by Equamax.

The second thing I want to comment on is that after Sandra Scarr's most fascinating talk. I say what next is the mystery of the geno-threptic correlation, and I will explain what it is. *Threptos* is the Greek word meaning nurture, and I split environment into two parts. Environmental variance is the variance in the environment, not the variance in the individual. The variance in the individual is threptic variance. That is, the variance in the trait due to whatever environment exists. The environment variance is one thing and the threptic variance is another, and there are ways of calculating from one to the other. Now what I refer to is that 2 years ago by the use of the MAVA method, not the twin method, the MAVA method of evaluation of heredity, it was found that the geno-threptic correlations were all negative, all of them, over the abilities, over the traits of the 16PF, and so on. That means that environment works against the genetic deviation. Whoever emerges above is pressed down toward the average and whoever emerges below is pressed upward toward the average.

Well, I might pause to speak about the MAVA method, the "multiple abstract variance analysis" method, and it simply assumes, which I think is uncontrovertible, that the variance of various types of family relationships breaks down into six components—between-family and within-genetics, between-family and within-family environments, and the two between-within covariances. Now those covariances are missing in the twin method, which I therefore think is obsolete. The only way to get at it is by big researches, and these are going to involve large samples of people. We had to get 2,000 subjects, for example, in the last MAVA method analysis. We obtain very consistent result, it is true, that we obtain very similar results from the twin method—genetic values of 70% g_f and 40% g_c. But the MAVA method does gives you a chance to get at the covariances, and these covariances amazingly turn out to be all negative. Even intelligence among the 16 traits was negative.

Well, that doesn't fit in with what we commonly think of. We think of the bright child as stimulated, one who stimulates himself; a dull child will remain dull. But no, we have got to remember the classroom where the teacher has a job to do. So she pushes hard on the backward and rather neglects the bright who look after themselves. So that's the only explanation I can give. Because it is so general, it must be inherent in human culture to pressure people toward the mean. Some have suggested that TV is the cause of this pressure toward the mean. And it certainly illustrates that advertisers and people who make TV have made TV understandable to the average mind. So, the bright don't get exercised, and the dull get bemused by the upward pressure. But we need a repetition of the last MAVA experiment to verify that these correlations are indeed negative. Thank you.

Evegny Sokolov: I will speak, perhaps very subjectively. I want to emphasize new problems arising from concepts in neural nets. One extension of such study that I haven't mentioned is the creation of so-called semantic space. So instead of presenting the subject with visual tasks, you can present color names and ask the subject according to his memory the differences between respective names. And again we can view the same data as an independent axis of the matrix. And we have done experiments in Russian, Germany, Vietnamese, Rwandan, English, and we conclude that in all cases we have found an isomorphic relationship between perceptual space and semantic space. Color names are located on the hyper-sphere, the same structure, but we have different positions for the names, so this means they can represent different subsets of colors.

These studies, I believe, are also important for new types of testing, and these new types of testing might be based on the construction of knowledge base. The subject is presented with pairs of names related to particular knowledge and a semantic space is created. This semantic space of the student is compared with the semantic space for the same colors of the expert. We can organize a selective semantic space of the student in such a way that it can mesh with the knowledge space of the expert. I believe this is very important for new types of computerized testing of knowledge.

Finally, I want to emphasize this basic study needs understanding of genetics for all the processes we have discussed. So we have differentiated environment influences and genetics, and color vision in this sense this is a very exceptional example. Because now it is very well-known that genetics creates red genes, green genes, and blue genes, and we can study the perceptual space, and we can relate perceptual experiences to a genetic map with respect to pigments. This is, of course, a fairly long-range approach, but it is very promising because we can find a direct relationship between genes and subjective experience. As soon as genes are changed, the perception is changed because of the changes in the position of the pigments. I believe that this problem is important for the future.

Dick Snow: I have two points to make about the question of "What is next?" But you might have noticed yesterday that I have trouble speaking without pictures—I have a high "visual" and low "verbal" profile. But I don't have any pictures now, so I'm going to ask you to exercise your own visual thinking and remember. You might have noticed that Sandra Scarr showed a slide with *parental abilities* including a box labeled *student engagement,* and a box labeled *student achievement.* I think engagement connects up to what I think comes next. In the ability-situation interface there are dynamic activities in learning, and I do not think we know very much about how abilities map onto learned activities and engagement in learning tests. So that is in between the person-situation interface, and we don't have much of a handle on that. So that is one important line of research which comes next. But it's not just ability, it's engagement, motivation, personality and cognition and lots of other things we don't like to talk about as abilities because abilities are things we understand, and those things we don't. So that is part of the next step—you could call those micro-adaptive functions.

The second point is that we don't know very much about how to integrate individual differences and development. Until recently, most developmental psychology only studied one kind of individual difference—that was age. Until recently, most individual difference psychologists never studied development, they studied individual differences at one point in time. There are some people beginning to ask—what does it really mean to integrate individual differences in psychology and developmental psychology? Robert Case, some researchers in Geneva, and some in Greece who have been doing factor analytic studies across time—longitudinal, not just cross-sectional. I don't do that work myself, I'm not much of a developmentalist, but someone should do it—maybe someone here in the room will do it. In that connection, I also think we don't know much of anything about a part of that, which is the development of personal knowledge—idiosyncracy. We don't have good ways of thinking about the idiosyncratic personal knowledge, which is a very important factor in human learning and development like Ray Cattell made reference to. Thanks.

John Horn: So I'm supposed talk about what comes next. A lot of things should come next. It's interesting—in the last talk by Woodcock, we were looking at practical applications, and in other talks were looking at advancements in theory. I think we should pay attention to both of these things.

One thing important in the applied areas is the kind of thing Jack Mc-Ardle was showing in his NCAA work, which is how you can explicitly talk about what you want tests to do, what you want concepts from science to do. In applied situations, you should very carefully look at the utility structure that he outlined for us, so that you can make explicit what value judgments you are wanting to articulate. I thought he put it very nicely—once you become an advocate, you should know that you are an advocate. You should know what it is you're advocating and be clear about it, and then use the relevant science in a way that supports you advocacy. Now if we could just get that idea out into the political arena, get people explicitly talking about how the evidence relates to the values they wish to see put ahead, and the values they wish to see developed, then I think we would really see some progress in our society and culture. I don't think that's coming next, but I think the work that Jack McArdle has been doing in the controversy that has developed over the NCAA—the use of tests and the development of decisions about who will be eligible to play as freshman in college sports—this work, in a capsule form, has given us some extremely good ideas about what we should be doing in regard to a lot of other values and important kinds of decisions that we make and have been making for centuries in bad and ineffectual ways.

In the scientific realm, I think Jack Carroll yesterday summarized nicely what should come next. He outlined the kind of analyses that would further advance the understanding of the structure of cognitive capabilities. There is more work to be done along those lines and I think we should be encouraging such research. The other thing that I think needs to be done, of course, comes as no surprise, from my talk on process analysis, we need to understand much better the processes that are involved in the expression of these abilities, as well as their development over the course of childhood. I hope things go that way, but they usually don't go the way I hope.

Sandra Scarr: Since 1983 I have been talking about how people make their own environments. This has been variously interpreted as "blaming the victim" or that genes determine everything. I really didn't mean it that way. I mean that in many ways people do select and actually create their own experiences. I think though we can have different models of this in different domains. Certainly, we are already going in these directions, like exploring ways in which people create their own family environments.

For example, characteristics of parents affect the kind of child-rearing they do. There is a study some of our colleagues at UVA have been involved in, including David Reese, Mavis Heatherington, and Robert Plomin, of families of children with various degrees of genetic relatedness. In this large national sample, they have families with fraternal twins, families with identical twins, and families with step-siblings who are in one of three categories: genetically related as siblings, step-children who come from the parents' former marriages and are genetically unrelated, and children who are half-siblings in step-families because one child was born to the present parents. So you have all these different degrees of genetic relatedness, from all of your genes in common to none of your genes in common, in intact families. And one thing they've found of importance so far, and the study is far from analyzed, is very important genetic variability in the way people behave toward each other in their interactions, and the way people perceive their family environments—both actions and perceptions. That study I think will change the socialization literature forever. There is no way that can be avoided.

I want to talk about one more thing—this is from an article by Eric Turkheimer and Irv Gottesman, published in *Developmental Psychology*, in which they plot of a reaction range surface. The idea is that one needs to look at an effectively different range of environments across a range of genotypes and consider an effectively different range of genotypes across environments. For intelligence, which they mapped, based on the developmental literature of what we know about family effects, it is certainly the case that at the very low end of environment, it doesn't matter what kind of genotype you have, because your development is going to be poor no matter what. But in other areas of the reaction surface, genotypes appear to matter and environments appear to have much less effect. Because everybody goes to school, because everybody has access to public libraries, television for good and for worse, and public communications, the opportunity structure in Western societies is such that people bring their own intelligence to bear—their fluid intelligence—to their cultural opportunities and acquire what of it they are capable of, or want to, or are motivated for, or have a personal investment in. Therefore in their view and in mine, most environments that we observe that are correlated with people's personal characteristics are not making environmental differences in people's outcomes—they are in fact reflections of people's own personal characteristics in their choices of environments, in their use of opportunities.

With that in mind, I think it is very important for us to understand where that threshold of adequacy is, and to address interventions and our public policy concerns toward those children who do not have adequate opportunities, who are not allowed to fulfill whatever it is that they were able to become intellectually. With respect to Steve Ceci's work, raised by John Carroll earlier, I think he is romantically attached to some of the correlations we observe without being sufficiently analytic about where the causal effects come from.

Richard Woodcock: With respect to what comes next in test development, I have already alluded to some of this in my paper. Now I want to discuss two things. I want to talk about test construction and about the quality of research, the nature of research, which backs up or should back up the tests that we produce and make available for people to use when making often irreversible long-term decisions about other people.

In regard to test construction, I think in the near future we will see more batteries that are organized to measure abilities across the whole spectrum of abilities, as we think of them. Second, I would not be surprised to see more emphasis on what I call facilitators and inhibitors—in these tests, or in the way people are told they should use and interpret these tests. The third would be to see more dynamic models underlying both the interpretation of test results and the models upon which these tests will be built.

What should come next? With respect to the research that we provide about the validity of tests, I think there should be more attention paid to the design of factor analytic studies conducted by test developers. By this I mean that the studies should contain enough breadth and depth of markers to adequately describe the factorial structure of a new battery. There may need to be included some reference markers—well-accepted measures of different abilities—that are external to the new battery. This should be an expected component of the analyses intended to provide evidence of what a new battery measures or does not measure.

Another point with regard to validity studies, is that test manuals often include a series of validity studies that are nothing more than a series of paired comparisons. Test A, the new test, is compared to test B. Then test A is compared to test C in another group of subjects, and so on. The author may report that there were 20 or 30 validity studies carried out. The truth of the matter is that you can't compare the results of any one study to any of the others. It would require less data gathering to administer all of the tests to a single sample and provide the potential user with a matrix of correlations among all the other tests and the new test.

My final thought is that reviews of tests should be comparative reviews —*Consumer Reports* sorts of reviews—in which several products are taken and compared against a list of criteria. Perhaps these three points—proper factor analysis studies, convergent validity matrices, and comparative reviews—should assume the stature of consumer's rights. Perhaps some authors or publishers might resist these ideas as full disclosure about some tests may not be healthy for sales.

Jack McArdle: Thank you all. Now let's have some questions or comments from others.

Harvey Sterns: In the field of industrial psychology in the past few years there's been renewed interest in g as a predictor of work performance. There are those of us who ask the question "Would you like to have more dimensionality than just g to clarify what is happening in these relationships?" Can you give me some arguments to go back to my industrial colleagues so that I can provide a stronger argument than just not having such restrictive measures.

John Horn: I'd like to comment on that, but I want to say again, that I've said some things about Schmidt and Hunter's work on predicting job performance, and it might seem that I'm criticizing these findings. The criteria that your asked about today is to predict all by one factor. Now, in line with this question, it may be in fact that we only care about one factor.

Use this example: You're thinking about promoting people in say the Psychology Department. Now some of those people are very mathematically and statistically smart and they do research along those lines. Then there are other people who are not very smart on mathematical statistical things and they do things along the lines of experimental manipulations and don't even use statistics. You want both of those people to be supported, so you want a criterion which says "I want good people." You don't want to differentiate those people in that criterion. So the people you are talking to Harvey, possibly want a *g* criteria. If you want a *g* criteria you want a *g* predictor. And that is what Schmidt and Hunter are basing their evidence on. It doesn't require any differentiation of the multiple abilities at all.

Now is that a good thing to do? Well come back again and ask the kind of questions asked by Jack McArdle—"What is your utility structure?" and "What are you trying to do with that criteria?" And then if you're trying to do something different, then use a utility structure analysis of it. Do you really want to distinguish people who are statistically mathematically oriented from the experimentalist, and if you think that ought to be important in your outcome variable, then measure that and account for it. Earl Hunt said that it's just as hard to measure criteria, maybe harder to measure criteria as Herb Eber could tell us, than it is to measure predictors of those criteria. The measurement problems are in principle the same for the criteria as they are for the predictors.

Herb Eber: I'm going to second what you said because its directly relevant. If you really have a specific criteria like next semester's grades in mathematics, then the best predictor is probably last semester's achievement tests in mathematics moderated with *g*. No doubt that you can do it better with those two numbers than you can with just one. But if you are concerned about something in the long range future, or if you're concerned about something that is likely to change, as typically we are in education, then we come back to the fact that it works better with rougher measures, with more central kinds of measures.

Richard Gorsuch showed in personality that you can in fact predict twice as much variance with 16 first-order factors than with five second-orders if you have the criteria for those kinds of predictions. But if the criteria is much rougher than that than all of that goes out the window, so that may be what's happening in industrial psychology. Most of the jobs you are selecting people for didn't exist 5 years ago and half of the ones that exist today won't exist 5 years from now. And in that kind of world, how specific would you like to be?

John Nesselroade: I learned from my German colleagues that the chance to ask a question is really an opportunity to make a statement. Something that I'd like to have discussed a bit more is the fact that, many times, individual difference studies are not sensitive to the fact that we may be combining together the wrong kinds of people to try to draw inferences from. I think Ray Cattell's notion of a negative relationship regarding the *geno-threptic* correlation is simply indicating that the institution by nature is conservative and in order to stay alive they have to operate on a conservative principle. So it's not so surprising perhaps that these correlations appear negative when you look at them in the large context. But people don't do the same things. Individual differences in development may mean that some people develop in one direction and some develop in the other. Some have a high potential maybe that go even higher in terms or their phenotypic response.

I think when John Horn did a study 20 some years ago that reported on within-person variation in fluid and crystallized intelligence, this is an early exemplar of the kinds of questions we need to ask to get a fuller picture of what is going on. People ought not to be clumped together until you have some information that says this now makes a reasonable level of analysis.

Roderick McDonald: I've written a little one-page on the title "Cognition Has No Structure," and you have to decide how serious I am.

I'm happy with g_f because it captures Spearman's intelligence defined as known genetic power, the eduction of relations and correlates, and is generally recognized to be the foundation of propositional thought and generalizability. Especially after Richard Snow's nice clarification yesterday, I see no reason to think of g_c as intelligence of the second kind. It is just a mixture of achievement and aptitudes in situations, and continuously developed.

My second point is that I like Louis Guttman's first law of intelligence — that all cognitive competencies are positively correlated. I see no reason why wide-sense factor analysis should be able to find existent structure, as against creating structure by the variables and tests, within the positive manifold. I don't see why it should be able to find structure with just three or four levels of stratification, say two kingdoms, g_f and g_c, a handful of phyla, such as memory and reasoning, then the species and varieties of tests and items.

Factor analysis is a nice device, I'm fond of it, for checking the homogeneity, hence the reliability, convergent and divergent validity, and the generalizability of the atomic items researchers in psychology and education choose, for whatever reason, to write. The atomic items, or what I tend to call atoms, generally fill the manifold quite densely. I'm not denying the existence of distinct processes in cognition, but we do not need factor analysis to tell us that memory is distinct from reasoning and both are distinct from perception. And these would still be distinct processes if they displayed no individual differences at all.

Earl Hunt: Let me make a point I wanted to make for the last 6 or 7 years or more than that. I've been involved in looking at cases and projections in the work force and such and I'm struck with the tendency really nobody can get really limited behaviors if you restrict yourself to tests that take you 5 to 10 minutes. Not for the question of determining base structure because I think we fairly well handle those behaviors that can be illustrated within about 5 to 10 minutes of various tests. We have got a pretty good handle on that. Now when we start extracting to things like the work force, we get a set of new problems. First, it is very difficult to measure performance. While academic performance is easy to measure, it is much harder to measure work force performance because these people are busy. And it costs to measure. The best studies, which are probably mentioned here, have been done by the Department of Defense in the last 7 years. In addition to just taking ratings, they actually go out and see whether the Cook can cook and whether the Gunner can gun, presumably whether the Intelligence Officer can be intelligent.

I'm being a little facetious, but my point is that we get a five-factor structure of performance in the work force. It becomes very important to draw a distinction in performance between what a person can do and what a person will choose to do under the normal constraints. You get a very global rating if you look at supervisor ratings, as most of the studies have done. I have a lot of trouble actually taking very seriously supervisor ratings, except for the fact that it may be that success in the work force is not determined by how well you can do your job but by how well your boss thinks you can do it. Or by how well you choose to. I think by constraining ourselves to time pressure measures, we are getting a good type of pictures of some things and no factor pictures at all of the variables that are completely outside of that.

Bill Revelle: I'd like to add another point. Phil Ackerman, for instance, has done some interesting work looking at the importance of ability versus noncognitive resources. He has looked at change in the relative importance of ability versus nonability of performance on cognitive performance of task. Ability makes a big difference when you're learning a skill but conscientiousness is important when you're actually doing the job for the next 40 years. You don't have to be smart once you've learned. Once you've acquired certain skills it turns out a lot of job performance is not skill. It is conscientiousness and persistence that determine job performance.

Those of us who study executive functioning have very big circles for executive functioning and have little tiny circles for cognition. It is important for the ability people to also look at the nonability personality motivation sets. A lot of these findings are physiologically based and a lot of these are genetically based. Experimental psychologists are talking to individual difference psychologists, and vice versa. We need to think about how experimental psychologists could be of help here.

Steven Porges: Not being a human abilities psychologist but as a psychophysiologist interested in developing processes in individual differences, I come into this room with a different set of bifocals and tunnel vision. I noted that most of the talks really had an idea of the nervous system, that is to say some relationship to the brain was embedded somewhere in peoples' models. And if we're going to model toward the future, I think the whole notion of the nervous system becomes critical.

I want to go back in time a little bit, I want to go back to the mid 1970s when Raymond Cattell was just retiring and that's the last time I heard him talk, and I only heard him talk at the University of Illinois retirement banquet. And I thought to myself, this is very exciting, because here was a person interested in individual differences who has an appreciation for the nervous system and for physiology. He doesn't have any measures for it but he appreciates it. And what I noticed over decades in these areas is that people tend to think of the nervous system as a construct. It gets buried into the circle we call g, sometimes we call it g_f, but there's not a real emphasis in starting to measure it.

Then there's this other issue relating genes to behavior, this is more what both Sandra Scarr and Evegny Sokolov were talking about. Genes don't make behavior—you have an intervening variable called the nervous system that gets in the way. And that nervous system is plastic, and the nervous system develops. If we go back to some of other psychometric constructs, we find that Cattell's "provincial" variables are merely a notion of how the nervous system works through sensory afferents. The nervous system needs to develop, just like lifting muscles. And if we think about mental processes as motor actions, just like lifting weights, we develop those mental processes by stimulating afferents. Now the overall excitatory potential, I don't know what it is, I think that may be genetics, but the system will not work unless you stimulate it. If you want to see a nervous system deteriorate, you block the sensory pathways to that component. So what I'm really saying is that you have to be very careful about how we model genetic–behavior relationships. This is critical in my subdiscipline development psychology because we have some of our colleagues saying that things are genetic when all they've done is put a couple of electrodes on a person and measure a heart rate pattern. Physiological differences are not genetic differences, and Raymond Cattell even brought this up in his talk—you can injure your head and change your physiology, change your intelligence, change your temperament but you're not changing your genetic package. So we want to be very careful in relating genes to behavior and to intelligence.

The politics of science is changing and is changing very rapidly. The NIH is focusing mainly on molecular genetic research. Those of us interested in behavior find ourselves excluded from the intramural research programs. The area called mental health is going to end up as a bench-science studying brain tissue. The NIH is moving very actively on this human genome project. And so this whole issue of genes and behavior has become politically hot and scientifically relevant. As behavioral scientists, we have to posture and lobby and explain that the behaviors can be caused from a variety of things. We're in a period of time where people are beginning to believe that all we need to know is something about genetics, then the environment and even the processes of the nervous system are being neglected.

Earl Hunt: I would like to completely support Steve Porges' point that just making a reference to the brain or the nervous system doesn't help very much. I think there is something that was not mentioned here, as we look to the future, is the tremendous increment we have in noninvasive biological measures of specific functions. And they will exert a tremendous influence in the future. I can't imagine they won't. So that I see a need to expand the field, not by better factor analysis, I'm sorry but I don't think that's the issue at all. I think the issue is expanding by better measures on the molecular side with physiological measures, and on the workforce performance side, a much wider range of what are best called social variables.

Sandra Scarr: I want to remind everybody of Lee Cronbach's classic and wonderful paper on the two disciplines of scientific psychology. He described the science of general laws and typological theory, meaning experimental psychology, where mechanisms are the focus of inquiry. Where we want to know what causes what in a sequence; if it's not temporal but some ordered sequence, and that the focus is on individual development and the question is how does this operate, and it's often a very proximal kind of study. The other scientific discipline of psychology deals with populations and variability and individual differences. It has as its main focus understanding sources of variation. And when we shift from one framework to another we're shifting from one kind of scientific discipline to another.

Now bridges can be built, and I second what Steve Porges is talking about. But one kind of inquiry has not replaced the other essentially nor do I think it will. First of all, if you don't find that there are important sources of variability to be looked at, there's not much point in looking for mechanisms there. If we find that there are not important sources of variability in a particular development, let's say, even longitudinally, but that's there's no particular environmental variability that influences that, then there is not much reason to look in the population in general.

Now there may be specific kinds of individuals who are affected. The classic example being very low birth weight infants—if you're looking for causes of cerebral palsy, in low birth weight infants, you don't look at a population of normal birth weight kids and ask does cerebral palsy arise from low birth weight because you'll never find it in the population. You've got to look at very specific instances and look for mechanisms. But there are different questions, there are different approaches to understanding individual variability versus mechanisms of development. I'm not saying this as well as I'd like.

Steve Porges: I actually think there's a much closer mesh and I think a lot has to do with our basic training. Many people have gone into the area of individual differences and personality testing, and other people have gone into laboratory research and experimental manipulation. There is this schism in psychology, one is called soft science, one is called hard science, and I think we have to get rid of that. We can utilize the wonderful methods that develop in the individual differences psychology and the fine measurements derived from neurological assessments. I think that's what Earl Hunt is saying, that's what I'm saying. If we take low birth weight kids and look for cerebral palsy, yes. But if we take low birth weight kids and 50 percent of them have a attentional problems later in life, then we may learn something about attentional problems from that mechanism which we could then use on rural populations. So we can then kind of marry these approaches. What I'm basically saying is if we're interested in individual differences in behavior, we can get it using different methodologies, assess it, predict it, and we can utilize the powerful mathematical techniques that have been realized in the study of individual differences.

Sandra Scarr: May I comment a little bit back to the development argument. We in experimental psychology can show that development is plastic to the extent that when intervened upon in a prescribed way, one can change the course, usually for the worse, for development. But does it mean that that's the way it happens out there in the real world. And that the danger I see in suggesting tremendous amounts of plasticity or uncertainty between genetic programs for development and behavioral outcomes as mediated through anatomical or physiological structures is that it gives people the notion that development is so uncertain almost anything can happen. Well you know in principle that's true and especially if it is experimentally intervened upon. But in the real course of development in the real world under observable environmental conditions that actually exist, is not very uncertain. As a matter of fact, it's not uncertain much at all, because that's why we get these terribly high heritibilities for such measures as intelligence because the brain isn't just indeterminent in its development.

Steve Porges: What I'm really trying to argue has nothing to do with what you're saying. What I'm trying to argue is that our educational system has lapsed. As developmental professionals, developmental psychologists, and behavior scientists, I think we need to know both quantitative methods and we need to know some experimental methods, especially a need for physiology. Everyone who has spoken here and those of you who are in the audience have some type of construct that you are calling the nervous system, the brain biological system, or something. But most of you are not schooled in that area. So what I'm saying to improve our educational process to bringing more of the cutting edge work that is going on in those areas, we'll start finding that the methods we are using now to develop factor structures, the actual measures that we use, will now start incorporating physiological and psycho-physiological measures.

I have one other point, because Sandra Scarr brought it up very nicely, this distinction between two sides of the two psychologies. What I used to say is "Ones man's error is another man's data." In the area of factor analysis and the area of individual differences you study error, you try to partition variance, which is error variance in the experimental model. I have had amazing arguments with my colleagues over the years because when I start to tell them that science should not be defined as manipulation of variables, manipulation and observation as we have learned as freshman and undergraduates of biology classes, but science should be defined as the partitioning of variance, they say what are you talking about. And I think that's exactly what we're all interested in—We're interested in accounting for variance and there are different methods for doing that.

I'm saying you should learn more about the relative values of these methods and incorporate some sophisticated understanding of neuro-physiology into our models. Physiological measures have a distribution, they have error, they have individual differences, and they fit all the same assumptions and models that all these other variables do. All I'm saying is that gives you another handle.

John Horn: Steve, I want to ask you a question. You just made some very nice comments on the way in which science has become politicized. But I think one remark, if I heard you correctly, was to the effect that we've made as though it were a leap frog kind of movement from behavioral to genetic, overlooking the physiological. I think I agree with you in terms of what I've been able to observe. It seems to me a very serious scientific error that we've made there and I'd like to hear you talk more about why that happened. If you know that it happened or where that happened, where do you get your information?

Steve Porges: Yes this is true. It's quite clear just reading the journal *Science*. It's quite clear watching the shift in funding priorities. If you talk to David Johnson of the Federation of Behavioral, Psychological, and Cognitive Sciences, he'll can tell you exactly what's going on over at NIH. Both behavioral laboratories are scheduled to be closed at NIH. Our new NIH leader is Harold Varmus, and his lead quote is "Behavior isn't necessarily worthless, but it doesn't solve things like other area of sciences." So it is about solving real world problems I think. Genetic diseases are something to be treated by manipulation.

John Horn: So people understood. People finally have understood that genetics doesn't necessarily mean that you can't treat it, they've got that right.

Steve Porges: Right, but what I told them is that once the politicians understand this next leap, which is genetics to behavior, then NIH is going to be in trouble.

John Horn: Just one other thing—do you see any hope in this?

Steve Porges: The positive statement is that I believe that people studying individual differences incorporate more physiological sophistication, incorporate it, but their explanations and concepts have to be a little more realistic relative to a field like physiology. We have to be very careful about politics that start to talk about physiologic differences in being temperamental. Now we have colleagues and we can talk later about who these people are, who measure kids under specific behavioral situations and are getting physiological differences and those physiological differences could be determined by the individual differences in behavior at the time of measure and had nothing to do with any permanent neurological, let alone genetic, background. So we have to be very protective, we have to monitor what our colleagues are saying because they are literally destroying our playing field.

Sandra Scarr: That's why the two disciplines of scientific psychology are going to be around for a long time because the mechanisms underlying variation in normal human behavior are not, I think, going to be amenable to the kinds of molecular genetic analysis we know how to do on disorders. These are rather specific gene or chromosomal disorders. Now maybe we'll become so much more sophisticated in both our physiological analyses of what the gene products are and in a way of being able to have a computer or something run them off.

Robert Thorndike: I want to first offer the observation that I think this has been a very valuable and informative conference due to all of the speakers. I would particularly draw attention to something that Steve Porges just said—that one man's variance is another man's error, or another person's error. And to say that really what we're talking about is what you wound up at the end saying that is that error is unexplained error maybe potentially explainable. But I have a feeling that, in the last analysis, when we start talking about relationships between genes and behavior, we're really going to wind up in a position of chaos theory where a butterfly flaps its wings in China and it rains in New York, and the intervening cause of influences are so many and so complex that in a sense we are going to have to leap over at least until we become a whole lot more sophisticated than I expect my great-great grandchildren to be.

Mike Frost: I view myself as an outsider to these scientific talks because I am a teacher from Vermont and I might be looking at this from a very simplistic point of view. But it seems to me that the discussions here have incredible importance for what we will be doing tomorrow. There's a lot of shaping, reshaping of thinking going on here, but I see one basic question that's been asked about and addressed directly and indirectly. It is still the basic central question of what in the world are we talking about when we're talking about intelligence? What is this mystery thing *g* factor that we're talking about? And we've talked, John Horn has talked about clarifying what we're going to measure. Sandra Scarr has talked about clarifying to theory. What is it that thing we're measuring? I don't know, and I would wager to bet that we would all write a different definition of that mysterious thing that we call intelligence here in this Rotunda.

I say that sincerely because back in the public school system there are some teachers sitting there asking us, "Well if you're going to work with this kid, isn't it important that we know what the real IQ is?" There is some parent that's sitting there saying, "Well I want to know how smart my kid is." And there is some special educator sitting out there that's being required to write a program for a kid that has to know the difference, I think I should know the difference about what this so-called expert is talking about in regards to the discussion on intelligence, aptitudes, or abilities. I think the discussion has a very basic charge here in the points of view—we better get our heads together and define what it is we're talking about.

Earl Hunt: I'd like to make a comment on that. There is a great deal of discussion in the schools now at the national level, and virtually every state, on things like teaching reasoning and teaching problem solving. Let me take my own state of Washington, which has passed a law that says children shall be taught to reason. They have also passed a law that says you will not drive while intoxicated. The state patrolmen have very explicit directions as to how he will decide whether you are going to drive while intoxicated. If he should pull you over and check say, "lets see, you thought you were going to travel at 55 miles an hour and you have to be at the other end of the state and you only left there at that time—that looks like premeditated speeding to me." He can't do that, there is no way. There is no set of measures to decide if someone is thinking or reasoning. I think it's legitimate to be asked how are you going to do decide on these programs for teaching reasoning. I don't think Mike Frost's question can be answered until this question is answered.

Dick Snow: I agree with Sandra, and I agree with other people too, that genetic research has got to go on even though we're waiting for some physiological research to take place or vice versa. Behavioral research has to go on without waiting for genetics or physiology. Mike Frost in Vermont who has to interpret the Woodcock-Johnson test tomorrow is going to have to do that tomorrow without waiting for the rest of us to do our thing. What I think you can do is recognize that no one person can do it all and you keep looking for bridges. If you can't define intelligence for the parent, at least you can enrich their conceptualization or recognition about how they think about it. You can't wait for a definition or you'll wait all of your lifetime.

Raymond Cattell: I'd like to comment on the several speakers' remarks about manipulative experiments. You know when Wundt decided to free psychology from philosophy, he took the physical sciences of the 19th century as his model of a science. Now that was a binary manipulative model, and since then, we've done a good deal on the multivariate experimental method. I'm afraid psychology today is still 90% bivariate. You look at the journals, and they are not getting the underlying variables that need to be handled in bivariate experiments.

But on a different issue, my mind is that we're all arguing on insufficient data and I do feel that we need more solid data. But this takes hard work, and it's the kind of thing John Carroll has done. I'm particularly pained about the absence of repetition of the MAVA experiment, which was novel 10 years ago and it's high time that was verified or checked in some way. But no one in the field has done so.

It is true that science is democratic, of course, but it seems a bit too much talk. I'm reminded of Runnemead and the Magna Carta, and that three or four centuries elapsed before any man got up in Parliament, in the midst of vociferous debate and said, "Gentlemen, let's sit down and calculate." Now there is some kind of advance we need in science—we need more data. So I close with hope someone will go ahead and get genetic information as a basis for all the discussion about physiology and such. We've got to get the facts first. Thank you.

Jack McArdle: I have only a few closing words—I thank all of the participants for their stimulating contributions, and I look forward to predicting the future with you.

Author Index

Subject Index

A

Ability factors
  acculturation knowledge, 59, 62
  automatic processing speed (Gs), 138, 142, 151
  auditory ability, 83, 86
  auditory processing, 62
  auditory thinking (Ga), 138, 142
  comprehension-knowledge (Gc), 211
  cognitive speed, 83, 268
  crystallized ability (g_c), 58, 72, 73, 74, 85, 231, 263, 265, 279
  education of relations and correlates, 82
  fluency of retrieval from long-term storage, 62
  fluid ability (g_f), 58, 62, 231, 263
  general intelligence (g), 6, 21,78, 81–83, 320
  general factor, 80
  general fluid intelligence, 215
  Gf, 72, 73, 74, 82, 84, 85, 265
  Gf decline, 279
  Gf–Gc theory, 64, 65, 137, 243
  Gs, 84, 85
  Gv, 86
  inductive reasoning, 83
  long-term storage and retrieval (Glr), 60, 138, 142
  primary abilities, 69
  primary factor, 75, 76
  primary memory, 82

  primary mental ability (PMA), 57
  quantitative knowledge (Gq), 62, 138, 142
  reading-writing, 138, 139
  reasoning, 75
  short-term apprehension and retrieval (SAR), 59, 62, 84, 85, 268
  short-term memory, 82, 138, 142
  speed of thinking ability, 60
  TSR, 84, 85
  verbal-conceptual knowledge (Gc), 138, 142
  verbal IQ, 284
  visualization (Vz), 60, 74
  visuospatial thinking (Gv), 138, 142
  working memory, 83
Ability measures and tests
  carefulness, 83
  chronometric measures, 83
  correct decision speed (CDS), 138
  common word analogies, 266
  computerized testing of knowledge, 307
  concentration, 83, 267
  decision speed, 62, 84
  declarative knowledge, 151
  Detroit Tests of Learning Ability-3 (DTLA-3), 143
  Differential ability scales (DAS), 143
  digit symbol, 287
  Gf–Gc Diagnostic Worksheet, 154
  Kaufman Abilities Battery for Children (K-ABC), 141–143

HCA Conference Participants

Dr. Wayne Baughman
American Institutes for Research
Washington, DC
(202) 342–5109

Dr. Patricia Beckley
2069 Brookfield Road
Blacksburg, VA 24069

Dr. Victor Bergenn
Council on Educational Psychology
450 Park Ave.
Leonia, NJ 07605

Dr. John B. Carroll
409 N. Elliot Road
Chapel Hill, NC 27514–7628

Dr. Heather Cattell
622 Kalanipuu St.
Honolulu, HI 96825

Dr. Raymond B. Cattell
662 Kalanipuu St.
Honolulu, Hawaii 96825

Dr. Ruth Childs
American Institute for Research
3333 K St., N.W.
Washington, DC 20007

Dr. David P. Constanza
Department of Psychology
George Mason University
Fairfax, VA

Dr. Herbert W. Eber
Psychological Resources
74 Fourteenth St. NW
Atlanta, GA 30309–2802

Dr. Dave Ehrler
Albany, GA 31701

Dr. Dawn P. Flanagan
Department of Psychology
St. John's University
Jamaica, NY 11360

Dr. Mike Frost
EDS, Inc.
RR 2, Box 811
Woodstock, VT 05091

Dr. Mark Fugate
Div. of School Psychology
Alfred University
Alfred, NY 14802

Dr. John Gillis
Department of Psychology
St. Thomas University
Fredericton, NB, Canada

Dr. Bert Hayslip
Dept. of Psychology,
N. Texas State University
Denton, TX 76203

Dr. John Horn
Department of Psychology
University of Southern California
Los Angeles, CA 90089–1061

Dr. Earl Hunt
Department of Psychology
University of Washington
Bellevue, WA 98004

Dr. Shyla M. Ipsen
109 N. Harrison St.
Box 842500
Richmond, VA 23284–2500

Dr. David Johnson
Federation of Behavioral, Psychological and Cognitive Sciences
750 First Street, N.E.
Washington, DC 20002–4242

Dr. Kenneth Jones
Department of Psychology
Brandeis University
Dover, MA 02030

Dr. Timothy Z. Keith
Div. of School Psychology
Alfred University
26 N. Main Street
Alfred, NY 14802

Dr. Jack Martin
25039 Bridlepath
Farmington Hill, MI 48335

Dr. Roderick P. McDonald
Dept. of Psychology
University of Illinois
Champaign, IL 61820

Dr. Ron McGhee
304 Martindale Lane
Albany, GA 31701

Dr. Kevin McGrew
Department of Educational
  Psychology
St. Cloud State University
Clearwater, MN 55320

Dr. Barry Mehler
Dept. of Humanities
Ferris State University
Big Rapids, MI 40307

Dr. Marty Murphy
Psychology Dept.
University of Akron
Akron, OH 44325

Ms. Jennie Noll
Department of Psychology
University of Southern California
Los Angeles, CA

Dr. Steven Porges
Department of Psychology
University of Maryland
College Park, MD

Dr. William Revelle
Department of Psychology
Northwestern University
Evanston, IL 60201

Dr. Patti Robinson
Albany, GA 31701

Dr. Barbara A. Rothlisberg
Educational Psychology
Ball State University
Muncie, IN 47304

Dr. Suzanne Selph
Monitoring and Compliance
10310 Layton Hall Drive
Belle Willard Adman Center
Fairfax, VA 22030

Dr. Richard Snow
Department of Education
Stanford University
Stanford, CA 94305

Dr. Evegny Sokolov
Department of Psychology
Moscow University
Moscow, FSR

Dr. Harvey Sterns
Inst. for Life Span Dev. & Gero
University of Akron
Akron, OH 44325–4307

Dr. Ann Sweney
203 N. Third
Towanda, KS 67144

Dr. Arthur B. Sweney
203 N. Third
Towanda, KS 67144

Dr. David Thissen
Department of Psychology
University of North Carolina
Chapel Hill, NC 27514

Dr. Robert M. Thorndike
Department of Psychology
Western Washington University
Bellingham, WA 98225

Dr. Vicki Threlfall
Department of Psychology
George Mason University
Fairfax, VA

Dr. Lee Willerman
Deparment of Psychology
University of Texas–Austin
Austin, TX 78712

Riverside Publishing Representatives

425 Springlake Dr.
Itaska, IL 60143–2079

Dr. John Laramy
Ms. Catherine Lawrence
Ms. Evanglina Mangino
Dr. Elizabeth McGrath
Mr. John Oswald
Dr. Fred Schrank
Mr. Joe Shively
Ms. Barbara Wendling
Mr. Michael Young
Dr. Tom Hutchinson

UVa Department of Psychology Hosts

Department of Psychology
University of Virginia
Charlottesville, VA 22903

Mr. Steven H. Aggen
Mr. Steven M. Boker
Mr. Fumiaki Hamagami
Ms. Patricia A. Hulick
Ms. Gina Marshall
Mr. Thomas S. Paskus
Dr. Sandra Scarr
Dr. John R. Nesselroade
Dr. Richard Woodcock
Dr. Jack McArdle